Search Engine Optimization
SECRETS

Search Engine Optimization

SECRETS

DO WHAT YOU NEVER THOUGHT POSSIBLE WITH SEO

Danny Dover

with insights from Erik Dafforn

WILEY

Wiley Publishing, Inc.

EXECUTIVE EDITOR: Carol Long
ACQUISITIONS EDITOR: Mary James
SENIOR PROJECT EDITOR: Kevin Kent
PROJECT EDITOR: Kristin Vorce
TECHNICAL EDITOR: Tim Buck
PRODUCTION EDITOR: Rebecca Anderson
COPY EDITOR: Kim Cofer
EDITORIAL DIRECTOR: Robyn B. Siesky
EDITORIAL MANAGER: Mary Beth Wakefield
MARKETING MANAGER: Ashley Zurcher
PRODUCTION MANAGER: Tim Tate
VICE PRESIDENT AND EXECUTIVE GROUP PUBLISHER: Richard Swadley
VICE PRESIDENT AND EXECUTIVE PUBLISHER: Barry Pruett
ASSOCIATE PUBLISHER: Jim Minatel
PROJECT COORDINATOR, COVER: Katie Crocker
COMPOSITOR: Craig Woods, Happenstance Type-O-Rama
PROOFREADER: James Saturnio, Word One New York
INDEXER: Robert Swanson
COVER DESIGNER: Ryan Sneed
COVER IMAGE: © Chad Baker / Lifesize / Getty Images

Search Engine Optimization Secrets

Published by
Wiley Publishing, Inc.
10475 Crosspoint Boulevard
Indianapolis, IN 46256
www.wiley.com

This book is dedicated to my family
(That's you, Mom, Dad, Jessica, and Josh!) for their
support and encouragement. I love all of you!

It is also dedicated to my fantastic friend Ian Lauth,
(not you Kevin Tower :-p) for his patience and support.
Thanks for putting up with me buddy!

Last but not least, I am dedicating this to all of my
brilliant co-workers at SEOmoz. Without all of you,
this would have been an unpublished disaster!

I don't know what I did to get lucky enough to have all of
you in my life but I appreciate my time with you every day.

—Danny Dover

To my wife and children, who love me even
though I never finish working when I say I will.

—Erik Dafforn

About the Authors

Danny Dover is a passionate SEO and influential writer. During his tenure at SEOmoz.org (where he was the Lead SEO), he did SEO consulting for many of the world's most popular companies including Facebook, Microsoft, and Comcast. His expertise has been cited in *Time*, *PCWorld*, *Smashing Magazine*, and the *Seattle Post-Intelligencer* and has been translated into Japanese, French, Spanish, Italian, Chinese, German, and Hungarian.

Danny has spoken at numerous SEO conferences (spanning three continents) and his written posts and articles have been read over a million times and accessed online in more than 175 different countries.

Erik Dafforn is Executive Vice President and Director of Organic SEO for Intrapromote, LLC, a Cleveland-based Search and Social Marketing firm. At Intrapromote's blog and ClickZ.com, he's written over 200 articles on SEO strategy and techniques, many of which focus on architecture's effects on the crawling and indexing processes. Erik lives in Indianapolis with his wife and three children.

About the Technical Editor

Tim Buck worked for 15 years as IT Manager for a small software development company. Being the sole source of IT support there, he was responsible for server management, desktop support, web development, and software testing, and he wore many other hats as well. As a result, he learned a little about everything, including the basics of getting his company's website listed in Google's search engine results.

Now Tim works as a web application developer in state government; in this role, he continues to learn a little about everything, supporting legacy applications as well as developing new ones.

Acknowledgments

I would like to acknowledge the extraordinary efforts of Kevin Kent (Project Editor), Mary James (Acquisitions Editor), Carol Long (Executive Editor), and Jenny Watson (who originally found me for this book) for their work on this enormous and fun project. Your guidance and leadership made it possible for me to complete this book and I sincerely appreciate your patience and support.

I would also like to acknowledge the SEO community as a whole for creating the invigorating environment that made this book possible. Whether I met you in person, online, or not at all, you have been my driving force and an unconditional source of encouragement and important constructive criticism.

Thank you!

—Danny Dover

I would like to acknowledge the help and encouragement of several people who made my contribution to this book possible.

Thanks to Danny Dover for his hard work conceiving an excellent collection of content not typically found in SEO books. Contributing to the project has been an honor and a challenge.

Special thanks go to John Lustina and Doug Ausbury, co-founders of Intrapromote, LLC, for their encouragement during the writing stage; and to James Gunn, who was instrumental long ago in helping me understand fundamental SEO concepts and who continues to be a source of great insight and knowledge today.

Finally, I want to acknowledge the expertise and professionalism of the Wiley acquisitions, editorial, and production staff, including such excellent editors as Kevin Kent, Mary Beth Wakefield, and Mary James. They are an excellent team.

—Erik Dafforn

Contents at a Glance

Contents

Read This First

Why would someone like myself want to publish my SEO secrets for the world to read? Doesn't this destroy my competitive advantage? Won't I surely go broke and starve on the street? Won't my friends mock me and my family disown me?

For two reasons, the answer is probably not.

► The first reason is the size of the market. The Internet is incredibly large and growing at an astounding rate. The market for SEO is following a similar path. There is absolutely no way I could work for all of the websites that need SEO consulting. As such, I am happy to pass the work on to others and teach them how to succeed. It is no money out of my pocket, and it makes me feel like I am contributing to a greater good. I learned most of what I know about SEO from others and, as such, feel obligated to spread the knowledge.

► The second reason has to do with SEOmoz, the company I used to work for. SEOmoz provides tools to help SEOs do their jobs. As such, it is to my advantage to promote and train other SEOs. Just like Google benefits from getting more people online, I benefit from teaching others how to do SEO. You may choose to use SEOmoz's competitors' services or you may not. That is completely up to you, and I will do my best to show you all the available options.

WHO THIS BOOK IS FOR

This book is for the SEO who already knows the basics of SEO and wants to take this knowledge to the next level so that they can make more money. In the SEO industry, the best way I have found to do this is to do SEO consulting.

This book is written as a guide to becoming an SEO consultant or for those who want to use the strategies of professional SEO consultants. It clearly lays out the processes and perspectives I have used at SEOmoz when I did consulting for some of the most well-known websites on the Internet. It is intended for those who love the Internet and strive to influence how it operates.

WHY THIS BOOK IS BETTER THAN OTHER SEO BOOKS

Modern SEO is complicated, fast moving, and rife with misconceptions. This makes it extremely difficult to learn. When I began researching for this book, I read all of the major SEO books that were available. I quickly found that they were full of theory and lacked actionable steps to really help the reader master the subject.

I wrote this book with the goal of building the bridge between theory and action by bringing together all of the best sources of information I have found and putting them in a format that makes it easy to understand and, more importantly, do SEO like a professional. This emphasis on action follows the steps I originally used to learn SEO. I believe this focus on process followed by explanation is unique among SEO books on the market, and I believe it will make the difference that allows you to out rank your competition.

HOW I LEARNED THE SECRETS SHARED IN THIS BOOK

The brutal truth is that I do not work at Google or Microsoft and I have never read a single line of code that powers the search engine algorithms. Surprisingly, as an SEO professional, I am not unique.

So what gives me the authority to write a book about SEO? The answer is simple. I get results. I have dedicated years of my life to studying the search engines and have learned how to influence search engine result pages. I use my skills almost every day to help people improve their rankings and drive traffic to their sites. To me, there is no better feeling than helping people achieve their online dreams.

This book is the next step for me. Instead of helping others in a one-to-one fashion, this book will enable me to help others in a one-to-many fashion. That is where you come in. My hope is that after reading this book, you will choose to use your skills to help others (but be sure to look out for yourself first). Either way I support you.

WEBSITE SUPPORTING THE BOOK

You will find additional supporting material at the accompanying online resource at www.dannydover.com/search-engine-optimization-secrets/. This resource includes:

- ▶ Beginner's Guide to SEO
- ▶ A Comprehensive SEO Audit Report (Informational Website)
- ▶ A Comprehensive SEO Audit Report (E-commerce Website)
- ▶ A Center for Learning SEO
- ▶ Web Developer's SEO Cheat Sheet
- ▶ Internet Marketing Handbook
- ▶ 15 Minute SEO Audit Checklist
- ▶ Updates to this book
- ▶ Resources on how to learn more

FEATURES AND ICONS USED IN THIS BOOK

The following features and icons are used to help draw your attention to some of the most important or useful information in the book, some of the most valuable tips, insights, and advice.

▶ Watch for margin notes like this one that highlight some key piece of information or that discuss some valuable technique or approach.

> **SIDEBARS**
>
> Sidebars like this one feature additional information about topics related to the nearby text.

TIP The Tip icon indicates a helpful trick or technique.

NOTE The Note icon points out or expands on items of importance or interest.

CROSSREF The Cross-Reference icon points to chapters where additional information can be found.

WARNING The Warning icon warns you about possible negative side effects or precautions you should take before making a change.

Enough talk; it is now time to get started. Thank you, and best of luck with your Internet endeavors.

## CHAPTER 1

Understanding Search Engine Optimization

IN THIS CHAPTER

- ▶ Learning how search engines see websites
- ▶ Taking a look at popularity in SEO
- ▶ Considering the role of relevancy in SEO

At Google, search engineers talk about "80-20" problems.

They are describing situations where the last 20 percent of the problem is 80 percent of the work. Learning SEO is one of these problems. Eighty percent of the knowledge SEOs need is available online for free. Unfortunately, the remaining 20 percent takes the majority of the time and energy to find and understand. My goal with this book is to solve this problem by making the last 20 percent as easy to get as the first 80 percent. Though I don't think I will be able to cover the entire 20 percent (some of it comes from years of practice), I am going to write as much actionable advanced material as humanly possible.

This book is for those who already know the basics of SEO and are looking to take their skills to the next level. Before diving in, try reading the following list:

- ► `robots.txt`
- ► sitemap
- ► nofollow
- ► 301 redirect
- ► canonicalization

If you are not sure what any of the items in this list are, you should go over to the nearest computer and read the article "The Beginner's Guide to SEO" at

`http://www.seomoz.org/article/beginners-guide-to-search-engine-optimization`

This free article can teach you everything you need to know to use this book to its fullest. Done with that? Great, now we can begin.

THE SECRETS OF POPULARITY

Once upon a time there were two nerds at Stanford working on their PhDs. (Now that I think about it, there were probably a lot more than two nerds at Stanford.) Two of the nerds at Stanford were not satisfied with the current options for searching online, so they attempted to develop a better way.

Being long-time academics, they eventually decided to take the way academic papers were organized and apply that to webpages. A quick and fairly objective way to judge the quality of an academic paper is to see how many times other academic papers have cited it. This concept was easy to replicate online because the original purpose of the Internet was to share academic resources between universities. The citations manifested themselves as hyperlinks once they went online. One of the nerds came up with an algorithm for calculating these values on a global scale, and they both lived happily ever after.

Of course, these two nerds were Larry Page and Sergey Brin, the founders of Google, and the algorithm that Larry invented that day was what eventually became PageRank. Long story short, Google ended up becoming a big deal and now the two founders rent an airstrip from NASA so they have somewhere to land their private jets. (Think I am kidding? See `http://searchengineland.com/your-guide-to-the-google-jet-12161`.)

RELEVANCE, SPEED, AND SCALABILITY

Hypothetically, the most relevant search engine would have a team of experts on every subject in the entire world—a staff large enough to read, study, and evaluate every document published on the web so they could return the most accurate results for each query submitted by users.

The fastest search engine, on the other hand, would crawl a new URL the very second it's published and introduce it into the general index immediately, available to appear in query results only seconds after it goes live.

The challenge for Google and all other engines is to find the balance between those two scenarios: To combine rapid crawling and indexing with a relevance algorithm that can be instantly applied to new content. In other words, they're trying to build *scalable relevance*. With very few exceptions, Google is uninterested in hand-removing (or hand-promoting) specific content. Instead, its model is built around identifying characteristics in web content that indicate the content is especially relevant or irrelevant, so that content all across the web with those same characteristics can be similarly promoted or demoted.

This book frequently discusses the benefits of content created with the user in mind. To some hardcore SEOs, Google's "think about the user" mantra is corny; they'd much prefer to know a secret line of code or server technique that bypasses the intent of creating engaging content.

While it may be corny, Google's focus on creating relevant, user-focused content really is the key to its algorithm of scalable relevance. Google is constantly trying to find ways to reward content that truly answers users' questions and ways to minimize or filter out content built for content's sake. While this book discusses techniques for making your content visible and accessible to engines, remember that means talking about content constructed with users in mind, designed to be innovative, helpful, and to serve the query intent of human users. It might be corny, but it's effective.

That fateful day, the Google Guys capitalized on the mysterious power of links. Although a webmaster can easily manipulate everything (word choice, keyword placement, internal links, and so on) on his or her own website, it is much more difficult to influence inbound links. This natural link profile acts as an extremely good metric for identifying legitimately popular pages.

NOTE Google's PageRank was actually named after its creator, Larry Page. Originally, the algorithm was named BackRub after its emphasis on back-links. Later, its name was changed to PageRank because of its connections to Larry Page's last name and the ability for the algorithm to rank pages.

Larry Page's original paper on PageRank, "The Anatomy of a Large-Scale Hypertextual Web Search Engine," is still available online. If you are interested in reading it, it is available on Stanford's website at `http://infolab.stanford.edu/~backrub/google.html`. It is highly technical, and I have used it on more than one occasion as a sleep aid. It's worth noting that the original PageRank as de-scribed in this paper is only a tiny part of Google's modern-day search algorithm.

Now wait a second—isn't this supposed to be a book for advanced SEOs? Then why am I explaining to you the value of links? Relax, there is a method to my madness. Before I am able to explain the more advanced secrets, I need to make sure we are on the same page.

As modern search engines evolved, they started to take into account the link profile of both a given page and its domain. They found out that the relationship between these two indicators was itself a very useful metric for ranking webpages.

Domain and Page Popularity

There are hundreds of factors that help engines decide how to rank a page. And in general, those hundreds of factors can be broken into two categories—relevance and popularity (or "authority"). For the purposes of this demonstration you will need to completely ignore relevancy for a second. (Kind of like the search engine Ask.com.) Further, within the category of popularity, there are two primary types—domain popularity and page popularity. Modern search engines rank pages by a combination of these two kinds of popularity metrics. These metrics are measurements of link profiles. To rank number one for a given query you need to have the highest amount of total popularity on the Internet. (Again, bear with me as we ignore relevancy for this section.)

This is very clear if you start looking for patterns in search result pages. Have you ever noticed that popular domains like Wikipedia.org tend to rank for every-thing? This is because they have an enormous amount of domain popularity. But what about those competitors who outrank me for a specific term with a practically unknown domain? This happens when they have an excess of page popularity. See Figure 1-1.

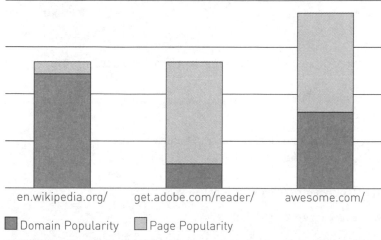

Link Popularity

en.wikipedia.org/ get.adobe.com/reader/ awesome.com/

■ Domain Popularity   ☐ Page Popularity

FIGURE 1-1: Graph showing different combinations of relevancy and popularity metrics that can be used to achieve high rankings

Although en.wikipedia.org has a lot of domain popularity and get.adobe.com/reader/ has a lot of page popularity, www.awesome.com ranks higher because it has a higher *total* amount of popularity. This fact and relevancy metrics (discussed later in this chapter) are the essence of Search Engine Optimization. (Shoot! I unveiled it in the first chapter, now what am I going to write about?)

POPULARITY TOP TEN LISTS

The top 10 most linked-to domains on the Internet (at the time of writing) are:

▶ Google.com

▶ Adobe.com

▶ Yahoo.com

▶ Blogspot.com

▶ Wikipedia.org

▶ YouTube.com

▶ W3.org

▶ Myspace.com

continued

(continued)

▶ Wordpress.com

▶ Microsoft.com

The top 10 most linked-to pages on the Internet (at the time of writing) are:

▶ http://wordpress.org/

▶ http://www.google.com/

▶ http://www.adobe.com/products/acrobat/readstep2.html

▶ http://www.miibeian.gov.cn/

▶ http://validator.w3.org/check/referer

▶ http://www.statcounter.com/

▶ http://jigsaw.w3.org/css-validator/check/referer

▶ http://www.phpbb.com/

▶ http://www.yahoo.com/

▶ http://del.icio.us/post

Source: SEOmoz's Linkscape—Index of the World Wide Web

▶ Not only that, but at any given time, the TbPR (Toolbar PageRank) value you see may be up to 60–90 days older or more, and it's a single-digit representation of what's probably very a long decimal value.

▶ Google makes scraping (automatically requesting and distributing) its PageRank metric difficult. To get around the limitations, you need to write a program that requests the metric from Google and identifies itself as the Google Toolbar.

Before I summarize I would like to nip the PageRank discussion in the bud. Google releases its PageRank metric through a browser toolbar. This is not the droid you are looking for. That green bar represents only a very small part of the overall search algorithm.

Just because a page has a PageRank of 5 does not mean it will outrank all pages with a PageRank of 4. Keep in mind that major search engines do not want you to reverse engineer their algorithms. As such, publicly releasing a definitive metric for ranking would be idiotic from a business perspective. If there is one thing that Google is not, it's idiotic.

In my opinion, hyperlinks are the most important factor when it comes to ranking web pages. This is the result of them being difficult to manipulate. Modern search engines look at link profiles from many different perspectives and use those relationships to determine rank. The takeaway for you is that time spent earning links is time well spent. In the same way that a rising tide raises all ships, popular domains raise all pages. Likewise, popular pages raise the given domain metrics.

In the next section I want you to take a look into the pesky missing puzzle piece of this chapter: relevancy. I am going to discuss how it interacts with popularity, and I may or may not tell you another fairy tale.

THE SECRETS OF RELEVANCY

In the previous section, I discussed how popular pages (as judged by links) rank higher. By this logic, you might expect that the Internet's most popular pages would rank for everything. To a certain extent they do (think Wikipedia!), but the reason they don't dominate the rankings for *every* search result page is that search engines put a lot of emphasis on determining relevancy.

Text Is the Currency of the Internet

Relevancy is the measurement of the theoretical distance between two corresponding items with regards to relationship. Luckily for Google and Microsoft, modern-day computers are quite good at calculating this measurement for text.

By my estimations, Google owns and operates well over a million servers. The electricity to power these servers is likely one of Google's larger operating expenses. This energy limitation has helped shape modern search engines by putting text analysis at the forefront of search. Quite simply, it takes less computing power and is much simpler programmatically to determine relevancy between a text query and a text document than it is between a text query and an image or video file. This is the reason why text results are so much more prominent in search results than videos and images.

As of this writing, the most recent time that Google publicly released the size of its indices was in 2006. At that time it released the numbers shown in Table 1-1.

TABLE 1-1: Size of Google Indices

DATA	SIZE IN TERABYTES
Crawl Index	800
Google Analytics	200
Google Base	2
Google Earth	70
Orkut	9
Personalized Search	4

▶ *This is especially true until Google finds better ways to interpret and grade non-textual media*

So what does this emphasis on textual content mean for SEOs? To me, it indicates that my time is better spent optimizing text than images or videos. This strategy will likely have to change in the future as computers get more powerful and energy efficient, but for right now text should be every SEO's primary focus.

But Why Content?

The most basic structure a functional website could take would be a blank page with a URL. For example purposes, pretend your blank page is on the fake domain www.WhatIsJessicaSimpsonThinking.com. (Get it? It is a blank page.) Unfortunately for the search engines, clues like top-level domains (.com, .org, and so on), domain owners (WHOIS records), code validation, and copyright dates are poor signals for determining relevancy. This means your page with the dumb domain name needs some content before it is able to rank in search engines.

The search engines must use their analysis of content as their primary indication of relevancy for determining rankings for a given search query. For SEOs, this means the content on a given page is essential for manipulating—that is, earning—rankings. In the old days of AltaVista and other search engines, SEOs would just need to write "Jessica Simpson" hundreds times on the site to make it rank #1 for that query. What could be more relevant for the query "Jessica Simpson" than a page that says Jessica Simpson 100 times? (Clever SEOs will realize the answer is a page that says "Jessica Simpson" 101 times.) This metric, called *keyword density*, was quickly manipulated, and the search engines of the time diluted the power of this metric on rankings until it became almost useless. Similar dilution has happened to the keywords meta tag, some kinds of internal links, and H1 tags.

▶ *Despite being more sophisticated, modern-day search engines still work essentially the same way they did in the past—by analyzing content on the page.*

Hey, Ben Stein, thanks for the history lesson, but how does this apply to modern search engines? The funny thing is that modern-day search engines still work essentially the same way they did back in the time of keyword density. The big difference is that they are now much more sophisticated. Instead of simply counting the number of times a word or phrase is on a webpage, they use natural language processing algorithms and other signals on a page to determine relevancy. For example, it is now fairly trivial for search engines to determine that a piece of content is about Jessica Simpson if it mentions related phrases like "Nick Lachey" (her ex-husband), "Ashlee Simpson" (her sister), and "Chicken of the Sea" (she is infamous for thinking the tuna brand "Chicken of the Sea" was made from chicken). The engines can do this for a multitude of languages and with astonishing accuracy.

Don't believe me? Try going to Google right now and searching related:www.jessicasimpson.com. If your results are like mine, you will see websites about her movies, songs, and sister. Computers are amazing things.

In addition to the words on a page, search engines use signals like image meta information (alt attribute), link profile and site architecture, and information hierarchy to determine how relevant a given page that mentions "Jessica" is to a search query for "The Simpsons."

Link Relevancy

As search engines matured, they started identifying more metrics for determining rankings. One that stood out among the rest was link relevancy.

The difference between link relevancy and link popularity (discussed in the previous section) is that link relevancy does not take into account the power of the link. Instead, it is a natural phenomenon that works when people link out to other content.

Let me give you an example of how it works. Say I own a blog where I write about whiteboard markers. (Yes, I did just look around my office for an example to use, and yes, there are actually people who blog about whiteboard markers. I checked.) Ever inclined to learn more about my passion for these magical writing utensils, I spend part of my day reading online what other people have to say about whiteboard markers.

On my hypothetical online reading journey, I find an article about the psychological effects of marker color choice. Excited, I go back to my website to blog about the article so (both of) my friends can read about it. Now here is the critical takeaway. When I write the blog post and link to the article, *I get to choose the anchor text.* I could choose something like "click here," but more likely I choose something that it is relevant to the article. In this case I choose "psychological effects of marker color choice." Someone else who links to the article might use the link anchor text "marker color choice and the effect on the brain."

▶ *People have a tendency to link to content using the anchor text of either the domain name or the title of the page. Use this to your advantage by including keywords you want to rank for in these two elements.*

This human-powered information is essential to modern-day search engines. These descriptions are relatively unbiased and produced by real people. This metric, in combination with complicated natural language processing, makes up the lion's share of relevancy indicators online.

Other important relevancy indicators are link sources and information hierarchy. For example, the search engines can also use the fact that I linked to the color choice article from a blog about whiteboard markers to supplement their understanding of relevancy. Similarly, they can use the fact that the original article was located at the URL www.example.com/vision/color/ to determine the high-level positioning and relevancy of the content. As you read later in this book (Chapter 2 specifically), these secrets are essential for SEOs to do their job.

Beyond specific anchor text, proximal text—the certain number of characters preceding and following the link itself—have some value. Something that's logical, but annoying is when people use a verb as anchor text, such as "Frank said . . . " or "Jennifer wrote . . .", using "said" or "wrote" as the anchor text pointing back to the post. In a situation like that, engines have figured out how to apply the context of the surrounding copy to the link.

Tying Together Popularity and Relevancy

So far in this chapter I have discussed both popularity and relevancy. These two concepts make up the bulk of Search Engine Optimization theory. They have been present since the beginning of search engines and undoubtedly will be important in the future. The way they are determined and the relationship between them changes, but they are both fundamental to determining search results.

▶ Popularity and relevancy are the two concepts that make up the bulk of Search Engine Optimization theory.

This fact is critical to SEOs. We have very little control over how the major search engines operate, yet somehow we are supposed to keep our jobs. Luckily, these immutable laws of popularity and relevance govern search engines and provide us with some job security.

SUMMARY

In this chapter, I explained the concepts of popularity and relevancy in relation to modern search engines. This information, along with your prior SEO experience, will make up the foundation for all of the SEO secrets and knowledge that you learn throughout the rest of the book. You no doubt have some questions. I'll start answering many of your questions in the next chapter, but you will likely form many more. Welcome to the mindset of a Professional SEO. Prepare to be questioning and Googling things for the rest of your life.

## CHAPTER 2

Relearning How You See the Web

When people surf the Internet, they generally view each domain as its own island of information. This works perfectly well for the average surfer but is a big mistake for beginner SEOs. Websites, whether they like it or not, are interconnected. This is a key perspective shift that is essential for understanding SEO.

Take Facebook, for example. It started out as a "walled garden" with all of its content hidden behind a login. It thought it could be different and remain completely independent. This worked for a while, and Facebook gained a lot of popularity. Eventually, an ex-Googler and his friend became fed up with the locked-down communication silo of Facebook and started a wide open website called Twitter. Twitter grew even faster than Facebook and challenged it as the media darling. Twitter was smart and made its content readily available to both developers (through APIs) and search engines (through indexable content).

Facebook responded with Facebook Connect (which enables people to log in to Facebook through other websites) and opened its chat protocol so its users could communicate outside of the Facebook domain. It also made a limited amount of information about users visible to search engines. Facebook is now accepting its place in the Internet community and is benefiting from its decision to embrace other websites. The fact that it misjudged early on was that websites are best when they are interconnected. Being able to see this connection is one of the skills that separates SEO professionals from SEO fakes.

In this chapter you learn the steps that the SEO professionals at SEOmoz go through either before meeting with a client or at the first meeting (depending on the contract). When you view a given site in the way you are about to learn in this chapter, you need to take detailed notes. You are likely going to notice a lot about the website that can use improvement, and you need to capture this information before details distract you.

▶ I highly recommend writing down everything you notice in a section of a notebook identified with the domain name and date of viewing.

KEEP YOUR NOTES SIMPLE

The purpose of the notebook is simplicity and the ability to go back frequently and review your notes. If actual physical writing isn't your thing, consider a low-tech text editor on your computer, such as Windows Notepad or the Mac's TextEdit.

Bare-bones solutions like a notebook or text editor help you avoid the distraction of the presentation itself and focus on the important issues—the characteristics of the web site that you're evaluating.

If you think it will be helpful and you have Internet access readily available, I recommend bringing up a website you are familiar with while reading through this chapter. If you choose to do this, be sure to take a lot of notes in your notebook so you can review them later.

THE 1,000-FOOT VIEW—UNDERSTANDING THE NEIGHBORHOOD

Before I do any work on a website I try to get an idea of where it fits into the grand scheme of things on the World Wide Web. The easiest way to do this is to run searches for some of the competitive terms in the website's niche. If you imagine the Internet as one giant city, you can picture domains as buildings. The first step I take before working on a client's website is figuring out in which neighborhood its building (domain) resides.

This search result page is similar to seeing a map of the given Internet neighborhood. You usually can quickly identify the neighborhood anchors (due to their link popularity) and specialists in the top 10 (due to their relevancy). You can also start to get an idea of the maturity of the result based on the presence of spam or low-quality websites. Take a look at Figures 2-1 and 2-2.

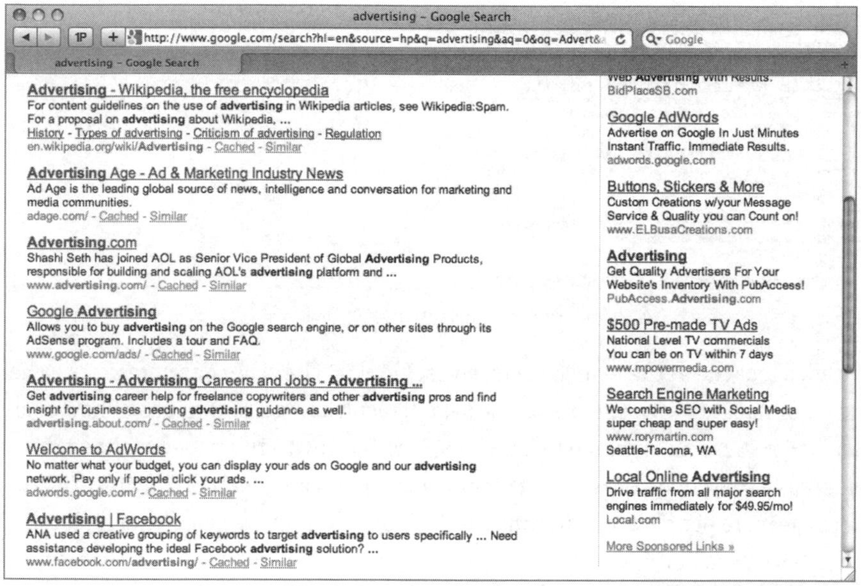

FIGURE 2-1: Google search result for "advertising"

Notice the difference in the maturity (quality) of the search results. In the second set of results (Figure 2-2), you see some of the same big names again (Wikipedia, for example, appears in both searches) but this time they are mixed with some sites that appear spammier (`iab.net`, `freewebdirectory.us`).

During client meetings, when I look at the search engine result page for a competitive term like *advertising*, I am not looking for websites to visit but rather trying to get a general idea of the maturity of the Internet neighborhood. I am very vocal when I am doing this and have been known to question out loud, "How did that website get there?" A couple times, the client momentarily thought I was talking about his website and had a quick moment of panic. In reality, I am commenting on a spam site I see rising up the results.

Also, take note that regardless of whether or not you are logged into a Google account, the search engine will automatically customize your search results based on links you click most. This can be misleading because it will make your favorite websites rank higher for you than they do for the rest of the population.

▶ To turn this off, append "&pws=0" to the end of the Google URL.

FIGURE 2-2: Google search result for "Internet advertising"

Along with looking at the results themselves, I look at the other data present on the page. The amount of advertisements on the search result gives a rough idea of how competitive it is. For example, a search for buy viagra will return a full page height worth of ads, whereas a search for women that look like Drew Carey won't likely return any. This is because more people are searching for the blue pill than are searching for large, bald women with nerd glasses.

In addition to the ads, I also look for signs of temporal algorithms. *Temporal algorithms* are ranking equations that take into account the element of time with regards to relevancy. These tend to manifest themselves as news results and blog posts.

TAKING ADVANTAGE OF TEMPORAL ALGORITHMS

You can use the temporal algorithms to your advantage. I accidentally did this once with great success. I wrote a blog post about Michael Jackson's death and its effect on the search engines a day after he died. As a result of temporal algorithms my post ranked in the top 10 for the query "Michael Jackson" for a short period following his death. Because of this high ranking, tens of thousands of people read my article. I thought it was because I was so awesome, but after digging into my analytics I realized it was because of unplanned use of the temporal algorithms. If you are a blogger, this tactic of quickly writing about news events can be a great traffic booster.

After scanning search result pages for the given website's niche, I generally get a sense for that neighborhood of the Internet. The important takeaway is to get an idea of the level of competition, not to figure out the ins and outs of how specific websites are ranking. That comes later.

EASY DE-PERSONALIZATION IN FIREFOX AND CHROME

Most SEOs perform searches dozens or hundreds of times per day, and when you do, it's important that de-personalized results appear so that you see what a "typical" searcher would see, as opposed to search results influenced by you own search history.

Firefox is a terrific browser for SEOs for many reasons, but one of its most helpful features is the ability to search right from the address field of the browser, the area at the top of the browser where you normally see the URL of the web page you're on. Better yet, with a little customization, you can easily perform Google searches that are de-personalized (although not de-geotargeted).

1. From the Bookmarks | Organize Bookmarks... menu, select any bookmarks folder in the left pane. (Do not simply select the All Bookmarks folder, because it won't work.)

2. Right-click the folder and select New Bookmark...

3. Add the following values to the fields:

   Name: Google de-personalized search

   Location: http://www.google.com/search?&q=%s&pws=0

   Tags: (Optional. Add any tags you want.)

   Keyword: g

   Description: (Optional. Use this to describe the search.)

4. Click Add.

That's it. Now, go to the Address field in Firefox (where you see a URL at the top of the browser) and type something like this:

```
g hdmi cables
```

continued

(continued)

This tells Google (g) to search for "hdmi cables". More important, because your Location field included **&pws=0**, that URL parameter will carry over to your search result. From now on, if you want to perform a de-personalized Google search, simply type "g" (no quotes) and the query term from your URL field.

Use this process for creating as many custom searches as you like, keeping these important factors in mind:

1. The Location field must contain the exact URL of the search result, with the exception of the **%s** variable, which will be replaced with your query term automatically.

2. The Keyword field is where you'll type before your search query to tell Firefox which custom query you'll be running. Be brief and accurate. I use terms like "b" for Bing, "tc" for text cache, and so on.

This functionality carries over to Google's Chrome browser too, because Chrome can import bookmarks from any other browser you use. If you're a Chrome user, simply import your Firefox bookmarks from the Chrome | Import Bookmarks and Settings menu, and you can search from the Chrome address bar just like you did in Firefox.

Action Checklist

When viewing a website from the 1,000-foot level, be sure to complete the following:

- ✔ Search for the broadest keyword that the given site might potentially rank
- ✔ Identify the maturity of the search engine results page (SERP) based on the criteria listed in this chapter
- ✔ Identify major competitors and record them in a list for later competitive analysis

This section discussed analyzing websites at their highest level. At this point, the details don't matter. Rather it is macro patterns that are important. The following sections dive deeper into the website and figure out how everything is related. Remember, search engines use hundreds of metrics to rank websites. This is possible because the same website can be viewed many different ways.

THE 100-FOOT VIEW—THE WEBSITE

When professional SEOs first come to a website that they plan to work with, they view it through a very different lens than if they were just idly surfing. They instinctively start viewing it from the perspective of a search engine. The following are the elements that my colleagues and I pay the most attention to.

How Important Is a Domain Name?

I could probably write an entire book on this subject. (Hear that Wiley Publishing? That's the sound of money.) From a marketing perspective, a domain name is the single most important element of a website. Unlike a brick-and-mortar company, websites don't have visual cues closely associated with them. Whereas potential customers can use visual cues to identify if a physical building is more likely a barber shop or a bank, they are not able to tell the difference between domain names. All domain names use the exact same format: http:// subdomain dot (optional) root domain dot TLD. Take, for example, `http://www.google.com` or `http://www.bing.com`. To an outsider, there is no reason to think that any of these resources would be a search engine. They don't contain the word *search*, and if their brands weren't as strong as they are, their gibberish names wouldn't mean anything to anyone. In fact, if you look at the top 100 most linked-to domains on the Internet, you see this trend over and over again: Wikipedia, YouTube, W3, Amazon, Macromedia, MSN, Flickr, Twitter, Digg, Technorati, IMDB, eBay—the list goes on.

This is where people get confused. They see websites like this and think that the domain name doesn't matter. They register domains that are hard to pronounce (SEOmoz) or hard to spell (Picnik) and figure they don't have to worry. The problem is they don't realize that the popular websites got popular not because of their domain names, but rather despite their domain names. Google was such an outstanding product with a plan that was executed so well that it could have had been named BackRub and still been successful. (Note: It was originally called BackRub. I am just amusing myself.)

As an SEO, if you find yourself in the position of changing or choosing a domain name, you need to make a difficult decision. How confident are you in the client's idea? Is it an idea that serves the entire world, or is it only useful to a few thousand people? If the website is world changing, it might actually benefit from a gibberish name. If the name is gibberish and very successful, people naturally start to associate its name with its service. For example, Google is now synonymous with "search." However, if the idea doesn't end up being world changing (and most websites aren't), a gibberish domain name can hurt the website. What are the odds that the general populous will type in spoke.com (a real website) to find personal profiles?

For the vast majority of websites, a "search friendly" domain name is best. The search engines will always be constrained by the fact that many people search for exact URLs when they want to go to websites. Of course, the most relevant and popular result for the query "myspace.com" would be www.myspace.com. You can use this to your advantage.

Say your clients own a hotel in Seattle. For them, the best domain name would be www.seattlehotel.com so that they could rank for the query Seattle Hotel. They should not worry about becoming a verb because the demand is not high enough for their service and the benefits of an exact match domain name outweigh the chances of their website changing the world. Need more proof? The domain names porn.com and sex.com sold for $9.5 million and $12 million, respectively.

> A nonsensical domain name can hurt a website, making it harder for people (and search engines) to find that site and associate with the concepts that the site focuses on.

> NOTE For a while, the most searched-for term on both Yahoo! and MSN was *Google*. People would search for the search leader in Yahoo! and MSN, click through to google.com, and then type their search query. This bothered Yahoo! so much that it eventually put a Yahoo! search bar as the number one result for Google.

But what if a killer domain name is not available? You are not alone. As of the time of writing all of the combinations for .com domains with three or fewer characters were already owned. If you can't get seattlehotel.com, you will just need to be more creative. To limit your ability to hurt yourself by being "too creative," I advise you to look out for the following when registering a domain name:

- **Avoid hyphens:** In domain names, hyphens detract from credibility and act as a spam indicator.

- **Avoid generic, uncommon top-level domains (TLDs):** Like hyphens, TLDs such as .info, .cc, .ws, and .name are spam indicators.

- **Avoid domain names longer than 15 characters:** People are lazy; don't try to make them type a novel just to access your website.

- **Be aware of permutations:** The owners of ExpertsExchange.com built a sizable brand before they realized their domain name could be misconstrued as ExpertSexChange.com.

This advice about domains applies mostly to people who are either starting out from scratch, or for whom purchasing a better domain is an option. If you're an SEO, you'll probably have clients that are stuck with the domain they have, either due to branding or financial constraints. If that's you, never fear. While a smartly chosen, keyword-rich domain is often an ideal situation, plenty of sites succeed without one. I doubt, for example, that Amazon.com is on the lookout for a more book- or electronics-based domain name.

Don't Fool Yourself, Looks Matter

I once talked to a website owner who had an 80 percent bounce rate on his home-page and figured it was normal. Can you imagine if 80 percent of the people who looked at you immediately ran in the opposite direction? This isn't normal. Web design is an element of SEO that many amateur SEOs miss. It doesn't matter if you can get high rankings if none of the searchers stays on the given webpage after clicking through.

SEO-friendly web design is a lot like getting a prom date; appearance matters. People make decisions about the credibility of a website the instant the page loads. Like people, credible websites have a very specific look and feel to them. They gener-ally have a clear logo in the top left, and a navigation bar horizontally on the top of the page or vertically on the left-hand side. They have less than five colors in their layout (not including images), and they have clear, readable text.

Would you feel comfortable leaving your children with a person in a bright orange prison jumpsuit? Of course not! In the same way, visitors to websites are not going to feel comfortable if they are greeted with pop-ups, loud music, and a multicolored skull logo.

Of course those are extreme examples. The common mistakes that I see are more along the line of the following:

- ▶ Lack of focus
- ▶ Crowded text
- ▶ Slow loading times
- ▶ Auto-playing music
- ▶ Unclear navigation
- ▶ Excess redirects

As an SEO, you need to stress the importance of good design. Though it may be fun and exciting to stretch the limits, it is not fun to be poor because 80 percent of your client's would-be customers leave the website directly after entering.

Duplication and Canonicalization

After analyzing a website's domain name and general design, my colleagues and I check for one of the most common SEO mistakes on the Internet, canonicalization. For SEOs, *canonicalization* refers to individual webpages that can be loaded from multiple URLs.

> **NOTE** In this discussion, "canonicalization" simply refers to the concept of picking an authoritative version of a URL and propagating its usage, as opposed to using other variants of that URL. On the other hand, the book discusses the specific canonical link element in several places, including in Chapter 5.

Remember that in Chapter 1 I discussed popularity? (Come on, it hasn't been that long.) What do you think happens when links that are intended to go to the same page get split up among multiple URLs? You guessed it: the popularity of the pages gets split up. Unfortunately for web developers, this happens far too often because the default settings for web servers create this problem. The following lists show the negative SEO effects of using the default settings on the two most common web servers:

Apache web server:

`http://www.example.com/`

`http://www.example.com/index.html`

`http://example.com/`

`http://example.com/index.html`

Microsoft Internet Information Services (IIS):

`http://www.example.com/`

`http://www.example.com/default.asp` (or `.aspx` depending on the version)

`http://example.com/`

`http://example.com/default.asp` (or `.aspx`)

Or any combination with different capitalization.

Each of these URLs spreads out the value of inbound links to the homepage. This means that if the homepage has 100 links to these various URLs, the major search engines only give them credit separately, not in a combined manner.

NOTE Don't think it can happen to you? Go to http://www.mattcutts.com and wait for the page to load. Now, go to http://mattcutts.com and notice what happens. Look at that, canonicalization issues. What's the significance of this example? Matt Cutts is the head of Google's web spam team and helped write many of the algorithms we SEOs study. If he is making this mistake, odds are your less informed clients are as well.

Luckily for SEOs, web developers developed methods for redirection so that URLs can be changed and combined. Two primary types of server redirects exist—301 redirects and 302 redirects:

▶ A 301 indicates an HTTP status code of "Moved Permanently."

▶ A 302 indicates a status code of "Temporarily Moved."

TIP You can read all of the HTTP status codes at http://www.w3.org/Protocols/rfc2616/rfc2616-sec10.html.

Though the difference between 301 and 302 redirects appears to be merely semantics, the actual results are dramatic. Google decided a long time ago to not pass link juice (ranking power) equally between normal links and server redirects. At SEOmoz, I did a considerable amount of testing around this subject and have concluded that 301 redirects pass between 90 percent and 99 percent of their value, whereas 302 redirects pass almost no value at all. Because of this, my co-workers and I always look to see how non-canonicalized pages are being redirected.

WARNING Older versions of IIS use 302 redirects by default. D'oh! Be sure to look out for this. You can see worthless redirects all around popular IIS-powered websites like microsoft.com and myspace.com. The value of these redirects is being completely negated by a single value difference!

Canonicalization is not limited to the inclusion of letters. It also dictates forward slashes in URLs. Try going to http://www.google.com and notice that you will automatically get redirected to http://www.google.com/ (notice the trailing forward slash). This is happening because technically this is the correct format for the URL. Although this is a problem that is largely solved by the search engines already (they know that www.google.com is intended to mean the same as www.google.com/), it is still worth noting because many servers will automatically 301 redirect from the version without the

▶ Other redirect methods exist, such as the meta refresh and various JavaScript relocation commands. Avoid these methods. Not only do they not pass any authority from origin to destination, but engines are unreliable about following the redirect path.

▶ It's not just semantics. How a page is redirected (whether by a 301 or a 302 redirect) matters.

trailing slash to the correct version. By doing this, a link pointing to the wrong version of the URL loses between 1 percent and 10 percent of its worth due to the 301 redirect. The takeaway here is that whenever possible, it is better to link to the version with the forward slash. There is no reason to lose sleep over this (because the engines have mostly solved the problem), but it is still a point to consider.

> **CROSSREF** The right and wrong usage of 301 and 302 redirects is discussed in Chapter 3. The correct syntax and usage of the canonical link element is discussed in Chapter 5.

Robots.txt and Sitemap.xml

After analyzing the domain name, general design, and URL format, my colleagues and I look at potential client's `robots.txt` and sitemap. This is helpful because it starts to give you an idea of how much (or little) the developers of the site cared about SEO. A `robots.txt` file is a very basic step webmasters can take to work with search engines. The text file, which should be located in the root directory of the website (`http://www.example.com/robots.txt`), is based on an informal protocol that is used for telling search engines what directories and files they are allowed and disallowed from accessing. The inclusion of this file gives you a rough hint of whether or not the developers of the given site made SEO a priority.

Because this is a book for advanced SEOs, I will not go into this protocol in detail. (If you want more information, check out `http://www.robotstxt.org` or `http://googlewebmastercentral.blogspot.com/2008/06/improving-on-robots-exclusion-protocol.html`.) Instead, I will tell you a cautionary tale.

Bit.ly is a very popular URL shortening service. Due to its connections with Twitter.com, it is quickly becoming one of the most linked websites on the Web. One reason for this is its flexibility. It has a feature where users can pick their own URL. For example, when linking to my website I might choose `http://bit.ly/SexyMustache`. Unfortunately, Bit.ly forgot to block certain URLs, and someone was able to create a shortened URL for `http://bit.ly/robots.txt`. This opened up the possibility for that person to control how robots were allowed to crawl **Bit.ly**. Oops! This is a great example of why knowing even the basics of SEO is essential for web-based business owners.

After taking a quick glance at the `robots.txt` file, SEO professionals tend to look at the default location for a sitemap. (`http://www.example.com/sitemap.xml`). When I do this, I don't spend a lot of time analyzing it (that comes later, if owners of that website become a client); instead, I skim through it to see if I can glean any information about the setup of the site. A lot of times, it will quickly show me if the website has information hierarchy issues. Specifically, I am looking for how the URLs relate to each other. A good example of information hierarchy would be `www.example .com/mammal/dogs/english-springer-spaniel.html`, whereas a bad example would be `www.example.com/node?type=6&kind=7`. Notice on the bad example that the search engines can't extract any semantic value from the URL. The sitemap can give you a quick idea of the URL formation of the website.

▶ URLs like this one are a sign a website has information hierarchy issues because search engines can't extract any semantic value from the URL.

Action Checklist

When viewing a website from the 100-foot level, be sure to take the following actions:

✔ Decide if the domain name is appropriate for the given site based on the criteria outlined in this chapter

✔ Based on your initial reaction, decide if the graphical design of the website is appropriate

✔ Check for the common canonicalization errors

✔ Check to see if a `robots.txt` exists and get an idea of how important SEO was to the website developers.

✔ If inclined, check to see if a sitemap.xml file exists, and if it does, skim through it to get an idea of how the search engines might see the hierarchy of the website.

This section dealt with some of the first elements of a site that I look at when I first look at a client's site from an SEO perspective: domain name, design, canonicalization, `robots.txt`, and sitemaps. This initial look is intended to just be a high-level viewing of the site.

In the next section I focus on specific webpages on websites and take you even closer to piecing the SEO puzzle together.

THE 10-FOOT VIEW—THE WEBPAGE

In the previous sections I analyzed webpages from a high level and ignored many details. In this section and the next I dig deeper and get more detail oriented. Roll up your SEO sleeves, things are about to get messy.

The Importance of Good Site Architecture

Before you start examining a website from this level, let me explain the importance of good site architecture.

While writing this book I am working with a large client that is totally befuddled by its poor rankings. (Note: This client had me sign a nasty looking non-disclosure agreement, so I am unable to reveal its name.) The company's homepage is literally one of the most linked-to pages on the entire Internet and at one point had the elusive PageRank 10. One of its current strategies is to leverage its homepage's link popularity to bolster a large group of pages optimized for ultra competitive keywords. It wants to cast a wide net with the optimized pages and drive a large amount of search engine–referred traffic to its product pages.

It is a great idea, but with the current execution, it has no chance of working.

The problem is that the website lacks any kind of traditional site architecture. The link juice (ranking power) coming from the hundreds of thousands of domains that link to this company's homepage has no way of traveling to the other webpages on this domain. All of the link juice is essentially bottled up at the front door.

Its content is located on at least 20 different domains, and there is no global navigation that leads users or search engines from the homepage down to catego-rized pages. The company's online presence is more like a thousand islands rather than the super continent it could be. It is an enormous waste of resources and is directly affecting the company's bottom line in a real way.

When explaining site architecture to clients, I start out by asking them to visualize a website like an ant hill. All of the chambers are like webpages and the tunnels are like internal links. I then have them imagine a little boy pouring water into the ant hill. He pours it down the main entrance and wants to have it fill all of the chambers. (As a side note, scientists actually have done this with cement to study the structure of ant metropolises. In one case, they had to pour 10 tons of liquid cement into an ant hill before it filled all of the chambers.) In this analogy the water represents the flow of link juice to webpages. As discussed earlier, this link juice (popularity) is essential for rankings.

The optimal structure for a website (or ant hill, if you must) would look similar to a pyramid (Figure 2-3).

This structure allows the most possible juice to get to all of the website's pages with the fewest number of links. This means that every page on the website gets some ranking benefit from the homepage.

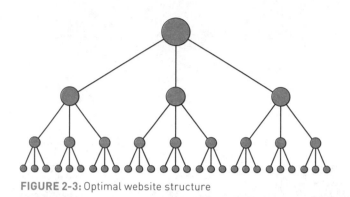

FIGURE 2-3: Optimal website structure

▶ A pyramid structure for a website allows the most possible link juice to get to all the website's pages with the fewest number of links.

> **NOTE** Homepages are almost always the most linked-to pages on a domain. This is because they are the most convenient (the shortest) URL to link to when referring to the website online.

Evaluating Homepages

Now that we are on the same page about site architecture, we can move forward. Once I get to this level of analysis, I start really looking at the site architecture. Obviously, this starts at the homepage.

Ideally, the homepage should link to every single category of pages on a website. Normally, this is accomplished with a global navigation menu (*global* meaning it is on every web page on the domain). This is easy to do with small websites because if they have less than 150 pages, the homepage could directly link to all of them. (Note this is only a good idea if the homepage has enough links pointing at it to warrant this. Remember the little boy and the ant hill; link popularity is analogous to the amount of water the little boy has. If he doesn't have enough, he can't fill every chamber.) Following are some good and bad examples of this.

GOOD EXAMPLES OF GLOBAL NAVIGATION

Figures 2-4 and 2-5 show two examples of good—that is, effective—homepage global navigation. In both cases, all of the high-level categories are linked to on the homepage. This maximizes the link value and spreads the value widely across the entire domain.

FIGURE 2-4: Amazon navigation

FIGURE 2-5: Rotten Tomatoes navigation

BAD EXAMPLES OF GLOBAL NAVIGATION

Figures 2-6 and 2-7 show two examples of bad, or ineffective, global navigation. In these cases, the hording of link juice is a bad strategy because it prevents subcategories and low level pages from benefiting from the link juice of the homepage. Without link juice, these pages wouldn't normally get indexed in the major search engine indices and wouldn't be able to refer traffic. So then why are Twitter and Facebook's pages indexed? Google is licensing APIs from Twitter and special casing Facebook. This is a good example of Google making an exception for big websites that they need to index. If these were normal websites, their indexation rate would suffer as a result of their global navigation.

© 2009 Twitter   About Us   Contact   Blog   Status   Goodies   API   Business   Help   Jobs   Terms   Privacy

FIGURE 2-6: Twitter navigation

Facebook © 2009 English (US)   About   Advertising   Developers   Careers   Terms   Blog   Widgets

FIGURE 2-7: Facebook navigation

As a result of site architecture, Amazon and Rotten Tomatoes are able to get the vast majority of their product/movie pages indexed in the major search engines. Meanwhile, Twitter and Facebook are having problems getting all of their content indexed, and the engines have begrudgingly been forced to work around their poor architecture. (Trust me, the engines don't do this often.) These two websites have plenty of links (water), but lack the tunnels (links and site architecture) to distribute them.

Evaluating Category Pages

If the website has more than 150 pages, it should divide its content into categories and link to those from the homepage. This is exactly what my former colleagues at SEOmoz look for on medium-sized websites. Ideally, these pages should serve both as a landing page for a searcher and a link juice router for search engines. Many webmasters mistakenly focus on one of these aspects while ignoring the other. As an SEO, part of your job will be making sure that both of these kinds of visitors are taken care of.

> ▶ A website with more than 150 pages should divide its content into categories that are useful to both humans and search engines alike.

Figure 2-8 shows a Netflix category page, a good example of a category page. This page links to subcategory pages that are both logical for humans to understand (genres) and helpful to search engines (fewer than 150 links).

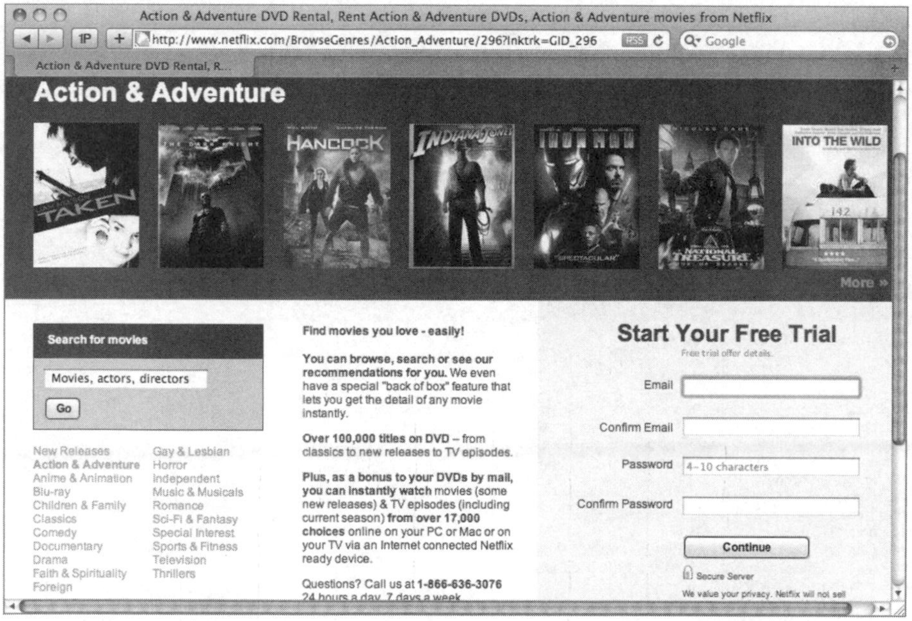

FIGURE 2-8: Netflix category page

Notice that the page has enticing images to click on and is very intuitive for first-time visitors. In this way, it is ideal for getting users to click through to a lower level page.

At the same time it is optimized for search engines by limiting the total amount of links on the page while linking to all applicable subcategories.

Figure 2-9 shows another example of a category page, this time from the Rotten Tomatoes website, and this one is less effective than the Netflix page.

MULTIPLE PATHWAYS TO CONTENT

Well-architected sites can get you to specific pages through multiple path-ways. For example, sites like Netflix or IMDb.com are models of cross-linking efficiency. Searching vertically through "Actors," you'll find the page of Zooey Deschanel, which will link to pages for Joseph Gordon-Levitt and *(500) Days of Summer*. Similarly, searching through romantic comedies will get you to (500) Days of Summer, which are only a click away from the two actors' pages. And so on.

A good site gets you to deep URLs through a logical path with minimal clicks. A great site gets you to deep URLs through any one of several logical paths, and the paths frequently cross throughout the journey. The difference between good and great means more rapid, more thorough indexing; a more appropriate distribution of page authority and authority; and more qualified traffic.

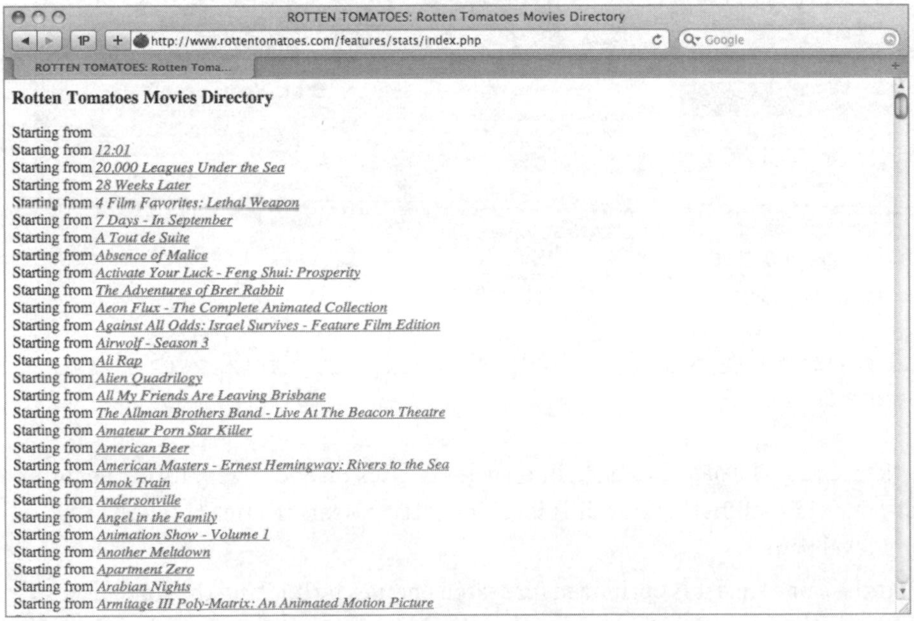

FIGURE 2-9: Rotten Tomatoes category page

Here is an example where the website is optimized for engines but not human visitors. This is a problem for two reasons:

▶ First, if a user encounters this page, it will be difficult for them to navigate, and they will likely return to the previous page. This is counterproductive for a navigation system.

▶ Second, search engine engineers preach building websites for humans not search engines. This is a clue to the long-term strategies of the search engines. This example does not appear to be built for humans and, thus, isn't a good long-term strategy for SEO.

It should be noted that this is not the main movies category page on Rotten Tomatoes, but it still serves a great example of what to avoid when recommending long-term SEO strategies. This page was built as a band-aid to make up for poor site architecture. It is far from optimal.

A good category page should do all of the following:

▶ Be useful for the user

▶ Direct link juice to all applicable subcategories

▶ Have enough unique content to be indexed by the search engines

Evaluating Subcategory Pages

If a website is very large it will need to break its categories into subcategories and link to them from the category pages. The subcategory pages should be set up exactly like category pages. The only difference is that instead of linking to more subcategory pages, they should link directly to content pages. Keep in mind that they have less link juice to pass than category pages (because they are more links away from the homepage), so subcategory pages should contain as few links as possible. This is because the amount of link juice a link passes is determined by both the link popularity of the given page and the number of links it contains. Similarly to category pages, subcategory pages should do the following:

▶ Be useful for the user

▶ Direct link juice to all applicable content pages

▶ Have enough unique content to be indexed by the search engines

PAGINATION SOLUTIONS FOR MULTIPLE OF CONTENT PAGES

What if your subcategory has 100 different products inside it? How should the link architecture look? "Information Hierarchy"—the process of configuring pages so that product and content pages get crawled effectively in large quantities—is one the most challenging aspects of SEO architecture work, and it requires a delicate balance of crawlability and usability concerns.

Having, for example, 100 products within one subcategory can be a challenge, and there are several techniques that can work by themselves or in combination to aid in the crawling and indexing processes for this much content.

First, you can start with the assumption that having all 100 products on the subcategory page creates a negative user experience, and that your preferred number of products per page is closer to 10. If that's the case, consider some of these options:

▶ **Think outside your preferred comfort zone.** For some reason, product pages often default to a very small number of results (or products), and I think this is due to bandwidth restrictions that existed long ago. If the links to product pages aren't particularly image-heavy, consider returning 20, 30, or even 50 products. If the page loads quickly, users don't mind scrolling vertically.

▶ **Create sub-subcategories.** Creating five sub-subcategories and linking to all of them from the subcategory page is really no different than linking to five separate content results pages. And it can help, especially if there is appreciable keyword demand behind the terms in the sub-subcategory.

▶ **Link to multiple pages showing limited numbers of links to content pages, but canonicalize to a "see all" version.** Have you ever seen a sub-category page that links to dozens or hundreds of different content pages by linking to the "next" page at the bottom of the page? This type of "chain" navigation is just about the least effective solution possible for getting hundreds of content pages indexed. Instead, offer users and engines a link to "see all," which links to a page showing all products (and thus linking to all content pages). Your navigation can still link to smaller pages showing fewer product links, but those smaller pages should all canonically point to the "see all" version.

Evaluating Content Pages

Content pages are the meat of websites. They are the reason visitors came to the site, and just like a good breakfast, these pages should leave those visitors feeling fulfilled and smelling of delicious bacon. (I made up that last part, but if a website really did smell like bacon, I would surely link to it.) The pages should be very specific to a given topic (usually a product or an object) and be hyper-relevant.

As an SEO you should be looking to see if the purpose of the page is directly stated in all of the following areas:

- ► Title tag
- ► URL
- ► Content of page
- ► Images

> **NOTE** Good content pages act as link magnets. They are much more likely to receive links than subcategory and category pages. Smart SEOs use this as an advantage and have content pages link back to their applicable category and subcategory pages. This then increases the amount of juice flowing to all of the content pages on the website and makes them all rank better.

GOOD EXAMPLE OF A CONTENT PAGE

Figure 2-10 shows an example of well laid out and search engine–friendly content.

The content page in this figure is good for a couple of reasons. First the content itself is unique on the Internet (which makes it worthwhile for search engines to rank well) and covers unique content in a lot of depth. If you have a question about Super Mario World, there is a good chance that this page will be able to answer your question.

Aside from content, this page is well laid out. As you can see in Figure 2-10, the topic of the page is stated in the title tag (Super Mario World – Wikipedia, the free encyclopedia); the URL (http://en.wikipedia.org/wiki/Super_Mario_World), the page's content (Notice the page heading, "Super Mario World"); and again within the alt text of the images on the page.

Imagine for a second you are a search engine engineer working at one of the main search engines. Your task is to organize the information on the Web and make it universally accessible. The problem is that the information on the Internet is not formatted in any specific format. This makes it incredibly difficult to write code that can read all of the information on the Internet, much less organize it. Now imagine you come to a page like that in Figure 2-10. The page uses multiple elements to describe what it is about. These clues are indispensible. By relying on these, you find it much easier to write code that understands what the page is about. Combine this with the fact that this page is part of a trusted and well linked to resource on the Web and it is easy to see why search engineers write code to make this example rank highly for relevant queries.

FIGURE 2-10: Wikipedia page on Super Mario World

BAD EXAMPLE OF A CONTENT PAGE

In contrast, Figure 2-11 shows a much less effective example of a content page. Notice how it differs from the first example.

This figure shows a less search engine–friendly example of a content page that is targeting the term *Super Mario World*. While the subject of the page is present in some of the important elements of the webpage (title tag and images), the content is less robust than the Wikipedia example, and the relevant copy on the page is less helpful to a reader.

Notice that the description of the game is suspiciously similar to copy written by a marketing department: "Mario's off on his biggest adventure ever, and this time he's brought along a friend." That is not the language that searchers query for, and it is not the type of message that is likely to answer a searcher's query. Compare this to the first sentence of the Wikipedia example, "Super Mario World is a platform game developed and published by Nintendo as a pack-in launch title for the Super Nintendo Entertainment System." In the GameFAQs example, all that is established by the first sentence is that someone or something named Mario is on an adventure that is bigger than his or her last (how do you quantify that?) and he or she is accompanied by an unnamed friend. On the other hand, the Wikipedia sentence tells the reader that Super Mario World is a game developed and published by Nintendo for the gaming system Super Nintendo Entertainment System.

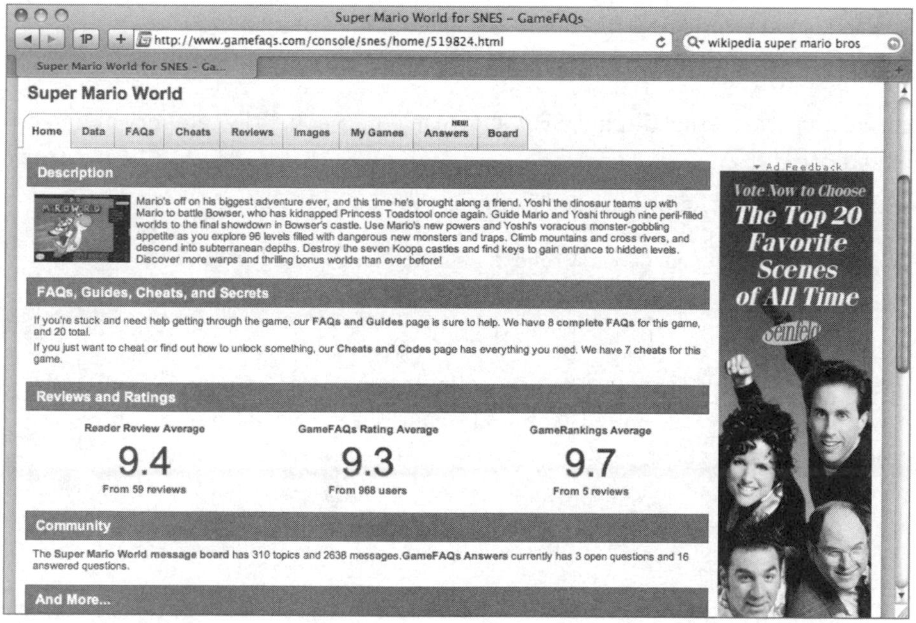

FIGURE 2-11: GameFAQs page on Super Mario World

If you were a search engineer, which example would you want to rank higher for queries related to this game? Search results show that Bing and Google engineers think the Wikipedia example should rank better.

AN IDEAL CONTENT PAGE

An ideal content page should do all of the following:

▶ Be hyper-relevant to a specific topic (usually a product or single object)

▶ Include subject in title tag

- Include subject in URL
- Include subject in image alt text
- Specify subject several times throughout text content
- Provide unique content about a given subject
- Link back to its category page
- Link back to its subcategory page
- Link back to its homepage (normally accomplished with an image link showing the website logo on the top left of a page)

Evaluating URL Structure

Along with smart internal linking, SEOs should make sure that the category hierarchy is reflected in URLs.

Take a look at the following good example of URL structure:

```
http://www.dmoz.org/Games/Video_Games/History/
```

> NOTE   Remember to consider case when you're considering URL structure. Different platforms capitalize terms in different ways. Remember that any case style is fine (lowercase, mixed case, and so on), but that whatever method you choose, you must stick to it and watch for unwanted variants being indexed. Two URLs with the same characters—but different case styles—are considered two distinct URLs by engines.

▶ An effective URL structure can help search engines understand how useful or relevant a given webpage is.

This URL is effective because it clearly shows the hierarchy of the information on the page (history as it pertains to video games in the context of games in general). This information is used to determine the relevancy of a given webpage by the search engines. Using the hierarchy, the engines can deduce that the page likely doesn't pertain to history in general but rather to that of the history of video games. This makes it an ideal candidate for search results related to video game history. Engines can speculate on all of this information without even needing to process the content on the page.

Now take a look at the following example of URL structure:

```
http://www.imdb.com/title/tt0468569/
```

Unlike the first example, this URL does not reflect the information hierarchy of the website. You can see that the given page relates to titles and is on the IMDb website, but you cannot determine what the page is about. The reference to tt0468569 does not directly imply anything that a web surfer is likely to search for. This means that the information provided by the URL is of very little value to search engines.

If you were a search engineer, which page would want to be included at the top of a search results page? The answer, of course, depends on the content and link profile of the given page, but instead of the URL supplementing this information, it is adding nothing.

> **NOTE** The IMDb example is interesting because the URL ranks so well for "the dark knight" despite its URL structure. One of the reasons this site is so authoritative is because its movie-specific pages begin to accrue links well before the release date of films, and this head start is able to overcome less significant factors like semantic signals from the URL itself.
>
> Still, true optimization requires examining all available avenues of improvement and weighing the benefit of implementing them. Could the IMDb page rank higher than the movie's microsite itself if the URL were simplified? And how would a more semantically clean URL affect click-through? Certainly not negatively.

URL structure is important because it helps the search engines to understand the relative significance of and adds a useful relevancy metric to the given page. It is also helpful for links because people are more likely to link with the relevant anchor text if the keywords are included in the URL.

Action Checklist

When you are viewing a website from the 10-foot level, be sure to check for and note all of the following:

- ✔ Homepage links to every category of pages on the website
- ✔ The ability of category pages to help the user and the search engines
- ✔ The presence of links on category pages to all applicable subcategories (if the given amount of page link juice can sustain it)
- ✔ The ability of subcategory pages to help the user and the search engines
- ✔ The presence of links on subcategory pages to all applicable content pages

✔ The relevancy of the given content pages to the given topic

✔ The ability of the URL structure to match category hierarchy and supplement relevancy

In this section I discussed what to look for when analyzing site architecture. I covered the different aspects that are important for category, subcategory, and content pages, and I included a lot of graphical examples (because picture books are easier to read than text-based books).

In the following section I want to dive down to the lowest level of webpages and examine individual pieces of content. If text is the currency of the Internet, consider the pieces of content to be dollar bills. Your mother was mostly right: money does not grow on trees, but it does grow on the Internet.

THE 1-FOOT VIEW—INDIVIDUAL CONTENT PIECES

▶ The content is the single most important element on the website.

You've made it! You are now low enough to see the actual content on the page. Are you excited? You should be. This is what visitors to the site come to see.

What Is Good Content?

In order to view content appropriately you need to know what you are looking for. So, what is good content? This question is so obvious, it seems silly to ask. Unfortunately, it is so broad, that a straightforward answer would be useless. Instead, I will answer it like most great geniuses who are posed with a difficult question; I will simply change the question. What is good content to an SEO? This is a much more realistic question to answer.

I have thought long and hard about this question and I believe that for SEOs, all good content requires two attributes. Good content must supply a demand and be linkable.

▶ **Good content feeds a demand:** Just like the world's markets, information is affected by supply and demand. The best content is that which does the best job of supplying the largest demand. It might take the form of an XKCD comic that is supplying nerd jokes to a large group of technologists who want to laugh. It also might be a Wikipedia article that explains to the world the definition of Web 2.0. It can be a video, an image, sound, or text, but it must satisfy a demand in order to be considered good content.

▶ **Good content is linkable:** From an SEO perspective, there is no difference between the best and worst content on the Net if it is not linkable. If people can't link to it, search engines will be very unlikely to rank it, and the content won't drive traffic to the given website. Unfortunately, this happens a lot more often than you might think. Have you ever been scrolling through an image-based slideshow and seen an image that takes your breath away only to realize that due to its implementation, you have no way to share that individual image? (This happens to me a lot on CNN.com.) Have you ever heard a song online that you wanted to share with a friend but were unable to due to copyright protection software? It is a frustrating experience, and it turns potentially good content into bad content.

So if that is good content, what is bad content? Bad content is just the opposite of good content. (I paid how much for this book?) It does not satisfy a demand and/or it is not linkable. It is rampant all over the Internet and a waste of time and other precious resources.

Good Content with a Bad Haircut

Every once in a while I stumble across good content that appears to be bad. Most often, this is because I immediately disregard it as an ad. SEOs view the Internet with powerful ad blinders. If something looks like an ad, it often simply gets ignored. Figure 2-12 shows good content displayed in a way that makes it hard to see for many SEOs.

FIGURE 2-12: Close-up of Bing Toolbox

Notice that the key call to action pieces on this Bing webmaster page are formatted in the same way as Google AdSense ads (clickable and colored link on top of unclickable black text, all of which is separated into small rectangle sections). This makes them hard to see and turns them into bad content.

When viewing websites from an SEO perspective, you sometimes need to remove your ad blinders to see all of the information available. Remember, as a student of the Internet, your perspective is jaded. Keep this in mind and try to be aware of it. Sometimes good content is right in front of you, and you just can't see it.

Action Checklist

When viewing a website from the 1-foot level, be sure to take notes on the following:

- ✔ Identify whether the content satisfies a demand
- ✔ Identify whether the content is linkable
- ✔ Make sure you are not missing something and viewing the page with a sharp eye

SUMMARY

In this chapter you completed your SEO first look at a site. You may be confused why all of these steps have been necessary. In fact, you probably feel exactly like Daniel from the *The Karate Kid* after waxing Mr. Miyagi's cars. There is a reason for all of these steps that will become clearer in the next three chapters. In the meantime, stick with me. Wax on, wax off.

In the next chapter, you use your SEO perspective and combine it with SEO tools. You will then have all of the resources you need to start identifying SEO problems on websites.

Picking the Right SEO Tools

Now that you have the correct SEO perspective on viewing websites, it is time to find out which tools SEO professionals use to dig deeper. Batman has his utility belt, generals have their massive armies, and as you are about to find out, SEOs have browser extensions and nifty websites.

This chapter is meant to be used as a resource for coming back to as you read the rest of the book. Its content is important to know up front (that's why it is located here rather than at the end of the book). It is completely appropriate to skim this chapter because it has a lot of technical information, but be sure to get a sense for the kinds of tools that are available and which ones are the most powerful. In my experience, the only way to learn how to use an SEO tool is to actually sit down and start using it. This chapter will be helpful for you when you start to do that by identifying for you which tools are useful for which situations and which metrics on each tool are important.

> **NOTE** A list of almost all of the tools I have used as well as all of the articles that I found most useful are available at **www.seomoz.org/dp/the-internet-marketing-handbook**.

Also, because this publication is in book form, some of the details and screenshots in this chapter will eventually be out of sync with the versions of the online resources that are available to you. I have done my best to focus on only the parts of the tools that are core features and won't be replaced. Having written that, I realize that this is next to impossible to predict, so I encourage you to use this as a basic foundation for the types of tools that are helpful and to explore to expand your SEO arsenal. Best of luck and Godspeed!

VIEW SOURCE

Oh, trusty source code. Did you know you can use it for other reasons than stealing images and mp3s? Whenever I come across a page that is not getting indexed, the first thing I do is view its source.

▶ Viewing a webpage's source enables you to see what the search engines see when they crawl the Internet.

> **TIP** I use Safari for surfing the Net (because for my uses it is faster), but as soon as I want to view source, I switch to Firefox. I do this because Firefox formats and colors source code so it is much easier to read. Specifically I find the added indentation of HTML tags useful for quickly navigating to the HTML **<head>** of the document. The **<head>** tag should be the first indented tag after the **<html>** tag, and in Firefox is colored purple if you keep the default settings. Once I have found the **<head>** of the document I look inside it at the meta tags (robots, description, and content-type) to see what settings the website has set for these options. You can read the best practices for these settings in Chapter 6.

Figure 3-1 shows viewing the source of a webpage in Firefox. Notice how the code is automatically indented and colored to make it easier to read.

Viewing source is a feature that is included in every major Internet browser that allows you to read the raw code returned by the requested website server when you view a website. This is important because this raw view is what the search engines see when they crawl the Internet. In general I use "View Source" when I want to:

▶ See how well a website's meta data is optimized

▶ Check for potential problems with webpage format

▶ Analyze global navigation

FIGURE 3-1: Image of viewing source in Firefox

Key Data Points When Viewing Source

When you view a webpage's source, you want to look carefully at several key data points to get an idea of how the search engines see the given page. The key data points below are the most important meta data of a page that the engines care about.

▶ **Meta description:** If you really did read the *The Beginner's Guide to Search Engine Optimization* (www.seomoz.org/article/beginners-guide-to-search-engine-optimization) mentioned in Chapter 1, you already know what a meta description is and why it is important. If you didn't, the quick definition is that a meta description is the textual description of a webpage that webmasters can write that search engines will include in search results. Thus, this content is important because it acts as a free ad for the given website. In the source code meta descriptions are written as

```
<meta name="description" content="Description Goes Here" />
```

The best meta descriptions are enticing and are written about the specific subject of the given page. (For example, all of the information you would ever need on adult diapers.)

OPTIMIZING FOR PEOPLE, NOT JUST SEARCH ENGINES

Remember that not all of your optimization should be aimed at search engine algorithms. In order to be successful, you need to optimize for the people that are going to read the search results that you optimize. Meta descriptions and title tags are your place to do that.

Meta descriptions are practically easy to write for people because they are not used directly for ranking purposes by the engines. Instead they are used to entice people to click the given search result. They should be reviewed by a marketing person (like an SEO) and optimized for people rather than engines.

TIP Meta descriptions are for people not necessarily for search engines. I have found the following textual additions very useful for increasing click-through rates in search engine results:

- ▶ Free Shipping
- ▶ Low Price Guarantee
- ▶ Reviews, Pictures, Samples
- ▶ Interviews
- ▶ Official Site

When reviewing meta descriptions, I find it useful to pull up the search result in the search engines and compare the meta description to that of the competition. I ask myself if I would click the result compared to others, and if not, I figure out why not and use this information to improve the description.

- ▶ **Meta robots:** Meta robots is a page-specific directive for controlling search engine crawlers. This is most useful for keeping specific pages out of the search engines indices while still being able to transfer their link value to other pages.

- ▶ In source code meta robots looks like this:

```
<meta name="robots" content="VALUES" />
```

Technically, robots is the value of an attribute called name. Because this is a mouthful, SEOs tend to refer to it as meta robots. Regardless of what you call it, it is better than `robots.txt` for keeping pages out of the search engine's indices because it disallows the engines from even listing the URL.

Figure 3-2 shows the result of using `robots.txt` to block a page that has inbound links to it. It's fairly rare to see a robots-excluded file show up in SERPs, but it's not unheard of (as Figure 3-2 shows), so remember that as you choose your exclusion methods. Notice that the URL is still shown in search engine results, but all of the meta data (title tag and meta description) is not shown. This makes this result essentially a waste, thus making it better to not include these blocked pages in the search engine indices at all.

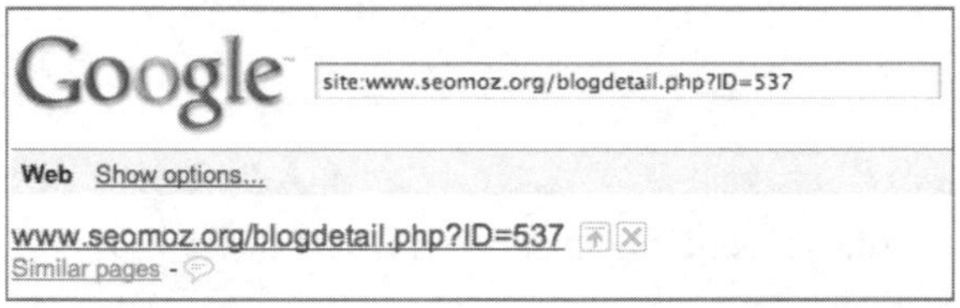

FIGURE 3-2: Google result showing page blocked by robots.txt

See how the URL is still present in the index? This is because it is blocked by `robots.txt` but still has links pointing at it. These links are now pointing at a page that the search engines can't access (SEOs refer to this as a black hole or an "uncrawled reference"), and the result is formatted in a way that is unlikely to be clicked by searchers. This is happening because behind the scenes search engines find this URL via links but aren't able to crawl it because it blocked via `robots.txt`. To make matters worse, since the search engines can't crawl these pages, they can't pass the page's link value through the links on the page, thus the black hole association. This means not only does the given page not get credit for its bound links, but it also can't pass this value to other pages that aren't blocked.

Alternatively, meta robots keep even the URL out of the indices and allow the links on that page to continue to pass juice (`"noindex, follow"`).

▶ **Frames:** A frame is a HTML technique for embedding one URL into another URL. A common example of this is a help center that keeps navigation separate from informational articles. Frames have very negative impact on SEO. Search engines treat frames as completely different pages (as they should) and do not share any of the page link metrics between two frames on a given page. This means that if a link goes to a given URL, it won't help any of the other frames on the page.

▶ From an SEO perspective, you should avoid frames at all times. If a client has them, you should educate them on alternatives like content displayed using AJAX.

AVOIDING BLACK HOLES

To avoid the black hole problems associated with **robots.txt**, meta robots should almost always be set to **"index, follow"**. (These are actually the default values; having no meta robots tag is the same as having one set to **"index, follow"**.) Exceptions include **"noindex, follow"**, which is appropriate for duplicate index pages, and **"index, nofollow"**, where the destination of links can not be vouched for (as in user-generated content). There is very little reason to ever use **"noindex, nofollow"** because you might as well maintain the value of the outgoing links.

In the source code a frame is identified by code like the following:

```
<frameset rows="70%" cols="50%">
    <frame src="left-frame.html">
    <frame src="right-frame.html">
    <noframes>
        <p>This is what is displayed to users who don't have
           frames and search engines in some cases.</p>
    </noframes>
</frameset>
```

or simply:

```
<iframe src ="example.html" width="100px" height="300px">
  <p>This text is read by engines but not people with
     frames enables</p>
</iframe>
```

▶ **Flash and Shockwave:** Although the search engines have gotten better at parsing Flash and Shockwave, it is still not a viable SEO-friendly option for a website. Not only is most of the content obfuscated, but linking is made difficult because websites made in Flash usually lack any kind of site architecture (from a URL perspective). Flash and Shockwave is usually identified in the source code with something similar to:

```
<object classid="clsid:D27CDB6E-AE6D-11cf-96B8-444553540000"
   codebase="http://active.macromedia.com/flash2/cabs/
   swflash.cab#version=4,0,0,0" id=inrozxa width=100%
   height=100%>
    <param name=movie value="welcomenew6.swf">
    <param name=quality value=high>
    <param name=bgcolor value=#FFFFFF>
```

```
<embed src="inrozxa.swf" quality=high bgcolor=#FFFFFF
   width=100% height=100% type="application/
   x-shockwave-flash" pluginspage=
   "http://www.macromedia.com/shockwave/download/
   index.cgi?P1_Prod_Version=ShockwaveFlash">
</embed>
</object>
```

Depending on the version, the code you see might be different but the main indicators are <embed> or <object> tags with one attribute pointing to macromedia.com or adobe.com (the maker of Flash).

THE PROBLEM WITH FLASH

The problem with Flash is it is hard for search engines to parse it and understand what content it contains. When you see Flash with valuable content inside of it, it is best to recommend to the client that the content be added to the HTML page so that the search engines can parse it or to use an alternative to Flash.

The best potential replacement of Flash may become HTML5. At the time of writing, HTML5 is in infancy with only a few major websites including it. HTML5 has some of the pros of Flash (animation) but is easy to parse like normal HTML.

▶ **JavaScript links:** At the time of writing, JavaScript links are dangerous because their ability to pass juice is not very clear. They can be written in a lot of different ways, and Bing and Google have not said which types of JavaScript links they support. We know that they are being crawled, are used for URL "discovery" by engines, and that they are passing some link juice, but the relative amount is unknown. This means that JavaScript links are not useful as an alternative to HTML-based links. They are implemented in JavaScript with the location object:

```
window.location.replace('http://www.example.com');
```

This is often followed by a .href or .replace depending on the implementation.

When you encounter JavaScript based links on clients' websites, it is best to try to replace them with standard HTML-based links.

▶ **Page title:** Even though you can see a page's title at the top of most browser windows, viewing the title tag from within source code can be very helpful. Does the page title appear within the <head> section and outside of any <script> tags? Does the page have only one title? (You'd be surprised.)

NOTE   Many people are confused by the relationship of Java to JavaScript. My favorite explanation is "Java is to JavaScript what Car is to Carpet." They are not related other than they are both computer languages. (Even that is a stretch because JavaScript is only a scripting language.) The name similarities are due to their respective creators really enjoying coffee (Java). It's as simple as that. Howard Schultz would be proud.

META KEYWORDS ARE OBSOLETE

What about meta keywords? Meta keywords refer to a specific meta tag that used to be used by search engines. This meta data is no longer an important metric. It is used by neither Bing nor Google. Don't waste your time writing it.

Common Questions Viewing Source Can Answer

Now that you know some of the key data points to look for when you are viewing source, it's time to consider some of the questions viewing source can help you to answer.

IS THIS PAGE NOT GETTING INDEXED DUE TO ON-PAGE ERRORS?

This is a fairly common situation. The key things to look at when trying to diagnose this are:

- ▶ Erroneous use of meta robots
- ▶ Use of Flash
- ▶ Use of frames
- ▶ robots.txt (not on the same page)

As HTML matures, the on-page giveaways of Flash (sounds and animation) will become less obvious. The surest way to see what is going on is to view source. When trying to answer this question, you simply need to look for an <embed> tag or <object> tag with an attribute that points to either adobe.com or macromedia.com. If you find this, the Flash-based piece of content is not being parsed by the search engines as easily as it could be if it was written in HTML.

IS THAT PIECE OF CONTENT IN A FRAME?

This is very important to avoid and easy to diagnose. Simply search the source code of the page for the `<frameset>`, `<frame>`, or `<iframe>` tags. Frames can be useful for some situations (as in Gmail and checkout processes), but they are almost never a good implementation for pages that depend on search engine–referred traffic.

ARE THESE NAVIGATIONAL LINKS PASSING JUICE?

As discussed in Chapter 2, site architecture starts with the homepage. I find myself viewing source a lot to see how global navigation is implemented. From an SEO perspective, the best implementation of navigation uses HTML lists and Cascading Style Sheets (CSS). When done well this looks like the following:

```
<ul>
    <li id="example-1"><a href="http://www.example.com/"
title="Example 1">Example 1</a></li>
    <li id="example-2"><a href="http://www.example.com/example-2.html"
title="Example 2">Example 2</a></li>
    <li id="example-3"><a href="http://www.example.com/example-3.html"
title="Example 3">Example 3</a></li>
    <li id="example-4"><a href="http://www.example.com/example-4.html"
title="Example 4">Example 4</a></li>
    <li id="example-5"><a href="http://www.example.com/example-5.html"
title="Example 5">Example 5</a></li>
    <li id="example-6"><a href="http://www.example.com/example-6.html"
title="Example 6">Example 6</a></li>
</ul>
```

If the navigation takes this form and the meta robot is set up to pass juice, then global navigation does pass juice. Notice that this code uses normal HTML-based links that are easy to parse. If these were obfuscated (that is, more complicated than necessary) with JavaScript or nofollows, the given links would not pass juice.

USEFUL SEARCH ENGINE QUERIES

The search engines have been gracious enough to give us special search commands for understanding their vast amount of data. The commands that I find the most useful are:

- ► cache:
- ► site:
- ► inurl:

▶ intitle:

▶ +

▶ -

▶ |

These commands, when used in combination, are powerful and sometimes prove essential for diagnosing SEO problems. To the search engineers that created these commands, I send my sincerest gratitude. You make my job much easier. (It should be noted that I have intentionally left out the search engine commands that I don't use. Because of this decision, I recommend that you don't treat this as a comprehensive list. It details only the commands that I find essential for SEOs.)

These commands are useful for filtering search results to show only pages that contain certain attributes. This means if you find a webpage that has an issue like a misspelling in a title tag, you can use the search engines to find all of the occurrences of this on your website and use this information to fix the problem.

Another example of this is for checking the effectiveness of keyword targeting. It is a common SEO problem to have multiple pages targeting the same keyword. This is a problem because then all of these pages must compete with each other for rankings rather than the best practice that would have all of these pages combined and one more powerful page competing for rankings. Figure 3-3 shows how these pages can be found by limiting a search to only those pages on Google.com with the phrase *lol* in the title tag of the document.

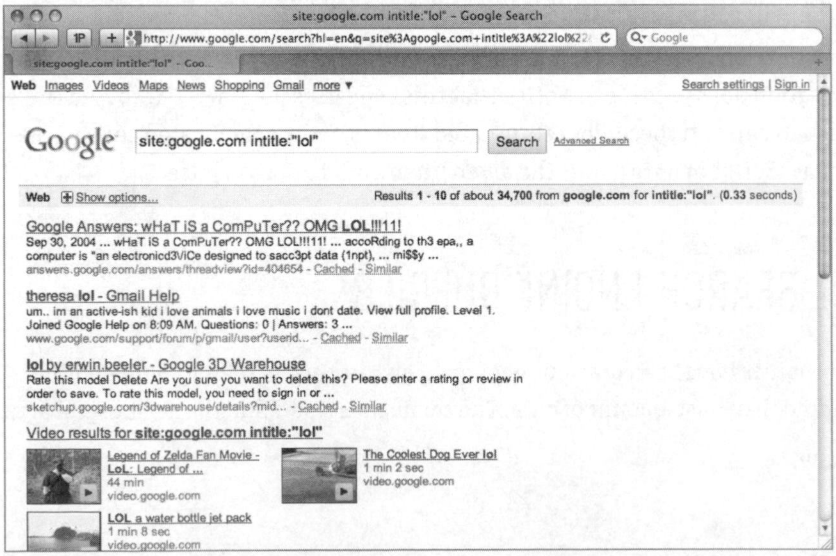

FIGURE 3-3: Image of combined search engine command query in Google

I use these search engine queries when I want to:

▶ Search for duplicate content

▶ Get a general idea for how well indexed a website is

Key Data Points Search Engine Commands Can Generate

You can query a search engine in the following ways to yield some useful data points:

▶ **Normal search:** What is the best way to see how the search engines will act? Run a normal search. According to my web history I search using Google about 17 times a day. This does not include the internal searches I do on Google properties like Gmail and YouTube or the searches I do on my phone. I have found that the best way to better understand Google is to continually and constantly use it. After all, our goal as SEOs is to improve our clients' rankings. What better way to do this than studying search results every day?

▶ **Quotes:** As I am sure you are aware, putting search queries in quotes limits results to exact matches. This extremely helpful when you want to see if a random page is in the Google index. Simply find a random sentence in the content, wrap it in quotes, and search for it. If it is long enough, odds are it has only been written once on the Internet and should return only one result. If it doesn't appear it means it isn't indexed. If it appears more than once, it means your client has duplicate content issues.

▶ **cache:** Cache is a copy of the file Googlebot downloads when it visits a website. As an SEO, this information is extremely important because it shows you exactly what Google sees. This is especially useful for determining crawl rate and diagnosing potential geo-location issues.

One of my favorite examples of the importance of cache use was when my former colleagues at SEOmoz were working with restaurant review website, yelp.com. Yelp was implementing a complicated system of geo-locating based on IP addresses and cookies to automatically redirect users to their applicable city version of yelp.com. For some reason, Yelp was having issues getting results in Google. Upon checking the cache, my co-workers saw that whenever Googlebot crawled Yelp, Yelp was automatically taken to the Mountain View, California, version of the site (home of Google headquarters). D'oh! After my co-workers pointed this out, this problem was quickly resolved and Yelp's traffic skyrocketed.

▶ *When viewing the cached version of a website, try clicking the link labeled "Text-only version." This shows a much better representation of what Google sees. I can't count how many hidden links I have found by using this trick.*

▶ **site:** The site command is used to limit a search query to a specific site. This is extremely useful for diagnosing indexing problems. I generally start by using the site command alone (`site:techmeme.com`). This simple query can tell you two important things:

   ▷ First, it gives you an idea of the major sections of a website. It also gives you an idea of how many pages are indexed in Google. If you know that a given site has only 100 pages, and this query returns 100,000 results, you know you have a duplicate content issue.

   ▷ Additionally, it makes you aware of some of the subdomains on the given site. This is extremely helpful for understanding how Google thinks a site is organized.

▶ **inurl:** This command limits search results to those where the query appears in the URL. This is most useful when combined with the site command (`site:www.seomoz.org inurl:"Rand Fishkin"`). Most SEO professionals find this technique most useful for identifying URL parameter–induced duplicate content (`site:www.example.com inurl:"sessionid"`). I use this after I identify a problematic parameter and I want to find all of its occurrences.

▶ **intitle:** Similar to the inurl command, the intitle command limits results to only those where the query is in the title tag. This can be helpful for many things including piracy (`intitle:"index of mp3"`), vanity searches (`intitle:"danny dover"`), and SEO-related things like duplicate title tag detection (`intitle:"my company: Best product ever page"`).

▶ **+:** The plus sign, when placed directly before a term, tells Google to search for exactly that term, not synonyms. For example, a search for `ghw bush` will return results that assume you mean "George Herbert Walker Bush". A search for `+ghw bush`, however, will return results that assume you want specific references to "GHW" in the results.

▶ **-:** The minus sign is a tremendous aid to filtering queries, and it can be used with specific query terms (`cubs -chicago -baseball` will show you results for "cubs" that do not contain Chicago or baseball) or in conjunction with specific operators discussed in this section. Searching for `"danny sullivan" -site:searchengineland.com` will return results about Danny Sullivan that appear anywhere except for SearchEngineLand.com. This operator works similarly to filter out title contents (`music -intitle:mp2`) and URL contents (`site:nytimes.com -inurl:pagemode=print` shows all indexed pages from nytimes.com that are not "print-friendly" versions).

▶ **|:** The pipe symbol symbolizes an "OR" search and can be used with regular query terms or with the commands listed in this section, primarily when you're looking for multiple items within a given dataset. For example, `site:example.com inurl:sessionid|jsessionid` will find URLs that contain either "sessionid" or "jsessionid" in indexed URLs from example.com. Similarly, `site:seomoz.org danny|rand` will return pages from SEOmoz.org that contain either "danny" or "rand" in the copy. (Pages that include both "danny" and "rand" will also be included with this operator, so it's a true "and/or" operator, not an "exclusive or" operator.)

▶ *The search engine commands in Google must be started with a lowercase letter or they won't work properly.*

Common Questions These Queries Can Answer

As I've already alluded to, you can use these queries to quickly answer some key questions.

IS THIS PAGE INDEXED?

To answer this question all you have to do is search for the URL preceded with the inurl command. For example, the query `inurl:"digg.com/users/jayadelson"` checks to see if the Digg profile for Digg's CEO is indexed. Hint: It is.

DOES THIS PAGE SUFFER FROM DUPLICATE CONTENT PROBLEMS?

If you have to ask, the answer is likely yes. To be sure, you can use any of the search engine commands previously discussed to check. Alternatively, you can use my preferred method and search for a full sentence from the page with the site command. For example, the query `site:google.com "Gmail stores, processes and maintains your messages, contact lists and other data related to your account in order to provide"` shows you that Google has its Gmail privacy policy posted on two different URLs. Tsk, tsk.

OMITTED RESULTS

Sometimes Google will mask similar results on searches. When it does this, it provides an indication of this with a link that says "omitted results". In these cases, it is important to click this to see the pages that Google has decided are duplicate pages.

ABOUT HOW MANY PAGES ON THIS DOMAIN ARE INDEXED?

This question can be dangerous because the number that is returned is not always accurate. The major search engines have data centers located in many places around the world that contain different versions of indices with different amounts of URL. This means that if you check the amount of pages indexed from one site, it can vary depending on which data center you happen to be accessing at that time. (Note: the data center you are accessing is not disclosed on the search result page.) If you are asked by a client for indexation numbers, you can generate a rough estimate by using the search site:example.com and using the number of results. If you do this, it is important to let the client know the problems with this metric.

▶ Be careful. If you are checking the amount of pages indexed from one site, that information can vary depending on what search engine data center you are accessing at a given time.

SEARCH ENGINE–PROVIDED TOOLS

As SEO has grown in popularity and as an industry, the search engines have started to provide more information about their data. It started with the queries listed in the preceding section and eventually turned into tools that are dedicated to making our jobs as SEOs easier. Bing offers a toolset called Webmaster Tools but it is not nearly as helpful as Google's Webmaster Central. The two most popular search engine–provided tools that are expected to exist for a while are Google Webmaster Central and Google AdWords Keyword Tool. (Bing, please catch up. We could use your help.)

> NOTE Also, I should note that a tool called Yahoo! Site Explorer existed, but because of Microsoft's takeover of Yahoo's search, and because of an uncertain future for the tool, I will not be writing about the tool in this edition of this book.

▶ **Google AdWords Keyword Tool:** This tool is available at https://adwords .google.com/select/KeywordToolExternal and is shown in Figure 3-4.

With Google AdWords Keyword Tool you can see Google specific information about how many monthly searches are performed on a given term. This is extremely useful for conducting keyword research and deciding which word a given page should target.

> NOTE If you do not have an AdWords account (which is required for full access to this tool's data), Google Insights for Search is another excellent tool that enables you to identify keyword trends and compare the relative popularity of up to five phrases at a time: www.google.com/insights/search/.

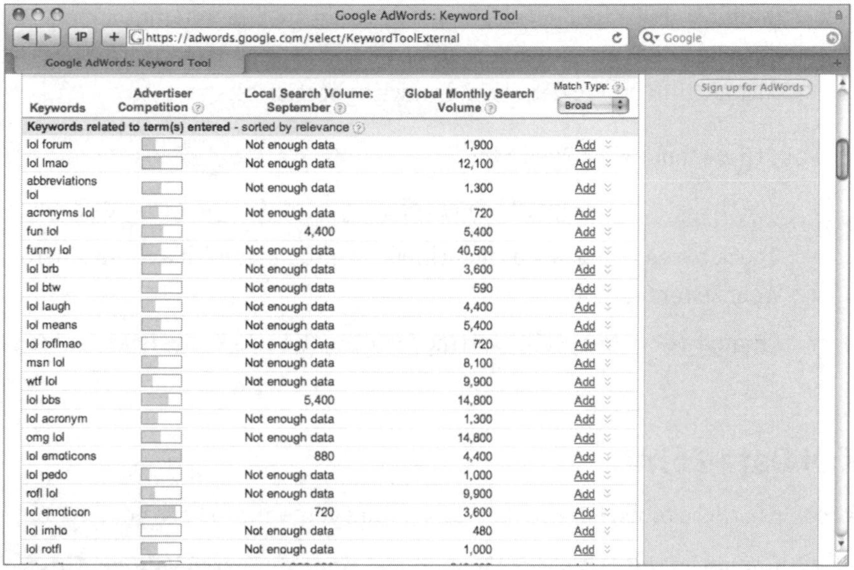

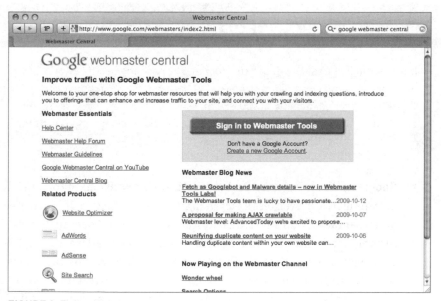

FIGURE 3-4: Google AdWords Keyword Tool

▶ **Google Webmaster Central:** This tool is available at www.google.com/
webmasters/ and is shown in Figure 3-5, and specific Webmaster Tools
reports are discussed in the next section.

FIGURE 3-5: Google Webmaster Central

Google Webmaster Central allows you to set specific settings for your website as well as see specific metrics of how Google sees your website. These metrics include link profile details and crawling statistics.

I use these tools when I want to:

▶ See the relative competitiveness of a keyword (Google AdWords Keyword Tool)

▶ Check to see if Google has identified any problems with a client site (Google Webmaster Central)

▶ Change a Google-specific setting for a site (Google Webmaster Central)

Key Data Points

As you use these tools, here are key data points you want to keep your eye on:

▶ **Google AdWords Keyword Tool: Global Monthly Search Volume:** This metric shows the approximate number of global searches for the given word or phrase. It is unclear how accurate this metric is but anecdotal evidence suggests that all of the data is relatively close to real. Unfortunately, this is the best we can do at this time. SEOs use this data to help determine keyword choices.

CHECKING VARIATIONS OF WORDS

It is extremely beneficial to use this tool to compare the relative worth of variations of the same word. For example, at of the time of writing the query "music video" is searched globally 11,100,000 more times than "music videos" In this case, and many others, the inclusion of an "s" makes an enormous difference.

▶ **Google AdWords Keyword Tool: Advertiser Competition:** Unfortunately for us, this metric is even less exact than the previous metric. It is depicted as a green bar rather than an artificially rounded number. Come on, Google! This information is useful for rough approximations of advertiser competitiveness. This applies only to advertisers bidding on Google keywords and merely correlates with the competitiveness of the natural search results. Professional SEOs use this in combination with the number of global searches to find high-volume, low-competition keywords. It is not an exact science, but again, it is the best we have right now.

Common Questions These Tools Can Answer

These two Google tools can help you answer two important questions.

WHAT IS THE BEST WAY TO WRITE A SPECIFIC KEYWORD?

The best way to answer this question is to use the Google AdWords Keyword Tool and both submit multiple variations of your keyword and check the "Use Synonyms" check-box. As I mentioned in the music video example earlier in this section, one letter can make a huge amount of difference in traffic.

GOOGLE WEBMASTER TOOLS

The Google Webmaster Toolset (GWT) is an excellent way of gathering Google-specific data about your site's performance and finding potential obstacles to Google viewing the site correctly. Some reports contain data that is not particularly actionable, while others show errors that you can repair immediately for nearly instant gain. The following sections discuss GWT at a high level, followed by a report-by-report synopsis of issues that GWT discusses—and what, if anything, you should be looking for.

Key Data Points

▶ **Google Webmaster Central:** This is an extremely important resource for all webmasters. It is essentially a control panel for websites in Google's index. At the time of writing, this interface offered tools for moving domains, setting locality preference, checking common SEO problems, analyzing link profiles, and exporting important SEO data. I highly recommend that every SEO sign up for this tool and verify their clients' websites. In doing so, they will likely gain new insight into their websites and how Google interprets them.

Common Questions Webmaster Tools Can Answer

These tools can help you answer the following questions.

HOW DOES GOOGLE SEE MY SITE?

This is a big question, and the individual reports that follow in this chapter all combine to give a pretty comprehensive look at how Google interprets the content on your site.

HOW DO I ASK GOOGLE FOR REINCLUSION IF I HAVE BEEN PENALIZED?

Google considers its index and services private and reserves the right to exclude anyone for any reason. When Google search quality representatives find a website they believe is violating the Google Webmaster Guidelines (www.google.com/support/webmasters/bin/answer.py?hl=en&answer=35769), they can either devalue applicable links, manually penalize a website's ability to rank, or remove the website from the Google index altogether. Common examples of penalty inducing actions are buying and selling links, cloaking (showing search engines one piece of content and showing normal visitors different content), keyword stuffing, and manipulative redirects. Luckily, if you have a client who feels their site is being penalized unfairly, you can ask Google for reinclusion.

> **NOTE** To request reinclusion into Google's index, go to www.google.com/webmasters/tools/reconsideration. Be sure that whatever got you penalized in the first place is fixed, and be ready to explain how it happened. This *mea culpa* form might be uncomfortable to answer comprehensively, but it's often the only way to get a banned site back into Google's index.

Google allegedly manually reads every reinclusion request it receives. From time of submission to time of action (assuming Google actually decides to act) is close to three months. It is best to check the site in question for any sign of breaking the Google Webmaster Guidelines *before* submitting the reinclusion request. Once you are sure your client's site is search engine friendly and abides by the Google Webmaster Guidelines, you can submit a reinclusion request through the Webmaster Central dashboard. After doing so, knock on wood, throw salt over your shoulder, and do a rain dance for 7 days for luck. You are going to need all of it that you can get.

> **CROSSREF** You can find a sample reinclusion request in Chapter 5.

Following is a deeper dive into Google Webmaster Tools reports. The section titles in the book correspond to the specific section names in the left navigation of Webmaster Tools. While some of the reports are fairly binary in their explanation of your site (an XML sitemap is either valid or invalid, for example), much of the data is technical and won't be easily labeled "good" or "bad" or offer specific recommendations. Instead, in most cases, Google simply shows you the data, and it's up to you to interpret and act on it. The purpose of the following sections is to help you decide which reports are critical to watch and the thresholds at which you should take action on improving various aspects of your site.

Dashboard

The GWT Dashboard gives a very quick snapshot of your site's performance, showing top-level data for the following issues:

- ▶ Top search queries
- ▶ Crawl error types and their counts
- ▶ Links to your site
- ▶ Keywords
- ▶ Sitemaps

Each of these report snapshots has a link to its full report counterpart, which is discussed in the following sections.

Messages

This page lists messages from Google to you, specifically about your site. Messages include notification of new verified owners to the site, changes to Sitelinks, and important notifications if your site is harboring malware or potentially running afoul of Google's quality guidelines. Check this area at least once per week for each of your clients' sites.

The Message center in the left navigation of GWT shows message for specific domains. If you have several sites verified in GWT, it's better to view all messages at the main hub of GWT, www.google.com/webmasters/tools/home. This page aggregates all messages about all domains in your GWT portfolio.

Site Configuration

The Site Configuration reports show how Google interacts with your site. The following sections discuss specific signals that your site and Google send to each other to optimize the user experience.

SITEMAPS

The Sitemaps report shows each sitemap that you (or anyone else who is verified for the site) have submitted, as well as most recent fetch date, status (either valid or invalid), and the type (general, mobile, and so on).

▶ The dashboard is best for quickly spotting anomalies, such as spiking search queries or crawling errors and spotting signs that your XML sitemaps are invalid.

It also shows the number of URLs indexed, contrasted with the number of URLs in your XML file. This is a helpful way to see what percentage of your sitemap's URLs is actually making it into Google's index.

Finally, you can submit sitemaps from this report, too, provided the actual files are on your domain's server. (In other words, you cannot upload sitemap files from your computer.)

CRAWLER ACCESS

This multi-featured report enables you to perform and diagnose all sorts of robots-related crawling rules for your site:

▶ **Test your robots.txt file:** This pane shows the HTTP status code of your current robots.txt file and the last time it was downloaded. The "Parse results" section, if it appears, goes through your file line by line and identifies any sitemap locations you've declared in your file, explains any disallow or user agent lines you've added, and identifies any coding errors. To test hypothetical changes to your robots.txt file, change the content of the "Text of http://www.example.com/robots.txt" field, add specific URLs to the URLs field, select a specific user agent, and click the Test button. The result will tell you whether your hypothetical changes will disallow the sample URLs you entered.

▶ Hypothetical because this report does not literally change your robots.txt file. It's simply a testing sandbox, and you must manually edit and re-upload your robots.txt file for actual changes to take effect.

ROBOTS.TXT ERRORS

There are a few things to watch out for while testing your robots.txt file. First, when you declare a sitemap location, a result of "Valid Sitemap reference detected" means only that the *location of the file* is valid, not necessarily the file itself. In other words, the URL that you gave as your sitemap location does exist. To know whether the XML is valid, you need to check the Sitemaps report.

If your robots.txt file was encoded as UTF-16, your "Parse results" section might show you a question mark as the first character in your file. This is a byte-order mark (BOM), and it usually renders the robots.txt file's first line incomprehensible for Google. Resave as UTF-8, re-upload, and you should be fine.

▶ **Generate a custom robots.txt file:** This pane will help you write a custom robots.txt file based on the actions, specific robots, and specific directories and/or files you want to control access to. Keep in mind that for any non-Google crawlers, you need to come prepared with the robot's user agent name. When you're done feeding it the roles, Google will create and let you download a file tailored to your needs, which you'll then need to upload to your server.

▶ **Remove URLs:** If you have certain URLs that appear in SERPs and you need them out of the index sooner than a 404 will accomplish it, use this tool. However, before it will work, you must first show Google (through a robots. txt file, meta robots tag, or 404 header code) that the content should not be indexed. Remember that this tool simply removes URLs from Google's index; it does not remove them from your server.

SITELINKS

This section shows the Sitelinks that Google has bestowed on your site for the home page and possibly other interior pages too. From this report, you can block individual Sitelinks so that they no longer appear on SERPs. Blocking a specific Sitelink does not remove the specific URL from the Google index; it ensures only that for queries in which Sitelinks appear, that specific link will not appear on the SERP.

> **WARNING** Weigh your options carefully while deciding whether to block Sitelinks. Remember that while you can block any Sitelinks you want, you cannot tell Google what link you would like Google to show in its place, and you can't even ensure that it will show anything at all. For example, if you block two of eight Sitelinks, Google may replace one or both Sitelinks with different Sitelinks, or it may simply show the remaining six.

CHANGE OF ADDRESS

The Change of Address tool is a supplement used when you're moving your site to a new or different domain. It does not take the place of old-fashioned 301 redirects from your old site to your new one, but it represents an additional signal for Google to help process the migration and is supposed to make the SERP transition faster for new URLs.

To use this tool, you must have both old and new domains verified through GWT and set up the 301s ahead of time. After those items are complete, you can use this tool to select the new domain that you're moving to.

> **NOTE** Currently, the Change of Address tool works only for root-level domains. In other words, your old and new sites must be either the "www" version or have no subdomain at all to be eligible for this tool to work.

SETTINGS

The Settings area has two sections:

- **General settings:** This tab lets you send Google three important signals about your content:

  - ▷ **Geographic target:** Use this to have URLs from your site appear in search results for only one country. The default is unchecked, which means your site can, in theory, appear for results in any country.

  - ▷ **Preferred domain:** Use this section to tell Google whether you prefer the "www" or non-"www" version of your URLs to appear in SERPs. This report is overridden by more overt actions like 301 redirects you perform yourself.

  - ▷ **Crawl rate:** This tool tells Google that you prefer its robot crawl your site at a rate faster or slower than it currently is.

- **Parameter handling:** This tab lets you pick dynamic URL variables from your site and tell Google to ignore those parameters when it crawls. For example, if your site has URLs /authors.php and /authors.php?sortby=lastname, you could tell Google to ignore the sortby parameter, which would help canonicalize any URLs that contain that parameter back to /authors.php. Google also lists dynamic URL parameters that Google *suspects* might be meaningless enough to create duplicate content on your site, but honestly, Google doesn't bat too well on this, often suggesting important parameters that create unique content.

▶ *Use this tool with caution, as an amped-up Googlebot can take down a server if it hits the server at full speed.*

Your Site on the Web

The "Your Site on the Web" reports show Google's interpretation of how users and other sites relate and interact with your site, including such metrics as query and linkage data. Following are the reports and how to get the most from them.

SEARCH QUERIES

This report shows queries for which your site appears in search results, along with estimates about how many times you get the click (CTR, or clickthrough rate). It also shows your page's "average position," which is the average rank for your site for a given query. While the impression and click numbers appear to be rounded estimates, they provide good insight into areas in which a little extra focus can provide additional traffic.

For example, you might have very low clickthrough for a high-demand query term in which your page's average position is 8. That makes sense, because anything ranked 8th will naturally receive a low percentage of clicks from a query. But with a little work, you can improve that page's ranking for the query and capture more of the clicks. This report helps you determine the high-return keywords, where the effort will provide the most return.

LINKS TO YOUR SITE

This report is valuable intelligence about the external sites that link to you most frequently, as well as the pages on your site that receive the most links. Like a lot of Google linkage data, you never quite know whether it's showing everything the engine knows about, so you may not be getting the precision that you'll see from tools like Open Site Explorer.

KEYWORDS

This report is conceptually very simple. It's the list of words, organized by frequency, that Google finds when crawling your site. Your top words should, therefore, be the terms that your site is focused on, whether category or specific products or services, along with some brand-focused phrases.

▶ Click a term and you'll see the list of pages that contain that term in greatest numbers, which is helpful for noticing pages that might refer to a specific term too often or not enough.

INTERNAL LINKS

This report lists your site's URLs in order of the number of internal links (that is, links from your own domain) pointing to them. This data is useful to help you ensure that your critical content is linked to more often than your non-critical content, which helps you manage the flow of PageRank and authority through the site.

In addition, this tool is a helpful way to spot duplicate content, because if you have two duped URLs (differentiated only by capitalization style, for instance), they will likely both show up on the report and help lead you to the page that is linking to the incorrect version.

SUBSCRIBER STATS

There's not a lot you can do with this information. It lists the number of Google users who have subscribed to feeds on your site using a Google-based RSS reader, such as Google Reader or iGoogle. If you run a feed on Feedburner, your subscribers won't be reflected here, because this tool reflects only subscribers to feeds on your own domain, not Feedburner.com.

Diagnostics

The Diagnostics reports specialize in pointing out errors and suggestions for improvement, along with raw crawling data that helps you identify server issues.

MALWARE

This section has content only if Google has detected your site has been infected with malware. If so, follow the instructions shown to clean your site and then inform Google to re-check it. Check this report once a week even if you are sure your site is clean.

CRAWL ERRORS

The Crawl Errors report is one of the most helpful reports and one of the biggest reasons GWT is so helpful. For both web and mobile content, Google shows you errors of the following type:

- ▶ **HTTP:** Generally a 400 or 403 error.
- ▶ **In sitemaps:** Shows URLs of multiple error types that are listed in your XML file.
- ▶ **Not followed:** Shows links that Google chose not to follow, usually because of excessive redirects or endless looping.
- ▶ **Restricted by robots.txt:** Check this to double-check whether your robots file is working the way you want it to.
- ▶ **Not found:** Traditional "404" errors.
- ▶ **Soft 404s:** "Page not found" errors that don't give a true 404 HTTP header code. These pages can lead to a lot of junk clogging up the index.
- ▶ **Timed out:** Usually due to the server being too busy to respond to Googlebot's request.
- ▶ **Unreachable:** Usually due to a server error.

Why is repairing these errors important? First, your users might be seeing the same errors as Google is. Second, there is a lot of spare PageRank and authority swimming around out there. If Google can't read your page, it can't see the architecture you built.

> **NOTE**   This applies especially to the "Not found" category. This report shows URLs on your site that other sites are actually linking to, but the 404 error is keeping your site from receiving credit for them. Repair the 404 errors (such as by redirecting the URL to an appropriate page on your site) and recoup that link.

CRAWL STATS

This report shows three graphs:

- ▶ **Pages crawled per day:** The number of distinct URLs that Google crawls by day. Expect spikes when you introduce a lot of new content, accrue strong links to your site, and submit new XML sitemaps. If this graph bottoms out consistently, it's likely due to crawl obstacles or penalties.

- ▶ **Kilobytes downloaded per day:** Similar to pages crawled per day, this graph frequently looks very similar to the one above it. Spikes and valleys can occur, however, if the pages downloaded by Google are particularly large or small.

- ▶ **Time spent downloading a page (in milliseconds):** This report reflects page-load time, and small numbers are better. This graph should not, in theory, correspond to the two preceding graphs. Relatively large spikes can suggest server problems or abnormally large file sizes.

HTML SUGGESTIONS

This section highlights pages for which Google has detected potential "issues" with your site's meta content, including:

- ▶ **Meta descriptions:** Highlights duplicates and descriptions that are too long or short.

- ▶ **Title tags:** Highlights URLs for which titles are missing, duplicated, too long, too short, and uninformative.

- ▶ **Non-indexable content:** Highlights content that Google can't read or interpret correctly.

It's worthwhile to look at this section with a critical eye toward your content. Google won't point out issues unless it feels they're giving users a poor experience, and its algorithm is all about enriching the user experience. It may be entirely appropriate on your site if five URLs share the same title, but this report nearly always highlights several areas to improve.

Labs

The Labs section of webmaster reports is where Google tests reporting structures before it considers them ready for prime time. But that doesn't mean their data is unhelpful. In fact, some Labs reports are as helpful in diagnosing site problems as reports in the other areas of GWT. Following are the Labs reports and a brief description of each.

FETCH AS GOOGLEBOT

This is Google's version of a "header checker," and it's quite similar to a long-time favorite tool of SEOs, Rex Swain's HTTP Viewer (http://rexswain.com/httpview.html).

Insert a URL from your site, and select whether you want it checked by Google's main crawler ("Web") or by its mobile crawler ("XHTML" or "cHTML"). Check back in a minute or two, and if Google has crawled the page, there will be a link called "Success" that you can click to see the code Google crawled.

This tool is very helpful for ensuring that your pages are showing the correct HTTP header code (200, 302, 301, and so on), and it's especially helpful for testing your site's mobile device detection and redirection. For example, testing your desktop site as Google's mobile crawler will help you know whether mobile devices are being redirected correctly to mobile content.

SITE PERFORMANCE

The Site Performance report shows a graph of random page-load times from your site over the last several months. Google has arbitrarily defined "slow" as the slowest 80 percent of sites on the Internet, and "fast" as the fastest 20 percent. This means your site could perform in the top 22nd percentile and still be considered "slow" by Google standards. Consequently, I recommend that you don't pay a lot of attention to those labels. Instead, pay attention to spikes that relate to your pages loading more slowly, and try to determine whether it's feasible to trim your load times.

Further, the report offers suggestions about how to cut the load time of your pages, including offering specific predictions about how enabling compression, combining and externalizing JavaScript and CSS files, and minimizing DNS lookups will affect the size of your pages.

VIDEO SITEMAPS

This report is similar to the Sitemaps report in the Site Configuration section of GWT, except its purpose is to diagnose and report on video content found in XML sitemaps. Currently the reports show very little information other than listing all of your existing XML feeds.

RELEVANCY DETERMINING TOOLS

As mentioned in Chapter 1, relevancy makes up a huge part of the search engine algorithms. As a result of this, SEO companies have developed tools to help make determining relevancy easier. The three I use the most often are Dave Naylor's Keyword Density Tool, SEOmoz's Term Target Tool, and Ranks.nl Keyword Density & Prominence Analyzer.

> NOTE The name of these tools is a misnomer. The metric keyword density by itself is not actually important to search engines. Don't let that confuse you; these tools are actually very helpful for determining how relevant a webpage is to a given keyword from a search engine algorithm perspective.

▶ **Dave Naylor's Keyword Density Tool:** This tool is available at `http://tools .davidnaylor.co.uk/keyworddensity/` and is shown in Figure 3-6.

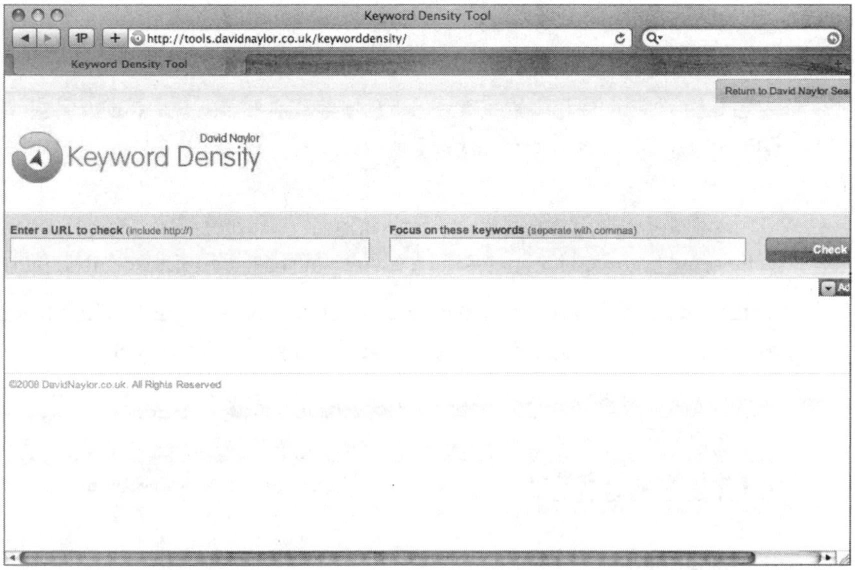

FIGURE 3-6: Dave Naylor's Keyword Density Tool

With Dave Naylor's Keyword Density Tool you can see metrics about the content and technical information about a given website. This is tremendously helpful for spotting potential spam signals (a specific keyword is used 300 times on a page whereas keywords are usually used 10 times on similar pages) and technical problems (a page is returning a 404 HTTP status code).

▶ **SEOmoz's Term Target Tool:** This tool is available at `www.seomoz.org/ term-target` and is shown in Figure 3-7.

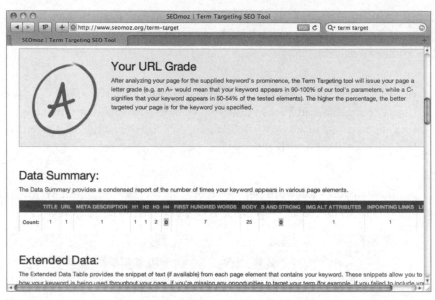

FIGURE 3-7: SEOmoz's Term Target Tool

SEOmoz's Term Target Tool helps determine how targeted a particular page is for a specified keyword by analyzing a variety of search engine–related factors.

▶ **Ranks.nl Keyword Density & Prominence Analyzer:** This tool is available at www.ranks.nl/tools/spider.html and is shown in Figure 3-8.

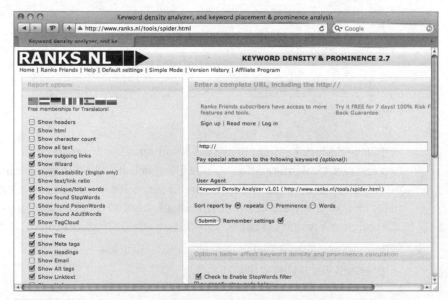

FIGURE 3-8: Ranks.nl Keyword Density and Prominence Analyzer

Ranks.nl Keyword Density & Prominence Analyzer is a robust tool that out-puts a large variety of search engine metrics for a specified page. It is shows more raw data than the other tools listed in this section, so it is good for data junkie SEOs.

> **NOTE** Ranks.nl Keyword Density & Prominence Analyzer shows more raw data than the other tools listed in this section.

I use these tools when I want to:

▶ See how relevant a page is to a specific keyword

▶ Save time while building client reports (I use the data from these tools in my reports)

▶ Gain a search engine crawler perspective on a webpage

Key Data Points

You can use each of these tools to focus on different important data points:

▶ **Dave Naylor's Keyword Density Tool:** This tool doesn't have a specific data point that is the most important. Instead, it provides a lot of data points that are useful when looked at as a part of a bigger picture. Some of the key sections I look at are as follows:

 ▷ **Keyword Analysis** to make sure the keyword is included in all of the appropriate places

 ▷ **Geolocation** to see where the server is located

 ▷ **External Follow Links** to get an idea about what type of links the website is willing to send outwardly

 I use this tool when I am trying to get a good idea of how the search engine's relevancy detectors see a specific page. That said, this tool doesn't provide enough data on anchor text, so although it shows the best view of relevancy of any tool available today, it still misses a major part of the equation.

▶ **SEOmoz's Term Target Tool:** The Your URL Grade feature this tool offers is great when you want to show a client a very simplistic view of how relevant a page is. It is straightforward and even the dumbest CEOs can understand its results. This works particularly well in the United States where the education system uses a scale of A, B, C, D, and F to grade students. Because this tool also uses this scale, people who are unfamiliar with SEO are able to use their prior knowledge to understand if the tool is reporting a good score or a bad score.

▶ **Ranks.nl Keyword Density & Prominence Analyzer:** This tool has a Ranks Wizard metric that is tremendously helpful for identifying the non-primary keywords on a page. This is useful when you are trying to do long-tail keyword analysis for a client. I use this when I am trying to leverage popular pages on a client's domain to attract new search traffic but don't want to change the primary keyword of the page.

Common Questions Relevancy Determining Tools Can Answer

These tools can help you answer for yourself (and explain to clients) the following questions.

HOW RELEVANT IS A GIVEN PAGE TO A GIVEN KEYWORD?

This is a big question that requires a lot of data to answer. If I am slim on time (as many professional SEOs are) and am in a meeting with a client I go directly to Dave Naylor's Keyword Density Tool or SEOmoz's Term Target tool. The Keyword Density Tool provides almost all of the data I need and loads very quickly, so I use it when what I need it for is a tangent for a larger conversation. For example, if I want to show a client that they are accidentally devaluing their ranking ability by ranking out too many times with the keyword they are trying to target, I use this tool to generate the actual percentages and show them examples of the foul links.

I use SEOmoz's tool when I am explaining the idea of relevancy to the client. I find that the simple letter grade this tool provides quickly communicates to the client how they are doing with regard to relevancy with an example from their webpage using an actual keyword they are trying to target.

WHAT DOES A GIVEN PAGE LOOK LIKE FROM A METRIC-BASED PERSPECTIVE?

This is similar to the first question except it changes the perspective a little bit. This version of the question comes up mainly when I am writing reports for clients. I use a combination of Dave Naylor's Keyword Density Tool and Ranks.nl's Keyword Density & Prominence Analyzer to harvest as much data as I can and then make judgments based on my findings.

SEO TOOLBARS

Remember at the beginning of the chapter when I half sarcastically compared Batman utility belt to SEO toolbars? The following is why I was only being half sarcastic: SEO toolbars are faster than traditional SEO tools (they run every page load) and can pack a surprising amount of information into their small space. The two toolbars that I have running (although not at the same time) are SEO for Firefox and the mozBar. Together, these toolbars provide me with the majority of the information I need for doing page-level SEO audits.

> **NOTE** I need to disclose that as a former SEOmoz employee, I am inherently biased toward the mozBar. That said, the reason SEOmoz built the toolbar was that my former colleagues and I were unhappy with the alternatives. Rather than overcompensate for my bias, I am going to tell you what I really feel and leave you with the responsibility of judging for yourself.

▶ **The SEO toolbar for Firefox** is available at `http://tools.seobook.com/firefox/seo-for-firefox.html` and is shown in Figure 3-9.

▶ **SEOmoz's mozBar** is available at `www.seomoz.org/mozbar` and is shown in Figure 3-10.

I use these tools when I want to:

▶ Quickly see the SEO-related properties of a webpage

▶ Get a context for a webpage on a domain

▶ Get a context for a domain on the Internet

FIGURE 3-9: SEO for Firefox

FIGURE 3-10: SEOmoz's mozBar

Key Data Points

These toolbars provide access to the following useful data points:

▶ **SEO for Firefox: PageRank:** Although Google's PageRank is only a very small part of the overall Google Search algorithm, it does provide a good insight for relative value of a page, and it can be a very fast indicator of whether a page is indexed. I include it in client reports as a benchmark but do not make it a basis for an important decision.

One important exception to this is when the PageRank of an established page is a zero. In this case, the page is being penalized, and I use it as a signal to tell me to look for manipulative practices. I also use this metric as evidence when explaining the downside of manipulative behavior to clients.

This gets complicated, but don't confuse "No pagerank information available," or a solid white bar, for a PageRank of 0. Deep or recently crawled pages may not have PageRank information available yet, but that doesn't mean they've been penalized or can't show up in search results.

▶ *A PageRank of zero indicates a page is being penalized. This is a clue to start looking for manipulative practices on the page.*

PAGERANK'S SCALE

PageRank is on a logarithmic scale. Roughly speaking, this means that a PageRank of 8 is ten times more powerful than a PageRank of 7. The takeaway is that getting from a PageRank of 1 to 2 is easy, but getting from a 7 to an 8 is incredibly hard. In both cases the way to boost this score is to get more inbound links from established websites. The difference is that the higher the PageRank of the client site, the harder it is to make an impact in popularity metrics.

▶ **mozBar: Root domains linking (page level):** Since the release of this metric, I have been incredibly impressed by how well it correlates to actual rankings. I highly recommend you watch this metric as you travel around familiar sites so you can get a context for its range.

One thing to note is if you see a large amount of pages linking to a webpage, but it has only one root domain linking, it means that all of these links are internal links and not worth as much (in the editorial voting sense) as normal external links.

▶ *Internal links are not worth as much (in the editorial voting sense) as normal external links.*

▶ **mozBar: Root domains linking (domain level):** Just like the metric on the page level, this metric displays the number of unique domains that link to a given domain. This is essential in determining how powerful a domain is in rankings. As discussed in Chapter 1, domain popularity is extremely useful for raising the power of weak pages. Even if the number of links to a given page is low, it can still rank highly if this metric is large. Currently, we see this all the time with Wikipedia.

> **NOTE** Current spammers use the leverage of strong domains to get their pages ranked highly. If you watch the search engine result page for the query "Buy Viagra," you will likely see this tactic at work. Generally, it takes the form of a profile on a well-known site that is targeted for Viagra.

▶ **mozBar: Analyze Page:** This is not an individual data point but rather an access point for a group of important data points. This button brings up a page that puts all of the relevant SEO on-page metrics in one place. As you can see in Figure 3-11, this makes it very easy to do a quick audit of a page without having to view source.

Page Analysis for
http://www.ford.com/

Link Data	Page Elements	Page Attributes		Export
Page-Specific	**URL**	**Domain-Level**	**Subdomain**	**Root Domain**
			www.ford.com	*.ford.com
Page Authority (PA)	96	Domain Authority (DA)	--	95
mozRank (mR)	6.85	Domain mozRank (DmR)	7.01	6.98
mozTrust (mT)	6.95	Domain mozTrust (DmT)	7.35	7.18
Total Links	213,914	Total Links	1,202,282	2,854,653
External Followed Links	176,703	External Followed Links	234,266	396,735

FIGURE 3-11: Analyze Page details

Common Questions SEO Toolbars Can Answer

Here are questions these toolbars are ideal for helping you to answer.

WHY IS PAGE A RANKING OVER PAGE B?

To a certain extent, this is what an SEO is hired to determine. Although the toolbars will not provide you with a comprehensive answer, they will get you close. The key metrics to look at are the ones listed previously: PageRank (to determine if there is a penalty, which can be indicated by a 0), root domains linking to page, root domains linking to domain, and the information provided by the Analyze Page button. Together these will give you a large indication of the popularity and relevancy of the given page.

HOW LIKELY IS IT THAT THIS PAGE IS BEING PENALIZED BY GOOGLE?

This is a very tricky question because many different types of Google penalties exist. These range from discrediting specific links to removing an entire domain network from the index. The only penalty you can be sure of is if the PageRank is 0 on an established domain, and the mozRank is still about a 5. If there is major inconsistency and the Google PageRank is lower, it usually means there is a major penalty in place.

HTTP HEADER ANALYZER

This Firefox extension is my secret weapon. I use it when I need to see exactly how a redirect is being implemented. I use this in client meetings constantly when I want to know whether the client has a 301 redirect or a 302, and I need to know how many pages load before I am directed to my final destination. Just for the record, my personal high score is a six-page redirect chain on a major and well-known site. It wasn't an accident; it was just a poorly designed tracking system.

Live HTTP Headers is available at https://addons.mozilla.org/en-US/firefox/addon/3829 and shown in Figure 3-12.

I use this tool when I want to:

▶ Know whether a redirect is a 301 or a 302

▶ Know all of the nodes in a redirect chain

Key Data Points

I use this tool often to bring up a couple key data points:

▶ **HTTP Status Code:** This is essential information to know as an SEO. This indicates the response code from a server to a browser. This is helpful for identifying "soft" 404 pages (404 pages that return a 302 or 200 HTTP status code) as well as redirects. As discussed earlier in the book, two different kinds of redirects exist: 301s and 302s. Though the numerical difference is one value, the SEO difference is enormous. A 302 redirect passes no link value, whereas a 301 passes between 99 percent and 90 percent of link value. This tool is the best option for accurately defining which redirect is present in a given situation. Better yet, this tool is extremely fast.

▶ **All files being downloaded from a page:** Live HTTP Headers can show the browser request and server response for each file downloaded on a webpage. This helps to identify exactly what is happening on the page and helps to point out any unnecessary requests that take up valuable bandwidth and the precision time of the users. I, along with my colleagues, use this to get the fullest possible perspective on all of the elements of a page.

▶ Although viewing source is good for this type of analysis, it misses some loading that takes place in external files. This tool helps fill in the gaps of this viewing source shortcoming.

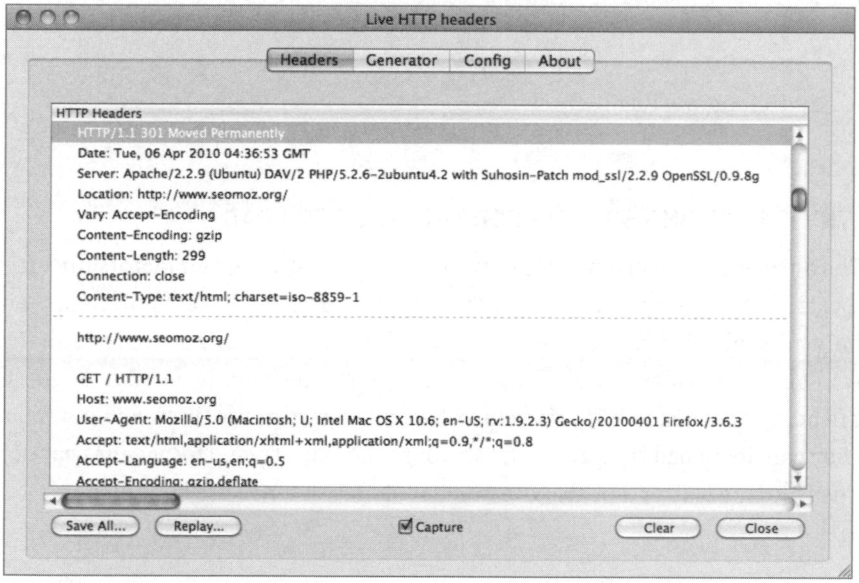

FIGURE 3-12: Live HTTP Headers

Common Questions an HTTP Header Analyzer Can Answer

I've already alluded to the two most common questions this type of tool can answer:

IS THIS REDIRECT A 301 OR A 302?

As I have mentioned several times, this is a very important differentiation. To find this answer, you can load this tool in Firefox, click Capture in the Headers tab, and load the page as you normally would in the browser. As soon as you do that, this tool writes all of the HTTP headers that are being transferred behind the scenes between the server and browser. Once the page has loaded, you can review this print out and see any redirects that may have occurred. These will be designated at the top of response blocks with HTTP/1.x 301 Moved Permanently or HTTP/1.x 302 Found.

NOTE Remember—301 redirects:

▶ Recommended SEO best practice for redirecting URLs

▶ Passes between 99% and 90% of link juice

▶ Permanent Redirect

302 redirects:

▶ Common SEO mistake made by web developers

▶ Passes 0% of link juice

▶ Temporary Redirect

WHY IS IT TAKING SO LONG FOR THIS PAGE TO LOAD?

▶ For more page optimization tips, see Yahoo's guide at http://developer.yahoo.com/performance/rules.html.

The answer to this question takes into account many different factors, including location of server compared to user's computer, latency, throughput, number of files being downloaded, size of files being downloaded, and many more. Though this tool won't be able to identify all of these factors, it can tell you the number of files that are being downloaded. This is helpful because browsers are limited in how many files they can download from a specific server at the same time. This means that not only does file size matter, but also the number of files that need to be served.

FIREFOX USER AGENT SWITCHER

As you surf around the Internet, your browser sends information to each server it connects to. One of these pieces of information is its user-agent string. The user agent string that my browser (Safari) sends to servers is Mozilla/5.0 (Macintosh; U; Intel Mac OS X 10_5_8; en-us) AppleWebKit/531.9 (KHTML, like Gecko) Version/4.0.3 Safari/531.9. This lets the server know that I am using Mac OS X on an Intel-based Mac and I use the browser Safari version 4.0.3. Based on this information, some websites choose specific versions of their content to send. Sometimes this decision is helpful as in when it provides the version of software that is compatible with the user's operating system. Other times this is used for cloaking. *Cloaking* is the practice of sending search engines one version of a website and users another. One way to detect this as an SEO is to switch your user agent to make you appear to be one of the search engine's crawlers.

TARGETING CRAWLERS BY IP ADDRESS

Smart webmasters will target crawlers by IP address rather than user agent because the former is much harder to fake. If you want to do this, you need to find a source online that keeps updated records of the search engine IP addresses. You can do this by searching `Search engine IP addresses` in one of the major search engines.

The Firefox User Agent Switcher is available at `https://addons.mozilla.org/en-US/firefox/addon/59` and is shown in Figure 3-13.

```
✓ Default User Agent

:: BROWSERS – Windows ::
MSIE 7 (Win Vista)
MSIE 6 (Win XP)
MSIE 5.5 (Win 2000)
MSIE 5.5 (Win ME)
Avant Browser 1.2
Opera 8.0 (Win 2000)
Opera 7.51 (Win XP)
Opera 7.5 (Win XP)
Opera 7.5 (Win ME)
Multizilla 1.6 (Win xp)
Netscape 7.1 (Win 98)
Netscape 4.8 (Win XP)
Netscape 3.01 gold (Win 95)
Netscape 2.02 (Win 95)
:: SPIDERS – search ::
Googlebot 2.1 (New version)
Googlebot 2.1 (Older Version)
Msnbot 1.0 (current version)
Msnbot 0.11 (beta version)
Yahoo Slurp
Ask Jeeves/Teoma
:: BROWSERS – Mac ::
Safari 125.8 (Mac OSX)
Safari 85 (Mac OSX)
MSIE 5.15 (Mac OS 9)
        ▼
```

FIGURE 3-13: Firefox User Agent Switcher

I use this tool when I want to:

▶ Search for evidence of cloaking content based on user agent

▶ Access a website that filters out standard user agents

Key Data Points

The two most important user agent strings for SEOs are listed in the following bulleted list. They are important because they are the strings that the two major search engines use to identify themselves:

▶ **Googlebot's user agent:** `Mozilla/5.0 (compatible; Googlebot/2.1; +http://www.google.com/bot.html)`

▶ **MSNbot's user agent:** `msnbot/1.0 (+http://search.msn.com/ msnbot.htm)`

Check `www.user-agents.org` for up-to-date user agent strings.

Common Questions the Firefox User Agent Switcher Can Answer

This tool helps with the following questions:

IS THIS WEBSITE CLOAKING?

I find that this question comes up fairly often. The best way to test this is to visit the suspected page with your normal user-agent and then switch to one of the search engine's user agents and hard refresh (browser-specific command that re-downloads the page rather than loading a cached version) the page. If the results are different, then yes, they are cloaking.

IP-BASED CLOAKING

The exception to this is if they are using IP-based cloaking. This is more difficult to detect unless you have the IP address that is being targeted. If this is the case, find a proxy server and try the page through that. If you suspect that the webpage is targeting the IP addresses held by the search engines, check the cached version of the website. Compare this to the version you see and note any differences.

IS THIS WEBSITE SENDING ME CUSTOMIZED RESULTS
BASED ON MY USER AGENT?

If you suspect that a website is sending you browser- or operating system–specific results, you can change your user agent. After you do this, do a hard refresh and see if the webpage changed.

FIREFOX RENDERING MODIFIER

Modern websites contain images, sounds, animation, and videos. These make websites exciting and more attractive to humans. At the same time, search engine crawlers are only sophisticated enough to understand a very small amount of this enticing information. As an SEO, you are going to find it sometimes helpful to view websites from a perspective that is closer to that of the search engines. You will find this makes it easier to understand why a search engine ranks a page like it does if you see it through the search engine's limited information perspective. The easiest way to do this is to disable all of the bells and whistles on your browser that usually make the Web so enjoyable to surf.

You can modify your website perspective using the Firefox Web Developer Toolbar. This tool makes it possible to enable and disable your browser's ability to render objects that can't be parsed by the search engines.

The Firefox Web Developer toolbar add-on is available at `https://addons.mozilla.org/firefox/addon/60` and is shown in Figure 3-14.

FIGURE 3-14: Firefox Web Developer's toolbar

Basically, I use this tool when I want to mimic the behavior of the search engine's crawlers

Key Data Points

The key data you are dealing with when you work with this tool are not those you want to see, but rather those you want to disable:

  ▶ **Disable JavaScript:** The script is a runtime scripting language that is useful for creating more interactive websites. Unfortunately, current search engines have difficulty parsing this language, and as of the time of writing, it can't be relied on from an SEO perspective. The Web Developer add-on has an option for disabling JavaScript, which is helpful to give you a better understanding of how the search engines see the website. In addition, because Flash is typically spawned from a JavaScript directive, disabling JavaScript usually shows a webpage without Flash elements running, which is a more accurate way of seeing a page the way an engine does.

▶ **Disable Meta Redirect:** One trick that many spammers use is instant meta redirects (such as the "meta refresh"). These are used to redirect users from the page they intended to see to a page that is more lucrative for the webmaster. Because these aren't always obvious, it can be helpful to disable them so your browser's behavior is closer to that of the search engine crawlers. The search engine crawlers detect when a meta redirect is in place, and if your browser automatically follows them, this can be hard to uncover.

▶ **Disable Cookies:** Cookies are small files that are stored on your computer after you visit specific websites. These are useful for storing information like login credentials so that you don't need to log in every time you visit the given website. Unfortunately, this technology doesn't work very well with the search engine crawlers. Disabling cookies via this add-on is another good way to more accurately mimic the search engine crawlers.

The most common SEO problem I see with cookies is websites storing the language version of a site after a user selects it from a splash page. (A splash page is a page the users see that ask them to perform a simple action. Examples of this include choosing their preferred language, verifying they are 18 or older, or choosing a color theme. Usually after users select this option once, it is stored in a cookie and they never see this page again.) Since the search engines don't crawl with cookies enabled, they never can skip the splash page, and all links going to the homepage are credited to the splash page. Since splash pages usually don't have enough content to rank well, it ruins the chances for the website to rank well.

▶ **Disable CSS:** The last key option on this add-on is the ability to disable CSS. CSS is used for formatting the visual components of a website. This includes layout, color, positioning, and some behavior. As you can imagine, CSS can be manipulated in many ways to fool the search engines, such as hiding content under other layers of content, positioning text outside the visible area of the screen, and making text invisible. As such, it is best to disable it when surfing like the major crawlers.

The most common example of search engine manipulation using CSS that I see is hidden links. This can be done either by manually positioning a link off the viewable portion of a screen or by simply hiding an entire div (section of a website). Disabling CSS allows you to see what the page looks like without these manipulations and makes it easier to find out why a page is being penalized.

The Common Question Firefox Web Developer Can Answer

Really this tool helps answer one key question:

HOW WOULD THE SEARCH ENGINES SEE THIS FEATURE?

This question comes up a lot during site audits. The best way to do this is disable all of the options in this section and see for yourself. This is easy and convenient because with the exception of disabled CSS, the features stay disabled as you navigate around different pages. If you want to be extra sure, and the website has already been crawled, you can view the search engine's cached version of the site and select the text-only option.

This is important because it helps you understand why the search engines are acting the way they are. One common problem it uncovers is global navigation that is written in complicated JavaScript and thus unparsable by the search engines. When this happens, you will not see the navigational links in the text-only cached version of the page, and you will know that the search engines are not able to connect these pages directly to the page you are looking at. This detracts from the popularity metrics of all of the pages on the domain.

▶ *Disabling CSS is another way for you to see what the page looks like from the perspective of the crawlers, which can make your job of finding out why a page is being penalized easier.*

SUMMARY

This chapter reviewed all of the tools that my colleagues and I use most often, and these tools are referenced in the chapters ahead. The best way to familiarize yourself with them is to bookmark them in your browser and use them a few times a week.

The next chapter discusses how to use these tools and the knowledge you gained in Chapter 1 to find SEO problems. This is a major portion of a professional SEO's daily work, so the upcoming chapter is very valuable. Good work so far; it is finally time to take what you have learned and find out how to apply it.

Finding SEO Problems

Now that you know what to look for and you have the tools to start working, it is time to get your hands dirty. This chapter discusses how to identify SEO problems. You can use these skills to impress and hook your potential clients. This chapter is extremely important, so no skipping pages! Enough chatter, let's begin.

THE 15-MINUTE SEO AUDIT

The basics of SEO problem identification can be done in about 15 minutes. When you are completing this audit I recommend you take notes based on the action items listed in each section. These simple notes can help you when you do a deeper dive of the website. This audit is not comprehensive, but it can quickly identify major problems, so you can convince your clients that your services are worthwhile and help you convince them to give you the chance to dig deeper. You may notice that the ideas in this section build upon the ideas expressed in Chapter 2.

> **CROSSREF** Chapters 8 and 9 presents a more comprehensive look at SEO audits, including samples from SEO audit reports.

Preparing Your Browser

Before you start your audit you need to prepare your browser to act more like the search engine crawlers. This action helps you to identify simple crawling errors. To do this, you will need to do the following:

- ✔ Disable your browser cookies
- ✔ Switch your user agent to Googlebot
- ✔ Disable JavaScript

DISABLING YOUR BROWSER COOKIES

When the search engines crawl the Internet, they do not accept cookies. This is behavior your client's website should expect anyway because certain users and certain browsers also do not accept cookies. By disabling them, you can uncover issues that relate to preferences you make on the page. For example, many websites store website-specific settings (like language preference, login name, shopping cart content) in cookies. While this is helpful for users, it can make it difficult for SEOs to understand why the major search engines are treating a page a certain way.

A good example of an issue that shutting cookies off might help uncover is a website that makes its users choose their primary language before entering the main site. (This type of page is also known as a splash page.) When the search engines (who don't store cookies) come to these types of pages they go to each language differentiated

> ▶ Disabling browser cookies is one way you can prepare your browser to see websites more as the search engines see them.

version of the website. This almost always causes duplicate content and geolocation problems. Having a page like this is extremely detrimental from an SEO perspective because it means that every link to your primary URL will be diluted because it has to pass through this splash page. Such a situation is a big problem, because as noted in Chapter 1, the primary URL (that is, www.example.com/) is usually the most linked-to page on a site.

In most browsers you can disable cookies by going into settings or preferences, looking for the privacy tab, and choosing clear cookies.

> **TIP** If you install the free Web Developer Toolbar (see Chapter 3) you can quickly and easily disable, delete, or clear cookies directly from the toolbar. This saves you time and lets you disable cookies without deleting them if that's what you want to do (Figure 4-1). Disabling cookies rather than deleting them is helpful because it keeps you from having to reenter all of credentials after you re-enable cookies.

SWITCHING YOUR USER AGENT TO GOOGLEBOT

You should change your user agent for similar reasons. Setting your user-agent to Googlebot increases your chance of seeing exactly what Google is seeing. It also helps with identifying *cloaking* issues. (Cloaking is the practice of showing one thing to search engines and a different thing to users. This is what sarcastic Googlers call penaltybait.) To do this well, you should perform a second pass of the site with your normal user-agent to identify any differences you see between the two. That said, going that deep is not the primary goal for this quick run through of the given website.

▶ As I discussed in Chapter 3, Firefox has a great User Agent Switcher add-on that can make this sort of switching a snap.

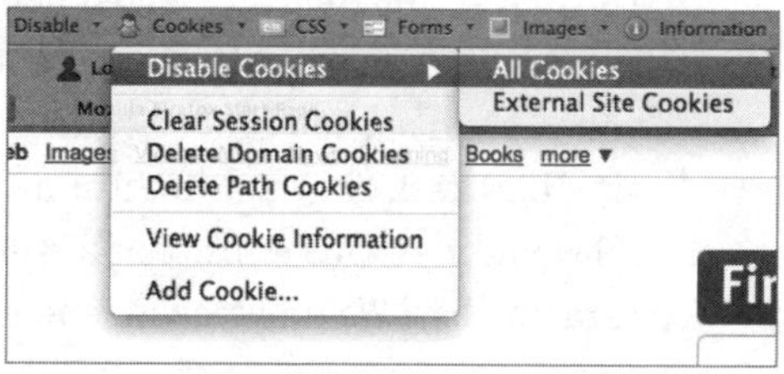

FIGURE 4-1: Disabling cookies in the Web Developer Toolbar

DISABLING JAVASCRIPT

Disabling your browser's ability to execute JavaScript is very important in helping you to see a site the way engines see it. Sites often use JavaScript to spawn instances of Flash or on-page content, or create special navigation schemes. By viewing a page with JavaScript disabled, you can see clearly whether those elements still remain viewable. If you can see an element on a page with JavaScript enabled but it disappears when

JavaScript is disabled, there's a very good chance that engines won't see that element, or that they'll see and process it differently from how you might expect.

> **NOTE** Google is getting better at parsing and following JavaScript code, but it's nowhere near an equal to old-fashioned HTML. Google does a decent job of looking at JavaScript code to "discover" URLs, but JavaScript environments are simply not as good at passing signals *about* those URLs, such as proximal and anchor text.

Assessing the Homepage

Next, go to the primary URL of the site and pay particular attention to your first impression of the page. Try to be as true to your opinion as possible and don't over think it. You should be coming from the perspective of the casual browser (this will be made easier because at this point you probably haven't been paid any money and it's a lot easier to be casual when you are not locked down with the client). Follow this by doing a quick check of the very basic SEO metrics. To complete this step, you will need to do the following:

✔ **Notice your first impression and the resulting feeling and trustworthiness about the page.**

The first action item on this list helps you align yourself with potential website users. It is the basis for your entire audit and serves as a foundation for you to build on. You can look at numbers all day, but if you fail to see the website like the user, you will fail as an SEO. When doing this, I try to ask myself if I would view this website as a reputable source. Would I give them my credit card number? Would I recommend it as a source to a friend?

✔ **Contrast content displayed with and without JavaScript.**

Carefully look at the page with JavaScript disabled, then re-enable JavaScript and refresh. While the *placement* of the content elements might be different, you want as many of the elements as possible to be viewable both with and without JavaScript enabled.

✔ **Read the title tag and figure out how it could be improved.**

The next step is to read the title tag and identify how it can be improved. This is helpful because changing title tags is both easy and has a relatively large direct impact on rankings.

TITLE TAGS AND CONTENT MANAGEMENT SYSTEMS

If your client uses a difficult Content Management System, then changing title tags may not be so easy; if this is the case then I wish you luck—you'll need it! When I have encountered this difficulty, I have picked the 25 most important pages on the domain and manually written the title tags. Unfortunately, in this case developers will need to manually add them to the pages. This isn't good for overworked developers, but it does usually boost rankings, clickthrough rates, and ultimately the bottom line.

✔ **See if the URL changed** (as in you were redirected from www.example.com/ to www.example.com/lame-keyword-in-URL-trick.html).

Next you need to direct yourself to the URL. First of all make sure there were no redirects. This is important because adding redirects dilutes the amount of link juice that actually makes it to the links on the page.

✔ **Check to see if the URL is canonical.**

The last action item is to run a quick check on canonical URLs. The complete list of URL formats to check for is in Chapter 2. Like checking the title tag, this is easy to check and provides a high benefit-to-work ratio.

▶ Sometimes redirects away from the root page are unavoidable due to initializing specific processes on a site. This is one of the rare cases in which a 302 is the SEO-friendly redirect.

▶ Checking and improving title tags and checking if URLs are canonical are two quick ways to do a small amount of work that could have a large impact on a website's rankings.

WHAT TO PUT ABOVE THE FOLD

Usability experts generally agree that the old practice of cramming as much as possible "above the fold" (that is, visible when the user first arrives at the page without scrolling down) on content pages and homepages is no longer necessary. While primary Calls to Action (CTAs) should be above the fold, there is no need to include all of the content. Many tests have been done on this and the evidence overwhelmingly shows that users scroll vertically. Because of this, there is no need to worry too much about "above the fold" malarkey.

Checking a Website's Global Navigation

After checking the basics on the homepage, you should direct your attention to the global navigation. This acts as the main canal system for link juice. Specifically, you are going to want to do the following:

- ✔ Temporarily disable JavaScript (if it's not disabled already) and reload the page.
- ✔ Make sure the navigation system works and that all links are HTML links.
- ✔ Take note of all of the sections that are linked to in the global navigation.
- ✔ Enable JavaScript.

▶ Disabling JavaScript has multiple uses. Earlier we did it to check content. Now we're doing it to check links.

As discussed in Chapter 2, site architecture is critical for a highly optimized website. The global navigation is fundamental to this. Imagine that the website you are viewing is ancient Rome right after the legendary viaduct and canal systems were built. These waterways are exactly like the global navigation that flows link juice around a website. Imagine the impact that a major clog can have on both systems. This review is your time to find these clogs.

Your first action item in this section is to disable JavaScript. This is helpful because it forces you to see your website from the perspective of a very basic user. It is also a similar perspective to the search engines.

After disabling JavaScript, reload the page and see if the global navigation still works. Many times it won't, and this simple step uncovers one of the major reasons the given client is having indexing issues.

Next, view source and see if all of the navigational links are true HTML links. Ideally, they should be because search engine testing performed by SEOmoz and other SEOs has shown that HTML links are the only kind that can pass their full link value. (This is as opposed to JavaScript-based links and server side redirects.)

▶ The most SEO-friendly global navigations don't use JavaScript at all. Instead, they are written in HTML and CSS that make use of <a> href pseudo-classes and descriptive anchor text.

Your next step is to take note of which sections are linked to in the global navigation. Ideally, all of the major sections will be linked in the global navigation. The problem is you won't know what all of the major sections are until you are further along in the audit. For now just take note, and keep a mental checklist as you browse the website.

Lastly, re-enable JavaScript. While browsing this way is not accurate to the search engine perspective, it does make sure that AJAX- and other JavaScript-based navigation works for you. Remember, on this quick audit, you are not trying to identify every single issue with the site; you are just trying to find the big issues.

Checking for Optimized Category Pages and Subcategory Pages

After finishing with the homepage, you need to start diving deeper into the website. In the waterway analogy, category and subcategory pages (if applicable to the website in question) are the forks in the paths of the website. As I have mentioned before in this book, these pages are the main pathways for a website's link juice. They help make it so that if one page (most often the homepage) gets a lot of links, the rest of the pages on the website can also get some of the benefit. You can make sure they are optimized by doing the following:

✔ **Make sure there is enough content on these pages to be useful as a search result alone.**

The first action point requires you to make a judgment call on whether the page would be useful as a search result. This goes with my philosophy that every page on a website should be at least a little bit link-worthy. (It should pay its own rent, so to speak.) Because each page has the inherent ability to collect links, webmasters should put at least a minimal amount of effort into making every page link worthy. There is no problem with someone entering a site (from a search engine result or other third-party site) on a category or subcategory page. In fact, it may save them a click and lower your abandonment rate. To complete this step, identify if this page alone would be useful for someone with a relevant query:

> ▷ Is there helpful content on the page to provide context? (Specifically, is there content on the page that would be worthy of a realistic search query? Does the page supply an information demand?)

> ▷ Is there a design element breaking up the monotony of a large list of links? (Is the page pleasing to the eye and easy to parse?)

Take notes on the answers to both of these questions.

✔ **Find and note extraneous links on the page (there shouldn't be more than 150 links).**

The next action item is to identify extraneous links on the page. Remember, Chapter 2 discussed that the amount of link value a given link can pass is dependent on the number of links on the page. To maximize the benefit of these pages, it is important to remove any extraneous links. Going back to my waterway analogy, these types of links are the equivalent of "canals to nowhere."

▶ *Category and subcategory pages actually stand a better chance of ranking for highly competitive phrases than their more common children content pages.*

✔ **Take notes on how to improve the anchor text used for the subcategories/
content pages.**

To complete the last action item of this section, you will need to take notes on
how to better optimize the anchor text of the links on this page. Ideally, they
should be as specific as possible. For example, if the given category page is
about dogs and the subcategory page is about English Springer Spaniels, the
anchor text for these sections should be "Dogs" and "English Springer Spaniels"
respectively. This helps the search engines and users identify what the target
pages are about.

THE IMPORTANCE OF CATEGORY AND SUBCATEGORY PAGES

Many people don't realize that category and subcategory pages actually stand
a better chance of ranking for highly competitive phrases than their more common children content pages.

If done well, these pages will have links from all of their children content pages
(popularity), the website's homepage (popularity), and provide a lot of information about a specific topic (relevancy). Combine this with the fact that each link
that goes to one of its children content pages also helps the given page and you
have a great pyramid structure (see Figure 4-2) for ranking success.

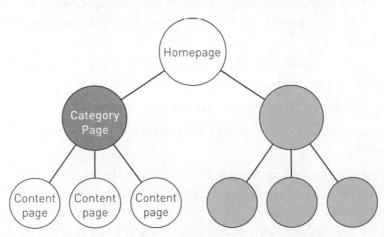

FIGURE 4-2: Diagram of category pages in relation to the rest of a site's
internal link profile

Auditing Content Pages

Now that you have analyzed the homepage and the navigational pages, it is time to audit the meat of the website, the content pages. To do this, you need to complete the following:

✔ **Check and note the format of the title tags.**

> The first action item is to check the title tags of the given page. This is important because it is both helpful for rankings and it makes up the anchor text used in search engine rankings. You don't get link value from these links, but they do act as incentives for people to visit your site.

FORMATTING TITLE TAGS

SEOmoz recently finished its first round of intensive search engine ranking factors correlation testing. The results were relatively clear. If you are trying to rank for a very competitive term, it is best to include the keyword at the beginning of the title tag. If you are competing for a less competitive term and branding can help make a difference in clickthrough rates, it is best to put the brand name first. With regards to special characters, we prefer pipes for aesthetic value but hyphens, n-dashes, m-dashes, and minus signs are all fine. Thus, the best practice format for title tags is one of the following:

> Primary Keyword – Secondary Keywords | Brand
>
> Brand Name | Primary Keyword and Secondary Keywords

Real-life examples include:

> Internet Marketing – Search Engine Optimization | SEOmoz
>
> Amazon | Apple iPod

As you look at the two preceding examples, it's important for you to objectively assess your brand awareness and decide whether it's worthwhile or advantageous to place your brand name ahead of your targeted terms. A site like Amazon could do pretty well for an "Apple iPod" query simply because the authority of the site outweighs the disadvantage of having its target terms further back in the title, and the user trust that comes by seeing "Amazon" near the front of the tag likely increases clickthrough. Chances are your site isn't as recognizable, so be very careful to assess the benefits and drawbacks of each approach.

You can see SEOmoz's most up-to-date research on title tags at `www.seomoz.org/knowledge/title-tag/`.

✔ **Check and note the format of the meta description.**

Similar to the first action item, the second item has to do with a metric that is directly useful for search engines rather than people (they are only indirectly useful for people once they are displayed by search engines). Check the meta description by viewing source or using the mozBar and make sure it is compelling and contains the relevant keywords at least twice. This inclusion of keywords is useful not for rankings but because matches are bolded in search results.

✔ **Check and note the format of the URL.**

The next action item is to check the URL for best practice optimization. Just like Danny Devito, URLs should be short, relevant, and easy to remember.

✔ **Check to see if the content is indexable.**

The next step is to make sure the content is indexable. To ensure that it is, make sure the text is not contained in an image, Flash, or within a frame. To make sure it is indexed, copy a sentence from the page and search for it within quotes in a search engine.

> **NOTE** If the sentence you searched for was indexed, that's great. But what else was indexed when you searched for that sentence? If that exact text string came up on a dozen other sites, either they're using your copy, *or you're using theirs*. Maybe it's as innocent as using the manufacturer's catalog copy to describe a product, but the bottom line is that your content must stand out from other sites to earn links that will help its ranking.

✔ **Check and note the format of the alt text attribute on images.**

If there are any images on the page (as there probably should be for the sake of users) you should make sure that the images have relevant alt text. In some testing at SEOmoz, we found that relevant alt text was highly correlated to high rankings.

✔ **Read the content as if you were the one searching for it.**

Lastly and possibly more importantly, you should take the time to read the content on the page. Read it from the perspective of a user who just got to it from a search engine. This is important because the content on the page is the main purpose for the page existing. As an SEO, it can be easy to become content-blind when doing quick audits. Remember, the content is the primary reason this user came to the page. It will either be helpful or the user will leave. When I do this, I ask myself the following questions:

▷ Does this content answer a relevant search query question?

▷ Would I recommend this content to a friend?

▷ Would I come back to this domain?

Analyzing the Links

Now that you have an idea of how the website is organized it is time to see what the rest of the world thinks about it. As you read in Chapter 1, links are incredibly important in the search engine algorithms. Thus, you cannot get a complete view of a website without analyzing its links. To analyze those links you need to do the following:

✔ **View the total number of links on the page (external and internal) and the number of root domains linking to given domain.**

This first action item requires you to get two different metrics about the inbound links to the given domain. Separately, these metrics can be very misleading due to internal links. Together, they provide a fuller picture that makes accounting for internal links possible and thus more accurate. At the time of writing, the best tool to get this data is through SEOmoz's Open Site Explorer (www.opensiteexplorer.org).

✔ **View the anchor text distribution of inbound links.**

The second action item requires you to analyze the relevancy side of links. This is important because it is a large part of search engine algorithms. This was discussed in Chapter 1 and proves as true now as it did when you read it earlier. You have two ways to get this data: you can use Google's Webmaster Central or SEOmoz's Open Site Explorer.

✔ **View the internal and external linking data and anchor text distribution for the site's competitors.**

If you know the link profile of your client's site and there are no "red flags" that appear, it might help very little if you have nothing to compare those numbers to. Examine the same linkage data that you did for your client, but do it for your client's top three or four competitors. The result will not be a comprehensive answer to all the site's ranking issues, but it will give you helpful context in which to discuss the potential work that your client may need to do in order to succeed in its market.

Checking a Website's Search Engine Inclusion

Now that you have gathered all the data you can about how the given website exists on the Internet, it is time to see what the search engines have done with this information. As an SEO, all of your work is completely useless if the search engines don't react to it. To a lesser degree this is true for webmasters as well. These action items can help you identify how the search engines react to the given website. Choose your favorite search engine (you might need to Google it) and do the following:

✔ **Search for the given domain to make sure it isn't penalized.**

The first action item is simple to do but can have dire effects. Simply go to a search engine and search for the name of your domain (Ex. Example.com). Assuming it is not brand new, it should appear as the first result. If it doesn't and it is an established site, it means it has major issues and was probably thrown out of the search engine indices. If this is the case, you need to identify this clearly and as early as possible.

✔ **See roughly how many pages are indexed of the given website.**

The second action item is also very easy to do. Go to either of the major search engines and use the site command (as defined in Chapter 3) to find roughly all of the pages of a domain that are indexed in the engine. For example, this may look like site:www.example.com. This action is important because the difference between the number that gets returned and the number of pages that actually exist on a site says a lot about how healthy a domain is in a search engine. If you find more pages in the index than exist on the page, you are facing a duplicate content problem. If you find more pages on the actual site than you find in the index, you are facing an indexation problem. Both are bad.

✔ **Search three of the most competitive keywords for which this domain likely ranks.**

The next action item is a quick exercise to see how well the given website is optimized. To get an idea of this, simply search for three of the most competitive terms that you think the given website would reasonably rank for. You can speed up this process by using one of the third-party rank trackers that are available.

CROSSREF I recommend SEOmoz's Rank Tracker, or see the other tools listed in Chapter 3.

✔ **Choose a random content page and search the engines for duplicate content.**

The final action item is to do a quick search for duplicate content. You can do this by going to a random content page on the given website and searching for either the title tag (in quotes) or the first sentence of the page (also in quotes). If there are more than two results from the given domain, then there are duplicate content problems. This situation is bad because the website is forced to compete against itself for ranking. In doing so it forces the search engine to decide which page is more valuable. This decision-making process is something that is best avoided because it is difficult to predict the outcome.

▶ *Duplicate content problems result in a website competing against itself for ranking and leave the decision of which page on the website is more valuable in the hands of the search engines.*

THE 5-MINUTE BRAND REPUTATION AUDIT

Many years ago branding was simply the act of marking one's cattle with a unique identifier so that they could quickly be sorted and would be difficult to steal. With the arrival of big corporations and the maturation of marketing, branding has evolved into something much more. Today, companies like Pepsi Cola spend hundreds of millions annually on their branding and marketing campaigns. With the popularity of search engines growing, SEO and Pay Per Click (PPC) have started to gain ground in these budgets. The following is a guide on how to perform an online brand reputation audit, which is necessary for measuring these growing resources.

Using the Brand Search Engine Result Page

Whenever I see top search query lists, I am always surprised at how often people search for exact domain names or brands. It is for this reason that the brand search engine result page (SERP) is so useful. The following actions can help you identify what improvements might be necessary for a branded term search result page.

✔ **Search for the brand name in the major search engines.**

To complete the first action item all you need to search for is the brand name of the given company. This will bring up a results page with about 10 results and some ads. This is one of the most important pages about the given company, and many otherwise smart company executives don't pay attention to it. For many searchers, this will be the front door to information about the company. Google knows this fact and has crafted algorithms to take advantage of it. Upon analyzing the SERP for a well-known brand name, you may notice some seemingly unusual results. This is because Google's brand-specific algorithms intentionally show more diverse results than they do for a normal search. These results tend to include reviews and websites that share opposing views.

To give you some context, the ideal brand search result page would have all of the following:

▶ An ideal brand search result page means no matter which link searchers click, they end up on a company-approved page.

- The main domain would have Sitelinks, a group of Google chosen links to primary sections of the given website in search engine results. (Figure 4-3).

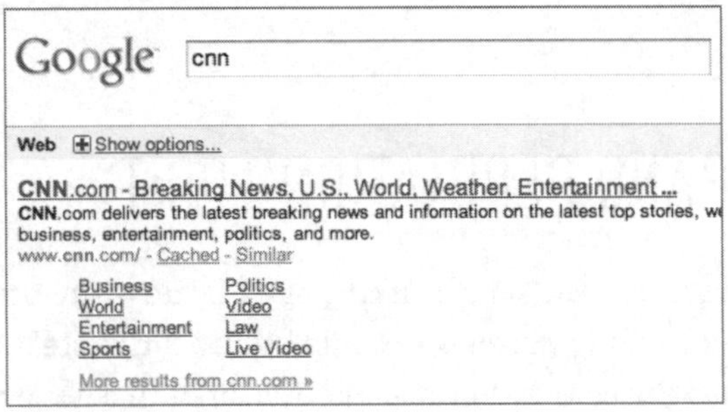

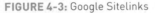

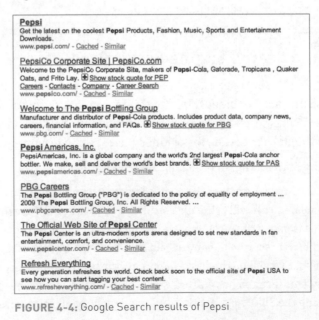

FIGURE 4-3: Google Sitelinks

- The first 10 natural results would be owned by the given company, as in Figure 4-4.

FIGURE 4-4: Google Search results of Pepsi

▷ The page would contain at least one positive review (Figure 4-5).

FIGURE 4-5: A positive review showing in Google Search results

▷ The given company would own all of the PPC ads for the query (Figure 4-6).

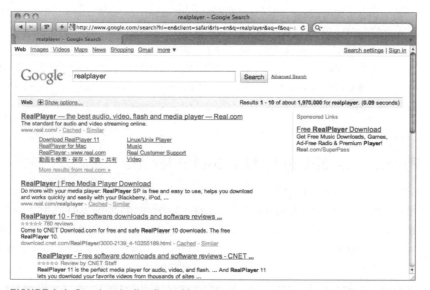

FIGURE 4-6: Google ads distributed by one company

The end result of a result page like this is that no matter which link the searchers click, they end up on a company-approved page. Although this isn't necessarily the best experience for the user, it is the best business tactic.

✔ **Search all of the following and identify potential problems (this is not a comprehensive list):**

▷ *Brand Name* Sucks

▷ *Brand Name* Scam

▷ *Brand Name* Cult

▷ *Brand Name* Problems

▷ *Brand Name* Issues

▷ *Brand Name* Support

▷ *Brand Name* Broken

▷ *Brand Name* Error

▷ *Brand Name* Review

The second and last action item on this list requires you to run a series of directed search queries to see if you can identify any problematic webpages. This list is not comprehensive and is only intended to be a starting point. I use this list in my work and customize it to my clients based on their product or service. (For example, if I was working for an oil company, I would run queries for topical negative queries such as "*Brand Name* environmental impact") This step is important both because it helps identify problematic sites early and because it mimics behavior that a skeptical user might do. Remember, if potential customers read even one negative review about a given company, they are significantly less likely to buy its product regardless of the source of the content.

Brand Searching in the Social Media

My sincerest hope is that by the time you read this book *social media* will no longer be the overused buzzword it is at the time I am writing this. It is definitely a very important part of the Internet, but it is not the be-all-end-all feature that may make or break your brand. It is merely a technological supplement. Remember, people were talking about brand on the Internet well before the creation of Facebook or Twitter. Use these services, but don't lose track of the real driving force behind brands—their products and services. The following list will help you glean some of the benefit these tools provide:

▶ Brand searching social media can help you respond to criticism as it happens or just shortly after.

✔ **Search Twitter for brand name mentions.**

This first action step is to search Twitter for any real-time (or near real-time) mentions of the brand. To do this, go to http://search.twitter.com and type the name of the brand into the search box. This step is important because it enables you to respond to criticism as it happens. Having been the guy that a corporation has contacted after I complained about them on Twitter, I can say that not only did it resolve the problem, but it left me giving the brand some well-deserved credit.

✔ **Search Google Blog Search for brand name mentions.**

This next item requires to you to search Google Blog Search for brand mentions. As the name implies, this searches only through the blogosphere. This is available at http://blogsearch.google.com and is quick and easy. For best results, narrow down the time span by clicking one of the available time filters. This action is important because it allows you to quickly see both what influential and beginner bloggers have to say about the brand. Bloggers' opinions can travel to many ears and make a large impact on overall brand, and you'll typically see company mentions on Google Blog Search prior to those stories going viral and spreading on Twitter and other social media sites.

✔ **Search Google 24-hour Search for brand name mentions.**

This third action point involves searching Google for brand mentions that happened within the past 24 hours. You can accomplish this by searching in Google, clicking Show options on the resulting page, and clicking Past 24 hours. This searches the Google web index for mentions that happened within the prior 24 hours. Taking this step is important because it gives you the chance to track down mentions before they are widely read. That said, on the Web, 24 hours is a long time and if you catch something too long after it happens, it might already be too late.

✔ **Search Google Realtime Search for mentions as they occur.**

Google Realtime Search (www.google.com/realtime) is a relatively new interface from Google that allows you to search for articles, posts, and tweets that reach the results page within seconds of going live. You can filter your search results by geographic location and by time, so it's very simple to track trends when and where they happen. Currently, most search results come from social media sites such as Twitter and Facebook (due to their sheer volume), but expect to see more sources represented soon.

✔ **Search Facebook for fake accounts and fan pages matching brand name.**

Facebook is unique in its ability to avoid looking corporate (with negative connotations) even when it is being so. This is largely due to the number of real-life friends who communicate on the site. So, the next action step has you search Facebook for fake user accounts and brand-related fan pages. To do this, simply log in to www.facebook.com/ and type the brand name into the search box as if you were searching for a person. You can then contact or browse through any of the information offered by that person or page.

✔ **Search Myspace for brand name mentions.**

Similar to the previous step, you should also search www.myspace.com/ for brand mentions. This social networking site is smaller than Facebook, but covers a lot of people who do not use Facebook regularly. To do this, log in to Myspace and search for the brand name as if you were searching for a friend or username. This will help you see how the given brand is being talked about by the Internet-savvy demographic that is largely different from Facebook members.

✔ **Search YouTube for brand name mentions.**

You should also search YouTube for brand name mentions. Though this isn't comprehensive (it doesn't detect words spoken in videos) it is the best video search available at this time. To do this simply go to www.youtube.com and search for the given brand name. This step is important because of the inherent nature of video on the Web. It is easy to consume and easy to share, so its potential for spreading is enormous. My favorite example of this working against a brand is a songwriter whose favorite guitar was ruined by United Airlines workers. He contacted the airline several times to resolve the issue, but they refused to reimburse him for his broken property. Upset by their lack of integrity he wrote a song and published it on YouTube. As I am writing this, the video has been watched more than five and half million times. The airline tried to respond to him, but the damage was already done (to his guitar and the United Airlines brand).

✔ **Search Digg submitted stories with brand name.**

This item involves searching Digg for submitted stories with the given brand name. To do this go to www.digg.com and search for the brand name in the search box. The trick here is that you are not necessarily looking for stories that have gone popular (because odds are they would have already turned up); instead you are looking for evidence of people who are trying to start something by posting negative brand stories to Digg. These people are especially important to find early so you can deal with their complaint before it erupts into a major problem.

✔ **Search forums for brand name mentions.**

The eighth action point is a bit more complicated than the ones before it. It requires you to go out and find industry-related forums and then search them for brand name mentions. The easiest way to find them is to search *Industry Name* Forum or *industry name* inurl:forum*. (The asterisk here indicates the search is for "forums" with an "s" or "forum" without, plural or singular.) This is important because forum members tend to be early adopters and more technologically advanced. This makes them very good people to impress.

✔ **Search Craigslist for brand name mentions.**

This action applies most to companies that sell products. It requires you to go to www.craigslist.org and search for brand name mentions. This helps identify aftermarket sales and sales opportunities. It is also a good way to find pirated or fake goods, which is important because it can directly affect the bottom line. If you do this, be sure to check all of the applicable localities because these are important filters on Craigslist. If the product is global, you can check just the major cities. It should give you an idea of how widespread the problem is.

✔ **Search torrent sites for brand name mentions.**

The final action item has you search BitTorrent sites for brand name mentions. BitTorrent is a protocol for sending large files over the Internet quickly. This makes it a very good protocol for file sharing. The easiest way to see if a given brand's product is being shared via torrents is to either search for `Brand Name torrent` or `torrent search engine` and search for your brand. This step helps identify which products are in demand for file sharers and shows you what people are saying about your product.

IDENTIFYING SEARCH ENGINE PENALTIES

Oh, the dreaded search engine penalties. They can single-handedly ruin your whole day. This section describes how to identify them. The next chapter tells you what you can do to treat them.

In my mind there are two broad types of penalties:

▶ **Algorithmic penalties**, which are algorithm identified patterns that search engineers have determined are indications of spam or dishonest tactics

▶ **Manual review penalties**, which are identified when a real person sees something he or she believes is against the search engine guidelines

Both of the penalties are implemented with algorithms but the detection methods differ. Keep in mind that the important thing is not to determine exactly how the page got caught, but rather what triggered the search engines to penalize the site and how to get rid of the penalty.

Algorithmic Penalty Symptoms

Algorithmically detected penalties are usually identified by one or more of the following symptoms:

▶ **A specific group of links stop providing any value:** This is the most common penalty that I see. It generally takes the form of weak pages with only a few strong links dropping out of the search results. This happens because the few strong links that these pages had stop passing value as determined by the search engines. Many times I have seen this when an entire link farm is removed from the search engine indices.

▶ **Website starts ranking lower for all keywords:** I have seen this happen a couple times, and it usually results in search engine referred traffic dropping by between 15 and 30 percent.

▶ **An entire domain ranks lower for all or most of its keywords:** This is a clear signal that the given website has done something that the search engines don't approve of. Many times (but not always) every keyword will rank 30 to 50 spots below where it did.

▶ **An entire industry of websites loses rankings for non-industry terms:** I have seen this happen twice. The first time it happened with the SEO industry and the second time it was with the automotive industry. The search results for the main keywords (*SEO* and *Car*, in this case) don't change but a lot of the long tail search results do. This seems to be linked to when the search engines update their algorithms in a way that redistributes the entire Web's link juice. This happens deep within the bowels of the Googleplex and the Microsoft campus and the details are never shared with the public. The only way to detect these types of penalties is to check the long tail search engine referring traffic via analytics software. The problem will appear as a loss in traffic, but the major keywords (non-long tail) will not show a decrease in referred traffic.

Manual Review Penalty Symptoms

Manual review penalties are usually much worse than algorithmic penalties. They are more severe and harder to recover from. Many times, the domain will need to be retired to resolve the issue. Manual review penalty symptoms generally look like the following:

▶ Although drastic, retiring a domain may be the only solution to resolve an issue involving a manual review penalty.

▶ **Key pages stop ranking entirely:** I have seen this mostly with homepages, but sometimes it happens with other key pages. This is generally a sign that the webmaster of the given domain did something like keyword stuff, buy or sell links, or implement a cloaking scheme that really upset the search engine's engineers.

▶ **Domain stops ranking for domain name:** Sometimes a domain will stop ranking for its name but continue to rank for its other keywords. I have only seen this once, but it should be noted that it was very difficult to fix.

- ▶ **Entire domain stops ranking for all keywords:** This is bad—very, very bad. This means that the entire domain has been removed from the search engine index. I saw one case where it took more than a year for the website to be reinstated.

DON'T PANIC

If you see symptoms of this (all or nearly all search-engine-referred traffic suddenly stops) happening to a client's site, be sure to check for common crawling errors before panicking. Sometimes this happens simply because someone blocked all search engine robots via robots.txt or an IP address range, or Google could have suspended your rankings if your server has had significant downtime recently.

Solutions to these problems are addressed in the next chapter.

Meeting with Clients Suffering from Penalties

When I first meet with clients in any of these situations, I use the meeting as an input session. The goal of the meeting is to find "the smoking gun" (that is, the cause of the penalty). I find out everything that they know has changed before and after the penalty started. This includes changes like implementing new navigation, changing URL structure, updating security, or any link building campaigns.

I also take this opportunity to let them know that although I have been able to help the vast majority of clients in this situation, Google, not myself, has the final say in these decisions and they may need to look into other alternative plans. (This is especially true if the entire domain has been removed from the index.)

In addition, I check for the most common mistakes that can cause results that look like penalties. Specifically, I check robots.txt to make sure the client has not accidently blocked the pages in question, and I check the meta robots tags on the given pages to see if the pages are blocking robots at a page level. I also look for evidence of cloaking by surfing the given website with the Googlebot user agent and comparing it to what I see while surfing the site as my normal browser user agent.

SUMMARY

Congratulations, you have come a long way in improving your SEO skills. This chapter taught you how to identify SEO problems. I build on this in Chapters 8 and 9 when I discuss comprehensive SEO audits.

You should now know all of the work that you should do before meeting with a potential client. I generally do the quick audits mentioned in this chapter and tell clients what I saw either the first or second time I meet with them. This is great way to show them that you know all about their site and that you know what you are talking about. Chapter 5 takes this to the next step and discusses how to fix the SEO problems you identified. If ignorance is bliss, you should be getting less happy at this point. Wax on, Wax off.

Solving SEO Problems

Now that you know how to identify SEO problems, you are ready to start solving them. Are you ready to learn the big secret of SEO? You have covered a lot of material so far, and this might be the most important concept covered in this book. Alright, here it is: most SEO problems are caused by a lack of links. You see, hyperlinks are the Swiss Army Knife of SEO. Assuming a few other conditions are met, links can fix almost any problem. The search engines need to index and rank content that people are naturally linking to. With that spoiler out of the way, this chapter is about fixing SEO problems and getting more links.

FIRST THINGS FIRST

The first thing I do when starting the actual job of fixing SEO problems is to check for the following common areas. I developed this list out of necessity after I wasted far too much time digging deeper into SEO problems than I needed to. Just like in software, sometimes the best SEO solutions are the simplest ones.

- ▶ **Identify the link profile:** The SEOs and computer scientists at SEOmoz believe that about 70 percent of Google's modern algorithm has to do with link metrics. This is based on large-scale correlation tests and first-hand SEO experience. The reason the engines focus so much on links is that they reveal a lot about a website. This is why the link profile is the first thing I examine when I start analyzing a website.

- ▶ **Canonicalization:** Canonicalization errors are extremely common and can be extremely hazardous to a website's ranking ability. The second thing I check when working with a website is whether its homepage is canonical.

- ▶ **Robots.txt:** The next SEO element that I check is the site's `robots.txt` file (located at the path `www.example.com/robots.txt`). Specifically, I am looking to make sure they did not block anything that shouldn't be blocked. You would think this is obvious but a lot of times it slips through the cracks, and a single misplaced keystroke can completely devastate a site's ability to be indexed. When I was running through this list with one of the top-10 most popular websites at the time (sorry, they have a nondisclosure agreement with me), I uncovered that they were accidently blocking all of their most important content from every search engine robot. This simple error potentially cost them an extraordinary amount of money.

- ▶ **Meta Robots:** For the exact same reasons as checking `robots.txt`, I check the meta robots tag on the homepage and content pages of the websites I do SEO work with. The parameters for this tag can be extremely confusing and can cause a lot of problems when done incorrectly. Specifically, I am looking to see if important pages are erroneously marked with either `"noindex"` or `"nofollow"`.

> **NOTE** Read the Meta tags in the `<head>` section of the page very carefully. `"noindex"` or `"nofollow"` attributes may not be assigned to the general "robots" attribute; instead, they might be pointed at engine-specific attributes such as "googlebot" or "msnbot". If you do a quick search for "robots" while viewing source code, you could miss something.

▶ **Site command in Google:** After I check for the important on-site domain factors, I check the search engine's point of view. I start out by running the site command in Google (for example, `site:www.example.com`). This gives you a rough idea of how many pages on the site are indexed in the search engine. Keep an eye out for either a suspiciously high number (duplicate content) or a suspiciously low number (crawler trap). The range will depend on the size of the website in question. A good indicator is to ask the webmaster how many pages he thinks are on his site and base your judgment on that number.

▶ **Text-only cached version of the homepage:** The last item on the list is perhaps the most important. Search for the exact URL of the homepage in the major search engines. If the page is not the first result, the site is likely being penalized and you have big problems. If it is the first result, click the link to see the cache version of the page. This is the copy of the page that the search engines have. In Google, I always make sure to click the link "Text-only version," because this filters out JavaScript-based page elements, CSS, and Flash, and it gives a more accurate indication of what Google sees when it views your page. Specifically, you are looking for spammy links or unclear navigational links. This text-only view is a great window into the perspective of the search engine crawlers.

> **TIP** Whenever I am asked to give free SEO advice on a website (like for a friend or acquaintance), I run through the items on the "First Things First" list. It is quick and easy and usually helps the person rank better.

FIXING POPULARITY PROBLEMS

The following popularity-related problems are almost always caused by a lack of links. These page problems are generally easy to identify but require a lot of work to fix.

Page Not Indexed

SYMPTOMS

A given page does not appear for any search result in a specific engine.

SOLUTIONS

1. First, verify that the webpage really is not indexed by using the site or info command in combination with the exact URL:

   ```
   site:www.example.com/products/bacon.html
   ```

   or

   ```
   info:www.example.com/products/bacon.html
   ```

   If no results are returned, the page really isn't indexed.

2. Next, check to see if the search engine crawlers are being blocked from the page. Be sure to check both robots.txt and the meta robots tag on the given page. (I have seen this happen many times.)

   robots.txt is located at www.example.com/robots.txt.

   Meta robot is located in the <head> of the document and takes the form

   ```
   <meta name="robots" content="follow,index">
   ```

   You are looking to avoid noindex as a parameter.

   If the page is blocked, simply remove the applicable line of code and wait for the engines to recrawl the page.

3. If the pages don't appear to be blocked and the page is still not indexed, try visiting the page while spoofing the user agent of the popular search engines. Sometimes, intentional or unintentional cloaking can prevent a page from being crawled.

   ▶ You can use the Firefox User Agent Switcher mentioned in Chapter 3 to visit a site as a search engine spider.

   > **NOTE** User agent spoofing is an effective way to mimic a search engine most of the time. Sometimes, however, servers react to IP addresses or other factors, not user agents. Viewing your server logs is the single most effective way to see how your server reacts to engine visits.

4. If the page is not indexed and the bots are not blocked, the problem is almost always caused by the domain not having enough links to get all of its pages indexed. The easiest way to fix this problem is make sure that the website has a proper information hierarchy. Your goal is to make it so there are as few clicks (on navigational links) as possible between the homepage of the domain and the unindexed page.

5. Find a random string of copy on your page and perform a Google search for that string in quotes. You might find a duplicate version of your URL from your site (or another site) that is considered more authoritative than your URL and that it has caused your page to not be indexed.

6. If improving the information hierarchy of the website is not an option, you can try adding a sitemap to the website if it doesn't already have one. Sometimes this proves to be the tool the search engines need to fully navigate a website.

7. The last solution is also the most effective. The best way to get a page indexed is to get it more links. Internal links (links coming from the same domain) are good, external links are better, but a combination of both is the best. Assuming the page and domain are not affected by penalties and there is content to crawl on the page, building more external links (links from other domains) will almost certainly get the page indexed. You can do this by using the tactics listed in the section titled "Link Building Techniques" later in this chapter.

> ▶ There are two distinct types of sitemaps—HTML (the traditional type with the look and feel of a regular site page) and XML (a long list of your site's URLs that users won't see). Having both can result in improved indexing.

Page Indexed but Not Ranking Well

SYMPTOMS

A given page does rank for terms but is suspiciously low in the results.

SOLUTIONS

1. If you run into this scenario, the first thing I suggest you check is the competition. Check their link profile (popularity) and page makeup (relevancy) and figure out why they are ranking above your client.

   To do this, I recommend identifying their link profile with either SEO Book's HubFinder (a tool that helps you find related sites in online niches) or SEO-moz's PRO tools (a group of tools that show you how your niche on the Internet ranks and gives you specific suggestions on how to rank higher). I also recommend analyzing the competitor's page for relevancy factors with SEO Browser or SEOmoz's mozBar.

   > ▶ Many times you can use the same tactics they are using to boost your ranking and combine them with your own tricks to outrank them.

2. If you don't see any obvious reason why the competition is outranking the given page, check to see if the page is being penalized. (See Chapter 4 for a discussion of search engine penalties). If it looks like the page is being penalized, follow the steps in the section "Fixing Penalties" later in this chapter.

3. If the competition does not have a noticeable advantage and the page is not being penalized, the solution might be improving the domain's information hierarchy so that the page is internally linked to more prominently. Remember, the best hierarchies are the ones with as few clicks (via navigational links) as possible between the homepage and any given page. (Remember the link pyramid mentioned in Chapter 2.) This is because link juice is diluted each time it flows through a link.

4. If the previous solutions don't help, I recommend focusing on making the page more relevant to the given term. Be sure that the term is included in all of the important SEO places. (See Chapter 2 and Chapter 6 for more information.)

5. If all else fails, you will need to get more external links to the webpage. In fact, this solution will prove more effective than any of the others on this list. Links are ranking power.

Page Indexed and Ranking Well

Though this isn't exactly a problem, it is not necessarily the final goal. What is better than ranking number 1? Ranking 1 through 10.

SYMPTOMS

A given page is targeted for a term, but it ranks much better for a different term.

SOLUTIONS

1. To get more positive mentions of the given page in the given SERP, try linking out to relevant articles that mention the given URL. Many times this will add the linked-to URLs to a given SERP and effectively make your URL dominate the given SERP.

   For example, if you are trying to shape the SERP for a new product, try linking to positive external articles that review the product and point to the product page. I usually do this under a section labeled "Media Mentions."

2. Occasionally subdomains can prove helpful for SEO (internationalization is one good example). If the given website has enough ranking power, it is possible to get several different subdomains on a given domain to rank for a given term. The best way to do this is to create a relevant subdomain and point as many links to it as possible.

▶ Used sparingly, subdomains can prove helpful for SEO.

WARNING Overdoing this tactic can lead to penalties. Making subdomains simply to catch exact match queries is an old spam tactic that has diluted power today.

If you have a URL for a specific product, it can be helpful to create a slight variation on it as a subdomain. For example, www.example.com/Product might be a landing page for the product and http://download.example.com/Product might be the place you actually download it from. (Again, use this tactic sparingly as it is helpful only for very powerful domains that use it judiciously.)

3. Another solution for owning all of the results for a given search term is to create what is a called a *microsite*. A microsite is a separate domain (usually containing a domain name that is an exact match for a given query) that has content on a very specific topic. This tactic can be helpful for controlling multiple results on a SERP.

One example of this is Open Site Explorer. This tool, which was created by SEOmoz, is located at www.opensiteexplorer.org rather than www.seomoz.org. This URL was chosen so that rather than piggybacking on the domain strength of seomoz.org, the tool gained its own links on its own domain, allowing SEOmoz to control two strong domains. This is helpful for rankings because the major search engines will show both of these results (SEOmoz.org and OpenSiteExplorer.org) for search queries when appropriate.

4. Even if you own all of the results on a page, you can still occupy more screen real estate. Buying ads from the search engines is an extremely effective tactic for getting relevant clicks. If you have not experimented with paid search engine ads, you should try to see how well it works for your niche.

BUYING THE WEBSITES OF COMPETITION

If you can't beat them, buy them. In fact, even if you can beat them, it is sometimes worth it to buy the websites of your competition. Remember that roughly 90 percent of clicks go to the first three results on a SERP. Depending on your niche, it may be financially worthwhile to buy websites from your competition.

Despite what this book often discusses about redirecting properly, this is one instance in which you should not redirect. You don't get more SERP real estate if you buy a domain simply to roll it into another domain. (You'll make your domain stronger by doing so, but you'll lose the chance of having more of your domains show up in results.)

FIXING RELEVANCY PROBLEMS

Now that you know how to fix the most common popularity problems, you are ready to learn how to fix some relevancy problems. You can rest easy; most of these are easier to solve.

Fixing Duplicate Content

Duplicate content is one of the most widespread SEO problems on the Internet. It is so much of a problem that the search engines have created a tool (rel="canonical") to help deal with the problem.

SYMPTOMS

Content appears on multiple URLs on either the same domain or on different domains.

SOLUTIONS

1. First you need to find all of the offending duplicate content. Choose a random string of text on the given page. In quotes, search for that phrase in the engines:

   ```
   site:www.example.com "this is text from the page"
   ```

   Alternatively, you can use the site command and search for the exact URL or use the intitle command and search for the exact title tag in quotes:

   ```
   site:www.example.com/exact/URL/of/suspected/page.html
   intitle:"This is the exact text from the title tag of a
   suspicious page"
   ```

   Figure 5-1 shows an example of what you probably see. Notice how these results for Facebook's domain are showing multiple versions of the same content. All of these URLs contain duplicate content.

   The site and intitle technique works to find duplicate versions of distinct URLs, typically illustrated by the inclusion of dynamic parameters after the filename. In some cases, however, the duplicate content will live on different base URLs and will not be caught by listing a full URL after the site command. To catch all suspicious forms of duplicate content on your site regardless of URL, it's often effective to simply show the URL of the home page after the site command, as shown here:

   ```
   site:www.example.com/ intitle:"This is the exact text from the
   title tag of a suspicious page"
   ```

FIGURE 5-1: A Google SERP showing Facebook with duplicate content

2. The best way to solve duplicate content problems is to use the
`rel="canonical"` tag:

```
<link rel="canonical" href="http://www.example.com/
    awesome.php?item=bacon" />
```

This tag acts as a strong hint to the search engines to help them make sense
of duplicate content. Insert this code into the <head> of offending pages and
this problem will largely be solved.

NOTE Check your canonical code carefully or suffer the consequences. You'll
probably use an automated system to add a canonical URL that strips extraneous parameters. Be sure it actually strips those parameters before it writes to
the **<head>** section of your code. It does no good to add a canonical URL code line
if the HREF value is the long, parameter-showing version that you want to avoid
having indexed.

TIP When engines combine forces to combat a problem such as duplicate
content, it's worthwhile to pay attention. This is their acknowledgment that their
algorithms are imperfect and need external assistance. In general, effort spent
on helping your content conform to what engines are looking for and helping
them overcome their own deficiencies will create opportunities for your site.

3. Sometimes you will run into a situation where you are not able to implement the `rel="canonical"` tag. I see this most often with legacy Content Management Systems, which are commonly built without regard to SEO. If this happens, it is best to either add the robots meta tag with `"noindex, follow"` to the offending pages (hard to do without accidently noindexing the canonical version of the page) or implement 301 redirects in an `.htaccess` file (Apache), as shown in Figure 5-2.

```
<meta name="robots" content="noindex, follow">
```

FIGURE 5-2: An .htaccess file 301 redirecting a page

4. If the duplicate content is caused by session IDs or tracking code in URLs, you can supply Google with the patterns to ignore (for example, `?tracking-parameter=123`). This is accomplished through Google Webmaster Tools.

I have had only mediocre results with this tactic.

> **NOTE** Yahoo came out with a parameter-handling tool 2 years earlier than Google did. Unfortunately, the concept didn't get a lot of attention until Google made its tool.

5. The other common situation I see is when the duplicate content is on third-party sites. In this case, you can simply ask the offenders to remove the content with a polite e-mail.

▶ When you choose a setting within a certain engine's webmaster tools, the change applies only to how that specific engine views your pages. That's different from a change you make to your actual site, which affects how all engines view your site.

6. Alternatively, you can ask the other webmaster to simply link back to your article. This helps the search engines understand where the original copy of the document is located and in some cases can actually improve your popularity metrics.

7. If a polite e-mail doesn't work and both websites are in the United States you can send a DMCA takedown notice (Digital Millennium Copyright Act). I have seen this work successfully on two occasions.

Fixing a Page That Ranks for the Wrong Term

On occasion, a page ranks for the wrong term. Though this isn't really a problem ("Oh no! I rank for too many terms!"), it is a situation that can be improved.

SYMPTOMS

A page is not ranking for the term you intended it to. This is different from the common situation where a page ranks for its primary keyword and a lot of other variations on its content (long tail).

SOLUTIONS

1. When this happens, it is almost always caused by inbound links (from strong external domains) linking with the offending word as the anchor text. Your best option is to make the page more relevant to its real keyword by including it in the URL, title, and text. You then need to build links with the correct anchor text.

2. If that solution does not work, you should consider changing the URL of the page. This negates all of the offending inbound links (usually a really bad idea) but gives you the opportunity to start fresh.

FIXING PENALTIES

Search engine penalties are the stuff a successful webmaster's nightmares are made of. One day you are top of the ultracompetitive SERP; the next you are completely removed from all listings. Luckily, there are things you can do.

Page with a Penalty

In my experience, this has been the most reported SEO problem from prospective clients.

SYMPTOMS

A page is either completely out of a search engine index or is ranking suspiciously low for a term it once ranked highly for.

SOLUTIONS

▶ Don't confuse "penalized" with simply not ranking well for your important term or terms. There is a difference.

1. Unlike other SEO problems, identification is not the first step toward finding a solution. The first thing to do when you suspect a page has been penalized is to figure out what changed. Many times it's a simple code change on the site. In my experience, these have included modified footer links and modified global navigation. Other times, the cause is a new group of inbound links from a bad source.

   In the worst-case scenario, it is an algorithm update inside the search engine black box.

   > **WARNING** Common examples of penalty-inducing tactics include:
   >
   > ▶ Sending a specific global navigation to search engines and a different navigation to people (cloaking)
   >
   > ▶ Unintelligible text used solely for boosting relevancy metrics
   >
   > ▶ Buying links
   >
   > ▶ Adding unrelated links to footers
   >
   > ▶ Keyword stuffing
   >
   > ▶ Automated link building
   >
   > ▶ Misleading redirects
   >
   > ▶ Misleading URLs
   >
   > ▶ Misleading title tags

2. The next step to remove the penalty is to fix every easily identified SEO problem on the given site. Your best bet in reversing a penalty is to stop doing anything that might be causing it.

This can include cloaking, spammy content, hidden content (either placed off the viewable page, layered under graphics, or displayed in a color that is identical or very close to its background), hidden links, paid links, link farming, misleading redirects, and misleading URLs. Simply put, if you wouldn't feel comfortable telling a search engine engineer at one of the major engines about a given tactic, stop doing it.

3. After you clean up your website, you need to make a backup plan. It is quite possible that the page in question will never be restored to its previous rank. (This situation occurs when the search engine algorithms themselves change as opposed to something changing on the given website.) You should warn yourself or your client about the possibility of not having the page return to its previous rankings.

4. After you have implemented all of the changes to clean up the given website, you can submit a reinclusion request to Google. Be as open and honest as possible in it. SEOs don't know what tools Google has to look into penalties, but we do know some of its resources:

   ▷ The search engines have a copy of your website and a list of all of the links going to it and how that list has changed over time.

   ▷ They have information on where it is hosted and who owns the domain name.

   ▷ They have information on the given website's competitors and allies.

   ▷ They have at least one snapshot of what the site used to look like.

   Your best chance for getting reincluded is to be honest and fix everything that you can.

   Reinclusion requests take between three weeks and three months to get processed. Google rarely responds to the requests, and there is no way (that I know of) to get ahead in line. *Do not submit multiple requests.* A lot of people do this, and it frustrates the reviewers. Put yourself in the position of the people who read all of the reinclusion requests. Write your request as if you are talking to a real person, not a gigantic corporation. (You can see a sample reinclusion request in the sidebar on the next page.)

5. Another approach is to try to contact a search engine spokesman. They make themselves available at search conferences and are sometimes able to fix a problem. This option has a better chance of working than a reinclusion request but is also very inconvenient. Googlers frequently hang out at the Webmaster Help forums (www.google.com/support/forum/). Inside, the Webmaster Central forum has a specific discussion category called "Crawling, indexing & ranking" in which people can ask for help diagnosing penalties.

▶ If you go the route of fixing these issues (and you should), be sure to keep records of what you changed. I have seen people waste a lot of time and money trying to find a nonexistent smoking gun.

SAMPLE REINCLUSION REQUEST

Do *not* copy this reinclusion request verbatim when sending your request to Google. It is extremely important that you personalize your message and use this letter only as an inspiration. It is very likely that some search engine employees will read this book and/or become aware of this template.

Dear Googler,

Thank you for taking the time to read this. I'm the JOB TITLE at EXAMPLE.COM, an INDUSTRY-TYPE startup out of CITY, STATE providing VALUE PROPOSITION.

Last week, our site, WWW.EXAMPLE.COM, lost all of our Google referred traffic. We had previously registered with Webmaster Central, but did not receive any notification as to why this happened. My co-workers and I are, put bluntly, freaking out. We try to be an honest team and to my knowledge have always acted within the Google Guidelines.

In the past week, we have worked with an SEO consultant to help figure out why we are being penalized. Here are the changes we have made on their recommendation:

List actual changes. Examples might include:

We were implementing a system of IP targeting that created a special case for Googlebot. We have since removed this feature in favor of more open practices.

We had 50 links in our footer that may have been considered spammy. We added them without knowledge of SEO best practices. We have since removed them.

We had a high percentage of key terms on our core pages. These may have been interpreted as keyword spamming. We have since removed the excess mentions.

I don't know if these were the problems that caused our ranking drop, but just in case we have stopped doing them. We have the best intentions and only want to be back in your search engine.

Thank you for taking time out of your day to read this.

Best regards,

NAME

▶ Fix every conceivable problem before submitting a reinclusion request. Do not fix one item, request reinclusion, wait for results, and repeat the process by fixing another item.

6. The last tactic that I recommend is complaining about the problem on a popular public website or blog. While lacking tact, I have seen this tactic work. Sometimes Google makes mistakes and if your case is one of them, Google gets pressured into fixing the problem.

Domain with a Penalty

On occasion, the major search engines penalize an entire domain. This is a worst-case scenario.

SYMPTOMS

Every page on a domain is ranking significantly lower than it used to or it is entirely out of a search engine index.

SOLUTIONS

1. If you are unlucky enough to encounter this situation, the domain likely did something that was very bad according to the search engines. Follow the steps listed under "Page with a Penalty."

2. Domains that are kicked out of an index can take anywhere from months to years to make it back into the index. If this is the case, it is almost always smarter to cut the losses and start a new domain.

▶ It can take months or even years for a domain that is kicked out of an index to make it back into the index. If you face this problem, it is almost always smarter to just start a new domain than to spend time trying to get the old domain back in.

Poison Links

Acquiring "poison" links—links from obviously spammy sources (for example, a link from http://cheap-drugs-for-sale.blogspot.com with the anchor text "buy prescription drugs online for free")—is an old tactic that while less effective than it used to be can still have negative consequences for the unfortunate target.

SYMPTOMS

A group of links from sites in "bad neighborhoods" (porn, prescriptions, casinos, hacks, and so on) are pointing at a page and causing it to rank lower.

SOLUTIONS

1. If you encounter this, your first goal should be to try to contact the website the links are coming from and ask them to remove the links. Due to the inherent factors behind poison links, this rarely works. That said, it is worth a try.

2. If you can't get the links removed, you should try to get the links discredited. Tell Google about the links via a reinclusion request. Again, be honest, polite, and open. The search engines actually benefit from this tactic because it helps them identify spam sources. This makes them more willing to help you.

3. If all else fails, you may want to change the URL of the page being linked to. This will make it so the page loses all of its inbound links, but it may help save the domain.

PENALTIES VS. FILTERS

Many SEOs and webmasters that I have talked to lump penalties and filters into the same category. Though these anti-spam methods have similar effects, they are actually fundamentally different.

▶ **Penalties** tend to be very severe. Many of them are implemented after manual review from search engine representatives. They are difficult to reverse and normally affect many pages on a website.

▶ **Filters** are different. They are usually triggered by algorithmic detection and are less severe than penalties. Many times they can be identified by standardized decreases in rank (for example, negative 50 positions).

The big takeaway is that both filters and penalties exist and when encountered should be taken seriously. Do not simply assume they will go away without you doing any work to fix them.

LINK BUILDING TECHNIQUES

Acquiring additional inbound links is the common solution that helps solve most of the problems that SEOs run up against. To make this difficult task a little easier for you, I have compiled a list of some of my favorite link building techniques. Not all of these techniques work for all people, but the list is long enough that you can almost undoubtedly find a technique that works for your case.

▶ Most of the problems SEOs run up against can be addressed by adding inbound links.

Low-Risk Link Building Techniques

▶ **Start a blog:** Your life is a story. Building a blog is extremely easy, and if you are able to find a way to differentiate yourself, you will have a limitless supply of link opportunities. Find something that you think other people (not just yourself) will find interesting and share it with the world. (Creating a business blog is similarly helpful if you are part of a large organization. Getting content approved adds some bureaucratic headaches, but it can be worth it if you stick with it. An honest, insightful blog about the inside of a corporation is relatively rare and is rewarded with quality links.)

▶ **Help bloggers:** Bloggers are great link suppliers. It is a natural part of their job. You can tap into this by helping them find the information they need. The easiest way to do this is to find recent articles where the blogger has made a mistake and send a polite e-mail with the correction. Many times the blogger will choose to link back to you out of appreciation.

▶ **Sign up for HARO (Help A Reporter Out):** Similarly, you can help online reporters do their job. This service connects reporters and content producers with the people who can answer their questions. You can be the expert they are looking to interview.

▶ **Contact business partners:** If you are running a business, you will undoubtedly have business partners. These partners will likely have links. Consider taking a link rather than payment for a simple task with a partner.

▶ **Ask customers:** No one likes your products more than your customers (after all, they paid money for them). Many times these customers have websites or blogs of their own. Try including a polite request for a link in receipts and confirmation e-mails.

▶ *You can make this process easier by providing customers with the code to do this.*

▶ **Ask friends and family:** Just like your customers, your friends and family likely have websites or blogs. These are some of the easiest links to acquire because the providers are likely to be more willing to help than general strangers.

▶ **Find links that your competition has and request linkers to consider your site:** This tactic is good for two reasons.

  ▷ First, the links are easy to find with tools like HubFinder and SEOmoz PRO.

  ▷ Second, these links will be considered relevant by the search engines because they are all from the same Internet neighborhood.

▶ **Write articles and submit them to content aggregators:** Many services online need content. Specifically, I have heard good things about About.com. After building up a reputation at these websites, feel free to include some links to your website when relevant.

▶ **Offer to write a guest blog post:** In my experience, professional bloggers always feel the need to post new content. Many times, they are willing to post other people's guest posts to fill this need. This has the benefit of building your credibility and link profile.

▶ **Do charity work and ask for a link in return:** This is a win-win situation. You get to help a charity with its website and you get a link from a trusted domain.

- **Code a simple calculator:** Calculators are deceptively simple to code in either JavaScript or PHP. Pick an equation that you know (human years to dog years, weeks to plant petunias, time to cook the perfect turkey based on size, price of a car after depreciation, and so on), build or contract someone to build the calculator, and optimize the page so it ranks for the term. People love to link to helpful resources.

- **Write a how-to:** Odds are you know how to do something that other people don't. Be it sewing a button, or optimizing engines, how-tos are great link getters.

- **Write a tutorial:** Similarly, to how-tos, tutorials are excellent link getting sources. Tutorials tend to be more technical than how-tos, which is great because more technical readers are more likely to link.

- **Make a screencast:** Screencasts are the lazy man's tutorial. They are easy to create (Quicktime 10 has a screen recorder built in) and even easier to consume. Also, due to their file size, they are more likely to be linked to rather than flat out copied.

- **Make or host a funny video:** This is easy to do and has the potential to spread virally.

> **NOTE** Don't host the video on Vimeo or YouTube, because you won't get the link benefits. Instead, sign up for Amazon Web Services (relatively inexpensive cloud computing) and host it yourself. Make sure that the video is embedded on a URL you own, not one owned by Amazon. (Amazon doesn't need any more links.)

- **Make or host a funny image:** Making and/or hosting an image is easier than doing the same for a video. Many reasonably priced hosting plans can handle the bandwidth, and for many funny pictures, the image editing quality doesn't matter.

- **Create a best-of list:** Even better than creating your own picture or video content is finding the best that other people have made. This is better for two reasons. First, it is easier because you don't have to come up with original ideas. Second, "best-of" lists attract more links because they are more useful than a simple list of resources.

- **Interview someone noteworthy:** If you have the resources to get in contact with someone famous or someone with a particularly interesting job or experience, you have the makings of a great blog post or article. These are great link sources because they tend to rank for the term that makes them interesting and thus drive a lot of traffic of potential linkers.

- ▶ **Aggregate helpful content:** Have you encountered a problem that after a lot of effort you were able to fix? If you have, post the solution online! It is surprising how many times people reinvent the wheel simply because the solution to the given problem is not readily available.

- ▶ **Write an entertaining or interesting quiz:** People like taking quizzes and showing off the results. Examples include the following: Which power ranger are you? What gadget are you most like? How long could you survive on a deserted island? How much is your brain worth? These types of quizzes are easy to build and are excellent link builders. (Just make sure they are relevant to your content, or you could run into penalties.)

- ▶ **Make an online game:** One of the best examples of a link magnet that I have ever seen is TravelPod.com's Traveler IQ Challenge. This simple flash-based game has earned them tens of thousands of links.

- ▶ **Participate in the comments of important blogs:** This is an indirect link acquisition technique. Do *not* post your own links in comments unless they are highly relevant and genuinely interesting. Instead, build your personal reputation with the writer and others in the community.

- ▶ **Go to industry events:** Linkers tend to prefer linking to people they know. Attending industry events not only puts you in front of the right people, but it helps you build your personal brand. In fact, at least half of the links to my personal website have come from mentions of me from blog posts talking about experiences at industry events.

Riskier Link Building Techniques

While I don't recommend any of the following techniques, I am including them because I have seen them work. I strongly believe that these do not make good long-term strategies because they are likely to be caught and discredited. That said, I have seen many websites rank highly (at least in the short term) using these techniques.

- ▶ **Buy links from directories:** If you choose to go this route, be sure to only buy directory links from pages that both pass juice and are highly ranked. (I recommend a mozRank of 5.00 or higher.) You want your link to be as few clicks from the homepage as possible and appear as legitimate as possible. Remember to measure the authority of page that will actually contain your link, not that of the home page of the site, and not that of the top category page that your link will be assigned to. If the category has 12 pages of links already, you'll be near the back, and the page is less likely to be authoritative and crawled frequently.

- **Buy links from link brokers:** Link brokers sell or lease space on highly trafficked and linked-to websites. This means they potentially can be helpful for both SEO and driving traffic.

- **Buy the help of social media influencers:** This is my favorite of my "not rec-ommended" link building practices. Most of the popular content on social media websites is controlled by a relatively small group of content submitters. These powerful people can often be bought, and while success of getting con-tent on the homepage of popular sites is not guaranteed, it is likely.

- **Buy natural links:** Do you have connections to someone at an important website? If so, you could potentially buy links from them. I don't recommend it, but if kept quiet, it will most likely help you.

MAKE EVERY PAGE LINK-WORTHY

Ten or fifteen years ago, the best web programmers were the ones who could balance visual effect and code economy. In other words, there was no reason for a line of code unless its result was a benefit to the site. Limited bandwidth created a value for fast-loading pages. For users with a limited bandwidth of, for example, 56 Kbps, every second was valuable and any extraneous coding simply wasted time.

Similarly, the philosophy behind link-worthy pages is that there's no reason to create a page if that page has no chance of ever being linked to for one reason or another, from some site or another. Because link juice and authority are both limited and valuable (like time and bandwidth were in the preceding example), there is no benefit to creating pages that will simply suck the site's authority and never earn their own.

This doesn't mean that all pages are therefore created equal and should get equal treatment from your architecture. Instead, it means that while you're deciding upon your content, you should similarly decide upon the level of authority that each page will be granted. While you may be forced to have a "Terms and Conditions" page, you can also decide that it will receive no link authority from your navigation (which is quite different from saying that it won't get any internal linkage).

Content for content's sake is a waste of resources and a distraction for users. It's far better, in terms of both SEO strategy and user experience, to have 12 pages of real meat than 100 pages of shadow and dust. If you're about to create a page but are unable to envision who would link to it or why, then you should reconsider creating it.

SUMMARY

Congrats! You should now know how to identify and fix the most common SEO problems. This puts you ahead of the game for most of your competitors. You just to need to remember to follow the steps outlined in "First Things First," verify the problem exists, use the search engine–provided tools (like `rel="canonical"`), communicate with the engines, and if all else fails, build more links.

In the next chapter you learn about the SEO consulting process that my colleagues and I use. As you will find out, it isn't enough to know the answers; you need to know how to get them implemented.

## CHAPTER 6

SEO Best Practices

- ► Maximizing information design
- ► Avoiding content creation pitfalls
- ► Understanding experts' recommendations

How do I build the perfectly optimized page? As an SEO, you will probably hear this question a lot. Sadly, there isn't a cut-and-dried answer, but you can draw from sets of best practices to help get close. In this chapter, I am going to teach you my top recommendations for achieving on-page, keyword-targeting "perfection," or, at least, close to it. Some of these recommendations are backed by data points, correlation studies, and extensive testing. Others are secrets based on my experience. Because this is in a form that I can't easily update, it will be your responsibility to take these suggestions and do your own research and testing to see if they are still the current best practice. To make this easier, I have tried to focus on big-picture ideas and skip the less important details. (That said, you can see current SEO best practices at www.seomoz.org/learn-seo/.)

PAGE-LEVEL INFORMATION HIERARCHY

Chapter 1 discussed the importance of relevancy and popularity. As you now know, a significant amount of the relevancy metrics that search engines use to rank pages comes from on-page elements. This section shows the best format for these metrics.

Best Practice

Figure 6-1 shows the best practice for optimizing a URL with a single keyword or phrase. Notice that the relevant phrase is located in all of the SEO page elements.

Reasoning

This page has the given keyword phrase in all of the appropriate places to make it as relevant as possible. It does this without spamming by mentioning the keyword in semantically helpful places without overuse. By that I mean, the page looks and reads like it was written for a human rather than a search engine.

This may sound overly vague, but the only "bad" place for using a keyword is where its mere appearance implies that it was done more for algorithmic benefit than for usability. That can happen anywhere, including titles, headings, body copy, figure captions, alt text, or anywhere else you can place copy.

You will find more details on this later in the chapter.

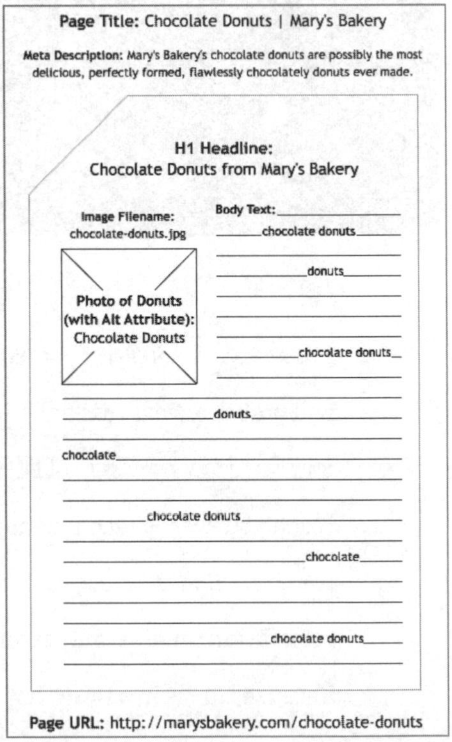

▶ There are some locations in which keywords will do nothing for you, regardless of the number of times you use them—inline comments in code, the meta keywords tag, and keywords inside a graphic image (such as a screen shot of text) to name a few.

Page Title: Chocolate Donuts | Mary's Bakery

Meta Description: Mary's Bakery's chocolate donuts are possibly the most delicious, perfectly formed, flawlessly chocolately donuts ever made.

H1 Headline:
Chocolate Donuts from Mary's Bakery

Image Filename: chocolate-donuts.jpg

Photo of Donuts (with Alt Attribute): Chocolate Donuts

Body Text: _____ chocolate donuts _____ donuts _____ chocolate donuts_ _____ donuts _____ chocolate_____ chocolate donuts _____ chocolate_____ chocolate donuts_____

Page URL: http://marysbakery.com/chocolate-donuts

FIGURE 6-1: Diagram of formatted page

Photo Credit: Rand Fishkin

DOMAIN-LEVEL INFORMATION HIERARCHY

Domain-level metrics of relevancy provide context. They are more complex than page-level metrics and for this reason are more often an SEO problem. This section describes how this hierarchy should be set up to maximize search engine benefit.

Best Practice

Make as few clicks (navigational links) as possible between the homepage and every content page. You can see an example of an optimal site structure using this philosophy in Figure 6-2.

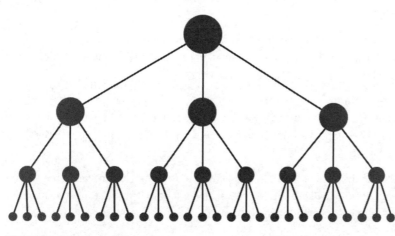

FIGURE 6-2: Link pyramid

This should be done while keeping the number of links per page below 50 for pages with mozRank 4.00 or lower, 100 links per page for pages with mozRank 6.99 or lower, and 150 links per page for pages with mozRank 7 and higher.

You can do this by simply not including extraneous links (my most common solution) or embedding the extra links in obfuscated JavaScript so that the search engines cannot parse them.

Reasoning

The depth of a website that a search engine crawler will travel is dependent on the link popularity of the given domain. See the section in Chapter 2 titled "The 100-Foot View—The Website," for more information.

URL

The URL of a page is important for search engine crawlers and humans alike. URLs should use as few characters as possible (to make it easier for humans to remember and to link to) and accurately describe the content of the given page.

USING HIERARCHY TO DISTRIBUTE AUTHORITY

It's a paradox, isn't it? The very notions of minimizing click path and limiting the number of links on a page are, by their definitions, conflicting and contradictory. Yet as the SEO, that is your challenge.

With a 5000-page site, you could completely minimize click path by simply linking to all 5000 URLs from the home page, and you'd have a truly "minimal" click path: All URLs would be only a single click away from the root.

Or, to completely minimize the number of links on a page, you could simply link to only a single URL from each page. Each destination page would get the full benefit of the linking page's authority, yet it would take 5000 clicks to get to the final page on the site.

Clearly, neither of these is optimal, so the trick is to find the right balance between the two. Simply advising you to create a pyramidal site structure may not be enough, so consider taking these extra steps:

▶ Segment your content (whether it's articles, products, category pages, or all of these) and identify the content with the most potential (as measured by demand, profitability of the product, and so on) and give it favorable hierarchical status. *Favorable hierarchical status* might mean prominent home page placement, top sorting location prior to paginating your content (if you have more products than will fit on one category page, for example), and linking to low-potential pages (privacy policy, terms and conditions, and so on) only from deeper pages, not from every page.

▶ Cross-link to similar pages. Take a lesson from Amazon's "Customers who bought this. . ." functionality and use the main body copy of your page to link to other products that the user might appreciate. These can be either similar products (such as a 2GB flash drive page linking to a 4GB flash drive page) or complementary (such as a camera page linking to a page showing a camera bag).

▶ Create multiple crawling paths where they did not exist before. We had dramatic increases in crawling, indexing, and ranking within a large news release library when we categorized releases by year, manufacturer, and product. This created multiple routes to each news release and increased their indexing (and then traffic) drastically.

Best Practice

The following examples show optimized URL structures. Notice how they include the given keyword and are formatted in a category-based system that helps users and search engines understand what the given page is about without having to visit it.

    www.example.com/item-name.html

Or

    www.example.com/category/item-name.html

Or

    www.example.com/category/subcategory/item-name.html

▶ The file extension is not important as long as it is an ISO standard that can be read by standard web browsers. Standard formats include (but are not limited to) .html, .htm, .aspx, .asp, and .php, depending on the format of the given file.

Reasoning

According to the correlation testing that SEOmoz has done, shorter URLs tend to rank better. The closer the targeted keyword is to the domain name, the better. Thus, example.com/keyword.html outperforms site.com/category/subcategory/keyword .html and is the most recommended method of optimization (though this is certainly not a massive rankings benefit).

With a little work, you can further pare down your URL and remove unnecessary clutter. In truth, the file extension, while technically informative, is completely unnecessary for engines. Creating an "extentionless" URL makes your URLs shorter, and more important, future-proofs your URLs against imminent platform change down the road.

Consider, for example, the URL for Honda's Odyssey minivan:

    http://automobiles.honda.com/odyssey/

This will, in theory, be the URL for this vehicle for as long as the vehicle is being manufactured. While the page is currently produced in an ASPX environment, its URL doesn't show that—and more important, the URL isn't confined to that. So down the road, a platform change to a different development environment that produces pages in CFM, PHP, or HTM will make no difference if the URL continues to be rewritten as it currently is.

URL rewriting is a simple process using products and modules like ISAPI Rewrite (for IIS), mod_rewrite (for Apache), and a host of rewriting plug-ins for WordPress environments.

▶ Hyphens are still the king of keyword separators in URLs, and despite promises from search engine representatives that underscores will be given equal credit, the inconsistency with other methods make the hyphen a clear choice.

▶ File extensions are technically informative but normally unnecessary for engines.

Lastly, the difference in SEO benefit between including or not including www (www.example.com vs. http://example.com/) is insignificant. Not including it can be confusing for some web users, but ultimately the choice is up the webmaster. As long as you pick one and only one format, it makes no difference in ranking whatsoever whether you put your site on a subdomain like www or choose to not have one. This practice is referred to as canonicalization and is described in depth in Chapter 5.

TITLE TAG

▶ Not only are title tags present in search engine results and in browsers, but they are increasingly used as anchor text of links from social media sites. So crafting SEO friendly title tags can help with both user experience and link relevancy.

At the time of writing, title tags are the most important single on-page factor in SEO. (I don't consider content a single on-page factor.) Implementing this best practice is a recommendation I give to all of my clients. It is usually easy to do and has quick and helpful effects on search engine rankings.

Best Practice

The following is the best practice for title tags for both search engines and people. Notice that the keywords are close to the beginning of the title and that the brand is included to increase click through rates.

Primary Keyword - Secondary Keywords | Brand Name

Or

Brand Name | Primary Keyword and Secondary Keywords

Reasoning

If you are trying to rank for a very competitive term, it is best to include the keyword at the beginning of the title tag. If you are competing for a less competitive term and branding can help make a difference in click-through rates, it is best to put the brand name first. With regard to special characters, I prefer pipes for aesthetic value, but hyphens, n-dashes, m-dashes, and minus signs are all fine.

As with much of SEO, the title tag has a dual purpose:

▶ To show the user what the page is about

▶ To show the engine what the page is about

While there is some evidence to show that engines read (and more important, factor into rankings) up through 80 characters or more, engines typically truncate the title tag at around character 65. This means that any character beyond 65 (or even earlier, if a word overlaps that character) will be turned into ellipses and will not even appear on most SERP. (Long-tail queries can sometimes have title tags longer than 65 characters.)

Beyond that, eye-tracking studies of search engine results suggest that even if title-tag characters appear in a SERP, users read fewer of them the lower your site appears in rankings. In other words, if your site is listed in the top organic spot, users might read its entire visible title. But if you rank second, third, or further down the page, they might read only two-thirds, half, or even a third of your title tag before skimming further down the page.

All of these facts point to the title tag representing very precious real estate, and in this real estate, the spot by the curb (the front end of the tag) is far more important than the tree line at the back of the lot.

> If possible, for very competitive terms, craft your titles so that your page's message is clear by the time you hit 35 or 40 characters.

I consider the title tag and meta description (discussed in the next section) to be the one-two punch of your URL's "elevator pitch." You have a few seconds (at most) to convince users that clicking your page will satisfy their query intent. Users will use the title and description to decide whether to click your result or someone else's, so they must be keyword-rich and serve a quick but memorable message.

META DESCRIPTION

Meta descriptions are the free advertisements webmasters get to include when their search results are included in a SERP. They should be optimized and tested just like traditional advertisements.

Best Practice

Meta descriptions are not directly used by the search engines to establish rankings. This means they are most helpful to webmasters when written like ads to entice clicks rather than for search engines to aid rankings.

This description is often done poorly by big clients. Notice in Figure 6-3 that the *New York Times* has a compelling meta description for the term United Nations while the United Nation's official website does a poor job (Figure 6-4).

FIGURE 6-3: The *New York Times* search result for "United Nations" with a good meta description

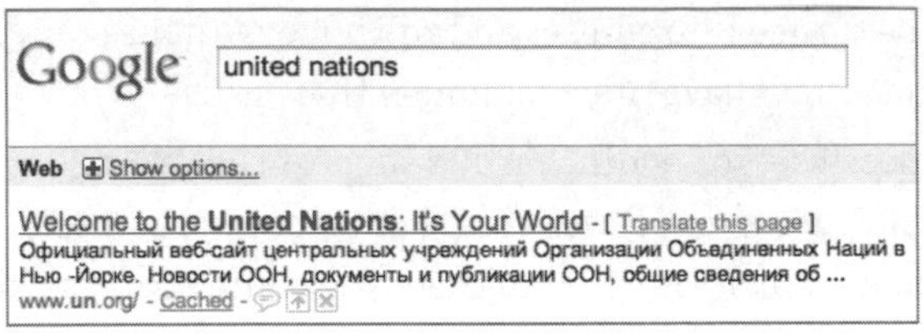

FIGURE 6-4: Official United Nations search result for English query "United Nations." This is a bad example because the meta description is in a foreign language and doesn't adhere to SEO best practices.

Other common mistakes with meta descriptions include keyword spamming (including a given keyword an unreasonable amount of times), misspellings, grammar mistakes, and odd capitalization.

Reasoning

Although meta descriptions are not used for ranking purposes by any of the major engines, they are an important place to use keywords due to the bolding that occurs in the visual snippet of the search results. Usage has also been shown to help boost click-through rates, which in turn increases the traffic derived from any ranking position. You've gone to significant effort to optimize your site structure, URLs, on-page content, and titles, so don't throw away all that work by creating a poor description that will cause users to turn away when they see your page on the SERP.

HTML HEADINGS (H1 – H6)

When HTML was first designed as a markup language for presenting information online, headings were essential for information hierarchy. As the Web has evolved, their impact has weakened because HTML was used in ways that it was not originally designed for.

Best Practice

Although HTML headings are still useful for human readers (think blog titles), they are no longer strong signals for search engines.

Google's Matt Cutts has warned against "overdoing it" when it comes to using H1 paragraphs too heavily (www.youtube.com/watch?v=GIn5qJKU8VM).

▶ Though they aren't "strong" signals, they're still signals. Optimization means taking every chance to convey your content goals to engines, so if creating an Hx structure is no more difficult than otherwise organizing your on-page content, use them.

META DESCRIPTIONS AND RELEVANCE

It's hard to believe, but as the SEO, not everything on the SERP is about you. The meta description is one good example. It does nothing for your ranking; instead, it's entirely for the user. Yet despite the description's lack of ranking influence, you're just as compelled to craft it carefully and diligently.

While engines typically pull the meta description to use as the descriptive "snippet" on a SERP, they aren't obligated to do so. There are several reasons that Google might not use the meta description as snippet text:

► The page does not have a meta description. If this is the case, the solution is simple: Write one.

► The page has a meta description, but it does not contain any of the words from the search query. Because its goal is to show correlation between the user's query and the ranked URLs, Google wants to use the descriptive snippet to show the user how the page answers the query. Often, if the meta description does not contain any of the terms found in the query, Google will pull small chunks of copy from various locations around the page that do contain the query text, such as headings, navigation, and body copy. This often leads to a very disjointed snippet, so it's imperative to include your targeted phrases in the meta description.

► To describe your home page, Google has historically used descriptive data found elsewhere, such as the page's introductory paragraph or the DMOZ .org or Yahoo Directory description of the site. You can't tell engines what text they must use for the descriptive snippet, but you can do the next best thing—tell them what text they cannot use. To tell engines that they cannot use descriptive text from DMOZ.org (the Open Directory Project, or ODP) or Yahoo's Directory (YDIR), insert the following code line in the `<head>` section of your home page.

```
<meta name="robots" content="noodp, noydir" />
```

There's no harm in putting this code on every page of your site, but DMOZ and Yahoo Directory rarely have entries devoted to deep pages, so the home page is typically the only affected URL.

Reasoning

The correlation tests that I was part of at SEOmoz showed that HTML headers do not carry the same ranking weight that we had originally presumed. My co-workers and I think they are very important for establishing information hierarchy and helping with algorithmically determined semantics, but they seem to be less important for search engine optimization. We recommend them on all pages as an aid for users but don't stress the importance when other opportunities for SEO improvement are available.

IMAGES

Images are fundamental tools of the modern Web. Although at the time of this writing computer scientists have made great strides in visual semantics, human aids are still needed for computers to understand images on large scales.

Best Practice

I recommend including the alt text attribute in all HTML code for images on all publicly accessible pages. This attribute declares what text should be shown if the given image is not able to be viewed by the user. For this reason, I generally suggest adding images with descriptive and keyword focused alt text to pages targeting competitive rankings. In addition, I recommend including relevant text directly before or after the images. This helps provide search engines with further context.

▶ *Ideally, this means the paragraph immediately preceding or following an image, as well as in an image caption if your design allows for one.*

When you have a "hot" image, one that links to another page, alt text is especially helpful and is the next best thing to anchor text when describing the content of the destination page to engines. For example, if you use an image to link to your "plumbing supplies" page, it's imperative that you use the alt text that describes what users (and engines) will find when they click the image. Using an image to link to a page is less desirable than using plain text, but if there's no other way to do it, write your alt text as if it's anchor text.

Reasoning

I have two reasons for these recommendations. First, I believe that all users regardless of limitations should be able to use the Internet. This includes people with disabilities as well as computers trying to use semantics to make information more useful. Second, the correlation data at SEOmoz showed that alt attributes were a surprisingly important metric for attaining high rankings. Though correlation is not causation, it seems unwise to ignore the data and my co-workers and I recommend the use of good images with good alt text for pages seeking to rank on competitive queries.

NOFOLLOW

Nofollow was one of the first search engine–specific attributes that was widely accepted on the Internet. (Meta keywords was the first.) Since its inception, its effectiveness has been debated widely and eventually largely discredited by major search engine representatives.

Originally, the stated purpose of the `rel="nofollow"` attribute was to keep a given link from passing authority. In other words, where a typical link is one page "voting" for another, the `"nofollow"` attribute simply removed the "vote" aspect. But it was not immediately clear that the tag also acted—at the individual link level—the same way the meta robots `"nofollow"` attribute worked, telling engines to not even crawl the link. Subsequent information from Google has expressed that notion as well.

Best Practice

The proper syntax for the `"nofollow"` attribute is to be inserted in an <a> tag alongside the `href` to which it refers:

```
<a href="/url-here.html" rel="nofollow">Anchor text here</a>
```

I recommend using `rel="nofollow"` for thwarting would-be spammers of user-generated content. I also recommend using it as an incentive for creating active users. (SEOmoz removes the `nofollow` of profile links after the user has earned 100 mozPoints.)

That said, I do *not* recommend using `nofollow` for PageRank sculpting as search engine engineers have claimed this is a waste of time and SEOs have not yet done definitive testing on this method. "Sculpting" in this context can refer to channeling authority of your internal pages away from low-potential content, PageRank "hoarding," or using `"nofollow"` on all external links – even those you consider authoritative.

Reasoning

An announcement from Google representative, Matt Cutts, on June 15, 2009, on his blog changed my policy. In essence, Google changed how it treats this attribute.

Whereas a nofollowed link used to be completely ignored by the engines, it is now included when calculating the number of links on a page but not used when calculating link popularity for the target page. See Figure 6-5 for a diagram of how nofollowed links are now treated by Google. Notice that the nofollowed links are still counted when the number of links on the page is calculated.

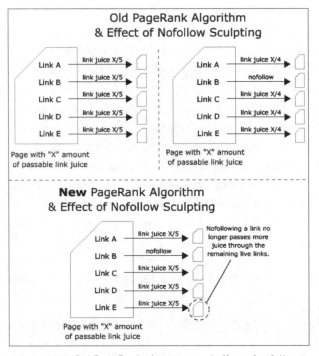

FIGURE 6-5: Old PageRank algorithm and effect of nofollow sculpting.

Photo Credit: Rand Fishkin

I think this search engine policy detracts from the overall health of the Internet, but I feel obligated to go along with it to make sure my clients get the best rankings in the search engines.

REL CANONICAL LINK ELEMENT

`rel="canonical"` is an HTML attribute that tells search engines which version of duplicate content is the main or canonical version. It has shown a lot of promise and has already worked well for some of my clients who suffered from duplicate content problems before implementing this attribute.

Suppose, for example, that you run a large electronics site, and you have a page of digital cameras. For the sake of your users, you can sort those cameras by price, user rating, manufacturer name, and so on. Users love this, but the unfortunate consequence is a slew of URLs that end with parameters such as &sort=price, &sort=rating, and so on.

This is a problem because in reality, it's all just the same group of cameras. Engines don't want a dozen different URLs when one will do. The rel="canonical" attribute was created to give engines a clue about which URL is the "authoritative" version.

Best Practice

The canonical tag is powerful but ultimately only useful as a hint to the search engines to prevent duplicate content. It is not the silver bullet that webmasters are looking for (nor the droids, for that matter), but it's very helpful in cases in which other authority-defining tools (such as 301 redirects) are not a logical solution.

The proper syntax for rel="canonical" is to place a code line in the <head> section of a page. It should be placed on all instances of duplicate content to show which version of the content should be shown in search engine results. For example, if you have an article at one URL (article.php) and a printer-friendly version of the same article on a separate URL (article.php?print=1), add this attribute to both pages with the URL of the original article so that the engines know to ignore the printer-friendly version and thus prevent detracting from relevancy metrics:

```
<link rel="canonical" href="http://www.yoursite.com/article.php" />
```

▶ It is not technically necessary to canonicalize a page to itself, but it helps remind you of the conventions you're using.

ABSOLUTE VS. RELATIVE URLS IN CANONICAL LINK CODE

You can use either fully qualified ("absolute") or relative URLs in your canonical link code. I recommend using absolute URLs because if your article is scraped and reprinted, scrapers often don't take the time to remove canonical tags. This will ensure that the scraped version will point back to your original article as the canonical authority.

Further, I recommend adding canonical tags to even the canonical version of a page. While this isn't necessary, it protects you from other users creating multiple versions of your URLs when they share them in social media environments. For example, if someone tweets your URL with &src=twitter at the end, having a canonical tag will ensure that only your original version of the URL will appear in SERPs.

Reasoning

This tool works well for getting duplicate content out of search engine indices. We know from public statements that this resource depletes link juice (ranking power) just like 301 redirects, but at the time of writing it is too soon to judge its value. When possible, I still recommend architectural solutions to prevent duplicate content.

> **NOTE** Canonical tagging is perfectly suited for situations in which you want the URLs to be accessible to analytics and the URLs have a decent chance of accruing external links. If you have affiliates driving links to your site—each one of which appends an affiliate ID to the URL for tracking purposes—then the canonical tag is perfect. A 301 redirect may keep the affiliate traffic from being counted correctly in your analytics program, and excluding affiliate URLs by `robots.txt` or robots meta tag would negate much of the link authority they could accrue.

META KEYWORDS

Meta keywords was the first search engine–specific HTML attribute. It once was a very powerful tool for manipulating search results. For this reason, it is no longer used by search engines.

Best Practice

I do not recommend using this tool for SEO.

> **WARNING** Be mindful, however, that some internal search engines (the algorithm that powers your on-site search feature) use meta keywords to help return searches from within your site. The Google Search Appliance, for example, can be configured to use meta keywords in its algorithm. So before you nuke all the keyword tags on the site (or recommend that no new tags be written), be sure they're not used for other purposes.

Reasoning

This webmaster resource was abused in the early days of the Internet and is no longer useful. It was used by Yahoo! as a very minor ranking metric but was and still is completely ignored by Google and Bing. If it is included, it provides a simple way for competitors to automate competitive analysis.

JAVASCRIPT AND FLASH

JavaScript and Flash are more complicated to parse for search engines than HTML. We know that while engines are growing more and more capable of interpreting the data within Flash files and JavaScript environments, they're not yet very good at doing it consistently or at using that information to allocate authority the way traditional HTML does.

Best Practice

I do not recommend using JavaScript or Flash for any website section that is important to search engines unless the Flash or JavaScript content is bolstered by an underlying technology that shows content to engines in a way that they can more reliably interpret.

▶ SWFObject (code.google.com/p/swfobject) is an example of a technology that enables Flash-heavy sites to show engines (and other users who do not have Flash or JavaScript enabled) traditional HTML content.

Reasoning

Although the search engines can crawl JavaScript and Flash, I choose not to add the risk of hoping they will correctly parse the code's structure. Their ability to analyze these languages is inferior to their ability to understand HTML, and choosing to code in the former can lead to lower search engine rankings.

301 REDIRECTS

301 redirects are the preferred method for redirecting URLs for SEOs.

Best Practice

I recommend 301 redirects as the best way to redirect URLs but warn that they do have disadvantages. The main disadvantage is that only between 99 and 90 percent of link value is transferred through these redirects. This is as opposed to the 0 percent that is transferred through 302 redirects.

Reasoning

Our tests and public statements from search engineers have made my co-workers and me reasonably certain that 301 redirects deplete between 1 percent and 10 percent of link juice (ranking power). This is an acceptable penalty if it is necessary to make one URL lead to another URL and other options are unavailable. It is also much better than the alternatives (JavaScript and 302 redirects), which pass very little if any juice at all. Meta refreshes, in our testing, appear to function similarly to 301s (from a juice/rank passing ability). However, because the engine engineers recommend 301 redirects over the alternatives, we do too.

> **NOTE** 301 redirects are preferred over 302 redirects in nearly every SEO situation. One instance in which the 302 is smart, however, is a redirect away from the home page. While it's always best if there's no redirect away from a home page, some sites require a redirect from / to a page such as `/default.asp` so that a process can initialize correctly. In this instance, a 302 is the correct redirect, because you don't want your site's root address dropping out of the index. Eventually, if that redirect can be removed, it's much better to have had a 302 in place so that you don't have to shift authority back to the root domain. In effect, it never really left.

BLOCKING PAGES FROM SEARCH ENGINES

There are many ways to block pages from search engines including the Robots Exclusion Protocol (`robots.txt`), IP blocking, and meta robots. While the first two work in most cases, meta robots is generally the best option as it keeps the pages out of the search engine indexes while allowing their links to pass value to other pages.

Best Practice

Meta robots (noindex, follow) is generally a better option than `robots.txt` because it keeps the given URL out of the search engine results (noindex) and allows all of the links on the page to send link value (follow). `robots.txt` files are useful but should be used sparingly and only if a meta robots tag is not an option.

Reasoning

`robots.txt` files stop search engine crawlers from visiting a web page, but they do not keep them from being indexed. Figure 6-6 shows an example of an "uncrawled reference"—a page that has been blocked via `robots.txt` but that still appears in a SERP. Notice how the URL is listed in the search engine results, but none of the content, like title tags or meta descriptions, is shown.

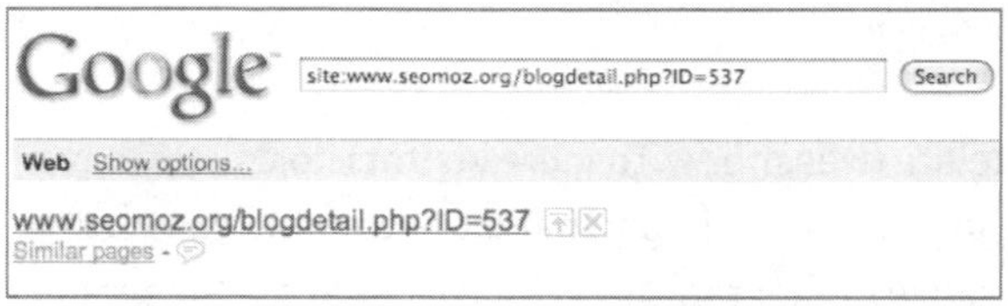

FIGURE 6-6: Image of Google Result for a page that is blocked by `robots.txt` but still listed as a result (although it doesn't have a meta description)

> **TIP** All things being equal, the robots "`noindex, follow`" command is the best way to keep pages out of search engine indexes. For certain instances, however, the `robots.txt` file can be a very flexible way to exclude thousands of pages (or more) from being indexed but it does remove the ability for search engines to credit internal links. For pages such as print-friendly versions of articles—pages that don't have a lot of link authority to offer anyway—you might be wasting Google's time (time that it could be spending crawling other, more important areas of your site) if you use the robots meta tag. Chapter 14 lists ways to use advanced Robots Exclusion Protocol commands to exclude massive swaths of content quickly.

Blocking via `robots.txt` also creates a black hole for link juice (the engines cannot crawl these pages to see any links on them and pass that juice along). Thus, I strongly prefer the meta robots option with the "`noindex, follow`" parameters for keeping pages out of the search engine indices. As an added bonus, this usage also allows link juice (ranking power) to pass to all links on the given page.

Normally, the more signals you can send to engines about content, the better. But in this case, stick to one method or the other. If Google sees a file is excluded in the `robots.txt` file, it won't crawl into the file to see the "noindex" tag. Consequently, the `robots.txt` file exclusion has hurt you and created a potential "uncrawled reference" situation.

▶ Avoid the temptation to use both robots "noindex" tags and the robots.txt file to exclude the same content.

TRAFFIC AND RANKINGS

As an SEO you will surely be asked if traffic has an effect on search rankings. My answer to this commonly asked question follows and may surprise you.

Best Practice

The metric of visitors to a given site is not used to help determine rankings.

Reasoning

Although traffic and rankings correlate (websites with more visitors do usually have higher rankings), neither causes the other. It is simply that more popular websites receive more links and more links cause higher rankings. I have heard statements from search engineers that "time on page" was used for a short time as a ranking metric but turned out to be a bad signal. Instead, modern search engines prefer the "absence of a click" on a search engine results page as a better metric for detecting when their results need upgrading.

THE PROBLEM WITH THE "UNIQUE VISITORS" METRIC

I believe that the metric of "unique visitors" (as opposed to total visitors) from web analytics software is fundamentally flawed. It relies on the visitor having cookies enabled and only visiting the given webpage from one browser on one computer. In practice, I think people visit the same site (Facebook, for example) from multiple browsers and computers enough to take away from the value of this metric.

Like Alexa.com traffic estimates, it is rarely accurate but frequently messaged. My suggestion is not to trust unique visitor counts nearly as much as raw visits for comparing the traffic sent to a site from various sources or comparing traffic growth from month to month. See www.seomoz.org/article/search-blog-stats for data that demonstrates the inaccuracies of this type of metrics.

PARAMETER-DRIVEN URLS

Oftentimes SEOs run into a situation where they are forced to work with parameter-driven URLs (for example, URLs like www.example.com/product?param=1&param=2). When this happens, it is best to follow my advice in this section to ensure that the search engines can accurately crawl the given website.

Best Practice

I don't recommend using this URL structure. If it is absolutely necessary (due to something like an established CMS configuration) I recommend no more than two parameters.

Reasoning

The search engines have been very clear on this. Their crawlers can parse and crawl parameter-driven URLs, but it is more difficult and often leads to duplicate content issues. This is backed up by SEOmoz correlation data, which showed that pages with static URLs tend to rank higher.

> **NOTE** Unlike 10 years ago, parameter-based URLs themselves aren't necessarily a problem. The problem is the issues that frequently appear alongside them—duplication based on parameter order within the URL, capitalization style, and so on. If you're invested in a parameter-based URL structure, it's not necessarily time to raise the white flag, but it is very smart to give your site a regular and thorough audit to ensure that it's not generating multiple URLs for each chunk of content on the site.

FOOTER LINKS

Footer links are hyperlinks that are included at the bottom of webpages. They are often a hot topic for the SEO community and frequently spammed as they are not as important to user experience as other more prominent links on a page. My advice on this topic is very clear and has not changed very much in the past.

Best Practice

Use footer links sparingly. I recommend no more than 25 relevant internal (and in some cases, external) navigational links. This number is not a hard limit and it is important to be mindful of intent when choosing keywords. Notice, for example, that the footer of Gawker.com links to all the sites within the Gawker Media "family." This is a perfectly legitimate use of cross-linking within a footer. It follows along the lines of "If you liked X, you might also like Y."

When the number of links in the footer increases significantly, however, and the anchor text starts to look a little too "optimized" (such as "payday loans" and "Seattle attorneys") and points to sites totally unrelated to the site on which they're sitting, it's probably time to reassess how the footer links are used.

Reasoning

I have seen many examples of Google penalties tied directly to abusive footer links (that *magically* lifted upon removal of footer links stuffed with keywords). Manipulative links in footers are easily detected algorithmically, and appear to have automated penalties applied to them by Google.

SUMMARY

This chapter discussed SEO best practices that are based on experience in the field, testing, and client results. You can see the latest research in this area at www.seomoz.org/learn-seo/.

That said, some of the big ideas in this chapter won't likely change for a long time. These include:

▶ The key to on-page SEO is making the page as relevant to a given query as possible.

▶ Ensure that there are no obstacles to engines seeing your content the way they should.

▶ For the best long-term strategies, SEOs should avoid tactics that they wouldn't share directly with search engine representatives.

▶ Building relevant and strong links is the most important thing you can do for a website.

If you follow these four rules, you will be an effective SEO for years to come.

## CHAPTER 7

The SEO Consulting Process

As an SEO consultant, your actual person-to-person communication will take up only a small portion of your time but will be the factor that makes or breaks your business.

This chapter outlines the SEO consulting process, one that I have used at SEOmoz and in my private business. The chapter is formatted like a framework to enable you to customize it to your needs. This chapter will not answer all of your questions (not even close), but it can give you the tools you need to be a successful consultant.

ANSWERING HARD QUESTIONS FROM CLIENTS

Before you can start a campaign, you first need to win the business. This frequently means that you must make a strong case for yourself (or your organization), your industry, and your specific methodologies by addressing some tough questions. Before getting to the specifics, you need to understand how to answer the hard questions. Clients usually ask surprisingly similar questions. This section covers those questions and the answers that often work the best.

BRING IT BACK TO THE CLIENTS

The trick to answering any difficult consulting question is to bring it back to the clients. How can you use their experiences to answer their own questions? No answer is better than one that clients didn't realize they already knew.

You can usually accomplish this by answering in terms of their business goals. For example, if a potential client says "I already rank on the first page, why do I need your help?" I answer, "How many of your leads come from your website?" If the potential client responds "50 percent," I might respond with "On average, the top three results for a given search get 90 percent of clicks. Imagine how your bottom line would be affected if I could get your website into that 90 percent. You said you get 50 percent of your leads from your website. What would happen if you got 60 percent or 70 percent by increasing the amount of qualified people who reach your website from search engines?"

Why Should I Care about SEO?

I usually answer this question by trying to make potential clients realize how important search is to their clientele. If they sell coffee cups online, I might ask them how their clients find them online.

I then bring up the Google AdWords Keyword Tool (see Chapter 3) and run some of their major keywords (coffee cups, coffee mugs, coffee gifts, Starbucks cups, cupware, and so on). They are usually surprised by how high the numbers are.

I then run a search on the most searched for term in the list and identify where the potential client ranks in the search engine result page (SERP).

In addition to examples like these, which focus on the keywords that should be important to the prospective client, many broader reasons outline why SEO should be important to anyone marketing a product or service on the Internet:

▶ **Search as a starting point.** About three-quarters of all Internet users looking for a product or service begin their quest at a search engine. Further, a site with a solid, comprehensive search strategy might derive anywhere from 50-80 percent of its web traffic from organic search. It's very difficult to make a case against a solid search strategy if you can make these numbers sink in.

▶ **SEO epitomizes "pull" traffic.** Search isn't a billboard, it's not a phone call that interrupts dinner, and it's not a commercial dividing up your favorite show. You don't come to searchers; they come to you, willing to learn and often ready to buy. This makes search traffic far more qualified than traffic from most other sources.

▶ **Organic search is a bargain.** In a study we did for one particular client in the medical information industry, we found that the same traffic earned in an organic campaign would have cost fourteen times the cost of our services, if it were purchased on a pay-per-click basis.

▶ **Your competitors are already using it.** As discussed throughout this chapter, it's easy to find instances of competitors outranking nearly any site for various veins of long-tail phrases (and in some cases, terms near the head of the curve.

This demonstration almost always convinces the potential client of the importance of SEO. However, after you've done this demonstration, you still need to make a couple more arguments to convince them to choose you to do their SEO. First, you need to convince the prospect that SEO should not be handled in-house. Second, once they've decided to outsource it, you want them to decide that the company to whom they should outsource it is yours.

What Is the Advantage of Outsourcing SEO to a Consultant?

When you're trying to win SEO business, you're not competing just against other SEO firms or consultants. You're often also competing against the client's reluctance to hire an SEO firm in the first place. Search strategy is still not a line item on many

> ▶ This can vary wildly from vertical to vertical. Sites with large TV and print budgets get a great deal of type-in traffic. This might make the percentage of search traffic look small, while the raw search numbers are still quite high.

> ▶ Unlike PPC, banners, and affiliate relationships, organic search is a residual, long-term value, because it continues far beyond when the SEO campaign ends.

corporate budgets, and when it's grouped in with broader marketing and advertising budgets, it can still be very challenging to convince clients that it needs its own presence in the budget.

Consequently, you need to make a case not just for yourself, but for your discipline in general. Fortunately, this is not difficult to do if you come prepared to discuss the following concepts.

FOCUSING TIGHTLY ON SEO

One of the largest complaints from in-house SEO workers is that they're spread too thinly and are not allowed to spend as much time on true organic SEO as they think is necessary. Instead, they become the "online marketing guy" or the "social media woman" and are forced to take on roles such as PPC management, social media strategy, and site development or to manage affiliate relationships.

This might work for a very small site, but medium to large sites need to have a person devoted full-time to SEO, if not a team. There's simply too much work and time involved in doing SEO right for it to be grouped together with other parts of IT or marketing.

As an SEO consultant, you and your company are paid to remain laser-focused on SEO, and the client will benefit because you won't get pulled away or distracted by other activities. Certainly you'll work with these departments, but only to facilitate the success of the SEO project.

REMAINING CURRENT ABOUT INDUSTRY TRENDS

Along with the time needed to simply attend to the work of a comprehensive SEO strategy, workers need time to remain up-to-date about the rapid changes in search.

To prove the value of remaining timely, go into your meeting with a firm understanding of the changes that have taken place in the SEO industry within the last week, day, or even the last few hours. Know which types of sites these changes will affect, and know how the prospective client's site fits into that scenario. You don't know what the prospective client is going to ask, but you can try to prepare yourself with topical answers.

If you look hard enough, there will have been something in the last few days that could affect the client, whether it's an update to XML site map protocol, image or video search, local and maps search, or analytics. Coming into a meeting with information about exactly how you'd address that client's strategy—especially if it relates to a change that the client hasn't heard about yet—will help reinforce the urgency of hiring an SEO firm.

Why Do I Need SEO if I Already Rank Number 1?

This is a really good question and can usually be answered in one of two ways. First, run a search to see for which SERP they are ranking #1. Typically, if a client dismisses the need for SEO based on a current top rank for a term, that term is mostly like what we call a "vanity" or "trophy" phrase that looks really good on paper. Often, however, this trophy phrase does not convert traffic at the rate of less popular but more focused phrases.

In addition, no matter who the client is, the site doesn't rank at the top for *everything*. Highlighting core terms for which the prospective client's positioning is less than stellar and having that prospective client see its competitors atop the list will bolster your argument for implementing a comprehensive search program.

Many times, there will still be significant opportunity either in the form of secondary results or long tail. For example, if they are the ranking number for "snow globe," you can use alternative domains to help them rank positions 2 through 10. If that is not an option, you can widen their reach by going after long tail terms by building pages, content, and links for those terms. If they are ranking for "snow globe" use their relevancy and current link profile to target terms like "holiday snow globe," "winter snow globe," and so on.

If this is not the case (say, if Wikipedia is the potential client) the answer may be that they really don't need your help. It is much better to under-promise and over-deliver than to struggle with a client who you can't help.

My Nephew/Cousin/Hosting Provider Already Does SEO, so Why Don't I Just Use Them?

This is an especially difficult question because it illustrates that the potential client doesn't value your skill set. If this is the case, you need to prove why you are better than your competition.

This can be accomplished by explaining your value proposition. I find it best to explain that SEO is an extremely fast moving industry and that a lot of your value comes from your network that keeps you up-to-date on the changing state of SEO. This might include big name friends in the industry or your participation in industry events like conferences. If possible, this is also an opportune time to point at testimonials from prior clients.

Then take the discussion one step further. If the prospect's cousin already does SEO, does the site reflect that? How many holes can you poke in the current strategy? Has the cousin read an article based on myth, and implemented tactics that will ultimately hurt the site?

Explain that as with most other service industries, you get what you pay for with SEO. Even if the client is getting shoddy advice for free, what happens when the cousin gets too busy to keep offering that shoddy advice? Explain that with your firm, beyond the expertise you bring, the client is also purchasing accountability and access, which means rapid response to questions, point-of-view research, and a team whose job depends on their ability to stay completely current with industry trends.

You need to sell SEO, like a lawyer would sell law. SEO is an important service and a big part of your job is selling it as such. You have the ability to drive a significant amount of traffic to your potential clients' websites. You need to make them realize the potential monetary impact of this.

What Do Google and Bing Think about SEO?

The easiest way to answer this question is to let the major search engines do it for you. Google has posted its position on SEO online at `http://www.google.com/support/webmasters/bin/answer.py?hl=en&answer=35291`.

Google and Bing gain a lot from SEOs who follow their search engine guidelines. For example, Google's mission is to "to organize the world's information and make it universally accessible and useful." In order to do this, it needs as much help as it can get. One of the primary jobs of an SEO is to make websites as useful and easy to index for search engines as possible. This is a win-win because it helps searchers find relevant information and it helps the engines provide these results.

Furthermore, all of the major search engines have SEO teams on their payroll. Their job is to make sure that the content their co-workers produce is as SEO friendly as possible. The search engines have many talented copywriters and engineers, but they still need the help of SEOs to make their content and products findable online.

If You Are Such a Good SEO, Why Don't You Rank #1 for "SEO"?

D'oh! I hate this question. The best way to answer this question is to be honest. For example, the reason SEOmoz doesn't rank #1 for SEO is largely because the word SEOmoz does not break down into two real words. Thus, seobook.com ranks above us because when its founder, Aaron Wall, receives a link with the anchor text "seobook," Google knows the word can be broken down into "seo" and "book." This is different than a name like SEOmoz because "moz" isn't a word, so the link goes to SEOmoz, not "SEO" and "moz."

The other reason is that this SERP is dominated by big name domains, not necessarily the most qualified domains. It is similar to how even though Nordstrom and Zappos.com might provide the best customer service in retail, they don't rank highly for the term "customer service retail" (see Figure 7-1). Likewise, even though NASA is the most qualified entity on earth (and beyond?) about spaceships, it doesn't rank in the top ten for "spaceships."

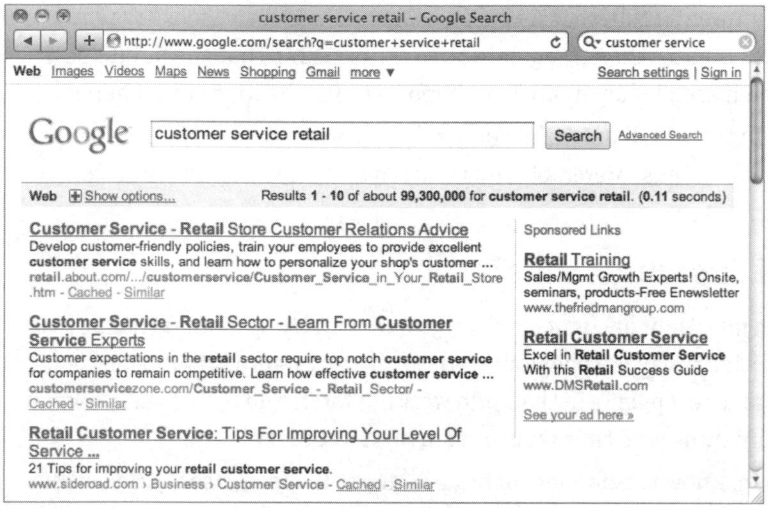

FIGURE 7-1: Google result for "customer service retail"

And finally, one reason that the vast majority of good SEOs don't rank particularly well for SEO-related terms is that they're so busy working with clients that they have very few resources to allocate to working on their own site.

Instead of prospects questioning your own firm's rankings, convince the prospective client to question your existing clients, read your case studies and articles, and to get a feel for what it's like to be a client of yours. Those are a much more accurate predictor of your prospect's results than your own firm's rankings for SEO.

> ▶ Be sure that your collateral material is current, your references are glowing (and ready to talk about you), and that you have case studies and references that match up with your prospect's general business type, such as "B2B manufacturing."

What Is Google's Algorithm?

As is the case with the previous questions, the best way to answer this question is to be honest. Remind the potential client that you don't work for Google, so you don't know what algorithms it uses. However, you can make educated guesses based on your experiences.

> **NOTE** You can also point clients to the SEOmoz annual industry survey called "Google Search Engine Ranking Factors," currently located at www .seomoz.org/article/search-ranking-factors. At the time of writing, this survey reports that about 70 percent of all ranking metrics are believed by industry experts to revolve around links.

How Do I Improve My PageRank?

I always try to answer this question by explaining the downsides of PageRank. PageRank is a poor metric because it lacks necessary precision and is updated infrequently at unpredictable times. It is on a logarithmic scale, so a PageRank of 8 is about ten times greater than a PageRank of 7. This means that the points past the decimal (which aren't shown) are very important for the higher numbers.

After I explain that, I tell potential clients that in order to raise their rankings, they need to get more links, preferably from trusted and well linked to sources.

▶ It's also smart to mention that because PageRank is one of over 200 different factors that go into the overall ranking algorithm at Google, focusing a lot of attention on PageRank itself is a very inefficient use of time.

Why Don't I Just Buy Links?

This is a common question for clients with large budgets. My opinion is that buying links in any traditional way is a poor long-term strategy. I remind them that Google has some of the smartest people in the world working for it, and it is to their advantage to detect paid links (and thus reduce spam in their index).

I then let them know the dangers of buying links. In most cases, paid links that are identified as such by the search engines are simply discounted. Other times (although less often), paid links can lead to penalties where they actually count against the target website.

Are Links Really That Important?

The short answer is a loud yes. When asked this question, I always refer back to the SEOmoz "Google Search Engine Ranking Factors" survey. This survey shows that industry leaders believe that about 70 percent of ranking metrics are related to links. This is backed up by my experience with SEO.

Do You Offer a Guarantee?

This question is discussed a bit more later in this chapter, but in general, it's not wise to offer a guarantee. Quite simply, you don't control enough of the variables in the SEO game to reliably guarantee significant results. You can't control the engines' tendency to change their algorithms, you can't control what users search for, and you can't control the level to which your client's competitors will aggressively optimize their own sites.

Guarantees in the SEO industry have traditionally been made by hucksters who make guarantees about showing a client a certain number of top rankings. The trouble is that those rankings usually pertain to queries that have little or no search demand behind them. In other words, the SEO company has proven its ability to make your site rank for terms that no one searches for.

That said, if you know the risks of making such a guarantee, your guarantee pertains to phrases that have both search demand and likelihood to convert on the client site, and you're not afraid to put it all in writing, then more power to you.

How Much Will My Traffic Improve?

Prospective clients ask this question all the time, and it's an amazingly frustrating question to answer. The variables involved make it so complicated that there's virtually no equation that can accurately predict the outcome.

It's not the prospect's fault. People want return on their investment, and it's their job to predict the amount of traffic—and ideally, revenue—that will come back from each dollar spent on marketing initiatives such as SEO.

If absolutely forced to come up with a prediction for traffic improvement, you can attack this problem from several directions, based on the specifics of the campaign. For example, a site that has had minimal, decent SEO work in the past will not see as much benefit from a new campaign as a neglected, nearly uncrawlable site will.

Trying to predict the outcome of an SEO campaign is a good exercise, because it also helps you formulate the foundation of the keyword strategy. Look for gaps in the prospect's referring keyword set. In other words, what should the site rank for, but doesn't? Compare the demand for the terms that the client does not rank for with the demand for the terms that it does rank for, and try to anticipate the traffic increase that would result from a top 5 rank for several terms within that set.

For example, check the ratio of branded to non-branded referring keywords. If the prospect's site currently heavily relies on branded traffic, there's a good chance that there is significant traffic potential with non-branded phrases (or vice-versa).

When you think you've created a predictive model that's as accurate as possible, give yourself some additional cushion. If your campaign ends up increasing traffic by 30 percent, would you rather your prediction have been 20 percent or 40 percent? As we describe elsewhere, under-promising and over-delivering are the key to successful client expectation management.

> ▶ Don't tie your contract to a specific, stated increase in organic traffic for the client. You simply don't control enough of the variables required to make an accurate prediction.

Switching from Parameter-Driven URLs Is Hard; Is it Really Worth All of the Work?

In this case (like most), the client is right. Switching from parameter-driven URLs (www.example.com/product?food=banana-pizza) to standard URLs (www.example.com/

product/food/banana-pizza/) can be a difficult technical problem. Not only does it require old code to be rewritten, but it requires new code to be written to handle the necessary 301 redirects.

When asked this question, I tell potential clients the story of when Amazon switched away from parameter-driven URLs to the more semantically clear URLs it uses now. (Note: It still uses parameters for tracking.) When Amazon made this switch, it doubled its traffic and was profitable for the first time in its history. While this might be a case of correlation rather than causation, this anecdote has helped me convince numerous clients to make the leap to SEO friendly URLs.

YOU TALK A LOT ABOUT GOOGLE, WHAT ABOUT BING?

When asked this question, I let them know that Bing is important in some markets and has some better technology (image search, airline ticket predictions) but Google still has at least 90 percent market share in the United States.

Additionally, most of the SEO best practices listed in Chapter 6 work well in both Google and Bing. It is best not to ignore Bing, but it pays more to focus on driving traffic from Google.

Is Company XYZ a Google Killer?

I always answer this question the same way. I have no idea what a Google Killer will look like, but I would imagine that it won't look anything like Google's current technology. The encyclopedia was overtaken by the wiki, which companies like Encyclopedia Britannica could not have seen coming.

Similarly, whichever company eventually overtakes the search giant will not function like Google and will likely only take the lead if Google fails to evolve.

Google is more than a good product. It's a good product with a substantial, loyal following. For a site to overtake Google, it needs to account for both of those factors. Consider the marathon metaphor: Suppose a great runner starts running a race. Suppose an equal (or even slightly better) runner starts the same race 2 hours later. That runner, despite being as good or better, will not catch the first runner due to the head start. The second runner will only succeed when he or she capable of inventing a new race and convincing people that the first race is no longer even worth watching.

PREPARING FOR THE FIRST MEETING

In the first meeting you have with a potential client, you want to cover three main areas. You want to:

- ▶ Learn about them
- ▶ Present them key information about you
- ▶ Communicate what you can do for them

Learning about the Client

The first time I meet with a client (either in person, over the phone, or via video conference) my priority is to learn as much about the client as possible. To craft the best SEO plan possible, I need to know what the potential client is trying to accomplish on a high level. At this point you should review the client's site with them and point out of the areas for improvement you saw in your earlier research.

▶ You did review the potential client's website before meeting with them, right? As discussed in Chapter 4, doing some quick audits of a potential client's website can yield valuable information you can use in your initial discussions with that client.

Most recently this tactic has been helpful for a training supplements company I worked with. I figured that they must already have a clear understanding of SEO because they ranked #1 for all of their products. Given their link profile and the competitiveness of their niche, their rankings surprised me—I suspected foul play. After our first meeting, I found out that they were actually manufacturing all of their products and they didn't actually have any direct competition on a product-by-product basis. This explained the rankings. If I hadn't learned this, I would have spent a lot of time looking for sketchy tactics that didn't exist.

Because of revelations like this, you always want to make sure to cover the following talking points in the first meeting:

- ▶ **What does your company do?** This is extremely important because it can reveal disconnections between the company and how the company's website presents itself. It also helps to identify company priorities and allows you to see what drives the potential client.

- ▶ **What do you want to accomplish with search?** I am almost always surprised by the answer to this question. Obviously every client wants more traffic, but this is only a means to an end. This question is designed to identify what that end is. Do they want to sell more products or influence more people? All of this information is extremely important when you do your keyword research later on in the process. For example, if the client wants to sell more products, your keywords will be product-related, but if your client wants to improve its reputation, you might not target a single one of their products. The answer to this question can make a big difference in how you spend your time.

▶ **How is your team organized?** This is helpful for logistical reasons. It helps identify paths for making changes to the website. You don't want to waste your time (and the client's) by explaining technical details to a copywriter or marketing tactics to a developer who doesn't care. This question helps you work more efficiently by giving you hints on how to communicate better with the potential client.

▶ **What is the process for getting recommended changes implemented on your site?** Beyond knowing the people involved, you need to know the process, too. Some clients can make changes to their site on the phone as you speak, while others have to create a development ticket, and you might wait a month or more to get changes implemented. Most are in the middle.

▶ **What is the SEO history of your site? What worked, and what didn't?** Asking this question can give you some insight into how the term "SEO" has been perceived within the organization throughout recent years. It's important to know whether you're the first vendor that the client has used, or whether the company is coming off a bad relationship with another firm. If the latter, your strategy and suggestions may face increased scrutiny as the client regains faith in the industry. You also need to know about any dodgy tactics that the client used in the past, as part of your time might be devoted to cleaning up the mess. If at all possible, read previous SEO audits and reports.

▶ **What is special about your company? What unique value do you provide your customers that your competitors don't?** The answer to this question is very important, and not just to make the client show confidence in the organization. A smart link-building program will use this unique value to generate the type of interest that will result in links. Whether the value is larger inventory, better prices, more attentive customer service, or something entirely different, the client needs to know that if they don't stand out, the SEO task will be significantly more difficult.

▶ **What sections are on your website?** This is one of the most important questions that I ask. When clients tell you about the sections on their website, they almost always reveal what the information hierarchy should be according to their priorities. This is extremely important when trying to see their website on a high level from their perspective. For example, if your client owns a website about widgets and he or she spends all their time talking about the

▶ Your ability to create value for the client is directly related to the speed and efficiency with which the client's team can implement your recommendations (and give you a valuable case study), so don't neglect this point.

different formats of widgets, it is very likely that their website should sort widgets by format.

- ▶ **What pages are your biggest moneymakers?** This helps you align your priorities with that of the client's. Your job should be to maximize your Return on Investment (ROI). The client is spending money on you, and in turn you should do your best to send as much qualified traffic as possible to the pages on the site that will make the potential client the most money.

- ▶ **What online resources (other domains) do you have to work with?** Many times clients will be sitting on powerful resources, and they don't even know it. I once worked with a media conglomerate that had no idea it would benefit from linking between its different child company websites. These websites happened to be some of the most widely linked domains on the Internet and their relationship to each other was being wasted.

- ▶ **Can I have access to your analytics?** This access is vital because it helps you in two important ways.

  - ▷ First, it helps give you an advanced view of how the flow of traffic reaches and moves through the given website. It allows you to see which pages are already driving traffic, which you can then use to your advantage.

  - ▷ Second, it gives you a measuring stick for your efforts. It provides you with the tool you need to show that you provided value to the potential client.

  > ▶ Don't take "no" for an answer when it comes to analytics access. You need it, period.

- ▶ **Is your website registered and verified with Google Webmaster Central?** If the answer is no, you should register it to see if you can identify any big problems. If the answer is yes, get access to it so that you can make sure all of the settings are set up properly. Specifically, you are going to want to look at the canonicalization settings of the homepage and the filtering of sitelinks. If no one from the organization has yet verified the site through Google Webmaster Tools, then sorting through GWT's diagnostics data can be one of the first valuable services you'll perform for them.

- ▶ **How many pages do you think you have on your domain?** Although the answer to this is usually only a rough estimate ("oh, about a million or two pages") it helps give you context when you start seeing how well the domain is indexed. If clients think they have one million pages and the search engines are indexing a completely different amount of pages, you have either uncovered a duplicate content problem (engines have more pages indexed than clients think they have) or an indexation problem (engines are not able to index all pages).

▶ One query that can be very helpful is site:domain.com -inurl:www. It can take a while and several subsequent refined queries, but it can show you all the subdomains on a site, at least those that are indexed.

▶ **What subdomains do you have on your domain?** This helps you identify the breadth of the domain. As a result of how the search engines treat subdomains, it can be hard to find them all without the client's help.

▶ **What areas of your site are off limits for me?** This helps you use your time more efficiently. I have run into situations where entire sections of a website are off limits because the developers that run them are in different departments. Furthermore, it helps you avoid making recommendations that can't be implemented due to legal problems with things like licensed content.

Presenting Yourself to the Client

Your first priority should be to decide if the potential client is worth working with. While you are determining this, the client is probably thinking the same thing about you. To be as transparent as possible, I try to include all of the following talking points to allow the client to size me up without hurting my chances.

▶ **Background on you and your company:** This might be the easiest talking point of all. In addition to striving to make a personal connection, I include this point because many times a potential client is interested to know how you got into as strange a niche as SEO. If you are like the majority of SEOs that I have met, you probably have a funny or interesting story of how you got into this profession. Good marketing is the art and science of telling stories. To prove that you are a good marketer, you need to prove that you can tell your story.

▶ **Your processes:** This is a good way to start to take the lead with a project. After finding out their priorities, I try reassure potential clients by letting them know how we can make their priorities a reality by using my process. I recommend being honest and flexible. If you plan to try something new to accommodate a special request, let them know ahead of time. It will help spread the risk and let the potential clients know they are being listened to.

▶ **Your impression on their potential:** This point is especially important because it sets the context of the entire professional relationship. If the clients have no chance of ranking number 1 for their desired keyword, let them know. As always, under-promise and over-deliver. SEO is an extremely chaotic profession where many variables are out of your control. Luckily for you, if potential clients are looking for an SEO consultant, their website probably has a lot of SEO potential. This will make your job easier and make the clients feel good knowing they have the possibility of positive change ahead.

▶ **Your impression of their priorities:** This is helpful in two ways. First, it shows the clients that you are listening and that you are taking what they are saying seriously. Second, it allows you to make sure that you are on the same page as the potential client. It is absolutely necessary that you clarify these points *before* you start doing any SEO work. This saves you and the client time and money.

▶ **Your priorities as they relate to the client:** The last point is possibly the most important one. Take the priorities discussed earlier and identify why you want to make them a reality. Is it because it will boost your career? Is it because you want a good testimonial? Don't be overly dramatic, but make sure potential clients understand why it is beneficial to you to help them accomplish their goals.

Communicating What You Can Do for the Client

The last step in creating the client relationship is to explain to clients in clear language what you can do for them. This is where you can sell your expertise and services.

▶ **Don't guarantee any specific results but do guarantee specific tactics:** Do not promise anything you can not absolutely guarantee. While it may be tempting to promise #1 rankings, don't fall into this trap. At this point you have not done all of your research, and there is very likely a competitor that you don't know about. Feel free to promise specific tactics, but don't over reach. Again, under-promise and over-deliver.

▶ **Let the clients know some context for how much SEO might help them:** This relates to setting expectations. After you have a firm understanding of what they are looking for and what resources they have to offer, give the clients some context for how much your work can expect to help them. I don't recommend mentioning any specific numbers but I do suggest giving them a vague idea of how well they might be able to do if they follow your advice. (For a more in-depth discussion about predicting results, see "How Much Will My Traffic Improve?" earlier in this chapter.)

▶ **Let them know what your initial game plan looks like:** Before wrapping up with potential clients, let them know what your next steps will be if they choose to hire you. Don't ask them if they will hire you, but instead move forward like they already have. Let them know that you will send them the paperwork and what your initial first steps will be. Don't be overbearing but make it easier to go along with your plan than to reject your services.

Explaining SEO Concepts to Clients

Clients often come in one of two varieties: Some want to know the wheres, whys, and hows of everything you're going to do for them, down to the algorithmic implications of hyphens versus underscores. Others are content simply knowing the basics of what you're doing and why, and they're more focused on projecting and documenting outcomes.

There are advantages and disadvantages of both types of clients. The trick is to capitalize on each client's level of investment to get the buy-in that you need to get the work done so that the results are able to speak for themselves.

▶ **Clients who want to know everything:** These clients are very process-oriented, and the key to effective communication with them is to make sure they're along for the ride in nearly every aspect of your work. Make sure they know you read the recent research on canonicalization, for example, so that when you make a recommendation based on it, they already understand the point behind it.

▶ **Clients who are content with a summary:** These clients either trust you fully or don't have time to focus closely on your methodology after the sales process is over. They're far more concerned with year-over-year growth than how to eliminate clicks between the home page and deep content.

In terms of time requirements, it's almost a wash. The first type of client consumes more time from day to day, but you'll spend less time rationalizing recommendations. The second type of client requires less day-to-day time but more time in explaining your recommendations and their projected outcomes.

Regardless of your client type, hone your presentation skills to best help them understand the SEO concepts you need to convey. Typically, it's far more effective to explain things visually. For example:

▶ **SERPs:** A screenshot of a typical search results page is one of the most effective tools you can use in explaining methods. For a target set of keywords, show who is ranking. Chances are your client won't be too fond of the leaders.

▶ **Graphs and clouds of keyword demands:** Showing clients the relative demand of specific keywords is a very effective way of explaining why you're pursuing different types of keywords. Dump relative demand numbers into a keyword-clouding application to really showcase the difference between two terms. Explain that this data is pulled from real humans doing real searches right now.

▶ **Impact on the visual portion of the site:** Clients frequently fear that if an SEO firm has its way, it will completely decimate the visual impact of the site. One question clients frequently ask is how recommended changes will affect the "look and feel" of the site they've worked years to cultivate. Showing a mockup of the site and highlighting affected areas usually assuages any fear that SEOs are trying to "slash and burn" the site down to the level of plain text. For example, meta descriptions don't affect the look and feel at all. URL structure, title tags, alt text, and navigation anchor text changes all have a minimal impact. Body copy and headings have more impact.

In any case, be happy when your clients are engaged. The worst type of client is a no-show—hard to reach, bad at responding, and stretched too thin to recognize the value you bring.

PAPERWORK: SETTING EXPECTATIONS

This section covers the standard paperwork that I recommend using as an SEO consultant.

> **WARNING**   This section is not giving you legal advice. I have no formal legal training. As such, I recommend you find a lawyer and get some advice before taking on a client. This section merely provides you with the basics; it will not be able to protect you if trouble arises.

Master Services Agreement

The *master services agreement* outlines all of the elements of the service (including the nondisclosure agreement and the statement of work) and defines any language that is used throughout the document. Its goal is to define the steps that should be taken if any given situation arises between the two parties agreeing to work together. (As you can imagine, this document is usually rather long.)

In general, the master services agreement has the following content (Note: This list is not all encompassing.):

Parties to the agreement: This section defines the two legal entities that are agreeing to work together.

Statement of work: This section defines the role and legal obligations set forth in the statement of work.

Terms of compensation and reimbursement: This defines the legal obligations of both parties with regard to compensation and reimbursement in the event of both a completed and interrupted business relationship.

Nondisclosure agreement: This section defines the role of the nondisclosure agreement in the master agreement.

Relationship of parties: This section defines the type of legal relationship both parties are entering. Many times this will be an independent contractor.

Termination of services: This section defines when the end of the agreement is and under what conditions it can be ended.

Disclaimer of warranties: This section defines all legal obligations that the given party is or isn't entering into with regard for warranties.

Indemnification and limitation of liability: This section defines indemnification of the client and the limit of their liability.

Use of trademarks: This section defines how each party can use each others' trademarks. This includes for use in self-promotion and in testimonials.

Disputes: This section defines what protocols will be used in case of disputes.

Attorneys' fee and cost of suit: This section describes which party will pay court and attorney fees in the event of a legal dispute.

Entire agreement: This section defines the given document and its exhibits (described next) as the entirety of the legal agreement.

Waiver: This section defines the ability of the client to waive liability in the case that the agreement is not upheld.

Enforceability: This section defines where and how this agreement will be enforceable.

Nondisclosure Agreement

A *nondisclosure agreement (NDA)* is a legal document that identifies and mandates what information is allowed to be disclosed or not disclosed to applicable parties and defines the terms in which this can happen. It is extremely important for creating a trusting relationship with clients because it sets the foundation for maintaining both of your privacy. It also gives the freedom to applicable representatives to talk openly about sensitive information that may help you both do your jobs.

In practice I have never had to use these against anyone but I have found it helps formalize the relationship with the client. I have found that after having the client review and sign this agreement they are more open with me about past behavior that may be affecting their ability to rank (for example, buying links, cloaking, keyword stuffing, and so on). This is essential for helping the client move forward. This makes this benefit as helpful as the potential protection this agreement would offer you if trouble arose.

In general, an NDA has the following content (Note: This list is not necessarily all encompassing.):

▶ **Purpose of agreement:** This section defines the purpose of the nondisclosure agreement. It also can define any broad definitions that are used throughout the document.

▶ **Definition of confidential information:** This section defines exactly what confidential information is in the scope of the agreement.

▶ **Length of agreement:** This section defines the length of the nondisclosure agreement.

▶ **Treatment of confidential information:** This section defines how confidential information must be treated. This includes general confidential information and the security precautions that are used when storing and transmitting it. In addition, it can discuss how that information (if in hard copy form) must be dealt with upon termination of the relationship, such as destroying or returning it.

▶ **Sharing confidential information with affiliates and representatives:** This defines who the given parties may disclose confidential information to and in what circumstances. It also can define how they may disclose this information

▶ **Disclosing confidential information if required to by law:** This section describes the obligations and protocols for the given parties if they are required by law to disclose confidential information.

▶ **General rights and obligations:** This section defines what both parties agree to if the nondisclosure agreement is broken.

> **TIP** If you are working with a well-known client whose business relationship with you might help you take on more business, you might find it useful to add language to the NDA specifically giving you permission to use their brand and logo on your marketing materials. Potential clients are easier to sign if you can list some of the better known brands you have worked with.

Statement of Work

▶ *This is the single most important document for consultants. Clear expectations make for more satisfied clients and thus more business.*

The *statement of work* outlines all of the work that will be done for a given project. It is extremely important that it is both thorough and specific so that both parties know exactly what is expected in the agreement.

You can solve many potentially problematic situations with clients who want more work or more hours simply by referring back to this document. If you need to, you can add more hours or deliverables, but this document makes it very clear that these tasks will be in addition to the contract and price they have already agreed to.

In general, the statement of work has the following content (Note: This is not necessarily all encompassing.):

Service agreement timeline: This section defines the timeline of the project. Many times it simply refers back to the master services agreement.

Project management: This section defines who exactly is in charge of managing the project on both parties' teams. It also provides job titles and contact information.

Project objective: This section defines the objective of the consulting service in terms of both parties' priorities.

Engagement outline: This outline is usually the longest section in the document and describes in detail each of the expected deliverables. It usually includes a lot of examples and requirements.

Compensation: This section defines who will be in charge of sending and collecting compensation. All applicable people should include contact information and job titles. This section also defines when compensation will be due and in what amount.

Deliverables schedule: This section defines when the above mentioned deliverables will be due.

DELIVERABLES

This section describes the different deliverables that I usually offer to clients. While I always make it a priority to offer clients whatever they need that is within my means, I have found it helpful to have a standard short list, as explained in the following section. Your list of deliverables might differ, but the important thing is that their contents, due date(s), and goals should be spelled out fully so that there is no misunderstanding about them.

Quick Hit List

This quick hit list identifies the easiest changes to the client's website that provide the most SEO value. It is organized in priority order and is usually two to five pages long.

Clients often find this document extremely helpful, so consider including it with all of your clients. They typically use it as a checklist they can send off to their development team. These changes usually provide quick results, which makes both developers and upper management happier. This makes the client look good to their colleagues and helps to get returning business.

This list varies depending on the needs of the client. The most common quick hit items I see are listed here:

▶ **Fix global navigation:** Many times I come across a situation where the global navigation on a website is preventing search engine robots from correctly crawling a website. Most of the time this is caused by difficult to parse JavaScript or flash navigation.

▶ **Implement SEO-friendly information architecture:** I see this problem frequently when a website has been forced to scale despite the design of its Content Management System. The fix for this is creating a navigation system that optimizes the link path between the homepage and each content page on the website.

▶ **Add a sitemap:** At the time of writing this tactic is useful for short-term boosts in traffic. It does this by allowing the engines to index more pages on a website than they might if they are forced to crawl difficult information architecture.

▶ **Implement better internal linking:** For sites that provide a lot of information on a niche topic, I recommend building pages that target important pages in the niche and creating internal links that boost this strategy. This is a lot like how Wikipedia does its internal linking to other articles.

▶ **Redirect duplicate content:** Creating duplicate content is a very common mistake. Use the tactics in Chapter 4 to find the duplicate content and redirect it or remove it with the tactics in Chapter 5.

▶ **Implement link building techniques:** Most websites on the Internet could benefit from more links. I offer this suggestion and tailor my specific recommended tactics to the niche of the client.

Comprehensive Site Audit

This site audit is a complete deep dive of a website, and when complete, it serves as the blueprint for the remaining work within the SEO campaign. It is usually more than 50 pages long and covers every aspect of SEO. You can see full-length examples of this type of report for different kinds of sites in Chapters 8 and 9.

ESTABLISHING PRICE POINTS

At this point you are probably wondering how much you can charge for your services. Unfortunately, this is a very difficult question. It depends on your skill level, your reputation, your local market, your currency, and the time of year. In this section I do my best to explain how SEOmoz came up with their prices, and I try to use a multiplier to help make this more useful to people in different circumstances.

Your Skill Level and Reputation (Multiplier)

Just like they do for a professional sports star or actor, your skill level and reputation as an SEO dictates how much you can charge. In this section I provide formulas to help you narrow down how much you can charge for a specific service. Table 7-1 shows rough guides for figuring out how much to charge for your services.

> **WARNING** Table 7-1 is based off experience but will vary greatly by your location and the state of the SEO industry at the time you are reading this. These rates are based on the state of the industry in the United States in the year this book was written.

▶ When doing consulting like this, you need to look into the tax implications of this supplementary income. You should meet with a licensed tax attorney to figure out what set up is best for you.

TABLE 7-1: Skill Level and Reputation Multiplier

LEVEL	DESCRIPTION	MULTIPLIER
Elite	An elite SEO is someone who works primarily with Fortune 500 corporations or equally influential websites. They frequently keynote marketing conferences and own big name SEO companies or are in-house SEOs for major brands. They have at least 5 years experience in doing SEO consulting.	$X = 4$
Advanced	An advanced SEO is someone who works exclusively with large companies and/or big budget websites. They frequently speak at marketing conferences and may have even keynoted smaller conferences. They own an SEO company, work at a big name SEO company, or are an in-house SEO for a large company. They generally have at least 3 years of experience doing SEO consulting.	$X = 2$
Intermediate	An intermediate SEO is someone who has worked with major companies but generally works with medium sized companies that are big locally. They have spoken at some SEO conferences but do so infrequently. They might work at an SEO company or are working in-house with SEO as their primary role. They generally have 2 to 3 years of experience in SEO.	$X = 1$

continued

TABLE 7-1: Skill Level and Reputation Multiplier   *(continued)*

LEVEL	DESCRIPTION	MULTIPLIER
Novice	A novice SEO is someone who is new to SEO and has held at least one part-time SEO position. They have attended a few SEO conferences but never spoken at them. They generally have less than a year of experience in SEO.	X = 1/2
Beginner	A beginner SEO is someone who is brand new to SEO. They maybe in their first SEO position or hold an Internet-related position and are looking into SEO as an interest.	X = 1/4

Report Price Ranges

The following price ranges are estimates and may vary depending on a multitude of factors including demand for SEO, geographic location, client knowledge of SEO, client size, client reputation, client resources, and/or time. All prices are in U.S. dollars.

QUICK HIT LIST

$1,250.00 * X

Additional factors:

- ▶ Length of report
- ▶ Detail of the report
- ▶ Amount of websites

COMPREHENSIVE INFORMATIONAL WEBSITE AUDIT

$4,250.00 * X

Additional factors:

- ▶ Length of report
- ▶ Detail of the report
- ▶ Amount of websites included
- ▶ Tools available
- ▶ Proprietary data available

COMPREHENSIVE E-COMMERCE WEBSITE AUDIT

$5,000.00 * X

Additional factors:

- ▶ Length of report
- ▶ Detail of the report
- ▶ Amount of competitors analyzed
- ▶ Tools available
- ▶ Proprietary data available

LINK BUILDING

$50.00 * X – per link

> **NOTE** This number is completely dependent on the quality of the link. The pre-ceding number would be for a relevant link that passes a mozRank of about 5.00.

REPUTATION MANAGEMENT

$3,000.00 * X

> **NOTE** This number is extremely dependent on popularity of the brand and the amount of work you do for them. This number is based on SEO brand SERP work and social media services. For example, this might include helping a website out-rank a competitor who is spreading damaging information about the given brand.

Additional factors:

- ▶ Current standing of reputation
- ▶ Size of brand
- ▶ Brand resources
- ▶ Difficulty of management requirements

SOCIAL MEDIA MANAGEMENT

$2,500.00 * X

NOTE   This number is extremely dependent on circumstance. For example, the proceeding number is based off a one-off social media audit along with the registration of relevant social media accounts. The audit covers social media impact on traffic and links. It does not involve reputation management or the design or development of creating social media accounts.

Additional factors:

▶ Which social media websites are being targeted

▶ Amount of profiles being registered

▶ Current state of brand

KEYWORD RESEARCH

$1,000.00 * X

Additional factors:

▶ Length of report

▶ Detail of the report

▶ Amount of keywords

▶ Amount of competition

▶ Difficulty of niche

▶ Popularity of niche

MISCELLANEOUS TASKS

$750.00 * X per hour

NOTE   This is completely dependent on the task and will vary widely. These tasks might include doing analysis of analytics, running training workshops, checking or writing code for search engine friendliness, gathering data, or writing up a SEO strategic plan. Price will depend on the specialized skills required for the task and the amount of time it takes to complete. The further outside the scope of traditional SEO deliverables, the higher the price.

A LA CARTE OR CAMPAIGN?

This section describes pricing for reports and activities on an *a la carte* basis. Many times, it makes sense to price projects in this format. Often, however, it makes more sense to group all of the reports into a global campaign that includes ongoing keyword research refreshing, refinements to recommendations, and regular analytics reporting. This is the way many search agencies price ongoing campaigns lasting a year or more.

In a long-term campaign, the client benefits financially because if priced separately, the reports and deliverables would cost far more than they do in an *a la carte* campaign. The SEO firm benefits by knowing that it will have incoming revenue for a defined amount of time.

WHAT TO GIVE AWAY FOR FREE

Most of my most productive and helpful meetings for my career have not directly made me any money. Instead, they made me connections or helped spread my personal brand. While an SEO's time is valuable, it is not something that should be locked up. You will likely find that your time is better spent when you are not directly making money.

Site Audits

The most useful training tool I ever experienced at SEOmoz was in-house site audits. (These are not the same as the comprehensive site audit reports.) These audits take place with a company that is interested in SEO services. In these cases, a company would come in and one of our consultants would lead a site audit with all of the other consultants at SEOmoz. This helped everyone in the room learn the trade and make connections with the companies that came in. SEOmoz did not charge the companies, and they were more than happy to recommend us to their friends and connections. These site audits were a win-win experience for everyone involved.

Lunch Meetings

I have had countless lunch meetings with people who are interested in SEO. During the meal we talk about the state of search engines, and I am happy to provide SEO advice and tactics that I think are useful. These meetings are great for making connections and helping people who might not otherwise use my services.

On a more personal level, I was able to meet a lot of people this way that I otherwise would not have had the chance to meet. I still find these lunch meetings fulfilling on a personal and professional level, and I am more than happy to have them at no cost.

Interviews

I have given a fair amount of interviews about different topics of SEO. I am more than happy to provide these free of charge (but to be honest, I doubt anyone would actually pay me for an interview) because it helps spread my personal and company brand and because it allows me to help people I might otherwise not have the resources to help.

General Advice

I give out free SEO advice all of the time. It makes up probably 30 percent of my e-mails daily and 70 percent of my industry related conversations. I don't do it because I expect to gain anything from it; I do it because I genuinely enjoy talking about SEO and helping webmasters fulfill their dreams via the Web.

I highly recommend making an extended effort to give away your advice and some of your time for free. In addition to it being a personally rewarding experience, the research required to consistently answer questions correctly keeps you very sharp and exercised the critical thinking skills necessary to perform top-notch SEO.

SUBSEQUENT MEETINGS

During the life span of a business relationship with a client you will have many meetings. Sometimes it can be difficult to determine which are business meetings and which would be more appropriately offered free of charge. Here are some examples of what I do in commonly confusing situations.

E-mail

I almost never charge for my time on e-mail. This is because I have trained myself to be exceptionally fast at answering e-mails. I recommend you practice answering e-mails where you spend no more than two minutes per e-mail. This has saved me a lot of time and given me more resources to get other work done.

For e-mails that require more than two minutes, I make a plan to get them done a specific point in the day. If these e-mails are for a client and they take longer than 10 minutes, I add them to my hours for that client.

Phone Calls

Phone calls with clients almost always take at least a half hour for me. This is because the clients that I deal with are as busy as I am and when we schedule time to talk, we usually both have a lot to say. It is also because phone conversations are more personal than e-mails and thus take longer to do well. In these cases, I charge for the hours of the call.

Wrap-Up Meeting

A day or so after I turn in the final deliverables to a client, I always schedule a wrap-up meeting to make sure that all expectations are met and that the clients know exactly what to do with what they have been provided.

This is helpful for both the client and me because it keeps us on the same page and leaves everyone feeling like they got their fair share from the business relationship.

Follow-Up Meeting

In some cases I will schedule a follow-up meeting with clients to see how my recommendations worked for them. This is both to ensure that the client was happy with my work and to make sure that my theories are working as I hoped they would.

▶ I highly recommend that you schedule these meetings because it helps boost goodwill and teaches you a lot about the effectiveness of your strategies and tactics.

SUMMARY

This chapter discussed the time-intensive SEO consulting process. It lays out a framework that can lead to successful consulting with your clients. This should act as a good starting point for you.

The next chapter covers SEO best practices. These will help you fill in many of the blanks in the framework you learned in this chapter.

## CHAPTER 8

Comprehensive Site Audit (Informational Website)

IN THIS CHAPTER

► Learning one sample format for a professional SEO audit
► Learning why each section is included
► Learning how to write an SEO report yourself

This chapter contains an annotated version of a professional SEO website audit. This report is based very closely on the reports I used to write for Fortune 500 companies when my former employer, SEOmoz, still did consulting. These are the same reports for which we used to charge $10,000 and more. I have included this as an example for you to build upon for your own consulting reports.

HOW TO READ THIS CHAPTER

This chapter is constructed differently than the previous chapters. It centers on a comprehensive SEO audit report, which is included in full at the end of the chapter, for a made-up website called MusicArtistDatabase.com. This chapter is intended to be a guide for writing your own reports. I have written from the perspective of a fake consulting company called Placeholder Consulting (I saved all of the creativity for the report, not on the name of the company). It includes the layout of the report, examples of how a similar report would be written, and an explanation of common SEO scenarios and recommendations that might be made. Put simply, this chapter focuses on the deliverable you can produce to make money as an SEO.

Like any respectable author (a.k.a. paranoid author) I want to offer one disclaimer. The copy of this book that you are reading is not the only copy in circulation and as such I don't recommend copying this report verbatim. (Doing so will make your work seem cheap.) This report is meant to be used as a framework. Though I am a fan of copying and pasting and encourage you to do so when appropriate, I want to remind you that your clients are paying you for your expertise, not mine. They want your opinion on their website and your advice on how to improve their rankings. As such, I recommend using the following chapter as guide but creating a report that you can call your own.

SITE AUDITS AND HOTEL ROOMS

Another way to think of a site audit is like a hotel room key. That key is very effective, but only for one room, and only for one fixed period of time. Similarly, a site audit is a customized document that applies to a single web site in a specific time in its life span.

It's normal to worry about complex audits getting into competitors' hands, but without the experience and perspective to understand how to apply specific principles appropriately, the report does them little good. The goal of these chapters is to not only show you what to look for and how to present it, but to offer the perspective needed to know under what circumstances it is—and isn't—effective.

Think of this chapter and the next as nerdy cookbooks. The best way to use this chapter is to read through it and the accompanying report once and then use it as a reference when you are writing your report.

SAMPLE WEBSITE

For this report I have made up a website called MusicArtistDatabase.com. This fictional website is a leader in the competitive celebrity information niche. It features artist biographies, photos, and gossip, along with album details and top charts. It gets 10 million daily visitors and ranks within the top ten for most musician name searches in the major search engines.

Informational Website

MusicArtistDatabase.com is roughly modeled on a combination of content-based websites for which I have done SEO consulting in the past. These types of websites tend to make money off ads and/or affiliate sales. Real-life examples of these types of informational websites include:

- ► www.imdb.com
- ► www.enclyopedia.com
- ► www.wikipedia.org
- ► www.census.gov
- ► www.about.com
- ► www.digg.com
- ► www.nytimes.com

My hope is that by using this report as a model, you will be able to write reports for websites that you work with that fall into this very populated website category.

SEO Scorecard

This report is based around an SEO scorecard. While doing consulting, my co-workers and I found this format especially good for bigger clients who tended to be more action focused, as opposed to smaller clients who wanted more detailed analysis so they could draw their own conclusions.

When I used this format, I usually used the scorecard included in this chapter as a base and added more sections as I found more problems. I would know which sections to add after spending several hours digging into the site trying to identify what aspects were hurting its SEO metrics. (See Chapter 4 for an explanation on how to do this.)

SAMPLE REPORT

The following is an annotated walkthrough of a comprehensive SEO audit. It should help answer most of the questions your clients are likely to ask.

Steps Before Writing the Report

Before you even start formatting your report, you will need a good understanding of the website for which you will be writing an analysis. To get this understanding, I take the following steps:

1. I usually run the 15-minute SEO audit described in Chapter 4. This helps familiarize me with the state of the given website.

2. After doing my initial run-through of the site I check the implementation (or lack thereof) of all of the SEO best practices listed in Chapter 6. This generally takes me about 2 hours.

3. I follow this up by investigating any problems I found via the 15-minute audit. Finally, I log in to the client's analytics program and Google Webmaster Tools to get an external perspective on the website. This generally takes me about 2 hours.

4. At this point I have spent about 4 hours investigating the given website and I am ready to fill out the SEO scorecard, which I then use as the basis for the report (see the section "SEO Scorecard" later in this chapter for more about the scorecard). Generally, it takes me 1 to 2 weeks to write the final report, which includes the time spent by other SEOs who peer review my work.

▶ Have other SEOs peer review your work if at all possible. Your peers can spot problems you didn't see and give criticism on assumptions you may have made. I have found a peer review makes my report more complete and better thought out.

> **NOTE** The rest of this chapter comprises descriptions of the sections of the SEO audit. Following the text of the chapter is the sample audit of MusicArtistDatabase.com in its entirety, which contains examples of all those pages discussed in the chapter. That way you can both read about what specific sections of an audit might entail and then go see what they might look like in an actual audit.

Cover

The cover of the report is extremely important for establishing credibility. It needs to clearly establish what the report is about, who wrote it, and who to contact if the client has questions.

Like any report cover, this page should include:

✔ Report Title (including the site name or URL)

✔ Report Author

✔ SEO Consultant Business Name

✔ SEO Consultant Business Address

✔ SEO Consultant Business Phone Number

> **TIP** You may or may not want to include an e-mail address depending on the contract you sign with your client. If you are providing ongoing consulting efforts, you will want to include it, but if this report is a one-off job, you might find it best to make it a little harder to contact you.

Table of Contents

Most modern word processing programs will be able to automatically create a table of contents based on a well-formatted report. See your software's user manual (or more likely Google) for information on how to do this.

> **TIP** Can't figure out how to make automated table of contents? The first step to doing this is formatting your report with the styles and information hierarchy available within your word processor. For example, section titles should be Heading 1 and subsections should be Heading 2. This is similar to HTML headers (h1–h6) and has many of the same benefits.
>
> Microsoft Word makes it very easy to insert a table of contents using either predefined styles or manual formatting. Search your version's Help menu to find the tool's location.

If possible, you should make the page numbers listed in your table of contents be actual links to pages within the report. This is helpful for when you export the report as a PDF. When you do this, the client will be able to click the page numbers in the TOC and automatically skip to the applicable section.

▶ For easy navigation of PDF versions of your report, make page numbers listed in table of contents be links to pages within the report.

SEO Scorecard

The SEO scorecard is a distilled version of the SEO analysis of the site. All of the most important SEO metrics are graded on scale from 1 to 5. This makes it easy for the client to prioritize changes and implement the most important fixes first.

The scorecard is a Microsoft Excel file that includes all of the sections in the report itself. It is split into columns that correspond to the major sections of the website. (For example, the optimization of Title Tags will be graded on a scale from 1 to 5 for each of the subsections on the website.) This is important both to provide context and to establish scope for the recommend changes.

At the bottom of the scorecard are relevant third-party metrics that are not necessarily on a 5-point scale. I found that these metrics are expected by clients who are used to hearing SEO described in terms such as link counts and unique monthly visitors.

> NOTE You can find a sample template for the SEO audit at www.dannydover .com/search-engine-optimization-secrets.

Most Pressing and Valuable Changes

▶ Invariably clients indicate that "Most Pressing and Valuable Changes" is the most important section of the report.

Time and time again I have had clients tell me that this section is the most important section in this entire report. For this reason, I always include this as the first content section of the report.

WHAT ARE THE COMMON SUGGESTIONS YOU MAKE IN THIS SECTION?

For this section I prioritize the SEO problems I found in my earlier analysis. Generally the problems I mention here are the same common SEO problems that I refer to in the "SEO Quick Hit List" described in Chapter 14.

In addition to simply listing the problems that I find, I include a link in each recommended change to a section within the report that describes the problem further and explains how to fix it.

On-Page/Content Optimization

On-page and content optimization is the practice of targeting search engine ranking factors toward both people and search engines.

WHY IS THIS SECTION NECESSARY?

This section covers the optimization of content and on-page keyword targeting. This is extremely important because this is the material that users came to see when they navigated to the given webpage. For this reason, it is also the most important information to the search engines when they are determining relevancy.

I include this section near the beginning of the report because I want to remind the reader that websites should be designed primarily for people, not search engines.

HOW DO YOU DO THE ANALYSIS FOR THIS SECTION?

For each of these sections I compare the implementation of the given factor to the SEO best practice of the time. You can read more about identifying how the client implemented the given factor in Chapter 2 and compare their implementation to the SEO best practices listed in Chapter 6.

Based on this information, you should be able to grade the clients' website and offer suggestions on how they can improve their on-page optimization. It's as simple as that!

WHAT ARE THE COMMON SUGGESTIONS YOU MAKE IN THIS SECTION?

Each of these topics is covered fully in Chapter 2, but generally I make the following recommendations.

KEYWORD TARGETING

Keyword targeting mistakes usually fall into two categories.

- The first category is targeting the wrong keyword. Finding the right keyword is a difficult and many times unintuitive process. Instead of choosing the keyword based on the narrow perspective of the author, it is best to use a keyword research tool to see what words or phrases actual people are using on Google. The best way to do this is to use Google's AdWords tool as discussed in Chapter 3. Remember, it doesn't matter if you have the most highly optimized page for a query if no one is searching for it.

- The other common mistake that people make is simply not targeting any keyword. This happens on many content pages where authors have written without presentation and information hierarchy in mind.

TITLE TAGS

Like keyword targeting, the common problems with title tags fall into two categories.

- The first category is the lack of targeting the correct keyword. Usually this is because the title tag is either simply stating the name of the website or it is written as sales copy. The solution to this is problem is to include the applicable keyword as close to the beginning of the title tag as possible.

> ▶ Remember that "keyword targeting" has nothing to do with the meta Keywords tag. Instead, it refers to the themes and specific phrases around which you shape the content of the page.

> ▶ Clients who have content pages that were written without presentation or information hierarchy in mind often have pages that don't target any keyword.

▶ The other common mistake I see clients make with title tags has to do with length. Title tags should be as close to but not greater than 70 characters. Short title tags almost never attract the same number of links as longer title tags. Similarly, title tags that are too long are truncated by the search engines and waste precious search engine results page (SERP) resources.

META DESCRIPTIONS

The most common mistake I see with meta descriptions is that they are not written as ad copy. Because they don't help with rankings directly, these are the client's opportunity to write copy solely to induce clicks. I usually include examples of good and bad meta descriptions from the given site to give clients some context on what they should be doing with this space.

H1 TAGS

I generally include a section on H1s in these reports because I have found that clients expect them. According to the research available to me at the time of writing, H1s are not particularly useful for rankings. That said, they are helpful for users, and as such I recommend making clear headings to help impatient readers get an idea of what the page they are looking at is about.

> **TIP** H1s can be a difficult factor for clients to understand (mostly due to the variety of ways they can be visually formatted) so I try to include an image of an H1 on their website so that they can see what element I am talking about.

BODY TEXT KEYWORDS

Body text keywords refer to the usage of keywords in the main content of the page. This is usually one of the easiest relevancy concepts for clients to understand, so I make a point of indicating how well they did.

The most common mistake I see in this area is keyword stuffing. It is common for inexperienced SEOs to increase the mythical search engine factor of keyword density in a futile attempt to help rankings. I point out this common spam filter and show them examples of this practice on their site if it exists.

▶ Let common sense—or better yet, an objective third party—be your guide if you're concerned about keyword stuffing. If a friend reads a page and notices awkwardness due to the number of times your phrases appear in various places, scale it back.

SUBSTANTIVE & UNIQUE CONTENT

A lack of substantive and unique content on a page is one of the more common SEO mistakes I see online. Usually the problem will be that the page is one of many pages that share a common template and there isn't enough content to warrant a whole new page. Sometimes people will try to supplement these pages by adding more photos. I generally recommend against this because the photos are difficult for the search engines to analyze and clients don't get the relevancy benefit they would if they were to include more unique textual content.

In terms of uniqueness, pull some random strings of text (8-10 words) and search for the string—in quotes—at Google. If you find multiple instances of the string on your client's site or other sites, chances are much of the copy is not original, or at a minimum, has been lifted by other sites.

IMAGE ALT ATTRIBUTE

You will find that many client websites do not take advantage of using image alt attributes for their images. At the time of writing including image alt attributes is one of the most helpful and least commonly implemented ranking factors. For this reason, I always recommend that relevant (and concise) alt attributes be added to applicable images.

This easy-to-make addition is one of the first "low hanging fruit" suggestions that I make to clients who can benefit from it.

▶ Including image alt attributes is one of the most helpful and least commonly implemented ranking factors.

URL Conventions

When someone develops a website, it is common to use IDs to represent content in URLs to make sure that each page on a website has a unique URL. This is necessary because when a web server queries a database for a specific piece of content, it needs to know exactly which row or rows of data to request. Thus, using IDs makes a lot of sense from a programmer's perspective, but it makes it difficult for people and search engines to understand what the content is about without parsing the resulting page.

WHY IS THIS SECTION NECESSARY?

I include this section in the report because I find that URL fixes are among some of the most powerful SEO fixes that I can recommend. They are generally harder than content-related fixes to implement (due to the redirects that are often needed after URLs are changed) but they scale better and usually need to be updated only once. This means they are a lot of work up front but have long-lasting benefits.

HOW DO YOU DO THE ANALYSIS FOR THIS SECTION?

I do two kinds of analysis for this section.

- ▶ First, I focus how the URLs change as I navigate the given website. I am looking for signs of parameter usage (www.example.com/?parameter=value) and use of unintelligible IDs (www.example.com/article/4853045/).

- ▶ Second, I look at the search results of the engines to see how they are indexing the URLs for the given website. (You can read more about this in Chapter 2 and Chapter 3.) Are they showing signs of canonicalization problems? Are the URLs longer than they should be?

WHAT ARE THE COMMON SUGGESTIONS YOU MAKE IN THIS SECTION?

The most common SEO mistake with URLs is websites generating URLs that are not easy to understand for users or search engines.

KEYWORD INCLUSION

The most common mistake I see with regard to keyword inclusion is the lack thereof. It is surprisingly common for URLs not to include the keyword the given page is trying to target.

I always recommend including the targeted keyword once and never more than twice in the given URL. This is to boost relevancy metrics and to avoid spam indicators.

URL LENGTH

I find that most URLs are of an acceptable length. Technically they need to be shorter than 2083 characters to be able to be parsed by Internet Explorer (I have never seen a natural URL longer than this), but this ranking factor is not a high priority.

▶ Unlike with page titles, there's no predictable point at which URLs are truncated on a SERP. Keep them short so you don't have to worry about it.

My normal recommendation in this section is to make sure that key URLs are shorter than 74 characters so that they are not truncated in SERPs. This won't likely have a major impact on rankings, but it is helpful for people who are sharing URLs with others and with click-through rates on the SERPs.

URL PARAMETERS

As I have mentioned several times in this book, URL parameters are not a recommended SEO-friendly tactic. Whenever possible, I recommend using semantic

URL structures (www.example.com/animals/dogs/springer-spaniels/) over URL parameters (www.example.com/?animal=dogs&kind=springer-spaniel).

▶ You want your clients to use semantic URL structures, not URL parameters.

Information Architecture

The information architecture and internal linking structure of a website helps to organize, identify, and prioritize the site's content for users and search engines.

WHY IS THIS SECTION NECESSARY?

The information architecture of websites is rarely planned out well from the beginning. As such, as a website grows, the relationship between its information becomes less and less clear. This is detrimental to both users and search engines.

Because of this natural tendency of large websites, it is important to include this section so that this can be addressed before it becomes an even bigger problem for webmasters and users alike.

HOW DO YOU DO THE ANALYSIS FOR THIS SECTION?

The best way to understand information hierarchy is to analyze the global navigation, URL structure, and internal link usage. The steps for doing this analysis are described in Chapter 2.

WHAT ARE THE COMMON SUGGESTIONS YOU MAKE IN THIS SECTION?

The most common mistakes I see with information hierarchy have to do with how information is organized and the anchor text that is used to link to internal pages. Luckily, these are generally easier to fix than the more common external SEO factors that are controlled by other website operators.

CONTENT HIERARCHY/ORGANIZATION

Most of the clients I have worked with put very little thought into content hierarchy as they developed their websites. For this reason I generally recommend answering very basic information hierarchy questions to get them on the right path to making semantic information relationships. These questions usually are as follows:

1. Are there clearly defined groupings of content?
2. Is there a logical page flow and organization of the content?
3. Does every page sit at the same level or are they in a proper hierarchy?
4. Does the content structure ensure that the number of clicks between the home page and deep content (the "click path") is minimal?

INTERNAL ANCHOR TEXT

The word choice of the anchor text of internal links is both very important for establishing information relationships and rarely done optimally. One exception to this is Wikipedia. I almost always use Wikipedia as an example in this section to show clients how internal anchor text usage can improve rankings.

This is usually so well understood to the clients that I have found that I need to warn them against the extreme of link stuffing when they use this tactic in extreme.

▶ In other words, consistency in anchor text is good, but complete lack of variation can be too much.

Robots Control Protocols

Webmasters can control the robots that crawl their sites in a number of ways. The only SEO-friendly way to do this is with meta directives and sitemaps.

WHY IS THIS SECTION NECESSARY?

Errors in robots.txt and meta directives can have dire consequences for rankings and, as a result, to the bottom line of the online business. Because of this, it is extremely important these two areas are analyzed when performing an SEO audit.

HOW DO YOU DO THE ANALYSIS FOR THIS SECTION?

Three items need to be checked when doing analysis on this section.

▶ The first is item is the most difficult because it is spread all over the website. Meta robots (as described in Chapters 3 and 5) are unique to each page on a website. They are the search engine–created mechanism for directing crawlers on a page level. This meta tag does not need to be included on the page unless the page should not be indexed or the links on it need to be nofollowed. See Chapters 3 and 5 for more information on the intricacies of this.

▶ The second item that needs to be checked comprises the robots.txt files on the different subdomains of a website. These are located in the root of the subdomain (www.example.com/robots.txt) and generally should contain very little information except for the location of the XML sitemap. You can learn more about this in Chapter 6.

▶ The last item that you should check is also the least important of the three. Sitemaps provide hints for search engines about which pages to index. By default search engines look for XML sitemaps in the root of the subdomain (www.example.com/sitemap.xml). You can read more about sitemaps in Chapter 2.

WHAT ARE THE COMMON SUGGESTIONS YOU MAKE IN THIS SECTION?

The most common mistakes I see in this section are the result of people listing pages in either their sitemap or `robots.txt` file that they do not intend to list.

▶ One causes overindexing, and the other causes underindexing.

META DIRECTIVES

Meta directives (also called meta robots) are the best way to block search engine crawlers from specific pages.

I have found myself recommending various uses of these in every SEO report I have ever written. For a full explanation of this see the section titled "Blocking Pages from Search Engines" in Chapter 6.

ROBOTS.TXT

The most common mistake I see clients making is using `robots.txt` to block pages rather than using the more search engine–friendly meta directives. You can read all about this in Chapter 6 in the section titled "Blocking Pages from Search Engines."

XML SITEMAP

The most common recommendation I make with XML sitemaps is adding one. I have consistently seen search engine traffic from sites rise and stay higher after implementing this tactic. You can use free or inexpensive plug-ins to generate these automatically.

▶ SEOmoz regenerates their sitemap once a week and uses the installable generator that is available at http://www.xml-sitemaps.com/.

Technical Issues

As the name implies, this is usually the most technical section of my SEO reports. This section covers all of the server and crawling errors that I and the search engines encounter when visiting the given website.

WHY IS THIS SECTION NECESSARY?

This section is important because it provides an easy-to-implement list of technical fixes. It is easy for developers to interpret and act on and usually makes a substantial difference in rankings.

HOW DO YOU DO THE ANALYSIS FOR THIS SECTION?

This section is actually one of the easiest sections to do the analysis for. This is because all of the information necessary for this section of the report can be found in either

Google Webmaster Tools or Open Site Explorer. Hooray for search tools! You can read about how to do this analysis in Chapter 3.

WHAT ARE THE COMMON SUGGESTIONS YOU MAKE IN THIS SECTION?

Almost all of my suggestions in this section involve 301 redirecting a broken page to a page that is working correctly.

SERVER RESPONSE CODES

This section covers what each of the different types of status code errors mean. I don't make any suggestions in this section.

404 FILE NOT FOUND

This section details a list of the most valuable pages that have links but are not found on the server. These are wasted resources, and I recommend first trying to fix the page if it is simply not displaying or redirecting the offending URL to a page that does render so that the links the broken page earned do not go to waste.

404 PAGE

▶ Largely, but not entirely. It is worth your while to fix these "soft 404s," as the engine engineers call them. Otherwise, you're at risk for severe overindexing of junk pages.

The most common mistake I see with 404 pages are pages that say 404 but return a 200 HTTP status code. Though this is a problem that has largely been solved by the search engines, it has secondary effects that are not fixed by the engines. Based on this, I recommend making sure that all 404 pages return an actual 404 HTTP status code in the HTTP headers.

The other common mistake I see is 404 pages that don't help the users find what they were looking for. This is easy to fix by simply adding a navigation and/or search field so that the user can find other useful content.

302 MOVED TEMPORARILY

The requested resource has temporarily moved to another location, but unlike with a 301, the browser should continue to request the original URL in future attempts to find the resource. The 302 redirect is only rarely the correct 300-series redirect to use for SEO purposes.

500 SERVER ERROR

More general and vague than a 503 (Service Unavailable) Code, the 500 response code means that for some reason (other than the page not being found and service being unavailable), the server is unable to fulfill the browser's request. This may, for example, be due to a server being unsure how to handle a specific browser request. Pages that repeatedly show Google a 500 response code will typically not rank for anything.

CRAWLING PROBLEMS

Crawling problems can be caused by many things. Generally the mistakes I see are related to errors in `robots.txt`, pages that are unavailable due to temporary server issues, or navigation and links that engines have trouble understanding.

For the `robots.txt` errors I recommend using meta robots and for the server issues I almost always find that the problem has been fixed by the next time I check the URL. When this is the case, I note that there was a problem in the past and make no further suggestions.

Search Guidelines and Spam Protocols

Every once in a while the search engine representatives come out with a new message that they want to make perfectly clear to the web community. This section covers these messages.

WHY IS THIS SECTION NECESSARY?

Most of the information we get directly from the search engines is broadly worded and difficult to interpret. Thus, when they come out with a strong new message with clear meaning it is something to take notice of. This section includes these messages and shows how they affect the given website.

HOW DO YOU DO THE ANALYSIS FOR THIS SECTION?

This section is the hardest to do analysis for because it relies on changing news from the search engine representatives. The best way to keep up to date on this is to frequently read the major search engine–focused sources. See the discussion of SEO leaders in Chapter 10 for information on who to listen to.

WHAT ARE THE COMMON SUGGESTIONS YOU MAKE IN THIS SECTION?

The most common suggestions I make are centered around keeping the given website in line with the search engine guidelines.

CANONICALIZED SITE VERSIONS

In this section I note the implementation of the various possible URLs for a website. Specifically I check for common canonicalization errors with the www vs. the non-www version of the website.

When I find a canonicalization problem (that is, `www.example.com` and `http://example.com` both render), I figure out which version has the most valuable links to it (via mozRank) and recommend that the other version be 301 redirected to the stronger version.

CANONICALIZED DUPLICATE CONTENT

In this section I check for duplicate content caused by non-canonicalized URLs. This generally happens when the www and non-www version of the website render and when URLs are case-sensitive. Because I usually focus on the www problem in the previous section, I use this section to discuss which content pieces should include the search engine–engineer created rel canonical tag. (This is an example of one of those rare, unusually clear search engine representative messages.)

This tag is recommended for any duplicate content pages where both URLs need to stay active (that is, a redirect is inappropriate). Most commonly this happens with print-friendly versions of content and with URLs that have important parameters attached.

"SEARCH RESULTS" PAGE EXCLUSION

The search engine representatives (see the discussion of SEO leaders in Chapter 10 for more details on who these people are) have been very clear about the engines not wanting to index pages that look like search results. They argue that searchers don't want to leave one search result page only to land on another.

For these pages it is best to add a meta robots tag with the parameter values `"noindex, follow"`. This keeps the pages out of the search engine indices but makes sure all of their links are still able to pass juice.

LINK ACQUISITION PRACTICES

This section is useful only for link building practices that have not yet been done by the client (it is extremely difficult to unbuild existing links). In this section I point the client to the existing search engine guidelines.

The engine representatives are very specific in not wanting paid links, link farms, and otherwise manipulated links in their indices affecting results.

▶ Of course it's still okay to have paid links point to your site; they just need to be designated as such, typically by the rel=nofollow parameter, so that engines know to avoid considering them for algorithmic benefit.

Inbound Links

Inbound links encompass the most important metrics for determining rankings. The first step to understanding these link profiles is to get lists of links.

WHY IS THIS SECTION NECESSARY?

This section contains a summary of the link profile for the given website. This is very important because it helps reveal the search engines' perspective of the given website. This is also important for the clients so that they can see what resources are really helping their website rank.

HOW DO YOU DO THE ANALYSIS FOR THIS SECTION?

I am able to do all of the analysis I need to do for this section using the free tool Open Site Explorer. This tool returns link profile summaries that are exportable to CSV and allows for filtering within the tool. From one report from this tool, I am able to get all of the data I need for this section of this report.

WHAT ARE THE COMMON SUGGESTIONS YOU MAKE IN THIS SECTION?

All of my recommendations for this section revolve around gaining more links of specific types.

OPEN SITE EXPLORER

Link profile problems usually fall into one of two areas.

- ▶ The most common problem is that the given domain simply doesn't have enough links to be competitive in its niche. The best way to determine if this is the case is to compare the given domain's mozRank or Domain Authority with that of its competitors.

- ▶ I also commonly see websites that have a lot of links but don't use targeted anchor text. This means they have raw link popularity but not relevancy. In this case I recommend they use some of the link building tactics listed in Chapter 5 to get links with predefined anchor text.

Link-worthiness

SEO experts estimate that the various characteristics of links make up about 70 percent of all Google ranking factors (www.seomoz.org/article/search-rank-ing-factors). As such, it is extremely important that the content of a website is worthy of receiving links.

WHY IS THIS SECTION NECESSARY?

As I have mentioned several times in this book, link-related metrics make up the majority of the search engine algorithm ranking factors. For this reason, it is extremely important to critique how well a given website's content is able to attract links naturally. This section does this by breaking link-worthiness into several categories.

HOW DO YOU DO THE ANALYSIS FOR THIS SECTION?

The analysis for this section is the most qualitative of the report. It relies on many human elements that are up to the discretion of the author to grade and make suggestions upon. While writing to this section I find it helpful to keep asking myself, "Would I link to this page?"

WHAT ARE THE COMMON SUGGESTIONS YOU MAKE IN THIS SECTION?

I find the best way to get through this section is to break the broad concept of link-worthiness into several smaller categories. These categories are listed in the following subsections.

DESIGN QUALITY

I find that many people underestimate the importance of web design when it comes to ranking well. It is true that actual graphical design is not directly quantified by the search engine algorithms but its secondary affects are certainly important to rankings.

Design makes an impact on whether or not someone is going to trust content. Trust is a major factor when someone decides if they want to rank to a given piece of content. For this reason, I commonly include some notes on how well designed I believe a given page to be.

USER EXPERIENCE

User experience is extremely complicated. For this section I usually simplify it by making some bulleted action items that are based on some obvious user experience problems.

These generally include making text more readable (spacing and color), directing the flow of the users as they navigate the website, and creating custom experiences for first-time users.

VALUE OF CONTENT

It doesn't matter how well information is designed and presented if it is not valuable to anyone. In this section I make recommendations on how to take the valuable information that I find on the given website and present it in ways that make it more consumable and more valuable to the average reader.

Generally I make suggestions like basing content on well-established magazine article styles (top ten lists, infographics, and so on). I also try to include some examples of related content that could be added to the site to make it more valuable.

SHARE-ABILITY/ACCESSIBILITY

In this last section I make suggestions on how the clients can take information that they have and make it more shareable and accessible to other people. The easiest way to do this is to include sharing widgets or include simple invitations for your users to share the content if they know someone who might enjoy it.

Many excellent sharing widgets exist, such as AddThis, ShareThis, and AddToAny. These third-party apps enable you to share your content across nearly every social platform available. In addition, most of the larger social networks such as Facebook and Twitter offer their own customizable widgets and plugins that allow your users to share and comment on data across those networks.

Metrics

Search engines use link popularity data to help determine if and when a website should rank for a given search query. The quality of backlinks is more important than sheer quantity, but it's important to track all of the link values. Because the numbers typically vary based on the tool used to calculate this metric, it is good to use a number of sources. Although the number of inbound links may vary from tool to tool, the relationships they reveal are extremely important.

WHY IS THIS SECTION NECESSARY?

This section is important to include because it shows some of the raw data points that search engines use to rank websites. (In the case where these metrics are publicly available, estimates based on SEOmoz metrics are provided.)

HOW DO YOU DO THE ANALYSIS FOR THIS SECTION?

To do the analysis for this section I use SEOmoz's Open Site Explorer. This report shows the top URLs that are pointing to your site, the internal page on your site that they point to, the anchor text used (or image alt text, if applicable), and the page and domain authority of the sites linking to yours. You can configure Open Site Explorer reports to show only internal, only external, or all links. In addition, you can show links coming to all pages on the entire top-level domain, only to the specific subdomain, or only to specific URLs.

WHAT ARE THE COMMON SUGGESTIONS YOU MAKE IN THIS SECTION?

In these sections I do analysis of the raw metrics and give suggestions on how they can be improved or leveraged elsewhere on the site.

LINKSCAPE LINKS

In this section I list the number of links pointing at each major section on a website and make suggestions on which sections are doing well and how they can be leveraged to boost other sections of the website.

GOOGLE PAGERANK

In this section I make it very clear that PageRank is not an accurate ranking factor in and of itself. It is merely one of several hundred methods that Google uses to rank webpages.

If they have any outliers (for example, a major section with a PageRank of 0 or 1 on a website where major sections average 5) in PageRank across their website, I mention the possibility of a penalty.

> **NOTE**   You can read more about fixing penalties in Chapter 5.

MOZRANK

mozRank is similar to PageRank in what it measures and how it correlates with rankings so I usually make similar suggestions as I mentioned in the previous section. The advantages mozRank has over PageRank are that it is more precise, updated more frequently, and when compared to PageRank, it can be used to spot a Google-specific penalty.

MOZTRUST

mozTrust is similar to mozRank, but it measures the trust of linking websites rather than the power of their linking profiles. This is also one of the major search engine ranking metrics and is useful for determining the presence of spam links. Spam links are indicated by low mozTrust and medium or high mozRank.

Conclusion

The conclusion is exactly what it sounds like—a conclusion to the report. It summarizes the findings in a few sentences and serves as a proper and enthusiastic segue between recommendations and the client's own implementation.

WHY IS THIS SECTION NECESSARY?

Professionalism demands that closure is included in every report. The most direct way to do this is to include a conclusion section to close out the report.

WHAT ARE THE COMMON SUGGESTIONS YOU MAKE IN THIS SECTION?

In this section I reiterate the some of the major improvements that the clients can make to their website and remind them about some of their areas of strengths. Reading a report about all of the problems on a website can be difficult for the website's owner. It is important to both restate the same important suggestions and reassure them about their past work.

Addendums

In each report I include several addendums of more detailed information to help the clients understand their website.

WHY IS THIS SECTION NECESSARY?

This section is important for giving the clients clear action items and for showing them the data on which the report was based. It is not enough to simply provide analysis; it is necessary to give them the tools so they can do their own analysis.

WHAT ADDENDUMS DO YOU USUALLY INCLUDE?

I include the following four addendums in all of my reports:

- ▶ A list of pages that 404 on the given site.
- ▶ A list of pages that are unreachable (due to server errors) on the given site.
- ▶ A list of pages blocked by robots.txt but have links.
- ▶ A list of links that are nofollowed on the given site.

AFTER COMPLETING THE REPORT

After you finish writing the report you will need to do some additional work to make sure you are able to provide the most value possible to the client.

Formatting the Report

When you finish the report it is important to deliver the final product in a suitable format. I recommend sending the client a hard copy (printed) as well as a PDF version of the report. The hard copy is for readability and professionalism and the PDF version is for distribution within the client's company and for searchability.

▶ Provide the client with a PDF version of the report for easy distribution and searchability.

> **WARNING**   Never send a **.doc** file. You should always send the client a PDF or hard copy of the report rather than a Microsoft Word file. This is because a Word file usually includes meta data that you don't necessarily want to include with the client. (Most notably, this includes tracked changes.) This is not to hide anything but rather to be as professional as possible.

Final Client Meeting

After I submit a report to a client I spend at least an hour going over the completed report with all of the applicable stakeholders. This generally takes place over the phone, but I have done it in person a few times.

▶ No matter how clear your report is, they'll ask a ton of questions. But be glad, because questions mean they're engaged and are more likely to take your recommendations seriously.

This final meeting is for the clients' benefit and allows them the opportunity to have all of their questions answered. It is not good enough to simply write the report; you need to also make sure that the client understands it and knows what actions to take and why.

SUMMARY

This chapter went through a comprehensive SEO audit for an informational website. It covered the layout of the report and the reasons behind its format. You learned how to make the information from earlier in the book useful and actionable.

The next chapter accomplishes similar tasks but is customized for an e-commerce website. I recommend using what you learned in this chapter and comparing it to the content in the next chapter. These reports are meant to be frameworks, and I have included two different kinds of reports so that you can pick and choose what you like about each of them and create something of your own.

Placeholder Consulting

Comprehensive Technical SEO Site Audit

MusicArtistDatabase.com

Prepared by Danny Dover

Placeholder Consulting

Comprehensive Technical SEO Site Audit

Overview

Search Engine Optimization is the process of creating, formatting and promoting web pages in a manner that ensures that they are ranked highly for chosen keyword phrases after a user performs a Web search in a search engines. Proper implementation of SEO allows a brilliant website to drive massive amounts of traffic.

MusicArtistDatabase.com is a substantial site with a great amount of unique content, many powerful links, decent on-page optimization and good use of robot control protocols. MusicArtistDatabase.com has carved a nice place for itself in its markry and has potential that its competitors should envy.

This comprehensive technical site audit digs deep into MusicArtistDatabase.com; analyzing the on-page optimization, URL conventions, information architecture, robots control protocols, technical issues, link-worthiness, and other factors. We have found many opportunities to improve what is currently implemented and help increase search engine traffic in addition to giving users a better experience.

We hope that you learn as much from reading through our recommendations as we have learned while writing them. MusicArtistDatabase.com is an excellent web property to start with and has exciting opportunities for improvement.

Sincerely,

The Placeholder Consulting Team

Placeholder Consulting

Comprehensive Technical SEO Site Audit

Table of Contents

1234 123th PL NE
Seattle, WA 98000
Phone (555) 555-5555

Placeholder Consulting

Comprehensive Technical SEO Site Audit

Placeholder Consulting

Comprehensive Technical SEO Site Audit

1234 123th PL NE
Seattle, WA 98000
Phone (555) 555-5555

Comprehensive Technical SEO Site Audit

Placeholder Consulting

Scorecard

We reviewed the site as a whole, but used 5 templates as examples for the scorecard. These templates represent entire sections of the website.

Type/Template	URL
Home	http://www.musicsrtistdatabase.com/
Top Charts	http://www.musicartistdatabase.com/top-charts/index.html
Artist Pages	http://www.musicartistdatabase.com/people/index.html
Album Pages	http://albums.musicartistdatabase.com/
Message Boards	http://forum.musicartistdatabase.com/

	Home	Top Charts	Artist Pages	Album Pages	Message Boards	Average
Overall Optimization	4	4	4	4	4	4
On-Page/Content Optimization	4	4	3	4	4	4
Keyword Targeting	4	4	2	4	5	4
Title Tags	5	4	4	3	5	4
Meta Descriptions	5	3	3	3	2	3
H1 Tags	3	1	1	1	1	1
Body Text Keywords	5	5	4	5	5	5
Substantive & Unique Content	2	4	4	5	5	4
Image Alt Text	1	4	5	5	5	4
URL Conventions	5	5	3	5	2	4
Keyword Inclusion	5	5	2	4	1	3
Length	4	4	3	5	3	4
Parameters	5	5	5	5	2	4
Information Architecture	5	5	5	5	5	5
Content Hierarchy/Organization	5	4	5	5	5	5
Internal Anchor Text	4	5	5	4	5	5
Robot Control Protocols	5	5	4	5	5	5
Meta Directives	5	5	4	5	5	5
Search Guidelines & Spam Protocol	2	2	3	5	5	3
Canonicalized Site Versions	2	2	3	5	5	3
Canonicalized Duplicate Content	1	2	2	5	4	3
Inbound Links	5	4	4	3	4	4
Linkscape	5	4	4	3	4	4
Linkworthy-ness	5	5	5	5	5	5
Design Quality	4	5	4	4	3	4
User Experience	5	4	3	4	4	4
Value of Content	3	4	4	3	4	4
Sharability/Accessibility	5	5	5	5	5	5
Metrics						
Linkscape Links	120535	125938	150993	153033	154500	141000
Google PageRank	5	4	5	5	5	5
SEOmoz mozRank	5.41	4.46	5.43	4.93	4.94	5
SEOmoz mozTrust	6.29	5.79	6.03	6.06	5.99	6
Technical Issues	3					
Server Response Codes	3					
404 File Not Found	2					
Crawling Problems	4					

Placeholder Consulting

Most Pressing and Valuable Changes

Based on Placeholder Consulting's assessment of MusicArtistDatabase.com, the following changes will make the biggest impact on rankings while taking the least amount of work.

301 redirect /cgi-bin/new/

Currently 13,000 URLs on MusicArtistDatabase.com return a 404 File Not Found HTTP status code. The vast majority of these URLs have at least one link pointing at them. In order to regain this link juice (ranking power), you should 301 redirect http://www.musicartistdatabase.com/cgi-bin/new/* (where * means anything that follows) to http://www.musicartistdatabase.com/*.

One example of this would be 301 redirecting http://www.musicartistdatabase.com/cgi-bin/new/artist/ to http://www.musicartistdatabase.com/artist/.

See the section titled '404 File Not Found' for more information.

Correct canonicalization of domain

MusicArtistDatabase.com renders at either http://www.musicartistdatabase.com/ or http://musicartistdatabase.com/. This is unnecessarily dividing the link value of the given URLs and creating duplicate content problems. In order to fix this, you should choose your preferred URL (http://musicartistdatabase.com or www.musicartistdatabase.com) and 301 redirect one to the other.

For example, if you choose the www version, you would 301 redirect http://musicartistdatabase.com/* to http://www.musicartistdatabase.com/* (where * means any file or directory that follows).

Placeholder Consulting recommends using the 'www' version because it is more familiar to web users and it results in fewer links being wasted due to the addition of a 301 redirect. Additionally, this is recommended because the 'non-www' version of the site has fewer links than the 'www' version and will lose less value when redirected. (301 redirects result in between 1% and 10% of link value being lost. See http://www.seomoz.org/knowledge/redirection for more information).

Correct canonicalization of subsections

Currently MusicArtistDatabase.com has canonicalization problems with its subsections. We recommend correcting this by 301 redirecting the "/" version of the URL to the index.html version of the URL. (This is because the "/" version of the URL has substantially fewer links than the index.html version).

For example:

Placeholder Consulting

- http://www.musicartistdatabase.com/artist/ should 301 redirect to http://www.musicartistdatabase.com/artist/index.html
- http://www.musicartistdatabase.com/top-charts/ should 301 redirect to http://www.musicartistdatabase.com/top-charts/index.html

Make meta descriptions more descriptive

The meta descriptions on MusicArtistDatabase.com are generally too short and not as enticing as they could be to potential website visitors. This has a dramatic effect on the amount of traffic that is referred from search engines.

We recommend making MusicArtistDatabase.com's meta descriptions more enticing to click but still under 155 characters.

See the section titled 'Meta Descriptions' for more information on how to do this.

Clear robots.txt and use "noindex, follow"

Robots.txt is great for stopping search engine crawlers but it does not keep URLs out of their index. Instead, it negates the value of the links on the page. We recommend clearing MusicArtistDatabase.com's robots.txt and instead adding meta robots "noindex, follow" to the applicable directories.

See the section titled 'Robots.txt' for more information.

Placeholder Consulting

Comprehensive Technical SEO Site Audit

On-Page/Content Optimization

Optimizing content is essential for ranking effectively in search engines. The principles covered in this section will help you understand how to do this.

	Home	Top Charts	Artist Pages	Album Pages	Message Boards	Average
On-Page/Content Optimization	4	4	3	4	4	4
Keyword Targeting	4	4	2	4	5	4
Title Tags	5	4	4	3	5	4
Meta Descriptions	5	3	3	3	2	3
H1 Tags	3	1	1	1	1	1
Body Text Keywords	5	5	4	5	5	5
Substantive & Unique Content	2	4	4	5	5	4
Image Alt Text	1	4	5	5	5	4

1234 123th PL NE
Seattle, WA 98000
Phone (555) 555-5555

Placeholder Consulting

Comprehensive Technical SEO Site Audit

Keyword Targeting

	Home	Top Charts	Artist Pages	Album Pages	Message Boards	Average
On-Page/Content Optimization	4	4	3	4	4	4
Keyword Targeting	4	4	2	4	5	4

Keyword targeting is the art of identifying and designing pages that are relevant to the keywords that potential users type into search engines when looking for products and services. A successful targeting strategy is based on competitive research, keyword popularity and relevancy measures. One of the most important on-page SEO factors is keyword usage and targeting.

In order to successfully optimize a website for search engines, keyword research must be employed to determine a keyword or set of keywords that will provide the most value for the page that targets it. These keywords should not be duplicated across multiple pages on the website, but instead exist primarily on the targeted page.

MusicArtistDatabase.com does an inconsistent job (/artist/) of targeting keywords throughout a page. To do this better it needs to use the same target keyword in the URL, title tag, meta description, and body content.

The lack of consistency in this area means there are opportunities to improve specific pages and sections. We've outlined these below:

Keyword Optimization
There are some pages on MusicArtistDatabase.com that are targeting too many keywords. This means that they are not able to target any specific keyword well. Some examples of these are provided below:

- http://www.musicartistdatabase.com/top-charts/top.html
- http://www.musicartistdatabase.com/top-charts/info.php?title=DrumAndBassAndJazzAndPolka
- http://www.musicartistdatabase.com/artist/britney-spears-justin-timberlake.htm

Notice that the keyword inconsistencies are leading to inconsistencies with the anchor text used in inbound links:

Most Common Anchor Text (http://www.musicartistdatabase.com/top-charts/info.php?title=DrumAndBassAndJazzAndPolka

Anchor Text	Total links
MusicArtistDatabase .com - Top Drum and Base	153
Jazz and Pola	103
Drums	45
Drum, Bass, Jazz and Polka	36
Polka Bass	29

Placeholder Consulting

A better optimization scheme would be:

Current URL:

http://www.musicartistdatabase.com/top-charts/info.php?title=DrumAndBassAndJazzAndPolka

Optimal URL:

http://www.musicartistdatabase.com/top-charts/drum-and-bass/

http://www.musicartistdatabase.com/top-charts/jazz/

http://www.musicartistdatabase.com/top-charts/polka/

Current Title Tag:

MusicArtistDatabase.com – Top Drum and Bass and Jazz and Polka!

Optimal Title Tag:

MusicArtistDatabase.com – Top Drum and Bass Artists of 2015

Current Meta Description:

Top artists!

Optimal Meta Description:

Find Out More About The Top Drum and Bass Artists of 2015. Interviews, Photos, Tickets and more.

Action Items
- Run tests on title tags and meta descriptions to find the optimal combinations.
- Do keyword research for product pages and articles and optimize on-page elements to be aligned with more relevant keywords.

Placeholder Consulting

Comprehensive Technical SEO Site Audit

Title Tags

	Home	Top Charts	Artist Pages	Album Pages	Message Boards	Average
On-Page/Content Optimization	4	4	3	4	4	4
Title Tags	5	4	4	3	5	4

The title tag is considered the most important on-page optimization element (behind content) and should have the most important keyword targeted by the page as close to the start of the tag as possible. Title tags should focus on the unique value of the page and not on the topic area of the website as a whole (with the homepage being a notable exception). They are the primary visible element in SERPs (Search Engine Result Pages) and should serve to both brand your site and provide a catchy, yet valuable headline that will entice visitors to click the link. The title tag should contain no more than 70 characters (including spaces).

The title tags on MusicArtistDatabase.com do not follow the recommended SEO best practices (http://www.seomoz.org/knowledge/title-tag). Specifically, the title tags contain sales copy that is usually reserved for meta descriptions. That said, these best practices are not necessarily the best option for all websites.

Because of this, Placeholder Consulting recommends running tests on select content pages to see if adhering to the best practices creates a higher click through rate in the search engines. Specifically, a test should be done on removing the sales copy from the title tags and putting it into meta descriptions. Example test:

Current Title Tag:
MusicArtistDatabase.com – The Beatles. The United Kingdoms Number One Band

Optimal Title Tag:
The Beatles at MusicArtistDatabase.com – Photos, Interviews, Songs, Discography

Current Meta Description:
The Beatles are the world's greatest band and have more number ones than any other band.

Optimal Meta Description:
The Beatles, one of the world's greatest bands, sang the singles X, Y and Z. On Sale Now!

Character Limit
Another area of improvement (although optional) would be to limit the characters of the title tag to 155. In most cases, after 155 characters Google truncates meta descriptions. This is a simple way to clean up your SERPs and help with click throughs to your site.

Comprehensive Technical SEO Site Audit

Placeholder Consulting

Action Items

- Run tests to find optimal title tags for each section on MusicArtistDatabase.com
- Implement site-wide title tag updates based on test results
- Check ranking movements after changes have been indexed

Placeholder Consulting

Comprehensive Technical SEO Site Audit

Meta Descriptions

	Home	Top Charts	Artist Pages	Album Pages	Message Boards	Average
On-Page/Content Optimization	4	4	3	4	4	4
Meta Descriptions	5	3	3	3	2	3

Meta descriptions, while not important for search engine rankings, are extremely important in gaining user click-through from SERPs. These short paragraphs are your opportunity to advertise your content to searchers and let them know you have exactly what they're looking for. The meta description should employ the targeted keywords intelligently in order to create a compelling description that a searcher will want to click. Direct relevance to the page and uniqueness between each page's meta description is key. The description should optimally be between 145 and 155 characters.

The meta descriptions are consistently too short for the pages on MusicArtistDatabase.com. This tag provides the content for free advertisements in search engine results. This makes them tremendously valuable. Below are examples of current meta descriptions as they appear in Google.

Good Examples:

The Beatles ☆
Detailed history with information on their music, movies, news, and latest projects. Images, related links, and a showcase for their albums.
Songs - Albums - Video - Store
www.thebeatles.com/ - Cached - Similar

The Beatles – Free listening, videos, concerts, stats, & pictures ... ☆
May 15, 2010 ... Listen to The Beatles: Come Together, Let It Be & more, plus 748 pictures. The Beatles were an iconic rock group from Liverpool, England.
www.last.fm/music/The+Beatles - Cached - Similar

Poor Examples:

The Beatles: Beatles, Beatles, Beatles! ☆
And now presenting...The Beatles! Great Beatles quotes...the FAB 4 still reigns.
www.musicartistdatabase.com/artists/beatles.html - Cached - Similar

The Beatles ☆
The Beatles were a great band that stunned the world and made it rock. They are best known for their groundbreaking singles which included such hits as ...
The Beatles discography - List of The Beatles songs - Breakup
www.musicartistdatabase.com/artists/beatles_2 - Cached - Similar

The Difference Between The Good and Poor Examples:
The biggest differences between good and poor meta descriptions are readability and the ability to entice users to click. The two good examples (above) meet these criteria because they look like they are written by a person (as opposed to a machine), are compelling advertisements, and get the keyword highlighted multiple times.

Comprehensive Technical SEO Site Audit

Placeholder Consulting

The poor examples do not meet these criteria because they appear spammy ("The Beatles: Beatles, Beatles, Beatles!"), don't entice the user to click ("And now presenting…"), or are cut off before listing important information ("which included such hits as …").

Action Items
- Find a way to programmatically create meta descriptions that are fuller and more enticing.

Placeholder Consulting

Comprehensive Technical SEO Site Audit

H1 Tags

	Home	Top Charts	Artist Pages	Album Pages	Message Boards	Average
On-Page/Content Optimization	4	4	3	4	4	4
H1 Tags	3	1	1	1	1	1

The H1 tag is considered the primary headline of a webpage in semantic markup. It is important for establishing information hierarchy on a webpage but is not largely significant for rankings. Its power is in helping users understand the content of a page for keyword targeting.

On most pages on MusicArtistDatabase.com H1s are not used. Although this does not likely have a huge ranking impact it is still detrimental to users. The following example is for the URL http://www.musicartistdatabase.com/:

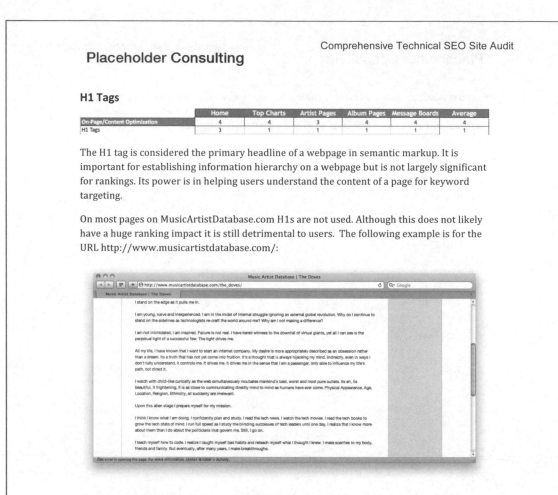

Though not as critical as it once was, HTML headers (H1-H6) should contain valuable keywords that describe the content on the page.

Action Items
- Use <h1> tags on the homepage, top charts, album pages, artist pages, and message board topics.
- Implement secondary HTML headers (H2-H6) when semantically correct.

Comprehensive Technical SEO Site Audit

Placeholder Consulting

Body Text Keywords

	Home	Top Charts	Artist Pages	Album Pages	Message Boards	Average
On-Page/Content Optimization	4	4	3	4	4	4
Body Text Keywords	5	5	4	5	5	5

A page's targeted keywords should be placed throughout the body text a minimum of 2 to 3 times without appearing spammy or "keyword stuffed". Although this isn't highly important for page popularity, it does potentially improve page relevancy and thus helps rankings.

We recommend putting a system in place so that content creators have a clear idea about how to choose search friendly topics and how to work targeted keywords into the text naturally. That said, it is always important to write content for people not just search engines.

Action Items
- Ensure that authors and editors (Album and Artist pages) have the article's keywords in mind while writing/reviewing the given article.

Placeholder Consulting

Substantive & Unique Content

	Home	Top Charts	Artist Pages	Album Pages	Message Boards	Average
On-Page/Content Optimization	4	4	3	4	4	4
Substantive & Unique Content	2	4	4	5	5	4

Search engines place high value on pages that have both substantive and unique content. Each page's content should be specific and relevant to that page's topic as well as add enough information for a user to understand what the page is about.

MusicArtistDatabase.com excels at having rich content (Album and Artist pages) by having many qualified authors.

Recency of Page Creation

The more often a site provides new unique content, the more frequent the search engine crawlers will likely return to the given website to check for new pages. This is beneficial because it reflects favorably on the website and gives it more potential pages to rank with.

One publicly documented component of Google's algorithm is called QDF or "Query Deserves Freshness". This piece of the overall algorithm prioritizes content for queries that are best answered with frequently updated content. When the engines recognize that the best results for a certain query may change frequently, they identify the query as QDF.

This helps promote new, related content from trusted sources (like MusicArtistDatabase.com) to the top of the SERP, even if it doesn't have a lot of links. For a full description of QDF see this Whiteboard Friday Video.

Action Items

- Create articles that target specific search queries. These should act like landing pages that help users find relevant content and products on MusicArtistDatabase.com.
- Write content based on news stories to attract QDF advantages.

Placeholder Consulting

Comprehensive Technical SEO Site Audit

Image Alt Attribute

	Home	Top Charts	Artist Pages	Album Pages	Message Boards	Average
On-Page/Content Optimization	4	4	3	4	4	4
Image Alt Text	1	4	5	5	5	4

Image alt tags, content close in proximity to the given image, and filenames are the primary ranking factors for image search traffic. Additionally, they can assist with traditional optimization for web search results.

Correlation tests at SEOmoz showed that the use of keyword rich image alt text correlates with higher rankings in for non-image search results. The correlation data showed that alt attributes were a much more important metric for high rankings than we originally thought. While correlation is not causation, it is unwise to ignore the data. Therefore, we recommend the use of good images with good alt text for pages seeking to rank on competitive queries.

For more information on this topic, see http://www.seomoz.org/knowledge/on-page-factors.

MusicArtistDatabase.com does an excellent job of ensuring that every image has alt text. The one notable exception to this is the homepage. When adding the alt attribute to images use keyword rich text that describes whatever is featured in the given image.

Action Items
- Add alt text to the images on the homepage.
- Ensure that alt text describes images in addition to being keyword rich.

Placeholder Consulting

Comprehensive Technical SEO Site Audit

URL Conventions

	Home	Top Charts	Artist Pages	Album Pages	Message Boards	Average
URL Conventions	5	5	3	5	2	4
Keyword Inclusion	5	5	2	4	1	3
Length	4	4	3	5	3	4
Parameters	5	5	5	5	2	4

There are a number of factors in a URL that can help or harm a webpage's ability to rank for target keywords.

Overall, MusicArtistDatabase.com scores relatively well for URL conventions with an average between 2 and 5. While most of the important URL factors are done according to SEO best practices, there remain some issues with the Artist and Message Board subsections.

Placeholder Consulting

Comprehensive Technical SEO Site Audit

Keyword Inclusion

	Home	Top Charts	Artist Pages	Album Pages	Message Boards	Average
URL Conventions	5	5	3	5	2	4
Keyword Inclusion	5	5	2	4	1	3

Placing keywords in the URL creates on-site relevancy, improves search engine result click-throughs, and provides good anchor text when URLs are copied and pasted on other websites. Where possible, the primary keywords should be used in the page filename and the secondary keyword should be used in subfolder names. (e.g. http://www.musicartistdatabase.com/secondary-keyword/primary-keyword.html).

Supersite

The supersite subsection could improve in its URL conventions.

Current URL:

http://www.musicartistdatabase.com/artist/britney-spears-justin-timberlake.htm

Optimal URL:

http://www.musicartistdatabase.com/artist/britney-spears.htm
http://www.musicartistdatabase.com/artist/justin-timberlake.htm

Message Board

Similarly, the message board subsection does not have the optimal URL convention. This is likely inherent to the message board CMS (content management system). If the opportunity arises to install a new message board CMS, creating better URLs should be a priority.

Current URL:

http://forum.musicartistdatabase.com/showthread.php?t=12075411

Better URL:

http://www.musicartistdatabase.com/forum/thread.php?t=title-of-thread&id=120875411

Optimal URL:

http://www.musicartistdatabase.com/forum/title-of-thread/

Action Items
- Consider moving Message Board to a subfolder rather than a subdomain.
- Consider migrating to a new message board CMS or finding a plug-in for the current one that allows for more SEO friendly URLs.

Placeholder Consulting

Comprehensive Technical SEO Site Audit

URL Length

URL Conventions	Home	Top Charts	Artist Pages	Album Pages	Message Boards	Average
URL Conventions	5	5	3	5	2	4
Length	4	4	3	5	3	4

According to correlation tests performed by our SEOmoz Linkscape engineers, shorter URLs tend to rank higher in Google than equivalent pages with longer URLs. Because of this, we recommend keeping URLs below 74 characters so the entire URL is displayed on SERPs without truncation. In addition to search result rankings, short URLs are better for usability, click-through rates, and linkability. The shorter the URL, the easier to copy and paste, read over the phone, write down, or use in any other unusual way.

MusicArtistDatabase.com scores an average of 4 on URL length. There is room for improvement moving forward, but changes should **not** be made to existing content. In the future, MusicArtistDatabase.com could improve URL length by thinking more about short and keyword filenames (page level), removing file extensions, and eliminating stop words from URLs.

Below are example pages on MusicArtistDatabase.com that have subpar URL lengths. The bold characters are in excess of the optimal 74 character limit.

- http://www.musicartistdatabase.com/artist/info.php?page=BritneySpears&ord**er= ORDER+by+date+DESC** (furthermore, a canonical tag should be added to these URLs that dictate sorting order)

- http://forum.musicartistdatabase.com/photo/showphoto.php?photo=32345753&u **ser=2108165**

Action Items
- Consider removing file extensions (e.g. .html)
- Eliminate stop words from filenames. There is a good list here of stop words.
- Add a canonical tag to URLs with parameters that dictate sorting order.

Placeholder Consulting

URL Parameters

	Home	Top Charts	Artist Pages	Album Pages	Message Boards	Average
URL Conventions	5	5	3	5	2	4
Parameters	5	5	5	5	2	4

Search engine representatives have been quite straightforward with regard to parameter usage in URLs. Their crawlers can parse and navigate parameter driven URLs but it is much more difficult (and thus less accurate) and often leads to duplicate content issues. SEOmoz correlation data also suggests that parameter heavy URLs are treated less favorably than those without. For this reason, parameters should be used sparingly.

MusicArtistDatabase.com scored well for URL parameters in all areas except Message Board. Unfortunately, this is common across the web as it is more convenient to implement forums with URL parameters than it is with other technical solutions.

Action Items

- Find and install a forum plug-in that reduces the amount parameters used in URLs going forward.

Placeholder Consulting

Comprehensive Technical SEO Site Audit

Information Architecture

	Home	Top Charts	Artist Pages	Album Pages	Message Boards	Average
Information Architecture	5	5	5	5	5	5
Content Hierarchy/Organization	5	4	5	5	5	5
Internal Anchor Text	4	5	5	4	5	5

The information architecture and internal linking structure of a website helps to organize, identify, and prioritize the site's content for users and search engines. The manner in which site navigation is handled, the frequency and relative weight/importance of internal links, and internal anchor text all play a critical role in search engine optimization effectiveness.

Information architecture, as it relates to a website, is an approach to content design that involves technical, aesthetic, and functional criteria. When done well, the focus of each page and subsection on a given website is clear and readily apparent. This requires particular attention to content, business needs, usability, interaction design, keyword usage, and web design. For effective SEO, it is necessary to have an appreciation of how a single website, as well as an individual webpage, relate to the rest of the World Wide Web.

Website information architectures are often organized into categories and sub-categories and reflected in a variety of ways, including navigational structure, breadcrumbs, URL sub-folder structure, sitemaps, and various linking practices. As each page serves a purpose within a website's page-flow and navigation process, it is important to view the page as a potential entry point from external traffic referral sources, such as search engines.

Placeholder Consulting

Content Hierarchy/Organization

	Home	Top Charts	Artist Pages	Album Pages	Message Boards	Average
Information Architecture	5	5	5	5	5	5
Content Hierarchy/Organization	5	4	5	5	5	5

The content hierarchy of a site can be outlined with a clear navigational structure. Generally this takes the form of breadcrumbs, URL sub-folders, and navigation menus. The following questions best define what an SEO might think when viewing a website from a content hierarchy perspective.

1. Are there clearly defined groupings of content?

2. Is there a logical page-flow and organization of the content?

3. Does every page sit at the same level or are they in a proper hierarchy?

MusicArtistDatabase.com does a great job of categorizing content into logical categories and sub-categories based on the subject level taxonomy and the URL structure that reflects the differences between the four major sections of the website.

That said, one of the most significant faults on MusicArtistDatabase.com is the lack of a universal global navigation menu. While each section has a its own navigation (on the left) and each major section is linked to (on the top) there is no interaction between the two navigation menus that gives the user some idea of where they are on the site in relation to everything else.

Action Items
- Consider adding a true global navigation to the site
- Limit links per page to less than 100

Placeholder Consulting

Internal Anchor Text

	Home	Top Charts	Artist Pages	Album Pages	Message Boards	Average
Information Architecture	5	5	5	5	5	5
Internal Anchor Text	4	5	5	4	5	5

Internal anchor text is the words used in links that point to another page on the same domain. They are important to humans and robots because they give some hint to where the link will take them.

For engines, internal links are especially important because they give hints on how information is related.

MusicArtistDatabase.com generally does a good job with this. Its only area for improvement would be implementing Wikipedia style internal links that link to special keyword specific pages every time they are used. This boosts the relevancy and internal popularity of a given website.

Action Items
- Consider implementing Wikipedia style internal links in Artist and Album pages to compete more for highly competitive terms.

Placeholder Consulting

Comprehensive Technical SEO Site Audit

Robots Control Protocols

	Home	Top Charts	Artist Pages	Album Pages	Message Boards	Average
Robot Control Protocols	5	5	4	5	5	5
Meta Directives	5	5	4	5	5	5

There are a number of ways that webmasters can control the robots that crawl their sites. The most SEO friendly ways to do this are meta directives, robots.txt, and sitemaps.

Placeholder Consulting

Meta Directives

	Home	Top Charts	Artist Pages	Album Pages	Message Boards	Average
Robot Control Protocols	5	5	4	5	5	5
Meta Directives	5	5	4	5	5	5

A meta tag with the "robots" parameter is used to control search engine robots on the page level. The meta tag should be placed within the <head> tag and each directive should be comma delimited. There are three main directives that we recommend using as needed:

```
<meta name='robots' content='noindex,follow' />
<meta name='robots' content='noydir' />
<meta name='robots' content='noodp' />
```

(Note that the "index, follow" directive is the default behavior and as such is not listed here. Including it on a webpage is not necessary.)

The "noindex, follow" directive is extremely useful because it keeps specific pages out of search engine indices while allowing the bots to crawl the links within the page. This ensures that the link juice flows throughout the site. This is a better choice than using robots.txt to keep pages out of a search engine.

The use of the meta robots tag protocol for "noydir" prevents a listing from the Yahoo! directory for your site/page from showing in the SERPs. Similarly the "noodp" directive prevents DMOZ.org listings from showing.

MusicArtistDatabase.com implements the following variation of this on many of its pages:

```
<meta name='robots' content='all' />
```

This tag tells search engine robots that they are allowed to index and follow all of the content on the given pages. This is the default behavior which means that the inclusion of this tag is useless. While it certainly doesn't hurt, it also isn't helpful. If bandwidth is an issue, it may be wise to remove this tag so that less code is on each page.

Action Items
- Consider removing the meta robots tag from applicable pages.

Placeholder Consulting   Comprehensive Technical SEO Site Audit

Robots.txt

Robots.txt allows webmasters to control how search engine robots access their sites. If a URL is listed in a properly setup robots.txt file, the engines will not index the content of the page but will still potentially include the URL of page in their search results. For this reason, we recommend using the meta robots tag with the "noindex, follow" directive for keeping pages out of the index.

The current robots.txt file on MusicArtistDatabase.com looks like this:

```
http://www.seomoz.org/robots.txt
+  http://www.musicartistdatabase.com/robots.txt          C   Q- Google

http://www.seomoz.org/robots.txt

User-agent: *
Disallow: /artist-profile/
```

As you can see this URL is still in Google's index:

Google   site:www.musicartistdatabase.com   Search
          About 1,590 results (0.20 seconds)   Advanced search

Everything   www.musicartistdatabase.com/artist-profile/
More   - Similar

Regardless of the reason for blocking these pages, the best way to ensure that they do not get into the search engine indices is to remove them from the robots.txt and instead add a meta robots "noindex, follow" tag to the applicable pages. This is a better execution of blocking robots because it keeps the URLs out of the indices and maintains the value of the links on the pages.

Action Items

Comprehensive Technical SEO Site Audit

Placeholder Consulting

- Set robots.txt to "Disallow:" (which means disallow nothing.)
- Add meta robots with the "noindex, follow" directive to the URLs currently listed in MusicArtistDatabase's robots.txt file.

Comprehensive Technical SEO Site Audit

Placeholder Consulting

XML Sitemap

XML Sitemaps assist the search engines with crawling and discovering of pages on a site.

MusicArtistDatabase.com currently does not have a sitemap:

This is perfectly acceptable given the indexation of MusicArtistDatabase.com's pages. No further action is required in this area.

Action Items
- None

1234 123th PL NE
Seattle, WA 98000
Phone (555) 555-5555

Placeholder Consulting

Technical Issues

Technical Issues	3
Server Response Codes	3
404 File Not Found	2
Crawling Problems	4

Many technical issues with MusicArtistDatabase.com can be found in Google Webmaster Tools. Fixing these errors will improve your site for both users and search engines.

Placeholder Consulting

Server Response Codes

Technical Issues	3
Server Response Codes	3

It is important to ensure that the correct server response codes are returned when crawlers and humans access a website. We provide brief specific details about each of the most common throughout this section. You can find more information about HTTP Status codes at http://www.seomoz.org/knowledge/http-status-code.

200 OK
The request has succeeded. The request is successful and the page displays correctly.

404 File Not Found
The server has not found anything matching the requested URI. No indication is given about whether the condition is temporary or permanent. This should occur any time the server couldn't find a matching page request. Often times, sites display 404 error pages but return the HTTP response code as a 200. This tells the bots that the page has rendered correctly and the page will get erroneously indexed.

301 Moved Permanently
The requested resource has been assigned a new permanent URI and any future references to this resource *should* use one of the returned URIs. The 301 redirect should be utilized any time you need to point one URL to another.

503 Service Unavailable
The server is currently unable to handle the request due to temporary overloading or maintenance of the server. The 503 should be used whenever there is a temporary outage. For example, if the server has to go down for a short period of maintenance, this would ensure that the engines know to come back soon because the page or site is only unavailable for a short time.

Action Items
- None

Placeholder Consulting

404 File Not Found

Technical Issues	3
404 File Not Found	2

MusicArtistDatabase.com has approximately 13,000 pages that are returning 404 response codes. As a result of this, none of these pages are indexed or spreading their link value. This is a high priority that should be fixed.

The table below shows the top 15 most important URLs according to the amount of links pointing at them. This is a sample that is intended to show you the amount of link value that is being wasted.

URL	Linked From	
http://www.musicartistdatabase.com/cgi-bin/artist/the-beatles.htm	199 pages	12/4/15
http://www.musicartistdatabase.com/cgi-bin/artist/Britney-spears.htm	189 pages	12/6/15
http://www.musicartistdatabase.com/cgi-bin/artist/madonna.htm	188 pages	12/4/15
http://www.musicartistdatabase.com/cgi-bin/artist/Justin-timberlake.htm	178 pages	12/4/15
http://www.musicartistdatabase.com/cgi-bin/artist/nsync.htm	178 pages	12/2/15
http://www.musicartistdatabase.com/cgi-bin/artist/backstreet-boys.php	169 pages	12/4/15
http://www.musicartistdatabase.com/cgi-bin/artist/miley-cyrus.htm	132 pages	12/4/15
http://www.musicartistdatabase.com/cgi-bin/artist/taylor-swift.htm	107 pages	12/11/15
http://www.musicartistdatabase.com/cgi-bin/artist/jayz.htm	98 pages	12/4/15
http://www.musicartistdatabase.com/cgi-bin/artist/pdiddy.htm	98 pages	12/4/15
http://www.musicartistdatabase.com/cgi-bin/artist/bob-dylan.htm	98 pages	12/4/15

Placeholder Consulting

Comprehensive Technical SEO Site Audit

http://www.musicartistdatabase.com/cgi-bin/artist/owl-city.htm	97 pages	12/4/15
http://www.musicartistdatabase.com/cgi-bin/artist/beach-boys.htm	97 pages	12/4/15
http://www.musicartistdatabase.com/cgi-bin/artist/del-la-vega.htm	96 pages	12/4/15
http://www.musicartistdatabase.com/cgi-bin/artist/bob-marley.htm	96 pages	12/4/15

Note: see addendum 404-pages.csv for complete list

Action Items

- 301 redirect the /cgi-bin/artist/ directory to /artist/ to regain these links.
- Wherever possible, correct internal link to a URL that doesn't result in an error.

1234 123th PL NE
Seattle, WA 98000
Phone (555) 555-5555

Placeholder Consulting

404 Page

MusicArtistDatabase.com's 404 pages are not as helpful to users as they can be.

A better 404 page would give suggestions to the user of what they might be looking for and highlight the internal search bar.

Action Items

- 301 redirect any highly linked 404 pages to relevant pages (see addendum).
- Wherever possible, correct internal links to pages that have errors.

Placeholder Consulting

Crawling Problems

Technical Issues	3
Crawling Problems	4

A site must be crawlable in order for the search engines to reach all of its pages. The data below is from Google Webmaster Tools and shows various crawl issues that Google encountered when crawling MusicArtistDatabase.com.

HTTP

According to Google, MusicArtistDatabase.com has five HTTP problems. They are listed in the table in this section. Note the erroneous spelling of 'artist' in the first 4 URLs. The fifth URL is likely a bad parameter link. Errors like this are typical with domains with as many pages as MusicArtistDatabase.com

URL	Detail	Detected
http://www.musicartistdatabase.com/cgi-bin/artisst/	403 error	Dec 5, 2015
http://www.musicartistdatabase.com/cgi-bin/artissst/search.htm	403 error	Dec 4, 2015
http://www.musicartistdatabase.com/cgi-bin/artisst/search/.http://message-board.MusicArtistDatabase.com	403 error	Dec 14, 2015
http://www.musicartistdatabase.com/artisst/.htm	403 error	Dec 8, 2015
http://www.musicartistdatabase.com/artist/cypress-hill.htm?nav=%3Chr%20noshade%20width=30%%20align=left%3EPentru	400 error	Dec 9, 2015

Not followed

MusicArtistDatabase.com has 125 URLs that were not crawled by Google due to redirection errors. We researched these and determined that these URLs are 301 redirected to themselves and as such caused an infinite loop.

See the table in this section for a sample of these errors. The complete list can be found in addendum no-follow.csv.

URL	Detail	Detected
http://www.musicartistdatabase.com/artist//history.php?Real_Old=%3C%207&start=110&Name=&Nerds=&Equip=Piano&Isolation=Compound&order=Kind	Redirect error	Dec 9, 2015

1234 123th PL NE
Seattle, WA 98000
Phone (555) 555-5555

Placeholder Consulting

URL	Detail	Detected
http://www.musicartistdatabase.com/artist//history.php?Real_Old=%3C=%207&start=110&Name=&MainMusic=Guitar&Equip=Piano&Isolation=&order=Kind	Redirect error	Dec 3, 2015
http://www.musicartistdatabase.com/artist/miley.php	Redirect error	Dec 12, 2015
http://www.musicartistdatabase.com/artist/mgmt.php?Equip=&MainMuscle=	Redirect error	Dec 4, 2015
http://www.musicartistdatabase.com/artist/disney.php?Equip=&Goo	Redirect error	Dec 2, 2015

Not Found

Google reports 13,220 404 errors on MusicArtistDatabase.com. Please see the section titled '404 File Not Found' for more information. The complete list of 404 error pages can be found in addendum 404-pages.csv.

Restricted by robots.txt

There are 891 linked to pages on MusicArtistDatabase.com that are blocked by robots.txt. Please see the section titled 'robots.txt' in Robots Control Protocols for more information.

The table in this section contains a sample of these pages. The complete list can be found in Addendum robots-txt.csv.

URL	Detail	Detected
http://www.musicartistdatabase.com/artist-profile/shakira.htm	URL restricted by robots.txt	Dec 2, 2015
http://www.musicartistdatabase.com/artist-profile/madonna.htm	URL restricted by robots.txt	Dec 14, 2015
http://www.musicartistdatabase.com/artist-profile/elton-john.htm	URL restricted by robots.txt	Dec 12, 2015
http://www.musicartistdatabase.com/artist-profile/michael-jackson.htm	URL restricted by robots.txt	Dec 2, 2015
http://www.musicartistdatabase.com/artist-profile/usher.htm	URL restricted by robots.txt	Dec 2, 2015

1234 123th PL NE
Seattle, WA 98000
Phone (555) 555-5555

Placeholder Consulting

Comprehensive Technical SEO Site Audit

Unreachable

Google indicated seven pages that were unreachable due to server errors. We checked these URLs and were able to reach all of the URLs except the ones that included "print-friendly.php".

See the table in this section for a sample of these errors. The complete list can be found in addendum unreachable.csv.

URL	Detail	Detected
http://www.musicartistdatabase.com/album/display.php?s=&id=31	Network unreachable	Dec 14, 2015
http://www.musicartistdatabase.com/album//pop.php?Name=Abba	Network unreachable	Dec 2, 2015
http://www.musicartistdatabase.com/album//pop.php?Name=MJ	Network unreachable	Dec 2, 2015
http://www.musicartistdatabase.com/album//print-friendly.php?Type=Artist	No response	Dec 14, 2015
http://www.musicartistdatabase.com/album//print-friendly.php?Type=Album	No response	Dec 12, 2015

Action Items

- Fix the 301 redirects in the section, Nofollowed
- Revaluate the use of robots.txt (See robot.txt section in Robots Control Protocols)
- Determine what is wrong with the pages in Unreachable and fix the problem
- Analyze the links listed in the addendums

Placeholder Consulting

Search Guidelines & Spam Protocols

	Home	Top Charts	Artist Pages	Album Pages	Message Boards	Average
Search Guidelines & Spam Protocol	2	2	3	5	5	3
Canonicalized Site Versions	2	2	3	5	5	3
Canonicalized Duplicate Content	1	2	2	5	4	3

This section covers a variety of factors that search engines have published stances on.

Comprehensive Technical SEO Site Audit

Placeholder Consulting

Canonicalized Site Versions

	Home	Top Charts	Artist Pages	Album Pages	Message Boards	Average
Search Guidelines & Spam Protocol	2	2	3	5	5	3
Canonicalized Site Versions	2	2	3	5	5	3

Canonicalization is the practice of making a given URL only accessible from one URL (i.e http://www.example.com and http://example.com,). When this does not happen, the search engines have to guess which version of a URL is the main (or canonical) version of a webpage. This commonly causes ranking issues.

Currently the 'www' subdomain of MusicArtistDatabase.com has a canonicalization problem.

We recommend making http://musicartistdatabase.com 301 redirect to http://www.musicartistdatabase.com. This will consolidate the links that are going to each version of the applicable pages. Looking at the link profiles of these pages shows that the 'www' version has considerably more links than the 'non-www' version. As such, we recommend 301 redirecting the 'non-www' version to the 'www' version URL. This is because when adding a 301 redirect, between 1 and 10% of the link juice is eliminated so the version with the least number of links (least potential loss) should be redirected.

URL	URL mozRank	Domain mozRank
http://www.musicartistdatabase.com/	6.55	6.37
http://musicartistdatabase.com/	4.75	5.16

Action Items

- 301 Redirect http://musicartistdatabase.com to http://www.musicartistdatabase.com.

Placeholder Consulting

Canonicalized Duplicate Content

	Home	Top Charts	Artist Pages	Album Pages	Message Boards	Average
Search Guidelines & Spam Protocol	2	2	3	5	5	3
Canonicalized Duplicate Content	1	2	2	5	4	3

If a unique piece of content is accessible at multiple URLs, these URLs should be canonicalized for search engines. This can be accomplished using a 301 redirect from the uneeded URL to the correct URL, or by using the rel canonical tag (when both URLs need to stay operational). (See http://www.seomoz.org/knowledge/canonicalization)

There is a current effort at MusicArtistDatabase.com to eliminate some of the duplicate content on the domain (print-friendly pages for example). This is a positive step in the right direction.

In addition to the ongoing efforts, it is also a good idea to canonicalize URLs that have differences in capitalization.

It is possible for users to link to certain pages on MusicArtistDatabase.com using the wrong URL character case. Currently, if a user gets to a URL in the wrong case they get the 404 page. When this happens, it is optimal to use the 301 in order to keep the link juice flowing and show the user the page they intended to see.

Some examples of this include:

- All of the articles in the /album/ directory (http://www.musicartistdatabase.com/album/) are case sensitive.
- All of the products in the /artist/ directory (http://www.musicartistdatabase.com/artist/) are case sensitive.

Action Items
- In the case where a URL with capitalization problems 404s, make it 301
- In the case where a URL with capitalization problems doesn't 404, add the canonical tag (This includes print friendly pages, sorting pages, etc...)

Comprehensive Technical SEO Site Audit

Placeholder Consulting

"Search Results" Page Exclusion

Based on Google's Webmaster guidelines, internal "search results" as content should be kept out of the search engine indices.

The internal search results pages for MusicArtistDatabase.com are being disallowed. We recommend adding the meta robots "noindex, follow" directive and removing the "search.musicartistdatabase.com" subdomain specific robots.txt entry to fully prevent the pages from getting indexed.

Erroneous robots.txt configuration for search specific robots.txt
(http://search.musicartistdatabase.com/robots.txt)

Action Items

- Remove the disallow at http://search.musicartistdatabase.com/robots.txt
- Add the meta robots tag to search result pages with the parameters "noindex, follow"

1234 123th PL NE
Seattle, WA 98000
Phone (555) 555-5555

Placeholder Consulting

Link Acquisition Practices

Buying links, selling links, employing link farms, link exchange programs, and manipulatively placing links on pages without the consent of the site owner are all against the search engines' terms of service and may result in penalization or banning. You can read more about this in the Google's Webmaster guidelines.

We haven't found any issues with MusicArtistDatabase.com's link acquisition practices. We recommend continuing the good work you are already excelling at.

Action Items
- None

Placeholder Consulting

Comprehensive Technical SEO Site Audit

Inbound Links

Inbound links encompass the most important metrics for determining rankings. The first step to understanding these link profiles is to get lists of links.

Open Site Explorer

SEOmoz's free Open Site Explorer provides a powerful way to look at link data. In addition to providing competitive link data to identify the strategies of other sites, Open Site Explorer also allows you to analyze the links to your site and look at dimensions such as link quality, link anchor text, and the most linked to pages on your domain. Listed below are the 25 most important links to MusicArtistDatabase.com according to Open Site Explorer.

#	Source URL	Target URL	mozRank Passed	Anchor Text
1	careers.musicartistdatabase.com/	www.musicartistdatabase.com/	6.39	
2	forum.musicartistdatabase.com/terms_of_use.php	www.musicartistdatabase.com/legal/	6.36	here
3	www.musicartistdatabase.com/	www.musicartistdatabase.com/career.htm	5.60	careers
4	www.musicartistdatabase.com/	forum.musicartistdatabase.com/	5.59	Message boards over 30 million posts and 1.8 million members! Get your questions...
5	www.musicartistdatabase.com/	www.musicartistdatabase.com/login.php?do=loctpw	5.59	forgot your password?
6	www.musicartistdatabase.com/	www.musicartistdatabase.com/artist/	5.59	Music Artists
7	www.musicartistdatabase.com/	www.musicartistdatabase.com/top-charts/index.html	5.59	Top Charts over 5,000 pages of top songs and albums
8	www.musicartistdatabase.com/	careers.musicartistdatabase.com/	5.59	careers
9	www.musicartistdatabase.com/	www.musicartistdatabase.com/sign-up	5.59	it's free!
10	www.musicartistdatabase.com/	www.musicartistdatabase.com/help.htm	5.59	help
11	www.musicartistdatabase.com/	www.musicartistdatabase.com/contact.htm	5.59	Contact us
12	www.musicartistdatabase.com/	www.musicartistdatabase.com/album/index.html	5.59	Over 8,500 album reviews
13	www.musicartistdatabase.com/	www.musicartistdatabase.com/search.html	5.59	search
14	www.musicartistdatabase.com/	www.musicartistdatabase.com/help/	5.59	feedback?
15	www.musicartistdatabase.com/top-charts/top.php	www.musicartistdatabase.com/career.htm	5.45	careers
16	www.musicartistdatabase.com/top-charts/top.php	www.musicartistdatabase.com/	5.43	home
17	www.musicartistdatabase.com/top-charts/top.php	www.musicartistdatabase.com/terms_of_use.php	5.43	terms of use
18	www.musicartistdatabase.com/top-charts/top.php	www.musicartistdatabase.com/album/about.htm	5.43	about us
19	www.musicartistdatabase.com/top-charts/top.php	careers.musicartistdatabase.com/	5.43	careers

1234 123th PL NE
Seattle, WA 98000
Phone (555) 555-5555

Placeholder Consulting

Comprehensive Technical SEO Site Audit

20	www.musicartistdatabase.com/top-charts/top.php	www.musicartistdatabase.com/cart/login_form.php	5.43	log-in
21	www.musicartistdatabase.com/top-charts/top.php	www.musicartistdatabase.com/search.html	5.43	search
22	www.musicartistdatabase.com/top-charts/top.php	www.musicartistdatabase.com/top-charts/listing.htm	5.43	products
23	www.musicartistdatabase.com/top-charts/top.php	www.musicartistdatabase.com/faq.htm	5.43	click for help
24	www.musicartistdatabase.com/top-charts/top.php	www.musicartistdatabase.com/email.htm	5.43	contact us
25	www.musicartistdatabase.com/top-charts/top.php	www.musicartistdatabase.com/index.html	5.43	store

Based on the above data from Open Site Explorer, we've discovered some notable aspects of MusicArtistDatabase.com's link profile.

First, MusicArtistDatabase.com is wasting a tremendous amount of link juice on its terms of use. This is likely a result of a footer link on every page. This is one extra link on every page that is going to pages that don't need to rank. The solution to this is to either remove the links (if legally viable) or embed them in obfuscated Javascript so that the engines can't follow them.

Secondly, your website is stifling a lot of potential by using and linking to the careers subdomain. This subdomain is being linked to in the footer of every page and on the sidebar of some subsections. This is a lot of wasted link juice as this subdomain is competing with other more important pages.

Thirdly, the most power links to MusicArtistDatabase.com are coming from within itself. This is due to its strength and use of subdomains. This shows that the domain could do much better if it got links from domains equal to or more powerful than MusicArtistDatabase.com. While this is always a good idea, it is a especially a good idea in MusicArtistDatabase.com's case because given its odd link profile (no links stronger than itself) it might lift any minor filters that are holding the domain back.

Action Items

- Obfuscate the links that are pointing at the career and terms of use pages. (Alternatively, you could redirect these pages to something related that you want to rank for)
- Redirect careers.musicartistdatabase.com to www.musicartistdatabase.com/careers/ or convert this subdomain into something that is worthy of ranking (a job board?)
- Focus link building efforts on getting strong links from domains stronger (in mozRank) than MusicArtistDatabase.com.

Placeholder Consulting

Comprehensive Technical SEO Site Audit

Link-worthiness

	Home	Top Charts	Artist Pages	Album Pages	Message Boards	Average
Linkworthy-ness	5	5	5	5	5	5
Design Quality	4	5	4	4	3	4
User Experience	5	4	3	4	4	4
Value of Content	3	4	4	3	4	4
Sharability/Accessibility	5	5	5	5	5	5

SEO experts estimate that links make up about 70% of all Google ranking factors. (Source: http://www.seomoz.org/article/search-ranking-factors) As such, it is extremely important that the content of a website is worthy of receiving links. This section explains how to do this.

Placeholder Consulting

Design Quality

	Home	Top Charts	Artist Pages	Album Pages	Message Boards	Average
Linkworthy-ness	5	5	5	5	5	5
Design Quality	4	5	4	4	3	4

This measurement quantifies how well the graphical representation of ideas and messages are able to communicate the given message. This takes into account text, images, page layout, and symbols.

Improving the design of MusicArtistDatabase.com would likely have very positive impacts on SEO. In particular, creating more visually compelling images on both album pages and individual artist pages would decrease bounce rates and increase revenue.

Artist pages could be further enhanced by visual representations of data such as images, charts, and graphs. Good examples of sites that do graphical data well include Mint.com (http://www.mint.com/blog/) and Zillow (http://www.zillow.com/local-info/WA-Seattle-home-value/r_16037/). These examples are extremely link worthy and as such have earned a lot of links and ranking value for their creators.

Action Items
- Use visual representation of data and include more relevant photos on artist pages.

Comprehensive Technical SEO Site Audit

Placeholder Consulting

User Experience

	Home	Top Charts	Artist Pages	Album Pages	Message Boards	Average
Linkworthy-ness	5	5	5	5	5	5
User Experience	5	4	3	4	4	4

In this context, user experience refers to the science of studying human interaction with websites. It includes elements of usability design and social science.

MusicArtistDatabase.com has a lot of great content but the discoverability and presentation of content could be improved. In addition to a cleaner UI (User Interface) and first time visitor treatments, a number of steps could be taken to improve navigation throughout the site. Some of the most important steps are listed in this section:

Recommend Target Areas:
1. Consider making the content section wider (like the message board). This will help keep the content from feeling cluttered.
2. Consider making a custom user experience for first time visitors. It shouldn't be invasive but should alert them of deals and helpful content and pages. It is important it is a helpful tool rather than a roadblock.
3. Make breadcrumbs more prominent (bigger and add more contrast). These could be very useful tools for the user but are currently hidden in the mass of text.
4. Reduce the ratio of text to non-text to increase whitespace and the readability of pages.

Action Items
- See Recommend Target Areas above

Placeholder Consulting

Comprehensive Technical SEO Site Audit

Value of Content

	Home	Top Charts	Artist Pages	Album Pages	Message Boards	Average
Linkworthy-ness	5	5	5	5	5	5
Value of Content	3	4	4	3	4	4

Highly valuable content attracts links and improves rankings.

Valuable content is one of the best aspects of MusicArtistDatabase.com. Discoverability and consumption, however, are each major areas that need improvement. Due to limitations in content presentation, the value of content is likely not being fully discovered by site visitors.

The biggest area of focus should be on improving the presentation of what is already great content. A couple of areas where content restructuring would be effective to increase perceived content value include step-by-step/how-to and news presentation.

Improve article consumption by including step-by-step and how-to articles formatting. A good example of a site that does this well is Gentleman Joe with its how to tie a tie (http://www.gentlemanjoe.com/how-to-tie.php) section. On MusicArtistDatabase.com a helpful example of this might be How to Legally Burn a CD.

The perceived value of the articles could be increased through more news-like presentation of data. This could include top ten lists, best articles, artist little known facts, common myths, and other interesting/helpful data.

Action Items
- Improve content consumption by including more step-by-step and how-to type articles.
- Strive for more news-like presentation of data and content. This is a format that the public has been conditioned to think is worth reading.

Placeholder Consulting

Share-ability/Accessibility

	Home	Top Charts	Artist Pages	Album Pages	Message Boards	Average
Linkworthy-ness	5	5	5	5	5	5
Sharability/Accessibility	5	5	5	5	5	5

Share-ability and accessibility refer to how easily a visitor can reach and spread content to other people through avenues like social media, e-mail, and word of mouth.

Currently MusicArtistDatabase.com does a great job of this. All of the content is open to the public and multiple share widgets are available.

Action Items

- Consider making the "sharethis" feature more prominent.

Placeholder Consulting

Metrics

Metrics	Home	Top Charts	Artist Pages	Album Pages	Message Boards	Average
Linkscape Links	120535	125938	150993	153033	154500	141000
Google PageRank	5	4	5	5	5	5
SEOmoz mozRank	5.41	4.46	5.43	4.93	4.94	5
SEOmoz mozTrust	6.29	5.79	6.03	6.06	5.99	6

Search engines use link popularity data to help determine if and when a website should rank for a given search query. The quality of backlinks is more important than sheer quantity, but it's important to track all of the link values. As the numbers typically vary based on the tool used to calculate this metric, it is good to use a number of sources. Although the number of inbound links is not necessarily accurate, the relationships they reveal are extremely important.

1234 123th PL NE
Seattle, WA 98000
Phone (555) 555-5555

Placeholder Consulting

Linkscape Links

Metrics	Home	Top Charts	Artist Pages	Album Pages	Message Boards	Average
Linkscape Links	120535	125938	150993	153033	154500	141000

Linkscape is the database that provides the data for Open Site Explorer. It provides access to link data from trillions of URLs across hundreds of millions of domains. Linkscape's link data offers webmasters the ability to analyze how many unique links are pointing at their domain, subdomain, and specific pages on their website.

According to this tool, MusicArtistDatabase.com has a tremendous number of links. It is obvious from this data that the current most link worthy sections on the website are:

1. The Homepage
2. Top Charts
3. Message Board

This illustrates what is working well for MusicArtistDatabase.com.

One thing that is not working well for MusicArtistDatabase.com is the use of niche anchor text. Most of the links that point at the MusicArtistDatabase.com domain use either no alt text or the term MusicArtistDatabase. While the latter is helpful for ranking for the phrase "Music Artist Database", it doesn't directly sell music. A better approach would be to get more links to the individual artist pages with their relevant keywords.

Action Items
- Increase the number of deep links from high quality domains to product pages rather than the homepage.
- Focus on getting more external links with keyword rich anchor text.
- Put primary emphasis on the total number of unique linking domains.

Placeholder Consulting

Google PageRank

Metrics	Home	Top Charts	Artist Pages	Album Pages	Message Boards	Average
Google PageRank	5	4	5	5	5	5

Google's PageRank measures link popularity on a logarithmic scale. It is a number that reflects the relative value of a given page. This data point can be useful for identifying potential site architecture issues and PageRank penalties but this metric is not the all inclusive ranking metric that some believe it to be. PageRank is only one of many metrics that go into Google's ranking algorithm. This means it is a relatively poor metric for determining rankings.

With a PageRank of 4 and 5 across all sections, MusicArtistDatabase.com already has relatively high authority and PageRank appears to be flowing well between the sections. Additionally, no PageRank penalties appeared to be affecting the domain.

Action Items
- None

Placeholder Consulting

mozRank

Metrics	Home	Top Charts	Artist Pages	Album Pages	Message Boards	Average
SEOmoz mozRank	5.41	4.46	5.43	4.93	4.94	5

mozRank refers to SEOmoz's logarithmically scaled 10-point measure of global link authority. mozRank is very similar in purpose to the measures of static importance used by the search engines (e.g. PageRank). Search engines often rank pages with higher global link authority ahead of pages with lower authority. Because measures like mozRank are global and static, this ranking power applies to a broad range of search queries, rather than pages optimized specifically for a few keywords.

The intuition behind mozRank is to leverage the democratic nature of the web. Every link to a page is a vote. Pages can cast that vote by linking out to other pages. Their vote then becomes diluted with more links; thus, pages which link to many other pages aren't able to overwhelm those which only link to a few other pages.

Throughout the entire website, MusicArtistDatabase.com has a higher mozRank than mozTrust. This is a sign that while the links pointing to MusicArtistDatabase.com have a lot of link worth they don't carry the same amount of authority and trust as its competitors. While this problem is not very big (The difference is less than 0.5), it is a spam indicator.

Action Items
- Increase number of editorial, trusted links. (From media publications for example)
- Increase links to deep content on the site.

1234 123th PL NE
Seattle, WA 98000
Phone (555) 555-5555

Placeholder Consulting

mozTrust

Metrics	Home	Top Charts	Artist Pages	Album Pages	Message Boards	Average
SEOmoz mozTrust	6.29	5.79	6.03	6.06	5.99	6

Just as links express global link popularity, they also express the trustworthiness of a given webpage. Receiving links from sources which have inherent trust (such as the front pages of university websites or certain governmental pages) is a strong endorsement of trust. mozTrust is a quantitative measure of this.

Like mozRank, trust-votes are distributed through links. To calculate this metric, trustworthy "seeds" are identified. Those websites that earn trusted links are able to cast (smaller) trust-votes through their links. Receiving a trust-passing link from a highly trusted source boosts your own trust.

mozTrust is expressed on its own 10-point logarithmic scale. While mozRank and mozTrust should not be directly compared, it can be interesting to consider how these two values relate to each other across several URLs. A URL with a large mozRank-mozTrust disparity may perform poorly against a lower mozRank URL but with a smaller mozRank-mozTrust disparity.

At the section homepages, MusicArtistDatabase.com is solid. That said, mozTrust decreases rapidly as pages get further from these subsection pages. This discrepancy reflects the fact that most high quality domains link to the section homepages, and therefore there is an opportunity to increase the number of deep links from high quality domains to sub-sections of the site. Doing so would have a positive effect on rankings.

Action Items

- Increase the number of deep links from high quality domains to product pages. The best way to do this would be to link to the most important pages in a section on section homepages (http://www.musicartistdatabase.com/artist/).

Placeholder Consulting

Comprehensive Technical SEO Site Audit

Conclusion

MusicArtistDatabase.com is an extremely powerful domain in an extraordinarily competitive Internet niche. It has collected an enormous number of links and contains a lot of valuable content and useful products.

It is for these reasons, that we at Placeholder Consulting are very excited about the potential of MusicArtistDatabase.com. This website has a lot of "low hanging fruit" (easy to accomplish tasks with high return on investment) that we believe will make a large positive impact on traffic and sales. (See Most Valuable Changes at the front of the report)

We wish you and your team the best of luck and appreciate the opportunity you gave us to work with you. Cheers!

Placeholder Consulting

Addendums

See attached Addendums for detailed lists:

1. 404-pages.csv

2. unreachable.csv

3. robots-txt.csv

4. no-follow.csv

## CHAPTER 9

Comprehensive Site Audit (E-Commerce Website)

IN THIS CHAPTER

► **Learning how to write a professional SEO audit**
► **Learning why each section is included**
► **Learning the intricacies of e-commerce site analysis**

Now that you have seen a report for an ad-supported website, I want to show you an important alternative. This chapter explains a report that is formatted for e-commerce sites. It shows much of the same information as the last report, but frames it from a different, more product-based perspective.

Specifically, you will notice that this report focuses more on the individual sections of the websites at the 10-foot view. (Remember Chapter 2?) This is done because the most important aspects of these types of websites are the products and landing pages. Get your note-taking utensils ready, this one's a doozy.

HOW TO READ THIS CHAPTER

In the preceding chapter I used the analogy of a nerdy cookbook to describe the best way to read these two chapters. (If it helps, try picturing Bill Gates with a French Chef mustache.) This chapter provides instructions for writing a report for an e-commerce site. Use the advice in this chapter and build upon it with your own ideas. Just like recipes are merely suggestions based on experience, the following report outline is merely a suggestion based on reports I have delivered in the past. When in doubt, make this your own by building upon the ideas I present to you. *Bon Appétit*!

SAMPLE WEBSITE

In this chapter our trusty fake consulting company, Placeholder Consulting, is up to bat again with a website called SellTheWidget.com. This website (which doesn't actually exist) is extremely popular and ranks in the top three for most of its products. It is the number-one widget seller in the world and has been online for many years. As such, it is a very large website with some serious navigational issues.

E-Commerce Website

As the domain name implies, this website is an e-commerce website that sells widgets directly to individuals. It is based on several e-commerce websites for which I have done SEO consulting work. Similar websites include:

- www.amazon.com
- www.ebay.com
- www.zappos.com
- www.buy.com
- www.etsy.com
- www.bestbuy.com
- www.costco.com

SAMPLE REPORT

Just like in the previous chapter, I walk you through an example report that describes each section and explains why it is important and what it should include. Use this information in combination with the sample report that follows the text of this chapter to help you write your own reports for your clients.

Steps Before Writing the Report

Before you start writing this report, you will need to fully analyze the given website. For an e-commerce site this means starting from the beginning of the buying process (usually search) and using the site just like a normal buyer would.

In addition to browsing the site like it is intended, you should do all of the analysis that is described in Chapter 4 and see how well the developers of the website implemented the SEO best practices (which are described in Chapter 6).

Again, I want to reiterate that this process takes a lot of time. I generally spend at least 4 hours analyzing the entire website before I sit down to write the report. This is an important process because it gives you a broad understanding of the website before you sit down and make recommendations on how to fix specific sections.

▶ Fully analyzing an ecommerce website may involve your going through the process of actually buying a product.

NOTE The rest of this chapter comprises descriptions of the sections of the SEO audit. Following the text of the chapter is the sample audit of SellTheWidget.com in its entirety, which contains examples of all those pages discussed in the chapter. That way you can both read about what specific sections of an audit might entail and then go see what they might look like in an actual audit.

Cover

The cover of the report needs to convey professionalism and value. I tend to go for more simplistic designs with lots of whitespace. I do this to show the client that the report is both serious and readable. Just like the previous report I recommend including all of the following on the cover of your report:

▶ Report Title

▶ Report Author

▶ SEO Consultant Business Name

- ▶ SEO Consultant Business Address
- ▶ SEO Consultant Business Phone Number

> **NOTE** Consider the pros and cons of adding your e-mail address to the cover also. An e-mail address is likely to draw a fair amount of contact from the clients after you deliver the audit (or their friends, to whom they're likely to show the report). If part of your price includes after-delivery consultation, then it's a logical addition. If not, then you might not want to risk a lot of free post-delivery consultation requests by including it.
>
> Still, it's likely that in negotiating the deal in the first place, you've already had a great deal of e-mail contact with the client, and your e-mail address is no secret.

Table of Contents

▶ *Browse this table of contents if for no other reason than to see the wide variety of issues the report discusses.*

The table of contents should be straightforward and easy to read. For your sake, it is easiest to have your word processor generate it. See the tips in this corresponding section in Chapter 8 to make this section both easier to create and easier to navigate for your client.

Most Pressing and Valuable Changes

This section is a list of five easiest SEO changes that will have the most impact on rankings.

▶ *For each recommended change, in the PDF version of the report you can include a link to the section in the report that describes the problem and how to fix it.*

WHAT ARE THE COMMON SUGGESTIONS YOU MAKE IN THIS SECTION?

For this section I prioritize the SEO problems I found in my earlier analysis. Generally the problems I mention here are the same common SEO problems that I refer to in the "SEO Quick Hit List" described in Chapter 14.

Search Engine & Third-Party Statistics

This section provides some of the raw data the search engines use to compute rankings.

WHY IS THIS SECTION NECESSARY?

This section is necessary because it provides the quick action points that clients like to pass to their development team. This is helpful because it allows the clients to make quick changes that will make at least some impact on their rankings right away.

NOTE As mentioned in the report, the raw numbers that these services provide is far from accurate. However, the data relationships between two or more sites are sometimes pretty close. In other words, if a third-party site says that your site had 100,000 visits one month, don't trust that number (instead, trust your analytics!). But if the site says that your site had twice as many visits as another site in a given month, it's more likely that measurement is somewhat accurate.

The same advice goes for data trends over time. Sites like Compete are typically pretty good at showing the general trend (rise or fall) of traffic, while the raw numbers are only an estimate. In other words, "Trust the curves, but not the numbers."

The rest of the report focuses on recommendations that will likely take longer to implement and take effect in the search engine indices. These long-term suggestions are more often implemented if the quick suggestions listed in this section make a positive difference in clients' rankings.

HOW DO YOU DO THE ANALYSIS FOR THIS SECTION?

This section is the result of the 4 hours (or more) spent analyzing the client's website before writing this report. I use this section to document the most pressing issues I find. I then refer to the applicable in-depth sections within the report in this section.

This section contains the overview of the problem; the later sections include more detailed explanations and solutions to these problems.

WHAT ARE THE COMMON SUGGESTIONS YOU MAKE IN THIS SECTION?

My most common suggestions are increasing the scores listed in this section. I do this based on what I see working for the website as reported by this raw data.

SEARCH ENGINE INCLUSION DATA

This section shows an estimate of the number of pages indexed in the major search engine indices. The most common problems I see in this section are either erroneously high or low page counts.

► If these numbers are abnormally high (as determined by the number of pages clients think they have on their website) then they likely have a duplicate content problem. Most often, this is caused by the search engines indexing unnecessary URL parameters.

▶ The other problem I commonly see is page counts that are suspiciously low. When this happens it is either caused by crawling issues (the crawlers can't access sections of the given website) or too few inbound links (which makes the engines think the pages are not worth indexing).

LINK POPULARITY DATA

This section includes the number of inbound links to the given website. The most common issue I see here is that Bing sees a lot of links and Google sees a lot fewer links.

This is usually caused by links on duplicate pages (low value) or links from link farms. In either case, the links are not likely helping rankings in Google and will likely be discounted by Bing in the future.

LINKSCAPE METRICS

Linkscape metrics provide raw insights into how the Web links to specific URLs. I usually see one of two combinations of metrics: high mozRank with low mozTrust or low mozRank with high mozTrust.

If you see either of these cases with your clients, it is likely they have a spammy link profile and it is affecting rankings.

CROSSREF See the section "SEO Toolbars" in Chapter 3 for more information.

BRAND & DOMAIN MENTIONS IN SEARCH ENGINES

In this section, I include metrics and graphs of domain metrics as reported by Google. The most common issue I see here is a lot of domain mentions but not very many brand mentions. This is a sign that a lot of automated mentions are being posted around the Web but very few actual people (and potential customers) are talking about the brand.

When this happens, I recommend that the client and I have a meeting about how to build a community and interact with the social Web. This discussion and the resulting plan usually take months to implement.

THIRD-PARTY TRAFFIC METRICS (MONTHLY)

This data is presented to show clients how inaccurate these third-party sources are compared to their internal analytics. I include these simply as a benchmark so that they can more accurately understand how their competitors and potential investors see their site.

Just because these numbers are inaccurate doesn't mean they are not important. A lot of very powerful and influential people use these numbers to make decisions.

Technical On-Page/On-Site Issues

This section covers factors (as reported by the search engines) that are negatively affecting this website.

WHY IS THIS SECTION NECESSARY?

This section is important because it covers some of the most common SEO mistakes that have the most impact on rankings. It is rather basic, but it makes it very clear what factors are holding the given website from potential rankings.

HOW DO YOU DO THE ANALYSIS FOR THIS SECTION?

The analysis for this section requires access to several tools and the knowledge of where to look to find potential problems. Luckily, if you have been following along, you should already know about these tools and where to look for these problems. (If you forget, check Chapters 3 and 4.) The 15-minute SEO audit (from Chapter 4) is usually sufficient to write this section of the report.

WHAT ARE THE COMMON SUGGESTIONS YOU MAKE IN THIS SECTION?

I find that the most common SEO recommendations are also the most impactful. This section covers these and offers advice on how to handle common situations.

REGISTRATION WITH SEARCH ENGINES

The vast majority of the clients I worked with had not verified their sites with the search engines and thus couldn't access their site-specific data. This is a problem because these webmaster tools are extremely helpful for understanding how the search engines see a given site and for instructing search engines on how to treat the site.

In this section I always walk the clients through what options are available to them via these resources and tell them what their optimal settings should be.

REVIEW OF ROBOTS.TXT

In this section I recommend that the client use meta robots instead of `robots.txt` and provide advice on each entry in the text file. See the section "Blocking Pages from Search Engines" in Chapter 6 for more information on this.

SERVER RESPONSE CODES

Most clients that I talked to did not understand the various HTTP status codes. I use this section to define common problematic status codes and offer suggestions on how to fix them.

Specifically I recommend converting 302 redirects to 301 redirects and either redirect pages that return a 404 response code or make them a better tool for helping users find what they are looking for.

SITE CANONICALIZATION

Site canonicalization is a very common problem that causes webpages on the same domain to needlessly compete with each other. This topic is covered in full in Chapter 6 in the sections "Rel Canonical Link Element" and "301 Redirects."

USE OF SITEMAP FILES

▶ When clients don't have a sitemap, I recommend they add one. They will likely see an initial boost in search engine referred traffic followed by a traffic level lower than the spike of that initial boost but higher than pre-sitemap traffic.

The most common situation I see with clients with big websites is that they already have XML sitemaps and update them weekly. This is the recommended best practice if it is not in place; I recommend adhering to it.

DUPLICATE CONTENT ISSUES

Most of the duplicate content problems I see are caused by canonicalization issues. Because these are usually easier to fix than other types of duplicate content issues (stolen content, URL parameters, frames, and so on) I focus on these and recommend 301 redirects and rel canonical when appropriate.

CRAWLING PROBLEMS

Crawling problems generally come in five types: plug-ins, forms, images, JavaScript navigation, and robot blocking. In this section I cover each of these when applicable and suggest alternatives.

Individual Section Reviews

This section does in-depth analysis of the major sections of the given website.

DUPLICATION, CRAWLING OBSTACLES, AND FAULTY INDEX COUNTS

The combination of duplicate content and crawling obstacles can result in engines showing index counts that are misleadingly close to the number of true pages on your site. I recently reviewed an inventory-heavy auto parts site with severe pagination-based crawling obstacles, yet the SKU pages that *were* indexed each had between two and four duplicates.

Together, these two "problems" combined to allow engines to index a number of pages that was suspiciously close to what the client believed the true page count was. So beware of numbers that look correct until you've had a chance to dive deeply into the specific of what is and is not indexed.

WHY IS THIS SECTION NECESSARY?

This section is important because it directly covers the most important sections of the given website. It makes specific recommendations on how to better optimize the on-page factors of these pages. This is both actionable and impactful.

HOW DO YOU DO THE ANALYSIS FOR THIS SECTION?

When writing this section I rely on the analysis I did before starting the report and dive deeper into each major section. As I am writing up the section analysis, I spend time surfing the given section and looking for SEO problems. I put most of my emphasis on on-page factors because they are easiest to spot when doing this kind of analysis.

> **CROSSREF** See the sections "10-Foot View" and "1-Foot View" in Chapter 2 for information on what to look for while writing this section.

WHAT ARE THE COMMON SUGGESTIONS YOU MAKE IN THIS SECTION?

In this section I review the title tag, meta description, meta keywords URL, and keyword usage of each major section of the given website.

HOMEPAGE

In many ways homepages are the anchor of websites. They are almost always are the most linked-to page and as such are the most important from an information hierarchy and link juice point of view.

My most common suggestions for homepages are related to keyword targeting. Homepages should directly target the main keyword of the website in all of their major on-page factors.

CATEGORY PAGES

Category pages are the forks in webpage navigation. They should be clear in their focus (specific categories rather than broad ideas) and target this keyword in all of their most important on-page SEO factors.

The most common problem I see with category pages is that they are not linked to from their parent (for example, homepage) and child pages (either product pages or subcategory pages depending on the height of the category system). This is a problem because it stunts the flow of link juice and makes it more difficult for users to navigate the website.

PRODUCT PAGES

▶ It's a challenge, but to get high index rates, e-commerce sites need to pay more attention to having unique, product-specific text on each of their product pages.

Product pages are the heart and soul of e-commerce websites. They are the salesmen of the website and should be optimized and tested for optimal results.

The most common problem I see with product pages is a lack of unique content. E-commerce sites usually have many products pages, and it can be difficult to generate unique text for all of them. Unfortunately, this is a problem that must be overcome in order to get high index rates in the major search engines. Successful tactics I have seen used are user generated reviews, additional product images, and editor reviews.

Keyword Targeting

Keyword targeting refers to the presence of a chosen keyword in areas of a page that are important for SEO.

WHY IS THIS SECTION NECESSARY?

This section is important because it gives specific recommendations that affect the ability for products to rank in search engine results.

HOW DO YOU DO THE ANALYSIS FOR THIS SECTION?

To see how well a keyword is targeted on a page I use SEOmoz's mozBar (see Chapter 3) and use the Analyze Page feature. This shows me all of the key SEO on-page metrics and how they are configured for the page.

WHAT ARE THE COMMON SUGGESTIONS YOU MAKE IN THIS SECTION?

In this section I make suggestions based on on-page factors.

TARGETED KEYWORDS

The most common problem I see with keyword targeting is that the client targets either too many keywords or one keyword that is too broad. In this situation the page has very little chance of ranking for its given keywords and the page should focus on targeting one term that is specific enough that it is in line with the amount of link juice the page has.

Visitor & Search Analytics

This section analyzes the clients' internal analytics to see what keywords are working for them.

WHY IS THIS SECTION NECESSARY?

What could be a better indicator of future success than previous and current success? This section determines which tactics have been working and shows how to monitor their progress.

HOW DO YOU DO THE ANALYSIS FOR THIS SECTION?

To do the analysis for this section you need to have access to your client's analytics program. Common programs include Omniture, Yahoo! IndexTools, and Google Analytics.

WHAT ARE THE COMMON SUGGESTIONS YOU MAKE IN THIS SECTION?

Analytics are the measuring stick of any e-commerce website's success. This section includes some of the measurements that should be monitored.

▶ Don't neglect taking note of what a site is doing well. Previous and current success can show you what has been working for a site.

IMPORTANT METRICS TO TRACK DAILY

There are many important metrics to track. These vary based on the website. Some common metrics that should be tracked daily by most e-commerce websites include:

- ▶ Daily Unique Visitors
- ▶ Referring Domains
- ▶ Natural Search Keywords
- ▶ Paid Search Keywords

TERMS & PHRASES LEADING TO CONVERSIONS

Many clients keep track of which natural and paid keywords are driving traffic but fail to take the extra step of seeing which keywords are driving actual conversions.

This additional insight is extremely important because it shows which keywords are actually generating revenue and thus provide the highest return on investment of time optimizing.

HIGH SEARCH VALUE TERMS AND PHRASES

These terms are the highest value (in terms of amount search traffic referred). I use these as a gauge for competitiveness in search engines and recommend them as a benchmark for the type of keywords to try to compete for.

THE BRANDED AND NON-BRANDED BALANCE

When you look at the list of top referring and converting keywords for a site, it seems like time after time, unoptimized sites come to us with a ratio of about 85:15. In other words, about 85 percent of phrases contain the site name in some way.

Branded queries certainly aren't bad, because when someone searches for your site, you certainly want them to find it. (And if they're searching for your brand and you don't show up on the SERP, you have serious problems.) But it illustrates a real opportunity for pulling in non-branded queries. There's no right or wrong ratio when it comes to branded:non-branded, but I like to shoot for raising the non-branded percentage to 40 or even 50.

When your branded percentage drops after you optimize, don't worry. That probably doesn't mean that you're losing branded queries. Instead, it usually means that you're beginning to pull in more non-branded queries, and the overall percent balance is beginning to shift toward more of an equilibrium. That's a good thing.

Information Architecture & Internal Link Structure

Information architecture and internal link structure are critical to how search engines index a given site. This section covers common recommendations I make to clients in these two areas.

WHY IS THIS SECTION NECESSARY?

This section is important to help clients understand the impact of planning websites to scale. It shows them what poor information hierarchy looks like and how it can affect their rankings.

HOW DO YOU DO THE ANALYSIS FOR THIS SECTION?

The analysis for this section takes place in the time spent surfing the website before starting the report. For a more in-depth discussion of this, see Chapter 2.

WHAT ARE THE COMMON SUGGESTIONS YOU MAKE IN THIS SECTION?

The most common suggestions I make for this section all have to do with factors that are on-page and thus within the control of the client. This is good news because it means these suggestions can be implemented from within the client's company as opposed to suggestions necessitating inbound links, which require the work of others.

INFORMATION HIERARCHY

Information hierarchy issues are usually within one of two categories: internal links and URLs.

▶ In the case of internal links, the recommendation I make most often is using keyword-targeted anchor text to point at pages targeting the same keyword. This might seem common knowledge but in practice it is rarely done. Websites should internally link to pages with the anchor text keyword they are targeting, not other text that happens to fit well in the context (for example, better internal anchor text would be "waterproof widgets" as opposed to "More information is available here"). You want to give search engines every hint you can to help them understand what search query the given page should rank for.

▶ The second case is with URLs. These addresses should use the keyword that is being targeted and reflect how that keyword is related to the rest of the site. Most commonly this should take the form of categories and subcategories titles reflected in URLs (for example, `www.example.com/colors/blue.html` rather than `www.example.com/pages/blue.html`).

Content Analysis

This section covers the value of unique content in demand by Internet users.

WHY IS THIS SECTION NECESSARY?

If you ever get the chance to go to an SEO conference (see Appendix A to see which ones to attend) you will certainly hear the phrase "content is king" over and over again. This happens because SEO speakers know the value of unique content.

It is essential to provide the search engines with content that is worthy of being placed at the top of results. Unique, relevant, and intriguing content is the best way to do that.

HOW DO YOU DO THE ANALYSIS FOR THIS SECTION?

The analysis for this section is the most qualitative of the report. It relies on many human elements that are up to the discretion of the author to grade and make suggestions upon. When writing to this section I find it helpful to keep asking myself, "Would I link to this page?"

WHAT ARE THE COMMON SUGGESTIONS YOU MAKE IN THIS SECTION?

Information, like the world's economic markets, is governed by the laws of supply (uniqueness) and demand (user need).

UNIQUE CONTENT

The most common problem I see with unique content is that it is not actually unique. Most of the time this takes the form of the same content being used on multiple sections of the same site. This makes it so the content must compete with itself and it devalues its relevancy.

Ideally each product page should contain at least three unique full paragraphs and a unique image of the given product. This is appreciated by both those who get the information they want and the search engines that get to index the information that searchers want.

USER NEED FULFILLMENT

Many times I see content that is unique but does not fulfill any user need. When this happens, I help identify what related information would fulfill a user's need (remember, a lot of people want to know a lot of different things) and recommend this to the client.

UNIQUE CONTENT FOR PRODUCT COPY

Sites that sell products that they don't manufacture often fall into the trap of using the exact same catalog copy that the manufacturer recommends for a particular product. This results in tens (or even hundreds) of catalog-based sites using the exact same on-page copy to market specific products.

You can do better. And if you want more search engine attention, you need to. If you print the exact same copy as 100 other sites, you're leaving your rankings up to other variables, like the footprint and authority of your site against those other 99 sites. Consider the folks at a site like woot.com and its hilarious narrative that surrounds its products. And the grand dame of products, Amazon.com, with its hundreds of user reviews discussing every facet of a product from unboxing to warranties.

Unique, engaging content draws links (not to mention viral passalong), and links draw algorithmic benefit. It's really that simple.

User Experience

If a user can't navigate or understand a website, its potential is extinguished.

▶ Usability and user experience are as important to the success of a webpage as search engine rankings.

WHY IS THIS SECTION NECESSARY?

This section is important because it covers the human side of SEO that many clients forget to address. The experience of the user on a website is the main characteristic that determines whether a user will buy a product. For this reason, this section is necessary in this report.

HOW DO YOU DO THE ANALYSIS FOR THIS SECTION?

The analysis of this section is based on my experience while navigating the site. This is covered in detail in Chapter 2.

WHAT ARE THE COMMON SUGGESTIONS YOU MAKE IN THIS SECTION?

Most of my suggestions for this section of the report are based on my initial reactions after loading the applicable webpage. This brief second is the key moment when users will decide if they want to continue onto the given website or click Back and look at a different search result.

DESIGN QUALITY

I find that many people underestimate the importance of web design when it comes to ranking well. It is true that actual graphical design is not likely directly quantified by the search engine algorithms, but its secondary effects are certainly important rankings.

Design makes an impact on whether or not someone is going to trust content. Trust is a major factor when someone decides if they want to rank to a given piece of content. For this reason, I commonly include some notes on how well designed I believe a given page to be.

USER EXPERIENCE

User experience is extremely complicated. For this section I usually simplify it by making some bulleted action items that are based on some obvious user experience problems.

These generally include making text more readable (spacing and color), directing the flow of the user as they navigate the website, and creating custom experiences for first-time users.

Link Building Opportunities

In this section I cover ways that the client can build links based on the content they already have.

WHY IS THIS SECTION NECESSARY?

This section is important because it shows clients how to leverage their current assets to build more links and thus get higher search engine rankings and ultimately sell more products.

I have heard many SEOs complain that link building is the hardest part of SEO. Though I think this can be true, I don't think it needs to be. When you already have something link worthy all you need is to get it in front of the right type of people to earn easy links. This section helps explain how to craft content to do this.

HOW DO YOU DO THE ANALYSIS FOR THIS SECTION?

To do the analysis for this section I use SEOmoz's Open Site Explorer. This tool gives me all of the link information I need for the client's website along with its competitors.

WHAT ARE THE COMMON SUGGESTIONS YOU MAKE IN THIS SECTION?

This section is broken down into two categories chosen to help the client understand their own link profile.

CURRENT INBOUND LINK TYPES

The most common suggestion I make in this section is to improve inbound anchor text. The most common anchor text for a website is almost always its domain name and its brand name. This is helpful for making it rank for those terms but not for better converting terms.

Competitive websites need to leverage their link building abilities by diversifying their link profiles (multiple keywords) and focusing their energies on anchor text that will help them rank for well converting keywords.

CONTENT CURRENTLY ATTRACTING LINKS

This section covers what content is currently doing well from an SEO perspective. My most common suggestion is to figure out why this content is working and spread these winning attributes to other content. Most of the time these sections are working because they offer content that is desirable to web searchers and is formatted in a way that makes it easy to consume.

Vertical Search Opportunities and Inclusion

This section covers suggestions for search verticals like image search and blog search.

WHY IS THIS SECTION NECESSARY?

This section is important for diversifying a website's link profile. Though standard search results are the most important, search verticals are helpful maximizing the reach of a given website's webpages.

HOW DO YOU DO THE ANALYSIS FOR THIS SECTION?

To do the analysis for this section, I check the inclusion of the given website in various search verticals and check the client's analytics for referrers from verticals.

WHAT ARE THE COMMON SUGGESTIONS YOU MAKE IN THIS SECTION?

For e-commerce websites, I generally only make search vertical suggestions on image and blog search. I have found that the common suggestions for other search verticals (local, news, real-time, and so on) don't apply to most e-commerce websites.

IMAGE SEARCH

▶ For e-commerce sites, the cons of image search, often in terms of stolen images, usually outweigh the benefits.

The most common suggestion I make for image search is to disallow it. Referrers from image search results have extremely low conversion rates for e-commerce sites.

BLOG/FEED SEARCH

Although the search engines are pretty good at auto-discovering popular blogs they are not good at discovering smaller corporate blogs. If this is the case for the given client, I recommend submitting the blogs to the search engines so that they start indexing them.

Glossary

This section contains a glossary that is helpful for clients who aren't familiar with SEO jargon.

WHY IS THIS SECTION NECESSARY?

The glossary of the report includes straightforward definitions of SEO jargon that is used in the report. Without these explanations, the client will have a difficult time understanding and ultimately implementing the suggestions made in the report.

WHAT ARE THE COMMON SUGGESTIONS YOU MAKE IN THIS SECTION?

The glossary contains the following SEO terms that I have found are the hardest for clients to understand:

Cloaking

Indexing-Crawling

Link Juice

Long Tail

SUMMARY

Well that doesn't seem so hard now does it? You should now know how to format an e-commerce–centric SEO audit report. Notice how much value is included in the 50 or so pages that make up these reports. If you have read all of the chapters thus far, you should be well on your way to taking your SEO skills to the next level.

The rest of the book is dedicated to taking the skills you have learned so far and supplementing them with some of the bigger-picture SEO concepts. In the next chapter you learn about the SEO industry and who came up with all of the ideas you have now learned.

Site Review for
www.sellthewidget.com

Prepared By Danny Dover

SellTheWidget.com is a major e-commerce website in a competitive industry. It has a great deal of ranking potential and is currently being held back by a poorly search engine optimized content management system. This report identifies the current search engine related problems affecting SellTheWidget.com and provides comprehensive solutions.

Date Created 2/27/15   All Content and Intellectual Property is under Copyright Protection | Placeholder Consulting

Placeholder Consulting

Site Review for www.SellTheWidget.com

Table of Contents

Placeholder Consulting

Site Review for www.SellTheWidget.com

Placeholder Consulting

Site Review for www.SellTheWidget.com

Placeholder Consulting

Site Review for www.SellTheWidget.com

Placeholder Consulting

Site Review for www.SellTheWidget.com

Top Five Most Pressing and Valuable Changes

Below are the most important upgrades necessary to optimize www.sellthewidget.com for search engines. Implementing these changes will lead to better search rankings for a multitude of important keywords.

http://sellthewidget.com/home.html should 301 redirect to www.sellthewidget.com/

Currently, http://www.sellthewidget.com 301 redirects to http://sellthewidget.com/home.html. This is an unintentional waste of Link Juice (ranking power) because each link that is redirected through a 301 is slightly diminished in value. Since more links are pointing at www.sellthewidget.com/ (1,805,384) than http://sellthewidget.com/home.html (30,559) it is recommended that you implement a 301 redirect to recapture a significant amount of link value.

Add list of widgets to category and subcategory pages

SellTheWidget.com does an excellent job of establishing a clear site-wide hierarchy to organize its massive amount of products. Each product category is linked to from the homepage (the page with the most incoming links) and thus capitalizes on a great deal of Link Juice (ranking power) by transferring it to each category page. Each of these categories then links to lower level subcategories. Adding links to top selling products on each of these category and subcategory pages has the potential to create the ideal internal linking structure.

Adding links to each applicable category and subcategory page will ensure that all of the links to the homepage will help boost the rankings of each individual product page. More information can be found in the section Information Architecture & Internal Link Structure - Information Architecture.

Exact match search queries on SellTheWidget's internal search should automatically redirect

Currently when a user searches for a product on SellTheWidget.com they are taken to a results page even if their query is an exact match for a product. For example, a user searching "Red Widget" is taken to http://www.sellthewidget.com/search?query=red%20widget. Placeholder Consulting recommends that in the event of an exact match, the user should be redirected to the product page. This will stop these internal search result pages from acquiring and wasting links as well as remove unnecessary pages from the major search engines' indices. As a result, more links and more ranking power will be aimed at applicable pages rather than the less user-friendly SellTheWidget search results pages.

Placeholder Consulting recommends that SellTheWidget add a meta robots tag to search result pages that don't return any results. The robots meta tag should only be added to SellTheWidget search result pages that are blank and NOT to search result pages that return results. The correct meta robots tag appears below:

<meta name="robots" content="follow, noindex" />

Make blank 404 error pages more useful to users

SellTheWidget.com's current 404 error page is a hindrance to users. The current version returns an incorrect HTTP response code (200 rather than 404) and does not help the user find the page they are looking to access. Users are simply left with a blank white page with the text '404'. Ex. http://www.sellthewidget.com/this-page-does-not-exist.html

At a minimum, this page should offer a message explaining the file is not found and suggestions on where to find the file. It should also include the website's global navigation menu and a search field.

Placeholder Consulting

Site Review for www.SellTheWidget.com

Search Engine & Third-Party Statistics (Identifying Strengths and Weaknesses)

The following metrics are reported by third-party sources (including the search engines themselves). They provide valuable insight into how various parties see SellTheWidget.com at a high level. They are time dependent and should only be used as estimations, not as exact measurements.

Search Engine Inclusion Data

www.sellthewidget.com	Result	Date	Source
# of Pages in Google	10,620,000	February 27th, 2015	site:www.sellthewidget.com
# of Pages in Bing	1,120,000	February 27th, 2015	site:www.sellthewidget.com

The number of pages on www.sellthewidget.com in the two major search engine indices

What does this data mean?

These metrics indicate that SellTheWidget is being properly indexed in Google but not in Bing. This is important information to know because the indexation of SellTheWidget in the major search engines strongly correlates to the amount of traffic the search engines send to SellTheWidget. Solutions for improving these index statistics are provided throughout this report.

Placeholder Consulting

Site Review for www.SellTheWidget.com

Link Popularity Data

www.SellTheWidget.com	Result	Date	Source
# of Links in Google Webmaster Tools	2,042,637	February 27th, 2015	https://www.google.com/webmasters/tools/externallinks?siteUrl=http%3A%2F%2Fwww.sellthewidget.com%2F&hl=en
# of Links according to Linkscape	2,001,159	February 27th, 2015	http://www.Placeholder Consulting.org/linkscape/intel/basic/?uri=www.sellthewidget.com
# of Links according to Google Blog Search	17,382	February 27th, 2015	http://blogsearch.google.com/blogsearch?hl=en&ie=UTF-8&q=www.sellthewidget.com&btnG=Search+Blogs
# of Links according to Nielsen Blogpulse	1,528	February 27th, 2015	http://www.blogpulse.com/search?query=www.sellthewidget.com&image22.x=0&image22.y=0

The number of links to www.sellthewidget.com as determined by various sources

What does this data mean?

To put these numbers in context, Google reports that www.sellthewidget.com has 1.7 million links and that www.widgetseller.com has 900,000 links. (Keep in mind that the numbers themselves are not necessarily accurate, but the relationships they reveal are extremely important.) This shows that SellTheWidget has the potential to outrank very competitive websites. In this case, the distinguishing factor between potential rankings and real rankings is very likely the anchor text and source of links pointing at SellTheWidget.

SellTheWidget's current anchor text profile reveals that it is targeting a large amount of very specific search phrases (long tail). For example, "Product XYZ at SellTheWidget". This is a good strategy that leverages SellTheWidget's links very well. However, given the competitiveness revealed by the above metrics, SellTheWidget could supplement its current anchor text strategy by targeting competitive search phrases like "Widget". This would work nicely with SellTheWidget's current PPC campaigns.

Placeholder Consulting

Site Review for www.SellTheWidget.com

Linkscape Metrics

www.SellTheWidget.com	Result	Date	Source
Domain level mozRank	8.17	February 27th, 2015	http://www.seomoz.org/linkscape/intel/basic/?uri=www.sellthewidget.com
mozTrust	8.92	February 27th, 2015	http://www.seomoz.org/linkscape/intel/basic/?uri=www.sellthewidget.com

Aggregate link information as determined by SEOmoz's Linkscape

What does this data mean?

Each of these results are on a log scale with a max of 10 and average 4.50 across the Internet. This confirms the competitive nature of SellTheWidget discussed above. SellTheWidget has a lot of potential to rank highly for very competitive search keywords.

It is also important to note that SellTheWidget.com's mozTrust is very high. mozTrust represents the amount of 'trusted' websites linking to a given target. Trusted websites are determined by the search engines independently but generally include respected .edu websites (http://www.harvard.edu/), important .gov websites (www.whitehouse.gov), and important news websites (www.cnn.com). Trust is a link metric that is completely separate from pure link counts but has been proven to improve rankings.

SellTheWidget's higher than expected mozTrust is likely coming from links from SellTheWidget's enterprise partners. This adds significantly to SellTheWidget's competitive edge.

Placeholder Consulting

Site Review for www.SellTheWidget.com

Brand & Domain Mentions in Search Engines

SellTheWidget	Result	Date	Source
# of Brand Mentions in Google Search	6,700,000	February 27th, 2015	http://www.google.com/search?hl=en&safe=off&q=%22SellTheWidget%22+-site%3ASellTheWidget.com&btnG=Search
# of Brand Name Mentions in Google Blog Search	12,992	February 27th, 2015	http://blogsearch.google.com/blogsearch?hl=en&ie=UTF-8&q=link;www.sellthewidget.com&scoring=d
# of Brand Name Mentions in Google News Search	65,400	February 27th, 2015	http://news.google.com/archivesearch?q=%22SellTheWidget&btnG=Search+Archives&hl=en&ie=UTF-8

The number of times SellTheWidget is mentioned in the media according to various sources

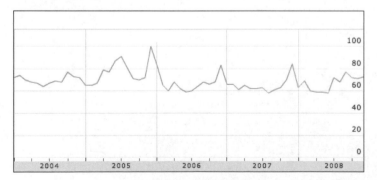

According to Google Insights, brand name mentions of SellTheWidget have stayed roughly at the same level since 2004.

Placeholder Consulting

Site Review for www.SellTheWidget.com

What does this data mean?

Given the popularity of widget news, these metrics are lower than they ought to be. SellTheWidget has clearly been successful in establishing itself as a widget platform (indicated by the high number of 'Brand Mentions in Google Search') but has not yet succeeded in effectively influencing the blogosphere and major news outlets.

As indicated by the Google Insights graph, SellTheWidget sees a spike of brand mentions during the last two months of every year (except 2004). These spikes, which are likely tied to the holiday season, highlight the effect of successful and newsworthy content. Analyzing what content was successful during these time periods could prove very helpful in crafting future content.

For example, analyzing HTTP referrers during these time periods in Internal Analytics highlights the success SellTheWidget saw from making itself the best place to buy Widgets related to the series finale of the popular TV show 'The Widgets'. Linkworthy content such as this is essential to driving links and traffic.

Placeholder Consulting

Site Review for www.SellTheWidget.com

Third-Party Traffic Metrics (Monthly)

www.SellTheWidget.com	Result	Date	Source
Traffic according to Google Trends for Websites	1,070,000	February 27th, 2015	http://trends.google.com/web-sites?q=SellTheWidget.com&geo=all&date=all&sort=0
Traffic according to Compete.com	30,000,000	February 27th, 2015	http://siteanalytics.compete.com/SellTheWidget.com/?metric=uv
Traffic according to Quantcast.com	20,800,000	February 27th, 2015	http://www.quantcast.com/SellTheWidget.com
Traffic according to Omniture (Analytics)	70,500,000	February 27th, 2015	Internal Analytics

Monthly traffic according to various sources

What does this data mean?

This information is important from a competitive analysis point of view. Competitors will likely rely on these erroneous metrics while analyzing SellTheWidget. It is to SellTheWidget's advantage to know the numbers are inaccurate and use their relative counts to serve as a baseline for conducting competitive analysis on SellTheWidget's competition. The large inaccuracies in these third-party traffic meters should serve as warning of trusting website traffic estimations in the news and elsewhere.

Placeholder Consulting

Site Review for www.SellTheWidget.com

Technical On-Page/On-Site Issues

The following data is taken directly from the search engines and reveals conditions that are negatively affecting search rankings for SellTheWidget.com. Generally, each of the problems below has easy solutions that can be quickly implemented.

Registration with Search Engines

The search engines offer a variety of tools to help webmasters explain to the engines how they would like their pages indexed by their crawlers. The tools also offer valuable feedback on potential problems the engines see on websites that couldn't otherwise be detected.

Google Webmaster Tools

Webmaster tools allow site owners to specify certain Google settings for websites. The most important settings are outlined below:

Geographic Target - Not Set

Geographic Target controls how Google targets users at SellTheWidget.com. For example, if SellTheWidget had a Japanese version of the site, this feature would be used to tell Google that the Japanese version of the site should have precedence in Japan. Since SellTheWidget does not have geo specific versions of its website, Placeholder Consulting recommends not setting this feature.

Preferred Domain - http://www.sellthewidget.com

SellTheWidget's current preferred domain contains "www.". This is as opposed to http://SellTheWidget.com. Placeholder Consulting recommends the version currently selected because it is what users most often understand and expect.

Image Search - Enabled

SellTheWidget currently allows its images to be crawled and included in Google's index. Placeholder Consulting recommends that this setting is kept as is. Including SellTheWidget's images in Google's index drives additional (although low converting) traffic to SellTheWidget and helps increase brand awareness.

Crawl Rate - Specialized by Google

Google's crawl rate of SellTheWidget.com has been manually set by the search engine. This generally only happens to large and complex websites. Server logs show that Google's bots crawl SellTheWidget extremely frequently compared to other test sites. This is good for SellTheWidget and shows that it included favorably in Google's index.

Registration with Bing Webmaster Tools

Webmaster tools allows site owners to specify certain Bing Search settings for websites. The most important settings are outlined below:

Overall

Bing does not report any major problems with SellTheWidget.com that could lead to it getting removed from its index. However, the search engines do indicate that SellTheWidget.com does suffer a lot from the URL tracking parameters.

Placeholder Consulting

Site Review for www.SellTheWidget.com

Site Status

These settings indicate the general health of real.com in Bing's search index.

Domain score - 5/5

Indexed Pages - 20,740,000

Blocked? - No

These data points indicate that SellTheWidget.com is strong and well in Bing's index. The domain score and blocked status are typical of non-spammy websites. The number of indexed pages is higher than expected and is most likely a result of the tracking parameters appended to SellTheWidget.com URLs.

Crawl Issues

File Not Found (404)

SellTheWidget.com has 1,500 404ing pages according to Bing. It is important to note that this is typical of a site with as many pages indexed as SellTheWidget.com. That said, if these can be fixed it would beneficial. Most of these occur on the subdirectories listed below:

- www.sellthewidget.com/temp/ (Ex. http:// www.sellthewidget.com/temp/juno.html)
- www.sellthewidget.com/news/ (Ex. http:// www.sellthewidget.com/news/content.php?id=60423)
- www.sellthewidget.com/product-description/ (Ex. http:// www.sellthewidget.com/product-description/data.html)
- www.sellthewidget.com/fr/ (Ex. http:// www.sellthewidget.com/fr/)
- www.sellthewidget.com/favorite/ (Ex. http:// www.sellthewidget.com/favorite/card.html)

Placeholder Consulting

Site Review for www.SellTheWidget.com

Review of Robots.txt

As of February 27th, 2015, www.sellthewidget.com/robots.txt contains the following:

```
User-agent: *
Disallow: /photos/
Disallow: /photos.html
Disallow: /newsletter/
Disallow: /privacy_policy*
Disallow: /*widget.html
```

www.sellthewidget.com/robots.txt

SellTheWidget's robots.txt file is currently blocking 874,182 variants of the regular expressions above. This is needlessly wasting a lot of links that otherwise could be helping pages rank.

/photos/

This is a potentially good idea because images found via search engines rarely lead to conversions. Normally it would be better to simply implement meta robots but since this folder only contains image files, this is best way to do this. In addition to blocking this folder it is recommended that images search be opted out of in Google Webmaster tools.

/photos.html

These pages do not need to be indexed and thus should be blocked from search engines. A better way of doing this would be to use the meta robots tactic (*<meta name="robots" content="noindex, follow" />*) on each of the applicable pages.

/newsletter/

This directory contains a lot of pages that contain useful and link worthy content. It is recommended that the decision to block this content be reevaluated. Unless there is a strong business reason to hide this content from search engines, these pages should be made indexable and act as landing pages for potential widget buyers.

/privacy_policy*

These pages do not need to be indexed and thus should be blocked from search engines. A better way of doing this would be to use the meta robots tactic (*<meta name="robots" content="noindex, follow" />*) on each of the applicable pages.

/*widget.html

This is a dangerous tactic as it means any file that ends with this pattern will be blocked. This includes widget pages that happen to end with "widget.html". A manual review showed hundreds of product pages that fit this pattern. (Ex. /red-widget.html, /blue-widget.html). It is recommended that this regular expression be edited to cover only the content that shouldn't be indexed.

Placeholder Consulting

Server Response Codes

SellTheWidget.com has several common but harmful server response errors.

404 File Not Found

SellTheWidget.com's current 404 error page is a hindrance to users. The current version returns an incorrect HTTP response code (200 rather than 404) and does nothing to help the user find the page they are looking to access. This is a problem because the search engines are indexing these 404 pages and the users who encounter them see a blank white page with the text '404'. Ex. http://www.sellthewidget.com/widgets/popular/new-releases.html.

At a minimum, this page should return a 404 error code and offer a message explaining that the file is not found and show suggestions of where they might find the file. The 404 page should also include the website's global navigation menu and a search field.

301 Moved Permanently

SellTheWidget.com has many incorrectly configured 301 redirects. According to Google Webmaster Tools, 106,413 of the 301 redirects on SellTheWidget.com redirect to non-existent (404) pages. Manual tests showed that these redirects worked for human users but not for Googlebot. Some examples of these URLs are included below:

- http://www.sellthewidget.com/goto?widget.10040677 (This pattern is observed over 100,000 times)
- http://www.sellthewidget.com/goto?product-description.10040677
- http://www.sellthewidget.com/goto?widget.description.10040677

These redirects should be fixed immediately in order to ensure that the search engines are able to crawl SellTheWidget.com correctly.

Placeholder Consulting

Site Canonicalization

www.sellthewidget.com's homepage has some common canonicalization issues. The two erroneous subdomains below should be 301 redirected.

- 'ww.sellthewidget.com' has 1,005 links pointed at it and should 301 redirect to www.sellthewidget.com/
- 'wwww.sellthewidget.com' has 2,987 links pointed at it and should be 301 redirected to www.sellthewidget.com/

Additionally, some secure pages are erroneously indexed in search engines. One example is:

1. https://www.sellthewidget.com/user/private/100076

As a security measure, all pages using the http protocol in combination with a secure socket layer (https) should contain the following meta tag in their HTML <head> section.

<META NAME="ROBOTS" CONTENT="NOINDEX, FOLLOW">

Placeholder Consulting

Site Review for www.SellTheWidget.com

Use of Sitemap Files

Currently, SellTheWidget.com does not host XML sitemaps. Instead it uses a non-standard HTML version located at www.sellthewidget.com/html-sitemap/. The current sitemap should also be supplemented with an XML version and made available at www.sellthewidget.com/sitemap.xml. This is the default location search engines look for sitemaps.

Sitemaps are used by the search engines to learn both the location and relative importance of webpages on a domain. Adding an XML sitemap to SellTheWidget.com will likely create a short term boost in the number of pages indexed by the engines.

The search engines provide three ways to identify the location of sitemaps.

1. Google and Bing will automatically search for sitemaps at www.sellthewidget.com/sitemap.xml. If the engines find a file there, they will use it as an aid in indexing www.sellthewidget.com.

2. Sitemaps can be specified in robots.txt. When search engine crawlers visit SellTheWidget.com the first file they parse is almost always www.sellthewidget.com/robots.txt. Robots.txt allows for a sitemap parameter for adding the location of sitemaps.

    2.1.   For example, adding 'sitemap: www.sellthewidget.com/sitemap.xml' will direct search engines to download the file located at that URL and treat it as a sitemap.

3. Lastly, sitemaps can be submitted directly to the search engines through their designed webmaster resources pages. Google's is located at http://www.google.com/webmasters/tools/.

All three of the methods work equally well. Additional information about sitemap protocol can be found at http://www.google.com/webmasters/tools/docs/en/protocol.html

Placeholder Consulting

Site Review for www.SellTheWidget.com

Duplicate Content Issues

SellTheWidget.com is self-imposing a lot of search engine related harm by serving the same content on both http://www.sellthewidget.com with plain URLs and http://www.sellthewidget.com with tracking parameters URLs enabled. This leads to a two-tiered problem. First, it dilutes Link Juice site-wide. Second, it increases the risk of search engines penalizing webpages on SellTheWidget.com.

Diluting Link Juice - From the perspective of the search engines, every time someone links to a given page on the Internet they are giving that page a small amount of ranking power (or Link Juice). Thus, from the perspective of a webmaster, the most important page for rankings should have the most links. SellTheWidget.com's tracking parameters are interrupting this system. When a user links to a page on SellTheWidget.com, they often include the tracking parameters in the link. This means that if two users each link to the same page on the website, the search engines will interpret their links as pointing at two separate URLs (due to the difference in tracking parameters) and the potential ranking bonus will be split two ways.

Search Engine Filters - Search engines use many metrics to identify spam. One of the most widely utilized spam indicators is duplicate content. When the engines encounter duplicate content they must make a guess as to which website is the original content creator. This guess leaves a chance for error. After the engines choose which copy is the primary source, they filter the remaining sources by devaluing their identical content.

Placeholder Consulting

Site Review for www.SellTheWidget.com

Crawling Problems

SellTheWidget.com has potential features that could prevent the search engine crawlers from properly indexing the website. The potentially problematic features are listed below with their best solutions.

Plug-Ins

SellTheWidget uses Adobe's Flash plug-in to stream audio and video. Since keeping this valuable product content behind the flash player is a competitive advantage for SellTheWidget, it is appropriate to not allow the search engines to index this media content. When the engines try to access the given content they are returned the text "Please upgrade your Flash Player by visiting http://www.sellthewidget.com/product-details/". This is the recommend behavior for both users and search engines.

Forms

Search engines are not able to use the main search form on the global navigation menu of SellTheWidget's website. Instead they navigate SellTheWidget.com by following internal links. SellTheWidget's internal search result pages can only be indexed if they are linked to either by SellTheWidget itself or by third-parties. These pages have been linked to nearly 10,000 times.
http://www.google.com/search?hl=en&safe=off&q=site%3Asellthewidget.com+%22Search+Results%22. Please see The Top Five Most Pressing and Valuable Changes - Stop Search Engines from indexing empty SellTheWidget search result pages for more information.

Images

SellTheWidget.com does an excellent job of including alternative text for every image. This is helpful to both blind users and search engines that can't interpret images in the same way that humans do. No additional changes are necessary.

Javascript

Search engines are not as capable at parsing Javascript as they are at parsing HTML. Many times this can cause indexing problems for websites that use Javascript for tracking and navigational links. However, the pages that SellTheWidget is using Javascript links for don't need to be indexed because they contain protected product files. No additional changes are necessary.

Placeholder Consulting

Site Review for www.SellTheWidget.com

Individual Section Reviews

The following are SEO audits for each of SellTheWidget.com's most important subsections. The recommendations below focus on the page elements that are most important to search engines. (See http://www.seomoz.org/article/search-ranking-factors for more information).

Overall, SellTheWidget does a good job of optimizing its basic SEO related metrics. The title tags are generally excellent and the meta descriptions are well optimized. SellTheWidget does make the common mistake of including the unnecessary meta keywords tag but need not worry about this hurting rankings. Further details are explained below.

Homepage

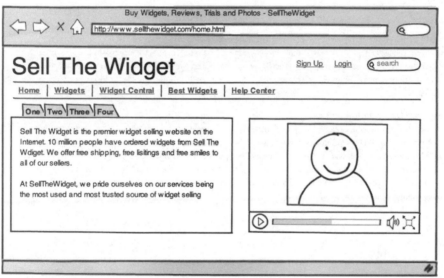

www.sellthewidget.com/home.html

Meta Data

Title Tag
<title>Buy Widgets, Reviews, Trials and Photos - SellTheWidget</title>

SellTheWidget.com's current title tag is well optimized for both humans and search engines. No improvements are necessary at this time.

Meta Description
<meta name="description" content="Buy widgets are the guaranteed lowest prices online - millions of widgets for sale, each including product reviews, samples, free trials, photos, latest trends and new styles."/>

Placeholder Consulting

Site Review for www.SellTheWidget.com

SellTheWidget's homepage meat description is very close to optimal. It is click worthy and contains many important keywords. Its only shortcoming is that the word "new styles" is cut off on some search queries due to character limits. Placeholder Consulting recommends that the meta description is shorted to less than 155 characters.

<u>Meta Keywords</u>
<meta name="keywords" content="widgets, buy widgets, widget videos, widget, widget reviews, widget photos" />

Currently the only search engine that uses the meta keywords tag as a ranking metric is Yahoo. It only uses it in certain cases with minor significance. Its main use today is by competitors to do keyword research. It is Placeholder Consulting's recommendation that the meta keywords be deleted from SellTheWidget.com to negate the risk of unintentionally aiding competitors.

URL
<u>www.sellthewidget.com/home.html</u>

It is Placeholder Consulting's strong recommendation that www.sellthewidget.com/home.html should be 301 redirected to <u>www.sellthewidget.com/</u> rather than the other way around. This is because each link that is redirected through the current 301 is slightly diminished in value. Since more links are pointing at SellTheWidget.com (105,384) than SellTheWidget.com/home.html (3,559) it is worthwhile to reverse the 301 redirect in order to save a significant amount of link value.

Keyword Usage and Targeting
SellTheWidget is currently doing a good job targeting its own name on its homepage. Placeholder Consulting recommends that SellTheWidget focus more on targeting more search related terms. These include widget, buy widgets, widget videos, and widget photos. As a rule of thumb, every well optimized webpage should have its most important keyword targeted once in the URL, twice in the title tag, and three times in the content. (One keyword in the content should also be bolded). For a page that targets multiple keywords, the keywords should be prioritized and/or targeted on other important pages.

Placeholder Consulting

Site Review for www.SellTheWidget.com

Widgets

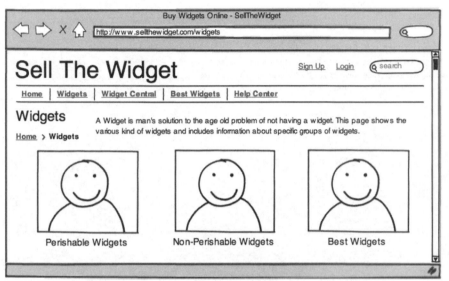

www.sellthewidget.com/widgets

Meta Data

Title Tag

<title>Buy Widgets Online - SellTheWidget</title>

SellTheWidget.com's current primary widget page title tag is well optimized for both humans and search engines. No improvements are necessary at this time.

Meta Description

<meta name="description" content="Watch millions of name brand widgets, widget accessories and more on SellTheWidget Online"/>

Placeholder Consulting recommends that "Watch thousands of name brand widgets..." is changed to "View thousands of name brand widgets". This is based on keyword research that showed that showed that "watch" was search 10X the amount that "view" was searched.

Meta Keywords

<meta name="keywords" content=" widgets, buy widgets, widget videos, widget, widget reviews, widget photos " />

Placeholder Consulting recommends that these be removed. Please see <u>Individual Section Reviews - Homepage - Meta Keywords</u> for more information.

Placeholder Consulting

URL

http://www.sellthewidget.com/widgets

No further action is required for this URL.

Keyword Usage and Targeting

This page is doing a decent job of targeting the keyword phrase "widgets". Placeholder Consulting recommends that the phrase is added to first hundred words of content in a P tag, H3, H4, bold, and in image alt tags. This will make the page more targeted toward the phrase and will increase its rank for applicable queries in the major search engines.

Placeholder Consulting

Site Review for www.SellTheWidget.com

Category Pages

www.sellthewidget.com/widgets/perishable

Meta Data

Title Tag

<title>Buy Perishable Widgets - SellTheWidget</title>

SellTheWidget.com's current category page title tag is well optimized for both humans and search engines. No improvements are necessary at this time.

Meta Description

<meta name="description" content="Perishable Widgets @ SellTheWidget. Free reviews, images and samples. "/>

Placeholder Consulting recommends that this meta description should be changed to "The best source for perishable widgets. SellTheWidget.com offers free shipping on all widgets" to gain additional traffic.

Meta Keywords

<meta name="keywords" content="perishable widgets, free shipping, widgets" />

Placeholder Consulting recommends that these be removed. Please see Individual Section Reviews - Homepage - Meta Keywords for more information.

Placeholder Consulting

Site Review for www.SellTheWidget.com

URL

http://www.sellthewidget.com/widgets/perishable

This URL is optimal for its current use. No improvements are necessary at this time.

Keyword Usage and Targeting

This page's keyword usage and targeting is optimal. No improvements are necessary at this time.

Placeholder Consulting

Site Review for www.SellTheWidget.com

Widget Central

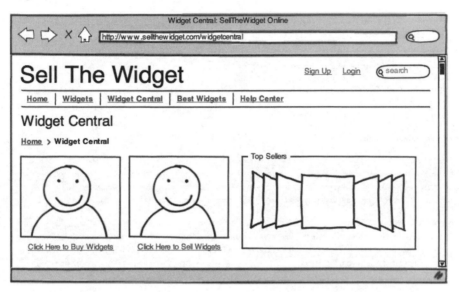

www.sellthewidget.com/widgetcentral

Meta Data

Title Tag

<title>Widget Central: SellTheWidget Online</title>

SellTheWidget.com's current widget central title tag could be better. Placeholder consulting recommends a more descriptive title tag like:

<title>Widget Central – Buy Widgets, Sell Widgets: SellTheWidget Online</title>

Meta Description

<meta name="description" content="Browse for free thousands of widget arrangements created by SellTheWidget users, our widget editors, and your favorite widget artists. Plus, widget reviews, new widget videos, artist photos and blogs."/>

This meta description is longer than the 155 character limit of most Google searches and is truncated. Placeholder Consulting recommends that the meta descriptions be changed to:

"Browse thousands of widgets created by SellTheWidget users, editors, famous widget artists."

Placeholder Consulting

This more enticing and concise meta description will likely drive more traffic than the current version.

Meta Keywords

<meta name="keywords" content="online widget, widget charts, top widgets, new widget releases, widget reviews, widget videos, online widget, widget lists, photos, lyrics" />

Placeholder Consulting recommends that these be removed. Please see Individual Section Reviews - Homepage - Meta Keywords for more information.

URL

www.sellthewidget.com/widgetcentral

This URL is optimal for its current use. However, if the name of the feature was changed more traffic could be driven. Keyword research showed that "widget lists" was searched for 5 million more times a month than "widget central". If possible, Placeholder Consulting recommends that the name of this feature be renamed to "widget list" (with the URL /widget-list/). Note: "widget list" was searched for 4.7 million more times than "widget lists".

Keyword Usage and Targeting

This page is doing a decent job of targeting the keyword phrase "widget central". Placeholder Consulting recommends that the phrase is added to first hundred words of content in a P tag, H3, H4, bold, and in image alt tags. This will make the page more targeted toward the phrase and will increase its rank for applicable queries in the major search engines.

Placeholder Consulting

Site Review for www.SellTheWidget.com

Best Widgets

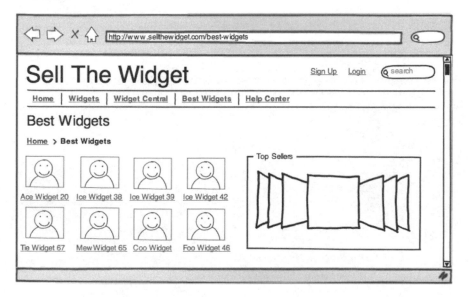

www.sellthewidget.com/best-widgets

Meta Data

Title Tag

<title></title>

SellTheWidget.com's current software title tag is blank and should immediately be added. Placeholder Consulting recommends "Best Widgets of CURRENT YEAR – SellTheWidget Online" (Where CURRENT YEAR is updated every year on different URLs so old years can still rank).

Meta Description

<meta name="description" content=""/>

SellTheWidget's current software meta description is blank and should immediately be added. Placeholder Consulting recommends "The best widgets of CURRENT YEAR as voted on by widget owners" (Where CURRENT YEAR is updated every year on different URLs so old years can still rank).

Meta Keywords

<meta name="keywords" content="" />

No further action is necessary at this time.

Placeholder Consulting

Site Review for www.SellTheWidget.com

URL

www.sellthewidget.com/best-widgets

Going forward it would be better to use URLs with the current year (best-widgets-2015) for individual "best of" pages and use "/best-widgets/" as an index page of all past "best of" pages.

Keyword Usage and Targeting

This page is doing a poor job of targeting the keyword phrase "best of". Placeholder Consulting recommends that the phrase is added to first hundred words of content in a P tag, H1, H2, H3, H4, bold, and in image alt tags. This will make the page more targeted toward the phrase and will increase its rank for applicable queries in the major search engines.

Placeholder Consulting

Site Review for www.SellTheWidget.com

Help

http://www.sellthewidget.com/-helpcenter

SellTheWidget's help center is currently blocked by robots.txt. Given the format of help center (frames hosted on a separate domain) Placeholder Consulting recommends no changes.

Placeholder Consulting

Widget Pages

www.sellthewidget.com/widgets/perishable/acme-widget-2300/

Meta Data

Title Tag

<title>Buy Widgets online including Acme brand - SellTheWidget Online</title>

SellTheWidget.com's current widget page title tags could be improved. Placeholder Consulting recommends the following title tag as an improvement:

"Acme Widget 2300 – Free Shipping | SellTheWidget Online"

Meta Description

<meta name="description" content="Buy Acme Widget 2300 with Free Shipping. Customer Reviews and product photos of the Acme Widget 2300."/>

SellTheWidget.com's current widget page meta descriptions are well optimized for both humans and search engines. No improvements are necessary at this time.

Meta Keywords

<meta name="keywords" content="Acme, Widget, 2300, but online " />

Placeholder Consulting recommends that these be removed. Please see Individual Section Reviews - Homepage - Meta Keywords for more information.

Placeholder Consulting

Site Review for www.SellTheWidget.com

URL

http://www.sellthewidget.com/widgets/perishable/acme-widget-2300/

SellTheWidget.com's current widget page URLs are well optimized for both humans and search engines. No improvements are necessary at this time.

Keyword Usage and Targeting

Widget pages do a great job of targeting the product names. The only recommendations Placeholder Consulting has to improve the keyword targeting is to add keyword (product name) as the alt text of relevant product photos. Additionally, it would beneficial to add the artist's name in bold at least once on the page.

Placeholder Consulting

Site Review for www.SellTheWidget.com

Photo Albums (http://www.sellthewidget.com/widgets/category/brand-name-model/photos.html)

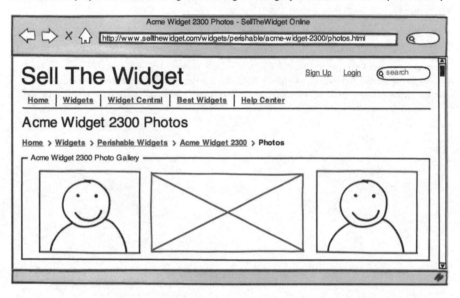

www.sellthewidget.com/widgets/perishable/acme-widget-2300/photos.html

SellTheWidget's widget photo albums at this URL are currently blocked by robots.txt. It is recommended that the applicable entry (Disallow: photos.html) be removed from SellTheWidget's robot.txt and that a meta robots directive is added to these pages.

<META NAME="ROBOTS" CONTENT="NOINDEX, FOLLOW">

Placeholder Consulting

Site Review for www.SellTheWidget.com

Photo Albums (http://www.sellthewidget.com/widgets/category/brand-name-model/random-number.html)

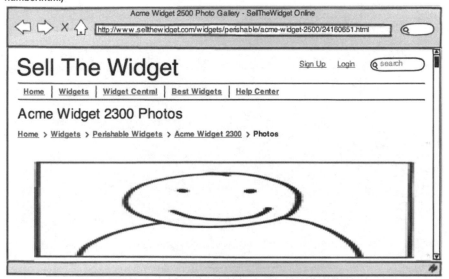

www.sellthewidget.com/widgets/perishable/acme-widget-2500/24160651.html

Meta Data

Title Tag

<title>WIDGET NAME Photo Gallery - SellTheWidget Online</title>

This title tag is well optimized but would be better if it was customized to each individual photo. Currently the title tag stays the same for every photo in an widget's photo album. It would be better for photo rankings if each photo did not compete with itself. If possible, Placeholder Consulting recommends that each photo title tag be customized to each photo. Ex. "Acme Widget 2500 Red - SellTheWidget Online".

Meta Description

<meta name="description" content="Check out Acme Widget 2500 photos on SellTheWidget"/>

This is a well optimized meta description. Placeholder Consulting recommends no changes at this time.

Meta Keywords

<meta name="keywords" content="Acme Widget photos, Acme Widget 2500, 2500, Widget, Photo" />

Placeholder Consulting recommends that these be removed. Please see Individual Section Reviews - Homepage - Meta Keywords for more information.

Placeholder Consulting

Site Review for www.SellTheWidget.com

URL

www.sellthewidget.com/widgets/perishable/acme-widget-2500/24160651.html

This URL is well optimized but could be better. If possible, Placeholder Consulting recommends that each URL is customized to each photo. Ex. "www.sellthewidget.com/widgets/perishable/acme-widget-2500/Red-Acme-Widget-2500-24160651.html".

Placeholder Consulting

Site Review for www.SellTheWidget.com

Keyword Targeting

The following information is about the targeting of keywords on SellTheWidget.com.

Targeted Keywords

The following are the terms on www.SellTheWidget.com's homepage that are found on the page elements that are most important to search engines. (See http://www.seomoz.org/article/search-ranking-factors for more information).

URL - www.sellthewidget.com/home.html

\<title\>Buy Widgets, Reviews, Trials and Photos - SellTheWidget\</title\>

\<h1\>SellTheWidget Online\</h1\>

\<h2\>BLANK\</h2\>

\<h3\>What Is SellTheWidget\</h3\>

\<h3\>Buy Widgets\</h3\>

\<h3\>Widget Reviews\</h3\>

\<h3\>New & Featured Widgets\</h3\>

\<h3\>Categories\</h3\>

\<h3\>Widget Review\</h3\>

\<h3\>Best Widgets\</h3\>

\<h4\>2011\</h4\>

\<h4\>2015\</h4\>

\<bold\>Buy Widgets\</bold\> (Same as \<strong\>)

Search engines use the above mentioned tags to help determine meaning and relative importance of page content. Specifically, the title and URL are the most important elements for search engines.

Placeholder Consulting

Site Review for www.SellTheWidget.com

h1

SellTheWidget's current h1 could be better optimized for search engines. Instead of restating the website's name it should include the most important keyword or keywords for the domain. See "Visitor & Search Analytics - Natural Search Keywords" below for more information.

h2

Currently the h2 on SellTheWidget's homepage is incorrectly configured! See below:

```
<h3 style="margin: 0; padding:0; font-size: 26px; color:#515f64;">What is SellTheWidget</h2>
```

The current version opens with an h3 tag and closes with an h2 tag. This error is causing search engines to not recognize this line as an h2. In addition to fixing this line, Placeholder Consulting recommends that all of the current h3s are converted to h2s. This will put proper emphasis on these keywords.

As a rule of thumb every well optimized webpage should have the keywords it is targeting once in the URL, twice in the title, and three times in the content. (One keyword in the content should also be bolded).

Placeholder Consulting

Site Review for www.SellTheWidget.com

Visitor & Search Analytics (Keyword Research)

SellTheWidget.com's current analytics provider, Omniture, is an excellent source of important and actionable data. Some of this data is covered below.

Important Metrics to Track Daily

There are several metrics that site operators should track on a daily basis.

Daily Unique Visitors

SellTheWidget.com has about 2,500,000 daily unique visitors. This number is important to watch so unusual spikes can be acted on. These irregularities can signal server errors, search engine penalties, and security compromises.

Referring Domains

SellTheWidget.com's top referring domains are:

1. www.google.com
2. www.yahoo.com
3. www.bing.com
4. www.google.co.uk
5. www.google.ca
6. www.amazon.com
7. www.cnn.com
8. www.live.com
9. www.aol.com
10. www.sellthewidget.com (self)

What does this data mean?

These websites won't likely change very often. If they do, immediate action should be taken to determine why they changed. More frequently, the fluctuations of the 'long tail' referring domains should be watched. These include domains 11 through 100 on the Omniture 'Referring Domains Report'. These domains will indicate areas of the web that are talking (either positively or negatively) about SellTheWidget.com. They should be scanned daily to identify conversations and promotions.

Natural Search Keywords

SellTheWidget.com's top referring natural search phrases and terms are:

1. "SellTheWidget"
2. "SellTheWidget.com"
3. "SellTheWidget widget"
4. "buy widgets"
5. "www.sellthewidget.com"
6. "free widget info"
7. "widget reviews"
8. "widgets"
9. "rent widgets"

Placeholder Consulting

Site Review for www.SellTheWidget.com

10. "widget"

<u>What does this data mean?</u>

These keyword phrases represent the wants (demand) of current SellTheWidget customers. 1, 2, 3, and 5 indicate the strength of the SellTheWidget brand with its users. 4, 6, 7, 8, 9, and 10 indicate potential new customers wants and their relationship to SellTheWidget. These keywords represent what users want from SellTheWidget. They want to learn more about widgets and read what other people have to say about them (reviews). These are the key wants of users and should be well understood and potentially profited from.

Paid Search Keywords

According to Omniture data, www.sellthewidget.com's top referring paid search phrases and terms are:

1. "SellTheWidget"
2. "SellTheWidget.com"
3. "SellTheWidget gift"
4. "www.sellthewidget.com"
5. "SellTheWidget widget"
6. "SellTheWidget gift subscription"
7. "SellTheWidget widget cases"
8. "SellTheWidget cases"
9. "SellTheWidget insurance"
10. "SellTheWidget case"

<u>What does this data mean?</u>

These keywords indicate the most successful (in terms of driving traffic) paid keywords in the major search engines. This list along with similar data reported by Omniture should be shared with SellTheWidget's marketing department and used to help plan future PPC campaigns.

Placeholder Consulting

Site Review for www.SellTheWidget.com

Terms & Phrases Leading to Conversions

These are the terms and phrases that most frequently lead to conversions.

- "SellTheWidget"
- "SellTheWidget.com"
- "SellTheWidget widget"
- "www.sellthewidget.com"
- "buy a widget"
- "widget reviews"
- "get a free widget"
- "widget"
- "widgets online"
- "free widgets"

<u>What does this data mean?</u>

These are the most important keywords to optimize for on <u>www.sellthewidget.com</u>. Natural SEO campaigns and paid search campaigns should focus on these terms. This list along with similar data reported by Omniture should be shared with SellTheWidget's marketing department and used to help plan future PPC campaigns.

Placeholder Consulting

Site Review for www.SellTheWidget.com

High Search Value Terms and Phrases

www.sellthewidget.com is naturally competitive for several highly valued search keywords. These include:

- "buy a product case"
- "free widgets"
- "widget reviews"
- "buy a free product"
- "widget"

<u>What does this data mean?</u>

These are the most competitive keyword phrases that SellTheWidget ranks well for. It is interesting to note that all but two of these phrases contain the word widget. These are less actionable than the other lists but are a good signal of competitiveness.

Placeholder Consulting

Site Review for www.SellTheWidget.com

Information Architecture & Internal Link Structure

Information architecture and internal link structure are critical to how search engines index a given site. When a search engine robot (or spider) first encounters a webpage, it has no understanding of how it is structured or how important the page is relative to the rest of the pages on the domain. This means that in order for a search engine robot to correctly determine the context of a website, it needs to find algorithmic clues on a website. The most important of these clues are URLs, internal links, and breadcrumbs.

Information Hierarchy

SellTheWidget does an excellent job of revealing its information hierarchy through obvious clues.

URLs

SellTheWidget's product pages have the ideal URL structure:

http://www.sellthewidget.com/widgets/perishable/red-perishable-widget/

No further changes are recommended.

Internal Links

SellTheWidget's information hierarchy is segmented with appropriate internal links. The navigation menu on the homepage lists all of the top level genres available on SellTheWidget (Ex. Perishable). These then lead to subcategory (Ex. Red) pages that contain relevant products and popularity charts. Each of these categories is linked to with optimal anchor text. This system could be improved by taking it one step further. Placeholder Consulting strongly recommends that links to all of the lowest level products are added to the second level sub-categories (Ex. Perishable -> Red) pointing to the top products for the applicable subcategory. This is helpful for users and for spreading Link Juice.

Breadcrumbs

The product and categorization pages on SellTheWidget currently don't include breadcrumbs. This makes it difficult for both users and search engines to determine their relative position when analyzing a webpage. Placeholder Consulting recommends adding the following breadcrumb structure to all category and product pages.

Widgets -> Category -> Subcategory -> Product

Where 'widgets' links to the homepage and 'category', 'subcategory', and 'product' point to their appropriate pages using the name of the given section.

Placeholder Consulting

Site Review for www.SellTheWidget.com

Content Analysis

www.sellthewidget.com currently has a lot of indexable unique content. This is great for both users and search engines alike. More specific information is available below.

Unique Content

Quality unique content is the cornerstone of any search engine optimized webpage. It provides incentive for people to link and boosts several of the metrics search engines use to rank pages.

Currently SellTheWidget does a good job of providing quality unique content on most of its pages. The homepage's "Top Widgets" feature updates daily and spreads Link Juice around to high selling products. The product pages contain unique descriptions of the widgets. Ideally, www.sellthewidget.com should contain at least three paragraphs of well-targeted keyword text per artist page to increase the chance of ranking well.

Placeholder Consulting

Site Review for www.SellTheWidget.com

User Need Fulfillment

People use search engines to fulfill a need. Sometimes this is the answer to a question, other times it is location of a resource. In SellTheWidget.com's case, the user's need is to review and buy widgets.

According to Omniture, the most popular pages on SellTheWidget are widget photo galleries. This doesn't necessarily mean that this is the primary use of SellTheWidget but it does indicate user intent.

Lastly, SellTheWidget does a great job of offering a giant selection of widgets to its users. It also offers a lot of unique information about products (reviews, photos).

Placeholder Consulting

Site Review for www.SellTheWidget.com

User Experience

Usability and User Experience are as important to the success of a webpage as search engine rankings. If a user can't navigate or understand a website, its potential is extinguished.

Design Quality

www.sellthewidget.com's design is slick, professional, and friendly. The use of familiar faces (celebrities) makes it inviting and comfortable.

The only recommendation that Placeholder Consulting has is to continue testing variations and making improvements based on the user feedback.

Placeholder Consulting

Site Review for www.SellTheWidget.com

User Experience

The homepage of SellTheWidget.com is overwhelming. There is no clear call to action, instead there are many buttons competing for the viewer's attention. The most prevalent of these include:

- "Search" - Header center
- "Shop for Widgets" - Blue button far right on navigation menu
- "Get SellTheWidget PRO" - Yellow horizontal banner
- Scrolling Widget Photos - Middle Left
- Advertisement - Middle Right

To a first time viewer of SellTheWidget.com's homepage, it is obvious that the website is about widgets but it is unclear what the user can gain from SellTheWidget. Ideally, this should be immediately made clear on the homepage without the user needing to scroll.

Most users (64% according to Omniture) reach SellTheWidget.com through search engines. This means they likely skip the homepage and land directly on product pages. While the product pages are more focused than the homepage, they still do not have a clear call to action. While it is good to have a lot of features for users, it is also important to prioritize them for users. This gives users a clear point to start at and allows them to explore on their own and discover what other features are available to them.

Placeholder Consulting

Link Building Opportunities

Current Inbound Link Types

It is important to understand the types of links SellTheWidget.com currently has in order to plan future link building campaigns.

The anchor text distribution is as follows for all of SellTheWidget's inbound links:

Anchor Text of Inbound Link	Unique Links %
SellTheWidget	31.8
Blank [Image]	8.1
Blank	2.3
SellTheWidget.com	2.2
SellTheWidget [Image]	2.2
www.sellthewidget.com	1.8
widget	1
SellTheWidget	0.9
Widgets	0.9
SellTheWidget.com	0.9

Distribution of anchor text of links pointing at www.sellthewidget.com/

What does this data mean?

From a purely link profile perspective, SellTheWidget no longer needs links with the anchor text of its brand name or URL. This is common of large websites. This information should be used when planning partnerships with other websites and when creating link worthy content. For example, a link coming from a website using SellTheWidget's services should stop using the anchor text 'Product Name on SellTheWidget' and instead use 'Buy Product Name'.

Placeholder Consulting

Site Review for www.SellTheWidget.com

Content Currently Attracting Links

The following are the most linked to pages on www.sellthewidget.com. This is important information to know because it illustrates what the most link worthy pages are on SellTheWidget.com. This information can then be used to plan new content.

Most linked to pages on *.SellTheWidget.com (Includes all subdomains)

Page	Approximate number of links
http://offer.sellthewidget.com/coupon/super-bowl	189,776
http://offer.sellthewidget.com/coupon/snl	178,624
http://offer.sellthewidget.com/coupon/oprah	135,591
http://www.sellthewidget.com/	135,394
http://offer.sellthewidget.com/coupon/verizon	63,965
http://offer.sellthewidget.com/coupon/tmobile	52,993
http://offer.sellthewidget.com/coupon/att	52,546
http://offer.sellthewidget.com/coupon/tullys	52,332
http://offer.sellthewidget.com/coupon/starbucks	36,875
http://offer.sellthewidget.com/coupon/costco	23,869

What does this data mean?

This data illustrates the SEO value of SellTheWidget's coupon program. It is very surprising to see that three partnership coupon URLs are being linked to more than SellTheWidget's homepage. This is likely due the size and placement of the partner links. These links are passing a large percentage of SellTheWidget's total link juice and should be carefully researched before removing.

Placeholder Consulting

Site Review for www.SellTheWidget.com

Most linked to pages on www.sellthewidget.com (Does not include subdomains)

Page	Approximate number of links
www.sellthewidget.com/	114,284
www.sellthewidget.com/widgets	17,468
www.sellthewidget.com/products	19,394
www.sellthewidget.com/myWidget	19,381
www.sellthewidget.com/widget-reviews	19,380
www.sellthewidget.com/myWidget/library	19,373
www.sellthewidget.com/SellTheWidget_faqs	19,362
www.sellthewidget.com/new-features.html	19,345
www.sellthewidget.com/special-offers	18,315
www.sellthewidget.com/help-center	13,184

What does this data mean?

This provides an important perspective on link worthy content on SellTheWidget.com. Other than the homepage, /widgets and /products are the most link worthy sections on SellTheWidget. These sections should be further promoted to gain additional links.

The section /myWidget is also noteworthy. This shows that user engagement is leading to a lot of links. This section has a great strategy that appears to making users stay on the page longer and link to their own pages.

The last important detail that this data reveals is the relative importance of /help-center and /SellTheWidget_faqs. Since this list only includes external links, this data point indicates that a lot of people off SellTheWidget.com are linking to sources of help on SellTheWidget. This generally happens when users are confused by the given website and resort to looking elsewhere for help.

Placeholder Consulting

Site Review for www.SellTheWidget.com

Vertical Search Opportunities & Inclusion

Vertical search offers webmasters a way to capitalize on certain types of search queries. Each of these verticals uses different signals and classifiers to create rankings. Below are the verticals that are most likely to help SellTheWidget.com drive additional traffic.

Image Search

Image search offers webmasters a way to drive an additional amount of traffic. Google uses the following signals to classify and eventually rank images. (This list is not comprehensive).

- Image filename
- Image alt text
- Text around image
- Links

SellTheWidget has already given Google permission to index its images (see <u>Technical On-Page/On-Site Issues - Registration with Search Engines</u> for more information). The next step to appearing in Google Image results is to make it easier for Google to classify images. Placeholder Consulting recommends SellTheWidget make the following changes to its photo pages. Ex. http://www.sellthewidget.com/photos/widget/blue-african-widget.html

1. Include product name in filename. Ex. "blue-african-widget-large.jpg" instead of "2356456-345234-large.jpg"
2. Add alt text other than the product name to all photos. SellTheWidget does this in some cases but for the majority of photos the alt text is only the product's name.
3. Add some kind of descriptive text to or around images.

Optimizing for Image search is usually a low ROI project but can generate additional traffic and can be utilized to improve brand recognition.

Placeholder Consulting

Blog/Feed Search

SellTheWidget.com appears to have two blogs associated with it. These blogs currently are not indexed in either of the leading blog search engines. (www.technorati.com and blogsearch.google.com)

- http://corporate-blog.SellTheWidget.com/ (Dormant)
- http://blog.SellTheWidget.com/ (Active)

Placeholder Consulting added http://blog.sellthewidget.com to both search engines on February 2nd, 2015 and it should be active within three weeks as long as it continues to post new content. Note: corporate-blog.sellthewidget.com was not added because it doesn't appear to be active at this time.

Placeholder Consulting

Glossary

Below are explanations of some of the search engine optimization jargon that is used in this report.

Cloaking

Displaying different content to search engines and human users. Depending on the intent of the display discrepancy and the strength of the brand of the person or company cloaking, it may be considered reasonable or it may get a site banned from a search engine.

Indexing (Crawling)

The process search engines use to download and catalog the Internet. Generally, it is done by writing a computer program (called a spider, crawler, or robot) that intelligently downloads website content, follows the links in that content to a new webpage, downloads the new page's content, and continues the cycle.

Link Juice

A theoretical metric developed by Google founder Larry Page. This metric represents a numerical unit of the worth for a given website. This worth can then be transferred to other websites through links.

Long Tail

"The Long Tail" is a phrase first coined by author Chris Anderson describing the typical distribution of search queries leading to a website. According to his widely accepted theory, most search referrer traffic actually comes from very specific search queries ("Widget I want to buy") rather than competitive and popular search queries ("Popular Widgets").

Understanding the SEO Industry

Like many niches within the technology sector, SEO developed from humble roots. This chapter describes these roots and discusses the current-day status of the SEO industry. It is a brief overview of a very complex industry but provides all of the basic information you should know while discussing the industry with fellow SEOs.

A BRIEF HISTORY OF SEO

To understand the current state of the SEO industry, it is important to know how it developed.

In the Beginning

SEO has always been about influencing the search results of search engines. Before the creation of modern search engines, there were a variety of search engines that helped organize the information on the Web.

Some of the earliest search engines made their debut in the early 1990s. These included the first versions of Yahoo! (which at the time was more like a directory than what people now think of as a search engine), ALIWEB, and Infoseek. Like Yellow Page influencers, early SEOs took advantage of alphabetical order to get to the top of rankings. This included listed pages with names like "AAA," "1ForU," and similar titles. In addition to this rudimentary tactic, early SEOs took advantage of chronological order by submitting websites at certain times (midnight), thus attaining the first result for the given query.

As the years progressed, new search engines debuted (Alta Vista, AOL, Inktomi) that started implementing more complicated algorithms. These algorithms used the metrics of keyword density (the number of times a specific word or phrase is used on a given page divided by the total number of words on the page) and meta tags like "keywords" to supplement their understanding of the content of websites. SEOs followed pace and started the process of keyword stuffing (artificially adding given keywords to a page) in order to be seen as more relevant. Although algorithms are much more complicated today, this cat and mouse game between SEOs and search engines continues.

In the early '90s, formal groups started forming around SEO (although it was not called that at the time). These discussions took place on mailing lists and in message boards. The actual phrase "Search Engine Optimization" was first coined in 1997 by an unknown person. Danny Sullivan (see "SEO Leaders") has noted that the first time he found the term used was in May 1997 in a meta tag on his website of the time, Search Engine Watch. He also admits that it is quite possible that it was used before that but has been unable to find any archived evidence.

Toward the end of the '90s, the major search engines started using metrics located off-page to rank websites. Although AltaVista claims to have been using link popularity metrics, Google differentiates itself with its PageRank algorithm. In this way, Google was able to filter out the unpopular pages that dominated the results of its competitors.

As a result of the success of the search engines, SEO started to become a more lucrative business. As such, SEO techniques at the beginning of the modern millennium started to become more sophisticated (link networks, paid links, content optimization, PageRank sculpting) and the search engines (mainly Google) started putting more resources into combating spam. This is the industry situation that exists today.

Coming of Age

As web search has gone more mainstream, so has SEO. It is now an established industry with large conferences and numerous professional organizations.

SEO conferences, including Search Marketing Expo (SMX) and Search Engine Strategies (SES), are now held in five continents and draw audiences in the thousands.

In 2009, Search Engine Marketing Professional Organization (SEMPO) estimated that more than 2 billion dollars would be spent on SEO services within the year. In the same year, Forbes conducted a survey titled "2009 Ad Effectiveness Survey" that showed that 53 percent of the senior marketing executives that participated planned to spend more than 1 million dollars on SEO services (more than any other form of Internet marketing).

Major corporations have taken note and now it is common occurrence for Fortune 500 companies to hire full-time SEO teams to work in-house. Following suit, small and medium businesses are doing the same. At the time of writing, a search for "SEO" on the popular job finding site, Monster.com, returned hundreds of results for United States companies looking to hire an SEO.

WHO ARE INTERNET MARKETERS AND WHERE CAN I FIND THEM?

As you get to know the SEO industry more, you'll inevitably find that *Internet marketing* is a rather broad term that applies to a lot of people. This section describes how people use the title, Internet Marketer, and how you can get involved with other marketers in your community. Remember, there is always a lot that you do not know about the Internet. Expanding your network is the best way to ensure that you have the resources you need when you find out they are necessary.

Understanding the Differing Views on SEO

Internet Marketer in the context of a job title can mean a lot of things. Just as a teacher can specialize in any one of many subjects (history, mathematics, science, and so on), an Internet Marketer can specialize in specific areas of online marketing (SEO, PPC, Affiliate, Analytics, and so on). In practice, this broad title can apply to anyone who tries to drive traffic to a given website. As you can imagine, this leaves a lot of room for interpretation.

BLACK HAT VS. WHITE HAT

Just like offline industries, Internet Marketing has its own unique code of conduct. We describe this on a scale going from black hat (sneaky marketers who use tactics clearly against the search engine guidelines) to white hat (marketers who follow the search engine guidelines word for word). Most people in the industry fall between these two extremes in an area people call *gray hat*.

To rank highly for the web's most competitive terms (pornography, prescription drugs, and gambling related), it is virtually essential to use black hat methods. These generally include manipulative link building tricks like parasite hosting (hosting content on a website without the permission of the site's owner), link farms (networks of websites built solely for the purpose of building links), content cloaking (showing one set of content to your visitors and another set to search engines), and other sneaky strategies. These marketers are typically less involved with their community partly because of the necessity to keep what they are doing a secret. Due to the competitiveness of their industry niche, they tend to be some of the most profitable marketers. They usually work against the grain of the search engines by focusing on finding loopholes and tricks to outsmart them.

White hat marketers work with the grain of search engines by following their guidelines and implementing long-term strategies. In my experience, I have never met an Internet Marketer who abides 100 percent by the search engine guidelines. As a result, the people who are identified as white hats in the industry are the ones who follow the guidelines the vast majority of the time. In my experience, the guidelines these marketers break are related to buying links and scraping search engine result pages. These marketers are often active in their industry niche communities and many times do very well financially with consulting for large corporations who are looking for long-term online marketing strategies.

> **TIP** As a reminder, you can see Google's search engine guidelines at www
> .google.com/support/webmasters/bin/answer.py?hl=en&answer=35769.

SEPARATING THE SPAMMERS FROM THE SEOS

Many people who claim to be professional SEOs are more like spammers than traditional SEOs. In the industry they are referred to as "Snake Oil Salesmen," a phrase referring to scammy salesmen from the past who sold snake oil claiming it had medical benefits. Today, these scam artists provide illegitimate "SEO services" and have cost a lot of people a lot of time and money. When interacting with SEOs, I recommend looking out for the following signs for someone who you don't want to do business with. Likewise, I recommend that you do not advertise the following services because they will hurt your credibility as an SEO:

1. Anyone who claims they can **guarantee** top rankings in search engines.

2. Anyone who claims they will submit a client site to a **large number of search engines**. (Remember from Chapter 2 the only search engines that are important to the vast majority of the world's Internet users are Google and Bing.)

3. Anyone who claims they do **mass directory submission**.

The people who do these things make up a small minority of the SEO industry. The rest of the industry is full of ethical people who are open to sharing ideas and working for the mutual benefits of their friends and colleagues.

▶ Unfortunately, the "outside world" often gets its perspective of SEO from clients who have been scammed by this minority.

Getting Involved

At first glance, SEO is a close-knit community with many niches full of smart and experienced people. This can make it very intimidating to enter. Luckily, the community is very open to new people and is constantly hosting networking events to make getting involved easier.

At the time of writing, SEO communities exist in most of the world's major cities. There are particularly active communities in San Francisco, Seattle, Vancouver BC, Toronto, New York, Miami, London, Munich, Stockholm, and Sydney. In each of these cities there are clubs and organizations dedicated to bringing SEOs together. These are mostly organized online and with only a few exceptions are open to the general public.

The easiest way to get involved with these communities and meet people is to interact with them online. I recommend starting to read and comment on SEO blogs. The most popular SEO blogs at the time of writing include:

▶ **Search Engine Land:** http://searchengineland.com/

▶ **SEOmoz:** www.seomoz.org/blog/

▶ **SEO Book:** www.seobook.com/blog/

▶ **Search Engine Roundtable:** www.seroundtable.com/

▶ **Search Engine Journal:** www.searchenginejournal.com/

▶ **Marketing Pilgrim:** www.marketingpilgrim.com/

▶ **Matt Cutts:** www.mattcutts.com/blog/

▶ **Search Engine Watch:** http://blog.searchenginewatch.com/

▶ **SEO Chat:** www.seochat.com/

▶ **SEO by the Sea:** www.seobythesea.com/

If that's not your style, you can try attending local events. To find SEO events in your city try some of the following queries in Google:

▶ SEO Events <City>

▶ SEO Meet up <City>

▶ SEO Club <City>

▶ Social Media <City>

▶ Social Media Meet up <City>

▶ Internet Marketing Event <City>

▶ Online Marketing Event <City>

▶ SEM networking <City>

If none of those queries uncover any events, you have just found a great opportunity. Hosting SEO events is easy, inexpensive, and great branding. Simply choose a location and spread the invitation via blogs, Twitter, and Facebook. For reference, most local events I have attended in Seattle have been free meet-ups at bars.

AIM FOR GENERAL MARKETING EVENTS, TOO

Consider speaking at more general marketing events, too—not just SEO-specific meetings. The American Marketing Association, for example, has chapters in most large American cities, and because the group caters to marketers from all branches of the discipline, online marketing—specifically SEO techniques—is often a topic that the members know little about. This makes your content even more valuable to the audience (and your reception quite favorable), and in general, fewer people are vying for the speaking slots.

My last suggestion for getting involved in the SEO community is a little more intimidating but is the most effective. Speaking at conferences and seminars is easier than it sounds and makes a big difference. If you have new knowledge to bring to the community, you may be able to share it by speaking at an industry event. You can apply to speak at major SEO conferences at the following URLs:

▶ **SMX:** http://searchmarketingexpo.com/speaking

▶ **SES:** www.searchenginestrategies.com/forms/ses_speakers.php

Before speaking, I recommend you learn a little about the community. The section "SEO Leaders" later in the chapter will help you understand who has had success speaking at conferences and should give you an idea of who you might be sharing a SEO panel with.

GETTING A SPEAKING GIG AT AN SEO CONFERENCE

Speaking positions at SEO conferences are one of those catch-22 situations where people who have spoken before usually are the ones who are invited to speak. This can make it very difficult for new comers to get invites.

The following are tactics that I have seen work for people new to speaking:

▶ **Create your own niche:** I have seen this work with a few different people. Cindy Krum, for example, is a very intelligent SEO who distinguished herself by being the first to focus on the Mobile SEO niche. In doing so, she made herself an authority and has been invited to speak at many conferences around the world.

▶ **Build a network and use it to connect people and highlight an already existing skill set:** This is the most popular way of breaking into the speaking circle. I have seen it done by many people who start out on a lot of different skill levels. The trick is to connect people who can help each other and when appropriate leverage your own skills and intellect to help those you can. Fellow marketer, Joanna Lord, an analytics and PPC expert, has used her network to connect people and earn a reputation that has gotten her many speaking positions.

▶ **Work for a well known company:** This tactic is harder to achieve but works extraordinarily well. I have seen people who have never spoken at conferences before break into the speaking circles by leveraging their employer and skill set to make a name for themselves. This is the tactic I used to get my first speaking position.

continued

(continued)

▶ **Leverage previously acquired knowledge and pitch your own topic:** Odds are you know something related to Internet Marketing. Jen Lopez is a SEO, formerly a developer, who has leveraged her development skills to present SEO concepts from the perspective of a developer. This has helped her pitches at developer and SEO conferences get accepted.

▶ **Leverage a strength that can supplement SEO strategies:** If you don't know much about SEO but do know a lot about another aspect of Internet Marketing, you can always try to pitch topics you do know at SEO conferences. Scott Willoughby is an e-mail marketing expert who has done well in both the SEO world and e-mail marketing by explaining complicated e-mail marketing tactics at conferences.

▶ **Divulge a secret that brought great success and can be repeated**: This tactic is done less regularly but when used is generally well accepted. Dennis Yu is a social media strategist who has leveraged his success with Facebook to travel the world and teach people how to use his methods to be successful.

▶ **Combine an expertise outside of SEO and explain how it relates:** One of the problems with SEO speakers is that they tend to know only one topic really well. You can use this to your advantage by taking a skill outside of most SEOs' skill sets and explaining how it can help them do their job. Sarah Bird, a lawyer based out of Seattle, has done a great job of this by teaching SEOs about how law relates to their job.

▶ **Pitch locally**: If all else fails, you can always try to leverage your hometown. I have seen people speak at conferences simply because they have been successful SEO in the area where the conference is held.

THE SEO PYRAMID AND WEARING MULTIPLE HATS

In addition to categorizing ethics by hats, Internet marketers refer to different abilities as different hats. Someone who calls himself an SEO might wear the hat of a web developer, paid search marketer, or social media marketer.

Many SEOs see their responsibilities in terms of the aptly named SEO Pyramid. (See Figure 10-1 for a graphical version of this.) Though this graphic illustrates the responsibility of a traditional SEO, it is common for Internet marketers to have overlapping skills from different niches (referred to as wearing multiple hats). These niches compliment each other and serve as building blocks for well-rounded online marketers. The job titles that follow are some of the most common niches (hats) that people in the Internet marketing industry have. Although a full explanation of the many niches in Internet marketing is beyond the scope of this book, I recommend learning as much about each of the following areas as possible so that you can execute the SEO process as illustrated in Figure 10-1 as well as the other jobs that specialize in other aspects of driving traffic online.

FIGURE 10-1: SEO Pyramid

Search Engine Optimizer (SEO)

SEO is an acronym that stands for both Search Engine Optimization and Search Engine Optimizer. People who have this job title generally only focus on organic search. They tend to be consultants who focus on link building and on-page optimization. They can be white hat, black hat, or within the large gray area in between. Although their ultimate goal is to have all of the skills outlined in Figure 10-1, many focus mainly on the two bottommost sections of the SEO Pyramid.

An SEO's typical strengths include information architecture, copy writing, link building, and keyword research.

Paid Search Marketer (Also Referred to as an SEM or PPCer)

PPC is an acronym that stands for pay per click. This refers to search engine ads where the advertiser pays only for those ads that are clicked. This type of marketer differs from SEOs in that they focus on paid search results rather than organic results. Although most of their ad-related duties fall outside the scope of the SEO pyramid, their keyword research skills are essential for constructing the entire shape.

Paid search marketer strengths include keyword research, ad copy writing, campaign management, and competitive analysis. At the time of writing, they have more of a presence in major corporations than traditional SEOs.

> **NOTE** Many SEO old-timers disagree about the proper usage of "SEM." While all agree that it stands for "Search Engine Marketing," it's sometimes used interchangeably as either the parent category of all search marketing (including elements such as organic, pay per click, and banners) or simply as a synonym for PPC. The latter perspective is especially prevalent among large advertising agencies and big brands. To hedge your bets and articulate your point to as many people as accurately as possible, I recommend referring to organic search as "SEO" and paid search as "PPC." This eliminates any problems associated with the varying definitions of "SEM."

Social Media Marketer (SMM)

A social media marketer is a relatively new job position. This title refers to someone who manages social media for the benefit of a website. They make up the newly formed tip of the SEO pyramid and are responsible for interacting with the online community and driving traffic. Whereas SEOs work in the arena of client websites and paid search marketers work in the arenas of Adwords and Ad Center (among others), social media marketers work in the arena of Twitter, Facebook, LinkedIn, Delicious, Digg, Stumble-Upon, and blogs. Their primary focuses are to build brand awareness, expand their network of friends, and to drive traffic.

Their strengths generally include their extraordinary social abilities, large social networks, and a large amount of influence. Many of these skills are displayed online as the number of friends, followers, or points.

Conversion Rate Optimizer (CRO)

A conversion rate optimizer is a person who focuses on raising the ratio of the number of people who visit a site to the number of people who eventually perform a specific action on a website (generally a purchase). Their role falls outside the scope of the SEO Pyramid but is essential for profitability. Whereas SEO helps people find a given site, CRO helps people perform an action on the given website after they find it. Conversion rate optimizers work on conversion funnels (the process of directing users to a specific action) and landing pages (webpages with a specific purpose or call to action). They do a lot of testing to find the combinations of elements that lead people to convert the best.

Their strengths include salesmanship, test creation, design, and buying psychology.

Affiliate Marketer

An affiliate marketer is someone who sells something online (product or service) by means of acting as a middleman. They make money by taking a commission for each item they sell. Like a conversion rate optimizer, their role falls outside of the SEO Pyramid but is essential for making the website profits. Affiliate marketers are generally more effective online marketers or salespeople than the manufacturer or provider of the product or service they sell.

Their strengths include salesmanship, web development, design, and conversion rate optimizing.

SEO LEADERS

An inherent side effect of the marketing industry is that regardless of the niche, the best marketers will rise to celebrity-like status. SEO is no different. The following is a list of the some of the biggest names in the SEO industry. This list will hopefully help familiarize you with some of the names you are sure to hear.

These names are included not so much to boost their egos but more to educate you. These people have important roles in the industry and are able to open many doors for the people who get to know them well. They are examples of people who have done exceptional jobs of personal branding. You can use the following bios to give you an idea of what has worked for them with their careers and use this as a reference for what might work for you.

Danny Sullivan (Search Engine Land)

Danny Sullivan began covering search engines in late 1995, when he undertook a study of how they indexed web pages. The results were published online as "A Webmaster's

Guide To Search Engines," a pioneering effort to answer the many questions site designers and Internet publicists had about search engines.

The positive reaction from both marketers and general search engine users caused Danny to expand the guide into Search Engine Watch, a website, where he served as editor-in-chief through November 2006. Now he heads up Search Engine Land as editor-in-chief, taking it into the next generation of search coverage. Danny also serves as Third Door Media's, the corporation behind major SEO events, chief content officer.

Matt Cutts (Google)

Matt Cutts is the head of Google's Webspam team and the spokesperson for Google's SEO policies. He is well known in the SEO community for enforcing the Google Webmaster Guidelines and cracking down on link spam. Matt also advises the public on how to get better website visibility in Google.

Rand Fishkin (SEOmoz)

Disclaimer: I used to work with Rand at SEOmoz, so I am admittedly bias. That said, while doing research for this chapter, Rand was included on every single SEO Leaders list that I saw.

Rand Fishkin is the CEO and co-founder of SEOmoz, a leader in the field of Search Engine Optimization tools, resources, and community. In 2009, he was named among the 30 Best Young Tech Entrepreneurs Under 30 by *BusinessWeek*.

Rand is a frequent speaker at Internet marketing conferences and has key-noted conferences on search around the world. He's particularly passionate about the SEOmoz blog, read by tens of thousands of search professionals each day.

Vanessa Fox (Nine By Blue)

Vanessa Fox is a Search Engine Optimization expert, writer, and consultant best known for her work creating Google Webmaster Central and as a Google spokesperson. Additionally, she is an Entrepreneur In Residence for Ignition Partners and the founder of Nine By Blue, a marketing consultancy with an emphasis on search.

Aaron Wall (SEOBook.com)

Aaron Wall is the author of SEO Book, a dynamic website offering marketing tips and coverage of the search space, free SEO videos, and free SEO tools. He is a regular conference speaker, partner in Clientside SEM, and publishes dozens of independent websites.

Barry Schwartz (Search Engine Roundtable)

Barry Schwartz is an SEO consultant, SearchEngineLand contributor, and iPhone app developer, but he's best known in the SEO industry for his stellar work on his own site, Search Engine Roundtable (SERoundtable.com). Barry is one of the most observant and objective people in the business, and he keeps a close eye on search engine news, obscure blogs, and forums where SEO news often originates. He is very careful to separate speculation from fact, and his is the first stop of the day for many big-brand SEOs.

Todd Friesen ("Oilman")

Currently the Director of SEO at Performics (a company that Google once owned but eventually sold off), Todd Friesen has worked on projects with Fortune 100 corporations, been an administrator at WebmasterWorld.com, moderated for Search Engine Watch, and is a co-host of SEO Rockstars for WebmasterRadio.fm. You can find Todd at just about any search engine conference speaking or networking with other SEOs.

Michael Gray (Atlas Web Service)

Michael Gray is the owner and president of Atlas Web Service; a New York–based Internet consulting firm. He has been involved in web development and website management since 1998. Michael has been involved with affiliate marketing campaigns for several years and does consulting work on a variety of topics such as SEO, social media, and blog management.

Bruce Clay (Bruce Clay, Inc.)

Bruce has operated as an executive with several high-technology businesses, and comes from a long career as a technical executive with leading Silicon Valley firms, and since 1996 has been in the Internet Business Consulting arena.

He has also been featured on many podcasts and WebmasterRadio shows, as well as appearing on the NHK 1-hour TV special "Google's Deep Impact." He has personally authored many advanced Search Engine Optimization tools that are available from the company websites.

THE PEOPLE AND TECHNOLOGY BEHIND GOOGLE AND BING

Though the people who lead the SEO industry are important, it is perhaps even more important to understand a little about the people who created search engines themselves. The decisions of the people who work at these companies have a deep effect on the lives of those of us in the Internet marketing industry. This section is about the people and technology behind Google and Bing.

> **NOTE** This behind the scenes information is much more important than simply as trivia fodder. It provides insight into why the important decisions at these companies are made.
>
> Understanding the culture at Google provides insight into why they are so adamant about only manually removing search results that violate their published guidelines rather than those that seem ethically unreasonable.
>
> For example, at the time of writing the third result for "Martin Luther King," a civil rights leader in the United States, is a white supremacy advocacy website. While this result does not seem like the best result for children searching for information about Dr. King, Google has refused to remove the result because it doesn't want to edit its index based on ethics. This makes sense given the idealistic and engineer-focused culture of the company. (The large exception to this policy is when Google is legally required to manually edit its index. In that case, they do manually modify results.)

Google

To many, Google represents a brand new paradigm for software. The company, which was started by two Stanford PhD dropouts, is operated like a computer science program at a major university. This is in direct opposition to the bureaucracy and closed wall structure of older software companies like Microsoft and IBM. Google is data company known for open protocols, geeky humor, simplicity in design, and great benefits for employees. More important than all of those things, though, Google is known for changing the world and pushing the Internet into the mainstream.

COMPANY CULTURE

Google's culture is unlike any major business culture that came before it. The company's founders made it a priority very early to try to make employees as happy as possible while at work. Their belief was that by doing this they would spend more time working and produce better work. As history shows, this plan worked.

Google employees enjoy gourmet food for meals (why leave the office if lunch is delicious and free?), laundry facilities, and toys and gadgets galore. One employee I talked to jokingly referred to the freshman 15 in reference not to college freshman gaining 15 pounds, but rather new employees at Google gaining 15 pounds due to the meal and snack selection.

Walking into a Google office is a lot like walking into a preschool classroom. The lobbies, hallways, and meeting areas are lined with toys, bright colors, and whiteboards with silly doodles (and complicated algorithms). This is a reflection of the company culture as a whole. The employees at Google tend to be playful while at the same time hard working and extremely intelligent. Most of the software engineers work in small teams and share offices. There is a management hierarchy, but it is less pronounced than at other companies. Like most leading software companies, the standard of work at Google is very high. What makes Google culture unique is that this is supplemented with a high standard of play.

SMART AND NEVER-ENDING

From the very beginning, Google has built an environment around regular improvements to its products and a reluctance to call anything a "final" version. In 2002, we went to the "Google Dance," a party thrown by the then up-and-coming Google, during the San Jose Search Engine Strategies Conference. There, we met a quiet young guy who was looming around the outskirts of the crowd.

We introduced ourselves and we asked him what he did at Google. "You know when you type the wrong word, and Google asks, 'Did you mean *this?*' "

"Sure," we replied, as Google's corrective suggestion interface had been added only the previous year (and dealt a blow to "typo spammers" in the process).

"I did that," he said modestly.

That particular interface feature stuck around and has evolved over the years, and it's a reminder that while people consider "Google" a singular force, it's made of many teams of experts in many different specialties. The sheer simplicity of Google's task and its interface is surprisingly complex.

PEOPLE

The people at Google are the force responsible for making the company what it is today. This is largely due to Google's ability to attract the best talent in the technology industry (this includes Vinton G. Cerf, who co-invented HTTP, the protocol that the Internet runs on). At the time of writing, Google has about 20,000 full-time employees. They work at any of Google's 70+ offices located all around the world. The people at Google tend to be young (many just out of graduate or undergraduate programs) talented, analytical, and high achievers.

The Googlers that I have met have all been very friendly and modest. I was once introduced to a Googler by one of his admirers. His friend jokingly introduced the Google employee as God. Red-faced, the Googler denied it. I followed with complimenting him on creating Earth and thanking him for allowing me to live here. Confused, he said "You're welcome?" I found out later that he was the one who started Google Earth. It turned out he really had created Earth! This conversation is a great representation of the reputation of Google employees. Their reputation is that of being intelligent, highly accomplished, and humble.

TECHNOLOGY

Although the employee benefits and company culture often gets press, the technology is what really makes Google a world changer. Google operates one of the world's largest global networks. It utilizes relatively unpowerful computers in parallel to create a distributed super computer. Google invented not only its own systems, protocols, and architecture, but also its own operating system (a modified version of Linux) and file system (GFS).

The company has data centers all over the world and a global infrastructure to connect them. When other companies find it easier to physically ship hard drives when transferring large amounts of data, Google utilizes the fiber optic cable it bought after the dot com boom to connect some of its data centers. The company works at a scale unmatched by any other company on the Internet.

At the same time, Google's technology is unbelievably efficient. Employees have leaked that their servers use half the level of energy for computations than industry standards. This is a level the EPA said was nearly impossible. This is incredible when a single search query in Google can use up to 1,000 machines in less than 0.2 seconds.

Microsoft

Microsoft is one of the original software giants. Cunning business tactics, smart employees, and ground-breaking software has made it one of the world's most recognizable and farthest reaching companies. Based in Redmond, Washington, Microsoft was originally started by Bill Gates and Paul Allen. The company, which originally started in Albuquerque, New Mexico with two employees, now employs almost 100,000. Microsoft dominates the software industry with its operating system (Windows), productivity applications (Office), and web server software (IIS and the .NET Framework). Its dominance in PC-based software has made great strides in recent years by moving online.

COMPANY CULTURE

Microsoft's culture varies widely from department to department. According to employees I have talked to departments like Microsoft Research and Microsoft Game Studios have cultures described as similar to a fun, well-funded start-up, whereas other departments have cultures where employees are subjected to meetings to plan upcoming meetings.

Many departments are very top-down management driven and communication via e-mail is pushed to an extreme. Though stringent, Microsoft is also an excellent place to grow a career. The company regularly promotes from within and salaries for most are generous. I have heard people who have worked at both Microsoft and Google describe the former as a less stressful workplace with more formal processes and easier upward mobility. I have heard these sentiments echoed by other employees who have worked at Microsoft and other major technology companies.

The company works with monetary and technological resources that are unimaginable at most companies, and the software the company produces helps power most of the world's computers. Microsoft has been described to me as "a thrill," "a headache," and "a rewarding company unlike any other."

PEOPLE

Generally, Microsofties are extremely intelligent and very technologically savvy. They range from high school graduates to well-known PhDs. Many of the employees invented the standards that run the technology sector today. My favorite example is former Microsoft employee, Vincent Connare, who worked on the fonts Arial, Web Dings, and the infamous Comic Sans.

The employees at Microsoft are generally tight knit within their teams and siloed by departments. An old professor of mine once told me a story about his time working on communication consulting for Microsoft. He referred to an experience with Bill Gates where the founder of the company blurted out in a meeting "Why can't the Windows people just talk with the Office people?" My professor, wide-eyed, responded, "You're Bill Gates! Can't you make them?" With a global company with more than

100,000 people and a strict hierarchy like that at Microsoft, this problem is a lot harder than one might think.

TECHNOLOGY

Microsoft has world-leading technological infrastructure. At the time of writing it just completed building the world's largest data center. On the Web side of the business it has made innovations like storing and running servers inside shipping containers for easy portability. On the software side it has developed an elaborate virus response team that many compare to S.W.A.T. On the hardware side of the company it has made innovations in infrared that has enabled it to build products like Microsoft Surface.

The company dominates many of the most lucrative software markets. Its Windows products make up 92.2 percent of the global operating system market (2010) and its Office and Internet Explorer products maintain similarly high market share in their markets.

IAYF

As far back as the very early 1990s, Bill Gates has preached a mantra of "information at your fingertips," commonly shortened to "IAYF." This summarized his goal for what Microsoft should produce—products that enable the rapid retrieval and dissemination of information across the globe. In fact, this philosophy is quite similar to Google's mission, which emerged nearly 10 years later: "To organize the world's information and make it universally accessible and useful."

In the last 20 years, Microsoft has been criticized for arriving late to several crucial games—browsers, search, and cloud computing, among others. The Microsoft Network (MSN) began as a combination of a closed-system Internet Service Provider and online network (similar to the roots of AOL, Prodigy, or CompuServe). It then slowly evolved into MSN as a search engine, first outsourcing its search results processing to Inktomi's technology, and later to Yahoo!'s algorithm. Using its own, homegrown search technology began in only 2005, which makes its current position in the market even more impressive.

So don't count Bing out just yet. Bing's technology has vastly improved since it was first launched, and with the recent merger with Yahoo!, the audience for its search technology is larger than ever. And while more people use Google than use Bing, nearly a third of all web pages run on Microsoft software—something that Google certainly can't claim.

And for the time being, Microsoft knows something important that very few people remember: You don't have to be number one to be profitable.

Microsoft is more secretive about its internal technology than many well-known technology companies, but its power and magnitude is hinted at by the company's ability to serve the world's computers. Its Windows Update system protects millions of computers worldwide. Even when its software is crashing, Microsoft's systems are working hard. Have you ever sent Microsoft an error report after a program crashed? I once spoke with an employee whose job was to build systems to store these reports en masse and create algorithms to see which problems were affecting the most people and in what circumstances. Microsoft's global systems are incredible in scale and growing exponentially with the advent of cloud computing and the rumored possibility of a version of Windows running entirely online.

At the forefront of Microsoft's online dominance is its search engine Bing. Launched almost a decade after Google, it has been relatively successful in catching up and in some cases surpassing its main competitor. The Bing team, like many teams at Microsoft, is very close lipped about its hardware and software. It's fair to guess that its systems run on modified versions of Microsoft's proprietary systems (.NET and Microsoft hardware). The only glimpse I have heard about the black-boxed search engine setup is that data storage requests (from engineers) start at a minimum of 50 terabytes. This gives some idea to the large scale of the system.

LONG-TERM PERSPECTIVE IN SEO

When you read the news and opinions of the experts in the preceding section, you'll find very few instances of exaggerated, hyperbolic claims that some new policy or algorithmic change is going to turn SEO on its head or somehow drastically alter the way we do business in the industry.

In the history of SEO, tactics frequently change, but strategy rarely does. In other words, the specific techniques you implement will evolve, but the goal is always—and probably always will be—to increase the number of qualified visitors to your site. Here are some additional examples:

- ▶ The tactic may have changed from directory submission to linkbait, but the strategy is still focused on accruing new links.
- ▶ The tactic may have changed from repeated site submission to XML sitemap generation and RSS pings, but the strategy remains getting your site's changes crawled as quickly as possible.

NOTE When you read about a new earth-shattering change that's going to fundamentally change (or better yet, kill) SEO, chances are the columnist or blogger is up against a deadline and has a word count quota to fill. Read it with caution. When you read a story about a policy or algorithm change with clear, calm direction about how (or whether) it will affect you and how you should adjust, keep reading.

In the last several years, plenty of changes occurred that promised to upset the SEO cart but never did. Depending on how long you've watched the space, the following list will either make you laugh or scratch your head in confusion. Either you remember these events, or you can't imagine they ever happened.

- **Google adds paid ads in the right margin of the results page.** This threatened the SERP as we knew it, and many rang the death knell of SEO because once you can buy your way into the results, what need does anyone have for organic?

- **Google adds premium paid advertisements above organic results.** Even worse! Now the mixture of paid and natural results in the same column will water down the algorithm's reputation and Google will lose all credibility. Right? Wrong.

- **Google adds Froogle (shopping) results between paid and natural results.** "Froogle?" Are you serious? It was the name Google gave its shopping engine (now simply called "Google Products") and when Google first added shopping results (with pictures, no less), Google was pronounced dead (again) for abandoning its spartan design.

- **Yahoo! uses Google to supplement its natural search results.** Realizing that search demand was larger than its ability to serve all its queries accurately, Yahoo! once outsourced some of its SERP processing to Google.

- **Yahoo! stops using Google to supplement its natural search results.** Eventually Yahoo! stopped doing this when it bought Inktomi and started showing its "own" results.

- **Google changes from its monthly Google Dance to the "Everflux" model.** Long ago, Google recalibrated its index monthly, and the SERPs were relatively static until the next month's change.

- **Google adds local and one box results of every imaginable flavor.** Anything that sends organic results further down the page causes an uproar. In the case of local and "one box" results, smart SEOs looked at changes as an opportunity to expand their presence.

► **Google inserts "see also" results in the middle of organic results.** How dare Google try to direct users away from a query that I worked so hard to rank for? What most SEOs didn't understand was that mathematical equilibrium predicts that you'll gain roughly the same number of visits as you'll lose when "related searches" are integrated into SERPs.

This list is meant to make you feel neither old nor young, neither green nor experienced. Its goal is simply to show you that over time, we've seen a large number of changes, each of which was going to shake things up significantly, and none of which really did. The next time you read about how "SEO is dead" due to the next big technology or site *du jour*, remember that all the preceding things were going to fundamentally transform SEO. But despite the predictions, life went on, and SEO didn't die. Not once.

SEO will be around as long as search engines are around. Search engines (although probably not in their modern form) will be around as long as people look for information. As discussed earlier, the tactics will change, but the strategy will remain the same: Create your content, get it crawled and indexed, encourage the clickthrough, and make the sale.

SUMMARY

Hopefully after reading this chapter you are ready to become part of the vibrant SEO industry. You should now have an idea of where we came from and start to have ideas about where we are going. You should also know who current leaders in the industry are and what they have done. The SEO industry is relatively young and fast moving, which means there is still plenty of opportunity to make an impact.

The next chapter contains information on search engines verticals. It is written to give you insight into the niches that exist in the SEO industry.

## CHAPTER 11

Search Engine Verticals

Online search has evolved along with the Internet to move beyond just text documents. Images and videos have become commonplace and made their way into the SERPs. As such, the search engines have started to look to humans for ranking metrics. These have included location and various metrics that strive to understand intent. Several examples of these new kinds of search results, called search verticals, are described in this chapter.

UNIVERSAL SEARCH

Universal or "blended" search is the term engines use to describe search results that include images, local results or maps, news, shopping, and/or videos mixed in with the normal blue and green text results.

For years, search engines offered users the ability to search for all types of media beyond simple HTML content. With a few clicks, users could view results specifically honed to news, images, shopping, local results, videos, and other vertical "silos" of content. In 2007 and 2008, all major engines took a leap forward and released versions of universal search. These presentation formats met with mostly positive feedback, and engines continue to constantly refine them.

Two significant factors played into engines' ability to create relevant blended search results:

▶ Relatively few users bother to perform "advanced" searches or search through different content silos, even when the ability to do so required a simple click on a refinement link in the standard navigation.

▶ Engines have dramatically improved their ability to predict search "intent" based on the type of query performed.

Universal search makes a lot of sense for some search queries and has made a big impact on SEO, simply because it has increased the number of content silos that marketers need to pay attention to. Take, for example, a search for "flowers" in Google. Flowers is a broad search query. It is not clear whether the user is looking for a specific type of flower, a local flower shop, or an image of a flower. Due to this ambiguity, Google shows lots of different types of results (search verticals) to best satisfy the user's search intent. You can see an example of this in Figure 11-1.

Universal search has huge ramifications for SEOs for two reasons. First, broad searches (also called short tail and head searches) are extremely common and drive a lot of traffic. Second, the inclusion of universal search means that SEOs can compete on several different playing fields in order to get the searcher's click. This takes these competitive terms and funnels the results into different verticals. To an SEO this means potentially more areas of the SERP to have a presence, but fewer spots available in each specific area. Game on!

> ▶ Google isn't the clear winner here. Ask.com also pioneered universal search, and Bing has very high-quality universal presentation, too.

> **NOTE** As more types of content appear in SERPs, Google has taken an opportunity to test different types of advertising alongside them, including AdWords with images or sitelinks, as well as enhanced business listings in Google Places (which show up in Map results).

FIGURE 11-1: Google Search result for "flowers"

LOCAL SEARCH

Local search encompasses searches done online where the results vary depending on the location of the searcher. From the engine's perspective, this is a much harder technical problem than a typical web-based search. Instead of simply running their standard algorithms to determine which result should rank based on relevancy and popularity, the engines are forced to first determine the searcher's location and then filter the results based on that information. This, as you can imagine, makes the process much more difficult.

In addition, engines must do their best to determine the intent of the query with little information to help them. That's why engines continue to experiment with showing varying levels of local and general information in a broad search (such as "plumber") whose intent is not easily discernable.

Determining Locality

Search engines determine a searcher's location in many ways, as discussed in this section.

SEARCH ENGINE TLD

Search Engine top-level domain (TLD) is the easiest solution. If users search for something on www.google.co.uk rather than www.google.com, they are likely in the United Kingdom rather than the United States. (Consider also that google.com automatically redirects to google.co.uk when accessed from an UK-based IP address.). While this is helpful from a broad sense, it isn't specific enough—they are in the UK but are they in London or Greenwich?

IP ADDRESS

When a computer connects to the Internet it needs to be assigned an IP address in order to make requests to outside servers. This process is actually quite complicated, but the simplified version is that the IP address ultimately comes from the ISP (Internet service provider) that the computer is trying to use to connect to the Internet. Because it is important that no two computers have the same IP address, ISPs needed to come up with a system for assigning unique IP addresses.

It is a problem for two computers to have the same IP address because when a given computer requests information, it needs to specify where that information should be sent. If this address is shared by two computers, information and connection conflicts occur.

The solution that ISPs came up with for distributing unique addresses was to issue ranges to certain regions and have other systems (routers) assign IP addresses within these ranges.

This means that a computer that connects to its local ISP in Seattle will share a unique range of IP addresses with other computers in Seattle that request IP addresses from the same ISP.

The search engines can store these ranges in their own databases and associate them with a physical place on earth. In this way, search engines can determine location down to the city level (sometimes it can even be closer than this).

USER-PROVIDED INFORMATION

Although IP addresses are better indicators of location than TLD, they are not perfect. These addresses can be spoofed and as IP ranges change, databases of IP addresses to physical locations go out of date.

For example, some cellular mobile broadband devices might have a "regional" IP address bank to pull from, but the result is having an IP address associated with a distant city. My IP address frequently points to a city up to 200 miles away from my actual location when I use my Verizon MiFi mobile hotspot.

This means that the search engines must find other information to supplement the IP address data. The easiest way to do this is to simply ask the users where they are searching from. This information can then be saved via cookie or associated with their account and used in the future. You can see an example of Google asking the searcher for their location in Figure 11-2.

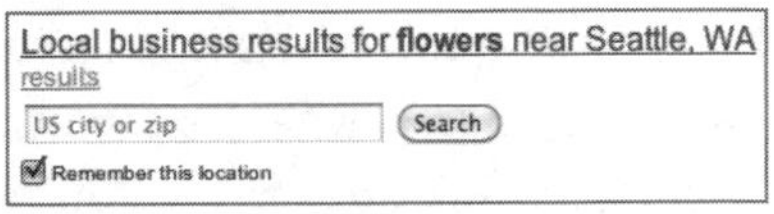

FIGURE 11-2: Google presenting textbox for zip code

Another source of location data that search engines use is past searches. This can be as simple as remembering if a logged-in user searches for something like "Seattle bars." It can also be a little trickier like remembering if a logged-in user searches for driving directions and associating the starting location with that user's account. Those search engineers are sly devils, aren't they?

WIRELESS ROUTERS AND GPS

Although the preceding tactics are great, the search engines can do better. If the searcher is accessing the Internet using a wireless network, the engines can sometimes use this information to target a person's location within a hundred feet (the range of a typical wireless router). The search engines do this by hiring people to drive around cities mapping the MAC (Media Access Control) addresses they encounter on publically accessible WiFi spots to GPS coordinates. In normal use a MAC address doesn't change. This system can be fairly accurate but requires a lot of maintenance.

MAC ADDRESSES

MAC addresses are unique numbers that are assigned to network adapters or network interface cards by the manufacturer of the hardware. These numbers don't usually change because they are built into the hardware (although technically it is possible to spoof these numbers). This makes it particularly useful for mapping to physical locations.

The best way to determine a user's location is through GPS. If users are accessing the Internet from a GPS-enabled device, they can voluntarily decide to send this information to the search engines. With GPS coordinates, the search engines can determine the user's location to an accuracy of within a few feet or less.

Ranking Factors

Once the search engines have identified where a user is located, they then need to rank the local results in a useful way. Local SEO expert, David Mihm, releases annual reports on what he and others who study local search believe are the most important ranking metrics. You can find the entire list at www.davidmihm.com/local-search-ranking-factors.shtml. This section of the chapter represents a synopsis of this report.

LOCAL BUSINESS LISTING ADDRESS IN CITY OF SEARCH

▶ *Search engines have started to shift the responsibility of business listing from themselves to the business owner.*

At the time of writing, the most important ranking factor for local search is the proximity of the searcher to the relevant address that is provided in the search engine's local business center.

CITATIONS FROM MAJOR DATA PROVIDERS

Because local business websites don't often attract links like more typical websites, the engines rely on citations from trusted data providers. These providers include local resources Yelp.com and CitySearch.com, and in some cases, citations may even include raw comments from users at the end of an article describing a local business. This is equivalent to the concept of popularity discussed in Chapter 1.

> **NOTE** At the time of writing, the Google Local algorithms for every city were the same, but it appeared that the algorithms for different business types varied. Because of this, it is important to see which major data providers are cited for businesses in your local area for your type of business by conducting an applicable search. After doing that, submit your business listing to those sources.

ASSOCIATING LOCAL BUSINESS LISTING WITH PROPER CATEGORIES

▶ *In Google you can associate your business with custom fields if it doesn't fit into a given category. At the time of writing, this tactic is very helpful boosting rankings in niche categories.*

In local business listing, business owners can choose from a hundreds of categories to associate with their business. While you can submit your business into five categories, Google sometimes places you into additional categories on its own, based on signals it gets from other sites. The engines then take this information into account when ranking local search results.

These human-powered categories assignments are used as relevancy signals for local listing and are heavily relied upon by the search engines.

GENERAL IMPORTANCE OF CLAIMING LOCAL BUSINESS LISTING

The engines tend to rank local results that are claimed in their systems higher than non-claimed results. Part of the reason for this is that in order to claim a business listing the business owner must verify the physical mailing address or phone number of the business. This makes the business listing more legitimate in the eyes of the search engines. You can claim a business listing by going to www.google.com/local/add and/or https://ssl.bing.com/listings/BusinessSearch.aspx and verifying that you own the business.

PRODUCT/SERVICE KEYWORD IN LOCAL BUSINESS LISTING TITLE

Just like exact match domains, the search engines must take into account the business name when determining rankings. If a user searches for Hilton hotels Seattle, the search engine will return Hilton hotel results before Marriott results.

GENERAL IMPORTANCE OF OFF-PAGE/OFF-LISTING CRITERIA

Once the search engines can start to map locations as being associated with a specific physical place, they can start using the information of virtual Internet neighborhoods as a link metric. For example, in the case of local search, a link from a local chamber of commerce website will help your rankings more than the exact same website that is associated with a different city.

VOLUME OF CUSTOMER REVIEWS ASSOCIATED WITH YOUR LOCAL BUSINESS LISTING

▶ This metric is very prone to abuse.

The search engines can also use the metric of customer opinions to rank local search results. Customers can choose to leave reviews of businesses on their online local business listing. This information can then be used to rank businesses.

Additionally, the search engines can use the number and sentimental analysis from reviews as a signal of whether or not a local business should rank well for a given query. This is a helpful metric because the nature of a business that has been reviewed four times versus a business that has been reviewed five times is completely different than a business that has never been reviewed at all.

GENERAL IMPORTANCE OF ON-PAGE CRITERIA

In a similar way to normal search, on-page criteria (relevancy) is important to local search. A page that has relevant information in the proper SEO places (title tags, URL, content, links) generally ranks higher than a page that does not. (This of course assumes that the effects of all the other metrics in the section are ignored.)

INCLUDING FULL POSTAL ADDRESS ON A WEBSITE CONTACT PAGE

Although this is prone to abuse, search engines look for the physical address listed in the contact page of a given website. This helps prove its legitimacy as well as its proximity to the searcher.

All of the metrics listed in this section help the search engines determine what locality a business website should be relevant for. Making this determination easier for the search engines improves the chances that your business website will be included in applicable results.

IMAGE SEARCH

At the time of writing image search is still in its infancy. The problem is that an image file is very different from a text document from the perspective of a computer scientist. The technology problems of searching for relevant text in a corpus of all text has largely already been solved.

Images are a completely different story for two primary reasons. First, image files are on average much larger than text files. Whereas a text document may be made up of thousands of 0s and 1s on the binary level, an image with the same dimensions may be made up of hundreds of millions of binary characters. This means that the computing power alone can become a bottleneck to solving the image search problem.

Secondly, algorithmically determining the meaning and contents of an image file is much more difficult than doing the same for a text file. Whereas a word may have only a few meanings and contain very little, an image can have millions of meanings and contain many objects. Imagine the difference between the word "crowd" and an image of a crowd. Although the word maps to the idea of a large group of people, the details of those people are not represented. This is not the same for an image of a crowd where the details of each person in the crowd are visible.

This of course is an oversimplification of the image search problem but it helps to illustrate its complexity. As a result of the complexity of these two factors (size and meaning/contents), search engines have relied on text-based metrics to rank images.

To make matters worse, these technical issues fail to address the social implications of image search. Whereas most search queries are done with the intention of getting information, the queries where images are the best result tend to aid people in stealing images. From an SEO perspective, this leads to the question of whether or not image search–referred traffic is even useful.

Is Image Search Traffic Useful?

This is the most common question I get when talking to clients about image search. They are right in that many image searches result in the user simply stealing the image and not giving credit to the owner or the site where it came from.

My initial answer to this question is two-pronged:

1. I have never seen an example where image search referrals provide enough value that it warrants making image optimization worthwhile.

2. At the same time, I think that everyone, regardless of limitation or disability, should be able to use the Internet. This includes humans and computers alike.

In order for this to happen, there needs to be a way to represent images for those who are visually impaired and those systems that can't understand them (which includes search engines). The best way to do that today is to optimize images just like SEOs do for a website as a whole.

OPTIMIZING FOR IMAGE SEARCH NOW

My final answer is that although image search traffic is not useful today, the demand for sophisticated image search will likely lead it to be useful in the future and thus is worth optimizing for now. I don't consider it a high priority but it is a good long-term strategy.

With that said, I recommend adding relevant keyword phrases to the alt attributes and filenames of images. (See the "Ranking Factors" section later in the chapter.) Additionally you should include these key phrases in the text that surrounds the image, including the copy preceding the image, and a caption if possible. These tactics make it easier for visually impaired people and search engines to understand what an image is displaying and have shown to boost the relevancy metrics for the page the image is embedded on.

Bing Is Winning

I am a big fan of the underdog. At the time of writing, Google dominates online search and advertising. Thus, I get excited when I see formidable competitors.

Bing, though much less popular than Google, is winning the race to build the best image search engine. It provides more relevant results in an easier to navigate interface. For example, Bing image search presents an AJAX driven result set that uses scrolling rather than pagination to view additional images (see Figure 11-3). This prevents unnecessary page loads and makes it easier to use (and it's one of the reasons why Google recently created a very similar image results interface).

This is a fact that more and more people are realizing. I always use it as my preferred image search engine, and its popularity is growing.

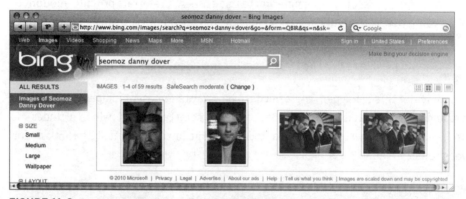

FIGURE 11-3: Bing Image Search result for "seomoz danny dover"

A lot of the technology behind Bing image search and Bing maps is coming from Microsoft Research. This think-tank style department has made amazing strides forward with image technology in the past few years. As an SEO you should be aware of this trend and not be blindsided when it makes an impact on future search-referred traffic.

Ranking Factors

Although there is much research on image search metrics compared to other search verticals, most experts agree the majority of image ranking metrics are related to those that are listed in this section.

ALT ATTRIBUTE (ALT TEXT)

The code to include an image file in HTML takes the following format:

```
<img src="http://www.example.com/image-filename.png" alt="Alt Text" />
```

The parameter in the alt attribute (in this example, Alt Text) is displayed in the event that the image cannot be represented. This happens when the technology accessing the tag cannot display the image. This is most common when the image is broken or when it is accessed by software like a screen reader.

This text typically describes the image and is a very good ranking factor.

SURROUNDING TEXT

Many times the text that surrounds an image in a web document describes the image. This can take the shape of a caption or introduction to the image.

This information is very useful for image search engineers. It is relatively common for an image to rank for a query that matches the text around an image.

FILENAME

In theory a filename should always describe its content. Unfortunately, this is not the normal case for image files. Many times they will be named by a computer (like a digital camera) rather than a human. This makes this a relatively poor metric for rankings.

That said, it does help to include descriptive words in image filenames because it is still used as a minor factor in image search rankings.

TRADITIONAL ON-PAGE SEO FACTORS FOR IMAGES

It is important to note that the search engines still use normal ranking metrics for images (relevancy and popularity). This is usually done on the page where the image is located. (Note this is different than the image URL.)

This means that by optimizing a page in the normal ways, you are also optimizing its images. It is a win-win situation.

VIDEO SEARCH

At the time of writing, video search is lead by YouTube with niche video competitors filling in the gaps of the enormous online video market. YouTube, which is owned by Google, got its start from ex-PayPal employees and combined superior video compression (which was Flash-based) and superior timing to beat its rivals. Its current competitors survive by focusing on video niches like HD and professional videos (Vimeo) and presentations with slides (Omnisio). YouTube is continuing to build upon its market lead by making strategic partnerships in niche video areas like music videos (Vevo.com).

From a technical perspective, video search is a lot like image search but with bigger file sizes. (Note that the storage is not the bottleneck, but rather the computing cycles necessary to analyze images and video.) It is immensely popular but still in its search infancy as search engineers figure out how to best determine relevancy and popularity for images and video.

Who Cares If It's Not YouTube?

I get this question a lot from clients. YouTube dominates the online video market. It is also owned by the company that dominates the online search market. So why should SEOs care about video search for videos that are not on YouTube?

In the past, they wouldn't need to. YouTube outranked all of its competitors when the same video was on both websites. They could go for the long tail but in video search that rarely converted to anything other than video views.

At the time of writing, the balance in video search is shifting. Video sites other than YouTube are ranking highly in video results in universal search, and blogs with links to posts are ranking in normal results. You can see an example of this happening in Figure 11-4.

FIGURE 11-4: Google Search result for "2009 auto tune"

This means that SEOs who work with video sites now have the ability to start competing in the SERPs without giving their content to YouTube.

Ranking Factors

According to expert Video SEOs (VSEOs) the rankings metrics for videos are very straightforward but are starting to include more social media and engagement attributes like the search algorithms as a whole.

TITLE

Like domain names for websites, the title of a video is usually included when linking to or describing a video. This makes it a powerful ranking metric because people tend to search using the same words or phrases with which they heard the video described.

DESCRIPTION

For the same reasons as the title, the video description is a good ranking metric. It has most of the benefits of a title but has the added luxury of being longer and more descriptive.

ENGAGEMENT

More and more engagement-based starts are appearing to influence video search results. Engagement metrics include actions like:

- ► Ratings
- ► Comments
- ► Favorite by users

While this is certainly new territory for search engines, it does fit in well with other engagement metrics that have been appearing in the SERPS (Yelp results, for example, occasionally show star ratings). It is also apparent that these metrics are harder to manipulate than classic metrics such as view count.

INBOUND LINKS

Inbound links are important for the same reason they are important for normal SEO. The links are an excellent indicator of popularity. Inbound links to video pages are treated very similarly to the standard links described in Chapter 1.

VIDEO SITEMAP

At the time of writing, I have seen tremendous success by including a video sitemap in addition to a standard sitemap on my websites. The newest video sitemap protocol right now includes the option of including the URL of the page where a video is embedded. I have found this helps both the video rank in video search and the page it is embedded on rank in universal search.

INSTANT SEARCH

In September 2010, Google added a horizontal dimension to search results with the introduction of Google Instant Search.

Google Instant really expands upon the role of an older, existing technology, Google Suggest, which is Google's "predictive search" engine. Predictive search works by using the first few characters or words typed in the query box to predict what the entire query is going to be. Google uses many different data types to predict what your full query will be, including your geographic location, your search history, as well as the search history of its entire user base.

In an instant search, Google pre-fills the SERP with results from the query that it predicts you are making. If and when you show Google that your query is not the one it is predicting, it automatically creates a second query prediction and repopulates the search results. It continues to re-populate the search results until you stop typing, hit Enter (or click the Search button), or until it can no longer make rational predictions based on your incomplete query.

SERP REFINEMENTS AND SEARCH ENGINE INNOVATORS

As mentioned about other SERP refinement features, Google isn't always the pioneer for new results features, and even when it is, it's not always the best.

Yahoo! released its predictive search feature, Yahoo! Search Assist, in 2007, and it was quickly heralded as one of the best predictive search features available. One of the things that makes Yahoo! Search Assist so good is that it shows search suggestions with your specific query term placed all throughout the suggested query—front, middle, and end. The vast majority of Google Suggest query suggestions, on the other hand, show your search term at the front of the search query.

Yahoo! Search Assist, therefore, might take your query term "Windows 7" and suggest a term like "how to reinstall Windows 7", where other, more front-loaded predictive search suggestion interfaces would not.

For example, consider the long-tail query "how to find a nanny". When the user types the first two words (as shown in Figure 11-5), Google automatically populates the search results as if "how to" were the final query.

FIGURE 11-5: Predictive search results for the query "how to".

As the user continues to type the query, Google Suggest kicks in and, as shown in Figure 11-6, pre-fills the query box with "how to find a job", when in reality, the user has typed only "how to find a". Based on its user data, Google has determined that "how to find a job" is the most likely end result of the user's query.

▶ In a Google Instant query box, the black type is what the user has typed, and the lighter, gray type is Google Suggest's prediction. That predicted query decides the current configuration of search results.

FIGURE 11-6: Predictive search results for "how to find a job".

Further down the list of search suggestions, you can see that Google thinks the query might also focus on finding a song, percentage, or a person.

Ranking Factors

> ▶ For now, your best bet might be to use Google Instant for keyword research to glean further insight about how Google knows what people search for and how they search for it.

Fully optimizing your rankings for Google Instant is easy to describe and nearly impossible to do. For instance, fully optimizing for the search "how to find a nanny" would require you to rank well for "how", "how to", "how to find", "how to find a", and, of course, "how to find a nanny". Then there are the "false" predictions that appear along the path to "how to find a nanny", such as "how to tie a tie", and "how to get rid of fruit flies".

You'll should not take this strategy far, as your content probably doesn't support all the query iterations from point A to point Z. Instead, watch your referring keyword reports to see whether your site is attracting users from shorter query strings than they used to. If your site's user behavior suggests that users are clicking over to your site before they've completed a query, then it's probably worth checking to see whether you can rank for other partial queries that relate to longer queries that have traditionally sent traffic to your site.

As of this writing, there's little evidence either way about what affect Google Instant is having on search habits. Are users looking intently at their suggested options, ignoring the box completely or somewhere in between?

SUMMARY

This chapter discussed the three most popular search verticals. You learned answers to common questions about them, and you also learned what the most important ranking factors were for each vertical.

In the next chapter you learn more about the niches and alternatives to traditional search. Specifically, you will learn about what other search engines exist and how you can use them to your advantage.

## CHAPTER 12

Optimizing for Alternative Search Engines

Google and Bing currently dominate the search engine market share in most countries in the world. (Two notable exceptions are China with Baidu and South Korea with Naver.) Because of this, they are usually the targets for typical SEO implementations. But what happens when you want to optimize for a niche product that is more likely to be found via different sources? The answer is to optimize for alternative search engines.

AMAZON

Amazon is the world's largest online retailer. (If you haven't heard of it, you should stop reading this and lock yourself in a room with a computer until your typing fingers hurt.) It organizes and sells millions of products to people all over the world.

As such it is a very high-impact search engine because the conversion rate (buy rate) tends to be much higher than that of standard search engines.

What Niche Is it Helpful For?

Amazon is useful for any SEO or webmaster looking to sell a product online. The vast majority of its products are physical, although recently it has been putting more of an emphasis on digital products to support its Kindle Empire.

If you are a webmaster or a work for a webmaster who wants to sell goods, Amazon is a great choice for you. It is highly optimized (Amazon is mentioned in every usability book I have ever read) and has an enormous customer base.

Ranking Factors

Although not all of the ranking factors for Amazon's search engine are known publicly, the following items cover the most useful known factors.

PRODUCT NAME

Amazon's search engine appears to work mostly off of relevancy metrics (as opposed to popularity metrics). This means that the product name is essential for ranking high in Amazon for a given search term or phrase.

The name of the product appears to be the most important ranking metric. (See Figure 12-1.) It is best to use user-friendly language ("chair" as opposed to "relaxation assistance device"). To aid in this, you can do keyword research in traditional search engine tools or through Amazon's predictive search engine. For example, when you start typing a query in an Amazon search box, a drop-down box begins to predict what you're trying to type. These searches are based on popularity, although Amazon isn't eager to divulge relative popularity numbers, the time period measured, and so on.

The product name and description can only be modified by the product seller, so it is best if they are optimized before they are sent to Amazon. This optimization should be done based on keyword research.

There is the option for customers to request to update listings, but at the time of writing that process is unreliable.

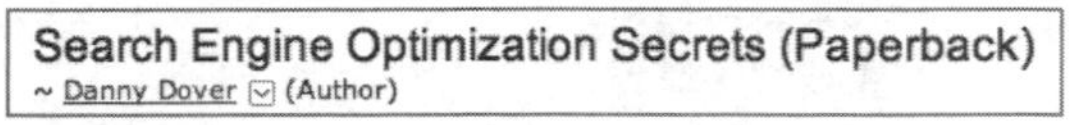

Search Engine Optimization Secrets (Paperback)
~ Danny Dover ☑ (Author)

FIGURE 12-1: Amazon product title for this book

TAGS

When a user tags a product on Amazon (on the product description page), it helps Amazon determine product relevancy. (See Figure 12-2 to see what the tag interface looks like.) This is an easy metric to influence and should be used but not abused. Every Amazon account can vote for a tag only once. I don't recommend creating ghost Amazon accounts to bypass this limit because spam detectors are surely in place.

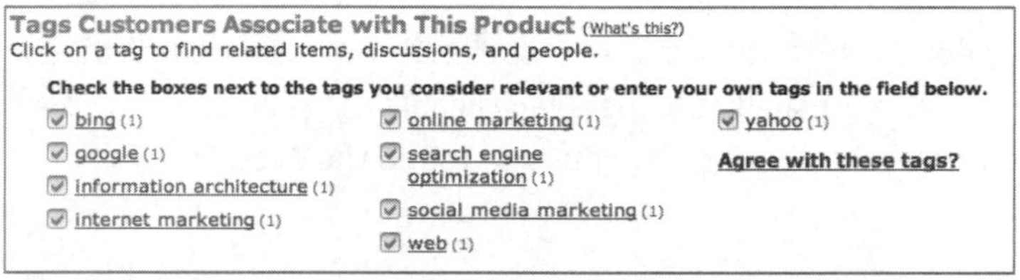

Tags Customers Associate with This Product (What's this?)
Click on a tag to find related items, discussions, and people.

Check the boxes next to the tags you consider relevant or enter your own tags in the field below.
- ☑ bing (1)
- ☑ google (1)
- ☑ information architecture (1)
- ☑ internet marketing (1)
- ☑ online marketing (1)
- ☑ search engine optimization (1)
- ☑ social media marketing (1)
- ☑ web (1)
- ☑ yahoo (1)

Agree with these tags?

FIGURE 12-2: Amazon tagging system

How Does This Alternative Engine Affect Primary Search Engines?

Amazon is one of the strongest domains on the Internet. As such, its pages rank for an enormous number of search queries. Combine this with the fact that these pages are highly optimized for selling and you can see their incredible value.

If it makes sense for your or your client's business model, it is a good idea to point relevant links to given Amazon product pages to help bolster the strong domain authority to make the page outrank your competition.

You may also want to look into leveraging Amazon's platform for selling your or your client's products rather than creating your own website. Though this will likely cut into margins (Amazon takes a percentage of each sale), it may prove worthwhile in some cases. (For example, this makes sense for book publishers and most gadget manufacturers.)

Further, Amazon can help some companies with reputation management problems. If your company or product is plagued by negative sites populating the SERPs for product-based queries, a strong Amazon page (owned by either you or an affiliate) will be a strong competitor to pages that disparage your product.

YOUTUBE

YouTube is by far the most popular video website on the Internet. It gets 1 billion page views a day from all over the world and is the result for millions of search queries. It is owned by Google and as such is integrated in Google search results with image thumbnails. Bing doesn't have this luxury (served!) and can only return YouTube results with standard text results. Its importance on the Internet should not be underestimated; it very likely will play an even bigger role in search in the years to come.

What Niche Is it Helpful For?

If you are optimizing videos or are a video content producer, you need to think about YouTube and its dominance. It is usually the first place people associate with online video and contains content from millions of producers around the Web.

▶ Promotions and ads in YouTube videos can drive traffic to other sites but as of now are not major mechanisms for routing traffic.

Ranking Factors

YouTube's primary ranking factors are:

- ▶ Video Title
- ▶ Video Description
- ▶ Video Engagement (measured with metrics like "views," "favorites," and comments)
- ▶ Inbound Links To Video Page

See the section "Video Search" in Chapter 11 for full descriptions and additional information.

How Does This Alternative Engine Affect Primary Search Engines?

YouTube video thumbnails appear on many relevant Google search result pages. These images have a higher clickthrough rate on average than traditional text results on these pages. For this reason, they drive an incredible amount of traffic.

Combine this with the enormous amount of direct traffic that goes directly to YouTube.com to watch videos and it is easy to see how popular videos can receive tens of millions of views in a matter of days.

> **NOTE** Google bought thousands of miles of fiber optic cables left over from the dot com bust so it could transfer data between data centers at a fraction of the normal cost. As such, its data transfer rates for YouTube and its millions of videos are far lower than if the video site was owned by another company. This helps explain the outrageous 1.65 billion dollar price tag Google paid for YouTube. They paid a lot up front but can run it for relatively cheap.

FACEBOOK

The most popular social network in the world, Facebook has not only affected the way people interact, but it's had a direct effect on search engine algorithms. While people don't use Facebook search the same way they use Google search (yet, at least), Facebook searches are increasing in number, and as an engine, Facebook has immense potential to match up users and intent based on the social web.

What Niche Is it Helpful For?

With 500 million users and counting, there are few niches for which Facebook *isn't* helpful. From animal lovers to foodies to high-tech products to polarizing politics, Facebook has a large number of members with every conceivable interest.

Ranking Factors

Facebook has two different types of search results, external pages (pages that live on domains outside of Facebook-owned domains) and internal pages (user profiles, Facebook pages, groups, and so on). External pages are indexed and ranked by Bing. These are typically shown under internal page listings and marked as Bing results. Internal pages, on the other hand, are the primary type of result for searches conducted on Facebook and rely on the technology of Facebook's internal search engine.

Facebook internal search is all about varying levels of connection. Consequently, the number of people who have "liked" a page has a strong correlation to how a page ranks in a Facebook search. It's a strong correlation, but it's not necessarily a direct relationship. Consequently, if you (or even those you are connected to) like a page, then that boosts that page's ability to rank for your search above results that simply have more likes from the general population.

Predictably, the most effective ways for your Facebook content to appear in Facebook search results are to do the following:

▶ Open up your content so that people do not first need to "like" or connect with you before they can see it

▶ Encourage people to like, share, and otherwise pass around your content within Facebook

▶ Engage with your community, which increases on-page content and encourages others to respond, which ultimately results in links to your content appearing in other users' timelines

How Does This Alternative Engine Affect Primary Search Engines?

Active Facebook profile pages have a great deal of ranking potential for branded, subject-based, and personal name-based queries at Google.

At Bing, however, Facebook has an even larger role. In October 2010, Bing and Facebook announced a partnership in which Bing would show personalized results on its SERPs. This personalization is based not on your past Bing search history like typical personalized results. Instead, the Bing algorithm considers in the likes of your connections to determine ideal results for queries such as movies, restaurants, and other topics.

▶ The Bing/Facebook collaboration represents an evolution of integrating social-graph data into mainstream search results; it's not the final step though. Expect many more agreements like this to weave their way into results pages for major engines.

DELICIOUS

In 2003 Joshua Schachter changed the way that people organize information online. He released http://del.icio.us (the most annoying popular URL in history) and introduced the world to social bookmarking. (The URL has since changed to http://delicious.com.)

Delicious is a repository for articles that users want to "save." Because a web browser's "favorites" or "bookmarks" feature is only as effective as a user's ability to always use the same computer and browser, Delicious is a way to have access to all your saved articles, blog posts, and reference material wherever you are, as long as you have an Internet connection.

When you "tag" an article at Delicious, it's as if you've saved it in a file folder with that tag name. In other words, an article about how to perform a 301 redirect on an ASPX site might be saved under the tags "301," "redirect," "IIS," "ASPX," "SEO," and other tags such as the author's name, name of the site or blog, and so on. Later, when a user performs a search at Delicious, the tags that other people have used to categorize URLs are a major factor in determining what pages Delicious returns in its search results.

What Niche Is it Helpful For?

Though it's doesn't have the popularity that it once did, Delicious is an exceptional traffic generating tool for those who write the correct kind of content. Delicious's user-base tends to favor web development and web design–related content. That audience is quick to bookmark how-to guides and top 10 lists.

This kind of content is relatively easy to get on the homepage of this site, which is viewed by a lot of people with the ability to link. This in turn helps search rankings and sends continuous traffic.

Ranking Factors

Delicious's system for ranking on its home page or Hotlist is painfully simple.

NUMBER OF BOOKMARKS IN THE LAST 3600 SECONDS

To the best of my knowledge, the only ranking factor that Delicious uses is the number of times an article has been bookmarked in the previous 3600 seconds (1 hour). A bookmark is counted every time a logged-in user clicks Save. It doesn't get as much simpler than that. Notice how the simplicity of the algorithm design is also reflected in simplicity of the layout design (Figure 12-3). Joshua Schachter realized the value of cutting away complexity so that the user can do what they came to the site to do.

FIGURE 12-3: Delicious's bookmarking interface

NUMBER OF BOOKMARKS OVERALL AND GENERAL SITE AUTHORITY

When you perform a search at Delicious's search box, the results are affected by how many times an article has been tagged with the query terms you use, but it's not always a direct correlation. In other words, the site most frequently tagged is not always the top result. Other, more authoritative domains, as well as the makeup of the user base that tags them, may also have an impact on which sites appear first.

If you want to rank well for queries within Delicious.com, the best thing you can do is make it very easy for users on your own site to bookmark the site at Delicious, including making suggestions about the tags they use. You can decide on those tagging suggestions by looking at current keyword research tools. If your content is extremely timely, suggest tags based on search topics or queries that are currently trending.

How Does This Alternative Engine Affect Primary Search Engines?

Delicious strives to keep nearly all of its content away from search engines. Its links are followed at the link level, but its `robots.txt` file excludes much of the site and most of its content pages (including user profile pages) are written with the robots meta tag set to `"noarchive,noindex,nofollow"`. And as if that weren't enough, when you try to crawl Delicious.com with a search engine's user-agent, the site serves a 404 error on most of the site's pages.

Delicious has a secondary effect on the primary search engines. The real value of this service comes from the audience it serves. This audience is generally tech savvy and very likely to link to good content in other social media websites beyond Delicious. These links then help search rankings in the same way that links help when social media isn't involved.

▶ Delicious's biggest asset is that it is a stage in which a lot of the right people watch the show.

FLICKR

Flickr was the world's first mainstream online social photo site. Facebook has since eclipsed it, but Flickr is still a valuable resource to SEOs and photographers alike.

What Niche Is it Helpful For?

As you likely deduced yourself, Flickr is helpful for photo search. At the time of writing Flickr is owned by Yahoo!. This means that its photos show up a lot in Yahoo! (via Bing) and very seldomly in Google. Google has tried to replicate the same photo repository with its Picasa product and acquisition of Picnik but at the time of writing has failed to achieve the market share and volume of Yahoo!'s Flickr.

Though not directly useful for improving Google search, it provides resources that can indirectly help in all of the engines. Flickr offers a search engine of its own that will filter images by license (www.flickr.com/creativecommons/).

▶ This is an excellent source for finding photos to spice up blog posts and webpages to make them more link-worthy.

Ranking Factors

Though not a lot is known publicly about Flickr's search algorithm, it is obvious through testing that the following metrics are the most important elements.

PHOTO TITLE

The best way to be found on Flickr is with an exact match photo title. It requires an exact match for a keyword search or partial match (one word) if the search query is a phrase. This is easy to customize when uploading images and should be done manually rather than simply using the file names given by your digital camera. You can see a good example of an optimized image title in Figure 12-4.

FIGURE 12-4: A Flickr image title

PHOTO TAGS

Flickr offers users the ability to tag photos to make them easier to find. This is a helpful for both searchers and those who want their content found. Like title keywords, Flickr looks for exact matches in tags. You can see a good example of this in Figure 12-5. Notice how the image is tagged with a lot of descriptive words that describe many aspects concerning both what the image is and how it was taken.

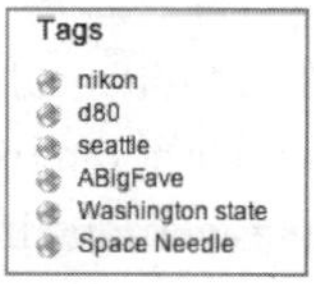

Tags
- nikon
- d80
- seattle
- ABigFave
- Washington state
- Space Needle

FIGURE 12-5: A Flickr image tag

PHOTO DESCRIPTION

Though not likely a primary factor, Flickr uses photo descriptions to determine relevancy. This fits well with the practice of helping search engines by helping users. You can see an example of a useful description of an image in Figure 12-6. Notice how it includes information about the photo, information on where to learn more and details of how to recreate the image with a precise URL.

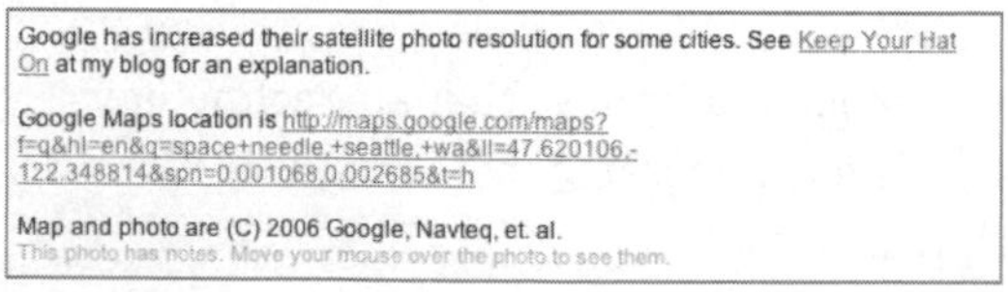

Google has increased their satellite photo resolution for some cities. See Keep Your Hat On at my blog for an explanation.

Google Maps location is http://maps.google.com/maps? f=q&hl=en&q=space+needle,+seattle,+wa&ll=47.620106,-122.348814&spn=0.001068,0.002685&t=h

Map and photo are (C) 2006 Google, Navteq, et. al.
This photo has notes. Move your mouse over the photo to see them.

FIGURE 12-6: A Flickr image description

How Does This Alternative Engine Affect Primary Search Engines?

When Flickr results are shown in the primary search results, they get there based on the metrics used by the major search engines, not that of Flickr's internal search. These results are concentrated in Yahoo! (via Bing) and can be a great way to jump start the image SEO efforts of a site focused on photos. Optimizing the image for Flick is easier than optimizing the image on a given website and can provide a lot of value without doing traditional image SEO.

> **WARNING**   As an SEO, you will very likely want to use Flickr images in your blog posts and in your presentations. Remember, just because a photo is included with a Creative Commons license in Flickr doesn't mean it was licensed that way by the image's owner. If this is the case, the owner technically can request damages.
>
> When in doubt contact the image owner.

TWITTER

Twitter has taken the Internet by storm. It is driving major traffic to popular twitterers and is being integrated into every major social media site. It is also becoming a main player in the important world of real-time search and is being integrated into the major search engine algorithms.

What Niche Is it Helpful For?

Twitter is a micro blogging platform where people can talk about any subject in 140 characters or less. Originally designed as a "status update" tool (the home page originally asked, "What are you doing right now?"), Twitter has since become used mostly for passing around random thoughts or, more frequently, links to content that the user finds useful. These short strings are called "tweets." This makes it applicable to almost all niches (I wouldn't try diagnosing patients via Twitter if you are a doctor).

The niches that are seeing the biggest benefits are those that are technology tech-savvy topics. As time progresses this is encompassing more and more niches. As of right now, the sky is the limit with Twitter.

Ranking Factors

Just like its service, Twitter's search algorithm is numbingly simple.

RELEVANCY

Twitter's search results are based entirely off of relevancy metrics (and time). It looks for exact matches between tweets and the searcher's query. The best way to be found via Twitter search is to tweet about exactly what people are searching for at the time they are searching for it. These topics can be determined by looking at Twitter's Trending Topics section or on its homepage when you are logged out.

Twitter's "follow" system regulates spam very effectively, because typically your tweets will be seen only by those that follow you. If you tweet out too much junk, you can expect to lose followers. But when users perform a search in Twitter, the results include tweets from all users. Inserting a hash tag (#) into a tweet is a way to group it with other tweets that focus on a particular topic. For example, adding "#nfl" to the end of your tweet about a particular game will result in your tweet appearing in any searches for "#nfl".

Tweeting relevant material about trending topics (and including a hash tag about that topic) is a great way to get traffic to your content, but remember that trending topics are trending precisely because so many people are talking about them. There's a chance that you'll get lost in the crowd with a single tweet.

TIME

Twitter is all about real-time communication. Tweets are instantly available online after they are received by Twitter's servers. Twitter's search engine finds all of the tweets that are relevant for a given query and prioritizes them by how recently they were posted. Currently, it only searches for tweets less than 3 days old.

How Does This Alternative Engine Affect Primary Search Engines?

Twitter results have a major effect on the primary search engine result pages. At the time of writing, both Google and Bing have access to Twitter's full API (called "The Firehose") and instantly crawl every tweet made on the system. These results are then used on search result pages for queries where real-time data is helpful, such as breaking news and other trending topics.

▶ Many times creating a Twitter profile, tweeting regularly with original material (or retweeting material that is important to your target audience), and continually building up your follower base is an easy way to secure a branded search term result.

Due to Twitter's domain authority, its profile pages also rank highly for relevant searches.

WHAT ABOUT DIGG.COM?

At the time of writing the only realistic way to get on the front page of Digg is to either pay a top submitter or be a top submitter. The site is not the democratic site it seems to be. While there are exceptions to this everyone once in a while, the chances of your content getting on Digg organically are so slim that it is not worth optimizing solely for this website.

SUMMARY

Alternative search engines are important for both niches and predicting the future of search. Websites like Amazon dominate product search, which means they can't be ignored when performing professional SEO services. This is one area that makes expert SEOs more successful than less experienced SEOs.

Learning the intricacies of alternative search engines is difficult but well worth the time investment when working in an applicable niche.

In addition to improving the bottom line, alternative search engines hint at the future of search. As any given alternative engine gains popularity, its data becomes more important to the traditional search engines. If these trends are caught early, SEOs can gain a competitive advantage that can devastate their competitors' rankings.

In the next chapter you take this to the next level by learning how to test the search engines so you can be aware of algorithm shifts before your competition.

## CHAPTER 13

Test, Test, Test

Testing the ways the search engines operate is the most important thing a Search Engine Optimizer can do. In fact, everything that we as SEOs know about the search engine algorithms is the result of testing. Testing is an ongoing process that must happen more frequently than the search engine algorithm updates. This chapter teaches you the skills you need to perform professional quality tests of your own so you can more accurately predict what types of techniques are required to improve your site's rankings. Although the following is designed to be performed on separate mini websites, the same principles apply to testing on your own website. Remember, SEOs can always be doing better and ranking for more terms.

SETTING UP A TESTING PLATFORM

To reverse engineer specific aspects of the major search engines, you will need to build a testing platform. (Note: If you are content just following the advice of the leaders in the industry and not performing your own tests, you can skip to the section "Running a Test" and perform the tests on your primary website.) The advantage of a testing platform over manually constructed web pages is that a platform will allow you to drastically cut down on the time it takes to set up a test and focus on interpreting results. This is because with a platform you do not have to rewrite code when you are performing a task you have already done.

When you're building a testing platform, it is important to implement a system that is both easily customizable and highly scalable. You will likely be performing many different tests at the same time and will find it necessary to customize your test pages in ways your might not expect up front. For this reason, it is important that the platform is more of a loose framework rather than a traditional tightly controlled Content Management System (CMS).

Picking a Web Server

Relatively few server resources are needed for a basic search engine testing platform. It is perfectly acceptable to find an inexpensive (less than $25 a month) shared hosting provider. I recommend a provider called Siteground (www.siteground.com), while other SEOs I respect recommend the more mainstream providers Slicehost (www.slicehost.com) and Media Temple (www.mediatemple.net). Regardless of which provider you choose, make sure it provides near 100 percent uptime at an affordable price.

> **TIP** Some shared hosting services claim to provide free hosting. They are able to do this because they place ads on your website, over which you have no control. This makes running variable driven tests impossible. As with all things on the Internet, if it sounds too good to be true, it probably is.

Domain Name

Choosing the best domain name for the websites on your testing platform is less important than you might think. Remember, you are not building these websites for traffic; you are instead building them for the purpose of blending in with the rest of the Internet. Avoid using excessive hyphens or inappropriate words that might get algorithmically detected by the engines. Similarly, avoid the spam-ridden TLDs (for example, .info). I recommend domain names that use real or plausible English phrases. For example, you could run tests on domain names like browncarrot.com, implodeddesk.com, or transordo.com.

The important thing to remember when finally making a purchase is to avoid domain names that look like spam. The search engines put a lot of time and effort into writing algorithms that can quickly identify spam based on factors like domain names. As a rule of thumb, find a name that you would feel comfortable putting on your business card.

▶ I use a website called domize.com to quickly search for available domain names. It is free, fast, and has helpful alternative suggestions.

TIP Most of the major domain registrars offer limited-time promotional discounts of domain names throughout the year. A large online community has formed around this money-saving opportunity and its members publicly post all of the available promo codes at any given time. You can find these by searching the name of the registrar and promo codes, for example, GoDaddy promo codes. I typically save about 15 percent on domains with the help of these secret communities.

PRIVATE REGISTRATION DOES NOT PROTECT YOU

Many registrars offer a service called "private registration." This service lists an escrow company in the public WHOIS database (the database that lists the owners of domain names) instead of its real owner. Although this is helpful to stop spammers from harvesting your information, it does not prevent the search engines from linking you to your domain name. Google, Microsoft, IAC (owner of Ask.com), and Yahoo are all registrars. They can view registration information even if it is "private."

Basic Information Architecture

It is important to make your website look legitimate so that the tests you run are applicable to other legitimate websites. One aspect of this involves creating a traditional information architecture. This means your test websites should contain at least the following pages:

- ► Homepage
- ► Contact Page
- ► Keyword 1 Page
- ► Keyword 2 Page

All of these pages should be linked to from a traditional global navigation bar either on the left side or top of every page on the site. Along with making the website look more legitimate, this helps to evenly distribute link juice so all of your tests can be indexed.

Figure 13-1 shows an example of a website testing the relative value of two links in the same paragraph. Notice that the text is randomly generated but uses all real words in grammatically correct sentences. This is to fool the search engines' natural language interpreters.

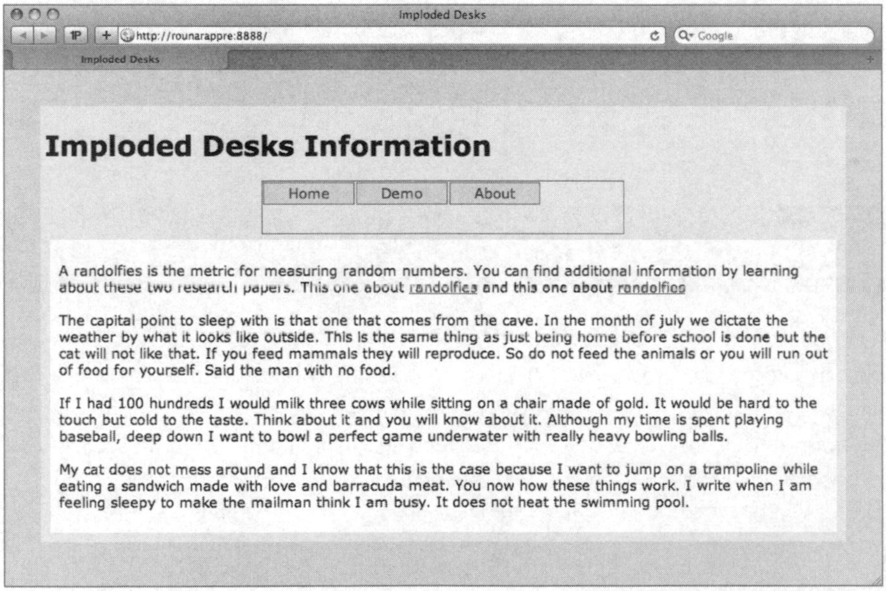

FIGURE 13-1: Example of a website testing the value of two links in the same paragraph.

Code

Finding the balance between code that works as a solid framework and code that can't be algorithmically detected as a match to corresponding test sites is very tricky. You don't want any of your websites to have identifying code that could be used to block all of them at once. This includes version numbers and "created by" attributions.

RUNNING A TEST

Testing is the bread and butter of staying up to date with SEO. Each of the following steps will help you build a test that is reproducible and helpful for furthering your SEO knowledge.

Planning a Test

Planning is the most important part of creating tests for the major search engines. The search engines use hundreds of metrics when analyzing a webpage for ranking. It is essential that the number of variables on a given test site are minimized. For example, on your test sites you must control the order in which links are placed on a page (some evidence shows links higher up in the code may get more value). Due to nuances like these, it is important to plan tests to make sure you are actually running equivalent tests between your trails.

I find it best to imagine the website not from the point of view of what you see in the web browser but from the point of view of the search engine crawlers. They parse the source code of the page linearly. This means that while a person looking at a site can easily get clues of information hierarchy from format and placement of text, the search engines likely can't. As a result, it is important to have the key parts of a website higher up in the source code. Through a series of tests I observed that the value of links are lessened the farther down they are in the code. The difference in link value was very small even in extreme cases, but this is an aspect of page design that needs to be taken into account when building test pages.

Setting Up the Test

If you used a system like the one I made available for download, you should be able to fill in a configuration file and a few keyword-specific pages. Set up your website to the specifications you came up with in the planning stage and work to get your website indexed. The easiest way to do this is to link to it from another website that is indexed and crawled at least once a week.

> **TIP** If you don't have the option of linking to your test page, you can submit it to a popular social media site such as Digg.com. These pages tend to attract a lot of links, and the search engines constantly crawl these websites to index content before it gets popular on the Internet. Use this to your advantage.

It typically takes less than a week for the major search engines to index the homepage of a brand new domain. After you finish configuring your test, wait for it to get indexed. You can check its status by searching for the unique title tag of your test site's homepage in any of the engines; for example, "This is my title tag."

Once the domain is in the index, record exactly how it appears in the search engine. (See the section "Recording Results" later in the chapter.) I recommend also taking screenshots and filing them with your test report.

Changing One Variable

Now it is finally time to run the test. Make sure you have everything recorded from the initial setup and go ahead and change one variable. This variable might be something simple like the position of a keyword or the location on the webpage of a link. Record exactly what you changed and wait again for the search engines to notice the difference.

At this point I recommend creating some kind of reminder for you to recheck the website's listing in the search engines after one week. I prefer to add a reminder to my calendar and make the changes manually, but it would be possible to automate this process instead.

▶ I learned this the hard way after one of my made-up keywords, "Aardvarkist," was used as an award on a popular website. The popular webpage quickly outranked my test website in the search engines and my three weeks of testing was ruined.

Redundancy

If possible, it is best to have multiple versions of the same test running simultaneously. This added layer of redundancy helps minimize the effect of unknown variables and prevents the entire test from failing if something unforeseen happens.

To help prevent test failure, I try to run three versions of the same test (only the keywords change) simultaneously. I have been happily surprised to observe that all versions of my tests report consistent results. This also has the added benefit of adding credibility to my tests when I share them with my colleagues.

THE IMPORTANCE OF REDUNDANCY

All the major search engines have data centers located all over the world. Each of these data centers contains a slightly different copy of the Internet. Thus, when you run a Google search in one place the results will likely be different than if you run it somewhere completely different. For the same reason, I have run a search on one computer and the same search on a computer three feet away and received different results.

Different results for different users can also be caused by search engines delivering "personalized" results (even if no one is signed into a Google account on that computer) or automatically geo-locating users to make their search results more relevant. For example, a search for "Lawyer" made in Seattle will automatically return results for Seattle lawyers even if the user did not type in the word "Seattle."

To compensate for these irregularities, it is best to run the multiple versions of a given test on servers in different geographic locations. It is best for all the tests to be run from the same country but with as much distance from each other as possible.

RECORDING RESULTS

All of your work performing tests will be futile if you don't take the time to appropriately record your results. I learned this the hard way when I was asked by a client about a specific test I had run six months earlier. I checked back through my handwritten notes and couldn't figure out the configuration of the test or what the results of it had been. I ended up having to rerun the entire test and redo all the work I had already done.

Although you can collect any data points you want, I suggest including at least all of the points in the following list.

- ▶ **Title:** The title of the test that clearly and succinctly identifies the test. For example, "The value of a 301 redirect compared to a 302 redirect."
- ▶ **Status:** It is also helpful to include the status of the test near the top of the document. I also recommend highlighting the status so the reader can quickly identify which tests are complete and which are still pending. For example, "Completed 12/21/2012."

- ▶ **Domain:** It is best to also include the domain names for the applicable tests so that the reader can quickly navigate to them and see the test firsthand.

- ▶ **Keyword:** Similar to including domain names, it is important to include the keywords used in the test so that readers can easily find the test online and see its results.

- ▶ **Start Date:** The date the experiment started.

- ▶ **End Date:** The date the experiment ended.

- ▶ **Question:** The question that is trying to be answered. For example, "Which type of server redirect passes more link value, a 301 or a 302?"

- ▶ **Setup:** It is helpful to include a paragraph explaining a high-level view of how the experiment was constructed. This is useful because it gives more credibility to the test and helps the reader identify problems the tester might not have thought of.

- ▶ **Null Result:** This is the result that would happen if the changed variable had no effect.

- ▶ **Alt Result:** This is the result that would happen if the changed variable did have an effect. Generally, there is more than one option here.

- ▶ **Hypothesis:** In accordance with the scientific method, it is useful to include a hypothesis to help establish goals and identify possible biases, which can sabotage test results. I have found this useful when colleagues have noted that my hypothesis lead me to create a test that inherently made the results lean one direction. Example hypothesis, "I predict that this test will show that 301 redirects pass more link value than 302 redirects."

▶ Since the outcome is helpful for those quickly scanning a report, if the outcome is known, it is often useful to include it right after the title of the test. For example, "301 redirects send more link juice than 302 redirects."

- ▶ **Outcome:** This is the actual change that occurred after the variable was changed.

- ▶ **Conclusion:** It is a good idea to write a conclusion after the test has completed. It is also the place to include any assumptions that were made and any conflicts that may have affected the results.

Figure 13-2 shows an example of a completed search engine testing report. Notice all of the data points that are included and how easy it is to understand the format of the report.

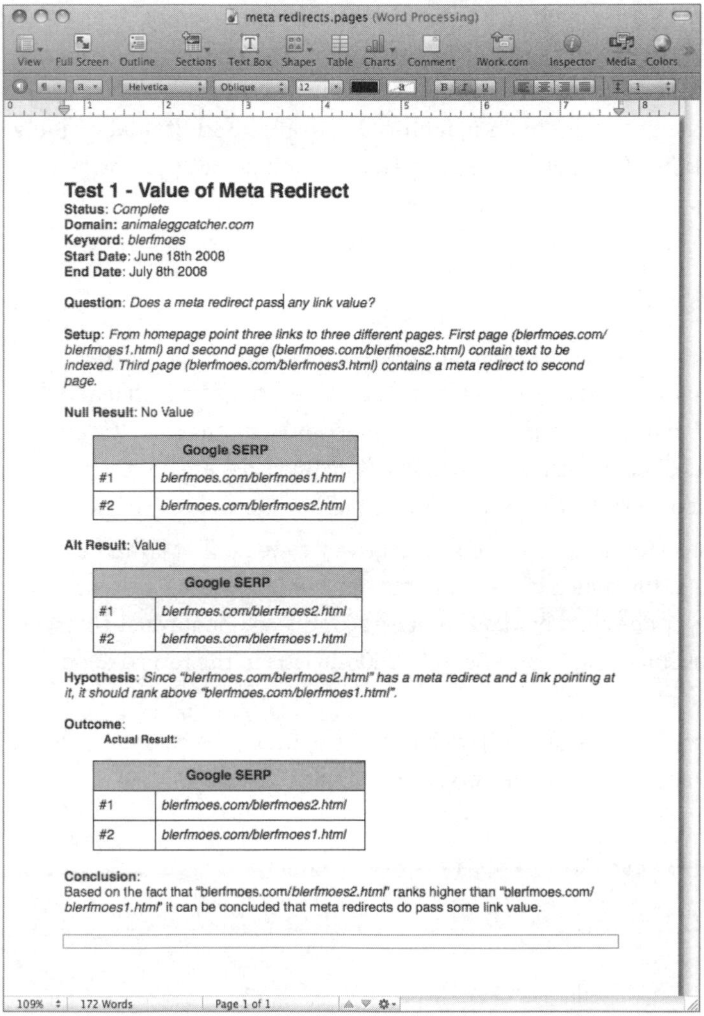

Test 1 - Value of Meta Redirect
Status: *Complete*
Domain: *animaleggcatcher.com*
Keyword: *blerfmoes*
Start Date: June 18th 2008
End Date: July 8th 2008

Question: *Does a meta redirect pass any link value?*

Setup: *From homepage point three links to three different pages. First page (blerfmoes.com/blerfmoes1.html) and second page (blerfmoes.com/blerfmoes2.html) contain text to be indexed. Third page (blerfmoes.com/blerfmoes3.html) contains a meta redirect to second page.*

Null Result: No Value

Google SERP	
#1	*blerfmoes.com/blerfmoes1.html*
#2	*blerfmoes.com/blerfmoes2.html*

Alt Result: Value

Google SERP	
#1	*blerfmoes.com/blerfmoes2.html*
#2	*blerfmoes.com/blerfmoes1.html*

Hypothesis: *Since "blerfmoes.com/blerfmoes2.html" has a meta redirect and a link pointing at it, it should rank above "blerfmoes.com/blerfmoes1.html".*

Outcome:
Actual Result:

Google SERP	
#1	*blerfmoes.com/blerfmoes2.html*
#2	*blerfmoes.com/blerfmoes1.html*

Conclusion:
Based on the fact that "blerfmoes.com/*blerfmoes2.html*" ranks higher than "blerfmoes.com/*blerfmoes1.html*" it can be concluded that meta redirects do pass some link value.

FIGURE 13-2: Example of a search engine testing report.

THE IMPORTANCE OF SHARING KNOWLEDGE

It may seem counterintuitive to share your test results with SEOs who might end up competing with you. This is true in some cases but as it turns out there are far more keywords available to optimize than there are SEOs. This means that it is quite normal to share knowledge with fellow SEOs without ever directly competing with them. It also means that the advantages of sharing knowledge outweigh the disadvantages.

Sharing data, test results, and ultimately, recommendations are very much like handing someone a key. The key was custom-crafted to fit a certain lock in a certain door. If a competing SEO firm is unwise enough to assume that this key will fit, as-is, in their client's door, then they risk looking foolish due to all the additional variables that exist with their client. The same complexity that challenges SEOs can often be an asset when it comes to publishing information.

Building a Reputation

Reputation is more important in the search marketing industry than any other industry I have worked in. It is still a young industry where word of mouth marketing is still the most effective way of getting a job. Everyone works on the same Internet, but the most successful SEOs (in terms of popularity and prestige) are not the ones who optimize the most pages; they are the ones who market themselves the best.

Coincidentally, I have found that the most effective way to market myself in the SEO industry is by using the same trick that Google has used for years. The secret is to work hard and give your product or knowledge away for free. Google does this with services like Gmail, YouTube, and Google Search. SEOs do this in the form of blog posts and forum comments.

Sharing information gleaned from hard work is, in my opinion, the best way to build a reputation and get clients in the search marketing industry.

NOTE   Google's policy of giving its main product away for free and thus attracting users and a strong reputation worked so well that the company didn't need to do any mainstream advertising until right before its IPO when it took out a full page ad in *The New York Times*.

Holding Search Engines Accountable

It took me a long time to realize that the major search engines make just as many mistakes as other companies. They are flawed and given their immense power, need to be held accountable for their actions and technology. By constantly testing the search engines, SEOs achieve this accountability.

The search engineers that I have spoken to have discussed the difficulty of removing spam from their search results without accidentally removing useful websites. They are forced to make judgment calls about whether they have been successful but don't have the manpower to fully check their work. These judgment calls can lead to errors that can have massive financial impacts for online businesses.

One example of this was when search engineers at Google discovered that URLs ending in ".0" were almost always spam. They decided to remove all instances of pages that fit this criterion from their search results but failed to realize the impact it made on the blogosphere. Unbeknownst to Google, many people had written useful blog posts with titles that ended in ".0". This included many articles on Web 2.0. It also included a popular Web 2.0 awards website that happened to be run by my company.

In this case, SEOs noticed the change relatively quickly and wrote blog posts condemning the problem. Google took notice of its mistake and updated its algorithm to reinclude these pages.

Few people understand the relationship between SEOs and the major search engines. Many believe it is like that of a host-parasite relationship, with engines being the former and the SEOs being the latter. Instead, it is symbiotic where both parties are essential to one another's well being.

SUMMARY

Just like many long and tedious processes in life, testing the search engines is a commonsense tactic that many people don't do simply out of laziness or lack of time and resources. For the professional SEO who is competing for the world's most competitive phrases, this is not acceptable. You will need to know the latest information in order to compete against others who are undoubtedly looking for a new way to outrank you.

Many critics argue that because of the number of variables involved (some that we know about and others about which we can only speculate), drawing foolproof conclusions in a real-world test setting is impossible. Maybe they're right, and maybe they're not, but the outcomes of lab-setting testing are undoubtedly helpful in making decisions about real-world content, coding, and architecture.

Luckily, with the steps outlined in this chapter, this is not a difficult task. You can use this outline, plan and execute a test, and use your own knowledge to make real progress. This, after all, is the goal of SEO. Testing is not as glamorous as SEO parties or a private conversation with a search engineer, but it is absolutely as important. SEO is still a new industry and learning from trial and error is your best way to ensure successful rankings.

## CHAPTER 14

SEO Resources

This chapter is a series of resources that I believe you will find useful while doing SEO and SEO consulting. It covers common SEO data, a time-tested checklist for switching domains, a quick hit list for doing SEO on the fly, and a quick guide on on-page optimization.

These are based on some of the paper resources I have hanging around my desk. A lot of memorization is required in the SEO industry and sometimes I find it easier to use a cheat sheet. I am guessing you will as well. Feel free to rip these pages out of this book and put them somewhere convenient (unless you are reading this in a bookstore!).

SEO CHEAT SHEET PART 1: ON-PAGE OPTIMIZATION

This first cheat sheet covers the basics of on-page optimization. This is essential for increasing relevancy and therefore boosting rankings. I have a blown up copy of this along with the other parts of this cheat sheet hanging in the public area of our office for everyone to reference.

IMPORTANT SEO TAGS

Element	Code

Title Tag	`<head>`
	`   <title>Keyword Phrase, Secondary Phrases</title>`
	`</head>`

HTML Headers (Very Limited SEO Value)	`<h1>Most Important</h1>`
	`<h2>Second Most Important</h2>`
	`<h3>Third Most Important</h3>`

Bold, Strong (Same SEO Value)	`<b>Keyword</b>` `<strong>Keyword</strong>`
Image (XHTML)	`<img src="keyword.jpg" alt="keyword" />`
Hyperlink	`<a href="http://www.example.com/webpage.html" title="keyword">Keyword in Anchor Text</a>`
Nofollowed Hyperlink (A Nofollowed hyperlink does not pass link value.)	`<a href="http://www.mysite.com/webpage.html" title="keyword" rel="nofollow">Keyword in Anchor Text</a>`

Canonical Link Element	`<head>`
	`   <link rel="canonical" href="http://www.domain.com/`
	`   canonical-url" />`
	`</head>`

The following table shows some guidelines to adhere to when recommending URL, title, meta data, and page structure. It's possible to fall outside these guidelines and still rank well and be indexed, but these numbers represent some best-practice recommendations.

SEARCH ENGINE INDEXING LIMITS

Element	Limit
Page File Size	No more than 150 kilobytes (before images, CSS, and other external resources)
Number of outbound links	No more than 150 unique links per page
Title Tag	No more than 70 characters
Meta Description	Roughly no more than 155 characters
Parameters in URL	No more than 2 `http://www.example.com/brands.php?nike`
Depth of URL	No more than 4 `http://www.example.com/category/keyword`

▶ *The limits in this table don't necessarily apply to websites with significant ranking power.*

SEO CHEAT SHEET PART 2: CANONICALIZATION ERRORS

This section of the cheat sheet shows common canonicalization errors. This is one of the first problems I look for when browsing a website. A website with incorrect canonicalization will suffer from duplicate content issues, and thus its relevancy will be diluted.

COMMON CANONICALIZATION ERRORS

Type	URL

Bad	`http://www.example.com`
	`http://example.com`
	`http://www.example.com/index.html`
	`http://example.com/index.html`
	`http://www.example.com/INDEX.html`
	`https://www.example.com/index.html`

Good	`http://www.example.com/`

NOTE The preceding table is a bit of a generalization. In truth, a "good" URL can be whatever you decide it should be, as long as it is easily understandable by both humans and search engines. "Bad" URLs are, therefore, everything else. If you need **https** or do not want a **www** subdomain, that's fine. Just be sure that you choose a system and remain true to it with your canonicalization techniques.

To condense the various default homepage URLs into one homepage, use 301 redirects (see the table named "301 Redirect in Apache" that follows) to correct for erroneous incoming links and make all internal links point to your domain using the syntax `http://www.example.com/`. Always include trailing "/" on folders.

The following table shows the code necessary to implement 301 redirects in Apache. This is useful for redirecting one URL to another and for correcting canonicalization errors.

301 REDIRECTS IN APACHE

Command	Description
`Redirect 301 /oldpage.html http://www.newdomain.com/newpage.html`	Redirect single file or directory to a new file or directory on a different domain.

`RewriteEngine on`
`RewriteCond %{HTTP_HOST}`
`^mysite\.com [NC]`
`RewriteRule (.*) http://www.mysite.com/$1 [L,R=301]`
	Redirect `http://example.com` to `http://www.example.com`. Affects entire domain.

`Redirect 301 / http://www.newdomain.com/`	Redirect entire domain to a new domain via 301 redirect.

To implement this code in Apache, create a file called .htaccess and include it in either the root of the public server or within whichever folder you have access to. The file is named only as an extension. Hidden files must be viewable in the operating system, and mod_rewrite must be enabled.

SEO CHEAT SHEET PART 3: META ROBOTS AND ROBOTS.TXT

Part 3 of this cheat sheet shows the different values you can include to direct search engine robots. These tools, meta robots and `robots.txt`, are powerful tools you can use to control which pages search engines are allowed to crawl and how they are allowed to crawl them.

The robots meta tag (or more popularly called "meta robots") is a page-specific tool for controlling robots. It applies only to the content on the given page and can be used to control both whether the page can be indexed and how its content can be used.

The syntax for the robots meta tag is:

```
<meta name="ROBOT NAME(S)" content="ARGUMENT(S)" />
```

Arguments can be combined and comma-separated within one tag, which means that content="noindex, noarchive" is a valid value. Robot names can either be "robots" (if you want the command to apply to all compliant user agents) or specific robots such as "googlebot" (if not all engines honor the directive or you don't want all engines to honor it). The following table lists the arguments and the robots that respond to them.

ROBOTS META TAG

Argument	Robot Name	Effect
noindex	robots, googlebot, bingbot	Don't index the page
nofollow	robots, googlebot, bingbot	Don't follow (crawl) any links on the page
noarchive	robots, googlebot, bingbot	Don't show a link to the cached version of the page
noodp	robots, googlebot, bingbot	Don't use DMOZ data for meta description or title tag (only for homepage)
nosnippet	robots, googlebot	Don't create a descriptive snippet to show on a SERP
nopreview	robots, bingbot	Don't create a descriptive snippet/preview to show on a SERP

robots.txt is a subdomain-specific text file that controls how search engines are allowed to crawl a given subdomain. It is important to note that this is not the preferred method for blocking search engine bots.

CROSSREF See Chapter 6 for more information about the preferred method for blocking search engine bots.

ROBOTS.TXT SYNTAX

Syntax	Description
User-agent: *	All robots
User-agent: Googlebot	Only Googlebot
Disallow: /private-folder/	Prevents crawlers from crawling specific folders and all subfolders and files
Disallow: /private-file.html	Prevents crawlers from crawling specific files
Disallow: /private-folder/ Allow: /private-folder/policy.html	"Allow" provides for exceptions to "Disallow" directives
Disallow: /default.aspx?sid=* Disallow: /months/j*/posts/	Asterisk stands for one or more wildcard characters and can be used, for example, session IDs (first line) or "january," "june", or "july" (second line)
Disallow: /*php$	$ prevents crawling of any URLs ending in the characters that precede $. Often used with asterisk wildcard.
Sitemap: http://www.example.com/ non-standard-sitemap-locaton/ sitemap.xml	Specifies where sitemap is. Standard locations listed in "SEO Cheat Sheet Part 4," the next section. Multiple sitemap locations (for video, mobile, and so on) may be listed.

▶ You can find some very good robots.txt documentation at http://www.robotstxt.org/.

SEO CHEAT SHEET PART 4: SITEMAPS

Part 4 of this cheat sheet includes all of the information you will need for standard sitemaps. These sitemaps are useful for getting short-term gains in traffic and can at least temporarily increase indexation rates.

SITEMAPS

Default Locations for Sitemaps
http://www.example.com/sitemap.xml http://www.example.com/sitemap.xml.gz http://www.example.com/sitemap.gz

▶ You can find more information about xml sitemaps at http://www.sitemaps.org. Additionally, you can find xml sitemap generators at http://www.xmlsitemaps.com so that you don't have to generate these manually.

Sitemap Syntax

```xml
<?xml version="1.0" encoding="UTF-8"?>
<urlset xmlns="http://www.sitemaps.org/schemas/sitemap/0.9">
  <url>
    <loc>http://www.example.com/</loc>
    <lastmod>1970-01-01</lastmod>
    <changefreq>monthly</changefreq>
    <priority>0.8</priority>
  </url>
</urlset>
```

Sitemap Syntax with Images

```xml
<?xml version="1.0" encoding="UTF-8"?>
<urlset xmlns="http://www.sitemaps.org/schemas/sitemap/0.9"
 xmlns:image="http://www.google.com/schemas/sitemap-image/1.1">
  <url>
    <loc>http://www.example.com/</loc>
    <lastmod>1970-01-01</lastmod>
    <changefreq>monthly</changefreq>
    <priority>0.8</priority>
    <image:image>
    <image:loc>http://www.example.com/image.jpg</image:loc>
    <image:caption>Caption of the image</image:caption>
    </image:image>
  </url>
</urlset>
```

News Sitemap Syntax

```xml
<?xml version="1.0" encoding="UTF-8"?>
<urlset xmlns="http://www.sitemaps.org/schemas/sitemap/0.9"
        xmlns:n="http://www.google.com/schemas/sitemap-news/0.9">
  <url>
    <loc>http://www.example.org/business/article55.html</loc>
    <n:news>
      <n:publication>
        <n:name>The Example Times</n:name>
        <n:language>en</n:language>
      </n:publication>
      <n:access>subscription</n:access>
      <n:genres>pressrelease, blog</n:genres>
      <n:publication_date>2008-12-23</n:publication_date>
      <n:title>Companies A, B in Merger Talks</n:title>
      <n:keywords>business, merger, acquisition, A, B</n:keywords>
      <n:stock_tickers>NASDAQ:A, NASDAQ:B</n:stock_tickers>
    </n:news>
  </url>
</urlset>
```

SEO CHEAT SHEET PART 5: USER AGENTS

Part 5 of this cheat sheet shows the user agent string for the major search engine robots. This is useful for identifying how and when the search engines crawl your website and for when you need to view websites as their user agent.

> **CROSSREF** See Chapter 3 for more a list of tools that make working with user agents easier.

IMPORTANT USER AGENTS

Who/What	User Agent
Google Search	Googlebot/2.1 (http://www.google.com/bot.html)
Google Search	Googlebot/2.1 (http://www.googlebot.com/bot.html)
Google Mobile Search	(compatible; Googlebot-Mobile/2.1; +http://www.google.com/bot.html)
Google Image Search	Googlebot-Image/1.0
Google Image Search	Googlebot-Image/1.0 (http://www.googlebot.com/bot.html)
Google News	Googlebot-News
Bing Search	msnbot/x.xx (http://search.msn.com/msnbot.htm)
Bing Search	MSNBOT/0.xx (http://search.msn.com/msnbot.htm)
Bing Mobile	MSNBOT_Mobile MSMOBOT Mozilla/2.0 (compatible; MSIE 4.02; Windows CE; Default)
Alexa/Internet Archive	ia_archiver
Alexa/Internet Archive	ia_archiver-web.archive.org
Alexa/ Internet Archive	ia_archiver/1.6
Ask/Teoma Search	Mozilla/2.0 (compatible; Ask Jeeves)
Ask/Teoma Search	Mozilla/2.0 (compatible; Ask Jeeves/Teoma)
Ask/Teoma Search	Mozilla/2.0 (compatible; Ask Jeeves/Teoma; http://about.ask.com/en/docs/about/webmasters.shtml)

Check http://www.user-agents.org/ **for updates.**

This finishes up the list of the most useful cheat sheets that I use as an SEO. The following sections include checklists I use when I need to perform SEO processes rather as opposed to simple tasks. These resources are practically indispensable when used together.

SWITCHING DOMAINS CHECKLIST

Moving domains can have a tremendously negative impact on search engine rankings. This is because the major search engines use metrics on both the domain level and the page level to determine rankings. When webmasters decide to switch to a brand new domain, they are resetting their domain metrics to zero whether they know it or not. Luckily, you can take the following steps to minimize and in many cases completely negate the effects of a domain move:

- ✔ Create an XML sitemap for your old domain.

- ✔ Create content (contact information, description of your company, indication of future plans) and something link worthy for the new domain. (You should start trying to build links early.)

- ✔ Set up the new domain and make it live.

- ✔ Register and verify your old domain and new domain with Google Webmaster Tools.

- ✔ Create a custom 404 page for the old domain that suggests visiting the new domain.

- ✔ In a development environment, test the redirects from the old domain to the new domain. Ideally, this will be a 1:1 redirect (`www.example-old-site.com/category/sexy-mustaches.html` to `www.example-new-site.com/category/sexy-mustaches.html`) unless you're also using the domain migration as an opportunity to create a new, more search-friendly URL structure.

- ✔ 301 redirect your old domain to your new domain on a page-to-page level.

- ✔ Submit your old sitemap to Google and Bing. The submission pages are within Google Webmaster Tools and Bing Webmaster Center. (This step will make the engines crawl your old URLs, see that they are 301 redirects, and change their index accordingly.)

- ✔ Fill out the Change of Address form in Google Webmaster Tools.

- ✔ Create a new sitemap and submit it to the engines. (This will tell them about any new URLs that were not present on the old domain.)

✔ Build a `robots.txt` file for the new site that lists the location of your new XML sitemap and ensure that all disallow directives are correct for the new site.

✔ Ensure that analytics are installed in the new site and that conversions are correctly registered and tested so that there are no gaps in reporting during the migration.

✔ Wait until Google Webmaster Tools updates and fix any errors it indicates in the Diagnostics section.

✔ Monitor search engine results to make sure the new domain is being properly indexed.

SEO QUICK HIT LIST

These are the SEO elements I check whenever I need to do a very fast SEO audit:

✔ Check canonicalization of domain (www versus non-www; http versus https; / versus /default.aspx (or other home page variations); etc.).

✔ Check global navigation (categories, subcategories).

✔ Check for the existence robots.txt (`http://www.example.com/robots.txt`) and ensure that it's not disallowing any critical content.

✔ Check for the existence of a sitemap (`http://www.example.com/sitemap.xml`) and ensure the content appears valid.

✔ Compare the cached text-only version of site in Google (search Google for given URL, click "cache," click "Text-only version") to the actual home page of the site and make sure the content elements of both are very similar or identical.

✔ Link Profile (mozBar, Linkscape).

▶ One more useful resource is David LaFerney's "A Complete Glossary of Essential SEO Jargon" at http://www.seomoz.org/blog/smwc-and-other-essential-seo-jargon. LaFerney's post is a good source for quick definitions of key SEO terms and phrases.

SUMMARY

This chapter included the cheat sheets and checklist that I use most often as an SEO. These have saved me countless Google searches and are permanently attached to the walls of my office. I hope that you find them as useful as I have.

Attending SEO Conferences

Internet marketing conferences can be either tremendously helpful for your career or an expensive waste of time. This appendix provides actionable information on how to make the most out of these conferences.

PICKING THE RIGHT CONFERENCE

It turns out that the Internet is available globally (you think!?). As such, numerous conferences in cities all around the world focus on marketing online. In this section, I review some the most popular search-related conferences so that you can pick the right one for you.

SMX

SMX, Search Marketing Expo, is a conference run by Danny Sullivan and Chris Sherman of SearchEngineLand.com. The conference is tailored for beginning to intermediate Internet marketers. At the time of writing, tickets range roughly from $1,600.00 to $2,300.00 and the conference takes place in New York, Seattle, Toronto, Santa Clara, London, Munich, Stockholm, Sydney, and China.

I have been to this conference many times and generally enjoy it. It attracts most of the big-name SEOs and is consistently attended by Google, Microsoft, and more recently, Facebook. Most of the material is beginner to intermediate-advanced.

PROS

▶ Attracts the big companies and names

▶ Many big announcements are made at SMX

▶ Held in many locations

CONS

▶ Expensive

▶ Sessions are rarely helpful for advanced SEOs

▶ *If you are an advanced SEO, this conference series is most useful as a place to speak and for its networking opportunities. Any big announcements that are made at the conference will be written about online and you can read them there for free.*

BOTTOM LINE

SMX is very similar to SES. It is one of the most mainstream Internet marketing conferences and attracts the biggest and best companies and speakers. Like SES, its sessions are primarily helpful for beginner and intermediate SEOs.

SES

SES, Search Engine Strategies, is a conference and expo run by the minds behind SearchEngineWatch.com. It is useful for beginning to moderately skilled Internet marketers. It usually attracts a larger number of participants than other conferences, and as such attracts many of the big-name SEOs and companies.

At the time of writing SES tickets range roughly from $900.00 (1-day pass) to $2,000.00 (3-day pass). SES takes place in Chicago, London, San Diego, New York, Toronto, San Francisco, and Berlin.

PROS

- ▶ Attracts the big companies and names
- ▶ Many big announcements are made at SES
- ▶ Held in many locations

CONS

- ▶ Expensive
- ▶ Sessions are rarely helpful for advanced SEOs

BOTTOM LINE

SES is very similar to SMX. It is one of the most mainstream Internet marketing conferences and attracts the biggest and best companies and speakers. Like SMX, its sessions are primarily helpful for beginner and intermediate SEOs. The sessions are usually redundant, but they do sometimes include small bits of wisdom. If you are in a situation were one of these small tips apply to you, it can make the entire conference pay for itself.

Pubcon

Pubcon is a conference put on by the minds behind WebmasterWorld.com. It focuses on social media, SEO, SEM, and affiliates. It is best suited for beginners to beginner-intermediates and is known for its venue, Las Vegas, and its lavish after parties. Tickets range from $400.00 to $600.00.

I have been to a few Pubcons and have enjoyed it every time. It is a long conference at four days but provides a lot of time for networking and lounging.

PROS

- ► Inexpensive
- ► In Las Vegas
- ► Fun crowd
- ► Great parties

CONS

- ► Session content is generally not helpful for advanced SEOs
- ► Four days is a very long time for a conference in Las Vegas

BOTTOM LINE

Pubcon is the most fun Internet marketing conference. What it lacks in useful sessions it makes up for tenfold in networking opportunities and extravagant after parties. It is the best conference for advanced SEOs because the environment of Las Vegas is particularly well suited for attracting expert SEOs and putting them in a mindset of being willing to divulge secrets. (This is a nice way of saying they drink too much and say things they normally wouldn't with competitors around.)

SXSW Interactive

SXSW, South by Southwest, is a three-part super conference that covers film, music, and interactive mediums. The interactive portion is five days long and covers websites, video games, and startup ideas. At the time of writing tickets ranged roughly from $400.00 to $550.00.

It is located in Austin, Texas, and attracts a very large crowd (11,000) from many technical fields.

PROS

- ► Includes a broad perspective on the Internet (not focused on search)
- ► Lots of events to attend and speakers to hear

CONS

- ▶ Large number of people
- ▶ The section called Interactive which covers topics related to SEO is only one portion of the bigger conference so it is not the main focus

BOTTOM LINE

SXSW Interactive is huge (with regards to attendance) but due to its lack of focus, is not a mainstream Internet marketing conference. In more recent years it has had more sessions on SEO-related themes and has had several big announcements that have affected SEO. (For example, Twitter was first introduced at this conference.) It is good for gaining a broad perspective for the Internet, but is not the best choice for someone who is looking for a conference dedicated to online search.

Other Conferences

Many other conferences take place all over the world and have a large variety of price points. They are great for meeting local people and local company contacts. If you are not around a major city, these conferences provide a great way to learn like the professionals.

These are especially good for learning about specific niches that can help bolster your SEO skills. In these cases, they attract major players in small industries and allow participants to make contacts they normally wouldn't be able to make.

My favorite niche conferences have been Y Combinator's Startup School (San Francisco), which centered around technology startups; SEOmoz Pro Training (London), which covered advanced SEO topics; and ROFLcon (New York), which covered Internet culture. The reason I really enjoyed these conferences was they focused specifically on my interests and allowed for easy access to the speakers who were not burdened by enormous crowds.

PROS

- ▶ Cover niche industries and interests
- ▶ Relatively inexpensive
- ▶ Small groupings of like-minded people

CONS

- ▶ Infrequent
- ▶ Don't necessarily attract large brands
- ▶ Locations can be inconvenient

BOTTOM LINE

These conferences are inherently very hit or miss. They have the benefit of being very focused but are generally less convenient to attend and aren't always well organized. That said, they are essential for the niche enthusiasts.

WHAT TO EXPECT

SEO conferences are a whirlwind of information and people. They are exhausting and overwhelming, but useful and fun. The sessions are generally very redundant and their quality is unpredictable. Many attendees, including myself, listen through a lot of old information in hopes of hearing one of the gems that emerge at these events. These usually take the form of tips, tricks, or tools.

The People

The social dynamic at marketing conferences is confusing but extremely interesting. Because all of the attendees and speakers are marketers, a huge amount of personal marketing goes on.

This has led to the creation of SEO "celebrities". (I use that word lightly and with a bitter taste in my mouth.) These are the people who regularly speak at conferences and/or work for well-known companies. They are usually constantly surrounded by people asking for advice and many of them can be extremely egotistical. It is a tight-knit circle and a lot of cross-promotion takes place inside of it.

In addition to these SEO celebrities, search engine representatives garner a lot of attention. They have direct knowledge of the inner workings of the engines and frequently say rehearsed lines that have been approved by their legal and marketing teams. They are great avenues for making real change in SERPs but are constantly surrounded by many people.

These niche celebrities are of course the minority. The vast majority of attendees are beginner SEOs who are simply looking to learn more about the industry so that they can do Internet marketing themselves.

The Venue

The venue of search engine conferences varies greatly. The big conferences (SES, SMX, Pubcon, and so on) are held in large convention centers. The sessions take place in individual rooms, while the big events (keynotes) happen in enormous rooms with temporarily constructed stages.

The medium-sized conferences (SEOmoz PRO training, for example) typically take place in hotel conference rooms. In this case, there are generally only a few different rooms where sessions can take place simultaneously.

The small-sized conferences (Startup School, for example) take place in auditoriums or clubs. They have the benefit of being more intimate and don't usually attract enormous crowds.

The Sessions

The sessions about Internet marketing conferences vary greatly in value and subject. They are usually comprise a few individuals speaking and an audience who is able to ask questions after the speakers finish.

Sessions tend to either take the form of keynotes, lectures, or panels.

- ► **Keynotes:** Keynotes are the main events of conferences. They generally take place right at the beginning and/or the end of conferences, are usually given by the biggest names at conferences, and typically don't include a question and answer section. The individual who lectures usually relates an experience he or she has had and how the audience can learn from it.

- ► **Lectures:** Lectures, in this context, are usually given by one individual at a time. They usually have one theme they try to convey through an audio/visual presentation. Their quality varies greatly but they are the best type of session for learning about action-based plans you can use to accomplish a task.

- ► **Panels:** Panels are usually made up of a group of experts who all share their opinions on a given topic. At search engine conferences these are typically made up of search engine representatives or well-known SEOs. They generally have one theme (Web Video, Social Media, Sitemaps, and so on) and almost always have more audience participation than lectures or keynotes.

The After Parties

The after parties at search engine conferences are networking events that usually take place at a popular bar, club, or restaurant. They range from the simple (a group of marketers talking to each other around a table) or the ultra lavish. (When Microsoft launched Bing it held a party at a park next to the Seattle Space Needle. Halfway through the party it used giant lights to color the space needle the colors of Bing.) These are great places to meet people and build your network. For me, these parties are the most valuable parts of conferences because of the people I get to meet and connect with later. SEO is a job that requires knowing more than is knowable by any single person. This means it quickly becomes essential to meet people who have pursued niches within SEO so that you can use their expertise when you experience a situation you are not familiar with.

> **NOTE** I have had this prove worthwhile many times. For example, while working with a client for a major music website, I saw that they could benefit from getting into Google News, but I was unfamiliar with the nuances of the news site submission process. Luckily, I had just come back from a conference where I met Brent Payne, SEO for the *Chicago Tribune*, and was able to e-mail and get trusted answers. Similar situations have happened when I needed sources for articles, stories for pitches, and people for job opportunities.

PREPARING TO GO

Before going to a conference, you should do everything you can to prepare for the event ahead of you. You will likely have very little downtime so you should figure out the logistics before leaving your home.

- ✔ **Get a Twitter account:** At search conferences there is always a conversation going on behind the presentation. Be involved and in the know by searching for the applicable hash tags (for example, #conference-name).

- ✔ **Know of the big names:** You are going to need to know who the big players are before you get to the conference. They will be talked about a lot at the conference and everything will make more sense if you understand the context.

- ✔ **Find restaurants nearby:** Knowing places to eat is always a great way to help you network. People unfamiliar with the area will be looking for someone who is in the know.

✔ **Bring an individual Internet source:** If you have the resources, bring an external Internet source (for example, a PC card). This will keep you connected if/when the Wi-Fi goes down. Additionally, it makes you a good person to know.

WHAT TO BRING

This section contains my packing list for conferences. You can use this as a base and build on it as you attend more conferences.

CLOTHING

✔ **Comfortable shoes:** You will be standing and walking around all day. Think function over fashion.

✔ **Branded clothing:** Become a self-serving billboard and wear your company's logo loud and proud.

✔ **At least two sets of dress clothes:** Many after parties will be at places that have dress codes. Be sure to dress to impress and you will be a success. (That last sentence was a mess but I digress...).

RESOURCES

✔ **Business cards:** I didn't have business cards the first time I went to a conference. It was both unprofessional and awkward. Don't make the same mistake as me. It is not necessary to get anything special; the person giving the card is much more important than the quality of the card. Unless you have superfluous design resources, I don't recommend spending significant time or money (no more than $20.00 USD) on your business cards.

✔ **Laptop/Notepad:** Make it easy for you take notes. You will be given a lot of information and it will be nearly impossible to remember it all. Bring something to takes notes and utilize it to its fullest.

✔ **Water bottle (Nalgene with a Carabineer is how we do it in Seattle):** You are going to be surrounded by hundreds of other heat-producing attendees. Be sure to always have a source of water on hand so you can stay hydrated and healthy.

WHAT TO DO

Once you are at the conference, it is important to use your time optimally. This section covers SEO conference best practices.

Show Time

As soon as you get to the conference it is time to start meeting people and talking shop. Remember, you are here to learn about SEO and meet new people, not to cower to insecurities.

- ✔ **Arrive early or late (not too late!) to avoid the registration lines:** Every person at the conference will need to register at the beginning of the conference to get in. Make sure you are not the one at the back of the line.

- ✔ **Wear your branded clothing:** You brought it, now wear it!

- ✔ **Network, Network, Network:** The relationships you make at conferences have much more potential than the information you learn in the sessions. Because almost every person at search conferences is there to network, meeting people is easy.

- ✔ **Skip one session block:** The big names at conferences got to where they are by knowing most of the things discussed in sessions. This means that they are unlikely to attend many sessions. Choose your least important sessions and skip them. Use this time to meet the big names in the industry. They will be much less bombarded and far more likely to really get to know you.

- ✔ **Go to popular booths:** Popular booths will feature more influential people and offer conversation starters for all the people you don't know.

- ✔ **At lunch, don't sit with friends:** This is hard because many people see lunch as a time to relax. However, this is not necessarily true for everyone. Network, network, network.

- ✔ **Drink a lot of water:** Keeping yourself hydrated keeps you energized and fully functional.

- ✔ **Use your notepad or computer:** Take a lot of notes. I recommend at least one new page/file per session.

✔ **Keep all of your random ideas in one place:** This can either be a separate text document or the last page of your notepad. This is helpful later when you are looking for post-conference motivation.

✔ **Collect cool swag:** Free stuff is great. Gather as much as you can and bring it home for friends and family.

Parties

Many people make the mistake of wasting industry-related parties by acting how they act when they party with friends. Although this is appropriate in small doses, your main goal at industry parties should be to improve yourself and your reputation. You have been warned.

✔ **Party hop:** Maximize your chances to network and learn from the more experienced attendees by going to as many party venues as you can.

✔ **Avoid useless conversations:** Make your impact but keep most conversations short and to the point. Here are a few things to bring up if the conversation stops:

▷ What do you not get to do enough of?

▷ Have you ever watched the Viagra SERPS to study black hat techniques? (Hint: "Buy Viagra" is much more interesting than simply "Viagra.")

▷ If all else fails, remember that people at start-ups *love* to talk about their company.

Before Sleeping

At some point in the night you will make it back to your hotel room (hopefully!). If you are able, now is a great time to spend 10 minutes and review the events of the day. This takes minimal effort and has a big impact on retention.

✔ **Review business cards:** Reviewing the business cards you received will help you remember all of the people you met.

✔ **Review notes:** This will likely help prioritize your work.

✔ **Create a To-Do list:** After a conference your motivation will likely be really high. Use this opportunity to define future tasks and goals.

AFTER THE CONFERENCE

Once you return home from a conference you still have more work to do. Don't let the connections you just spent so much energy creating disappear. This is the best point to reconnect.

- ✔ **Blog about it:** Not only will this help you keep a record of the event, but it also provides an avenue to cement connections with people.

- ✔ **Connect online:** Find people you met in real life and connect with them online. Specifically, I recommend finding people on Twitter, Facebook, and LinkedIn.

INFLUENTIAL MARKETERS AND GOOGLE ALERTS

The vast majority of successful Internet marketers keep Google Alerts for their name. This means that whenever Google encounters a blog or tweet or article that mentions someone with an alert setup they get an e-mail pointing them at the text that mentioned them.

You can use this to your advantage by driving influential eyeballs to your website. Use this secret sparingly because influential Internet marketers are excellent at detecting spam and disingenuous mentions.

SUMMARY

Hopefully after reading this appendix you are more prepared for Internet marketing conferences. If you haven't attended one you should now know what to expect and what to focus on. If you have attended conferences before, hopefully you picked up some tips.

The sessions at conferences are very hit or miss but the networking is always useful. Information can go stale but relationships can always provide resources if fostered properly.

Index

B

BackRub, 8, 21. *See also* PageRank
Batman utility belt, 43, 73. *See also* SEO toolbars
beginner SEO consultant, 172
The Beginner's Guide to Search Engine Optimization, 6, 45
best practices, SEO, 129–148, 396
  alt text attribute, 138–139
  blocking pages from search engines, 144–145
  domain-level hierarchy, 130–131
  Flash, 143
  footer links, 147–148
  HTML headings, 136, 138–139, 396
  images, 138–139
  implementation, comprehensive site audits and, 182, 261
  JavaScript, 143
  meta descriptions, 135–136, 137
  meta keywords, 142–143
  meta robots, 144–145
  nofollow attribute, 139–140
  page-level hierarchy, 130
  parameter-driven URLs, 146–147
  rankings and traffic, 145–146
  rel="canonical" tag, 140–142
  SEO conferences, 414–415
  301 redirects, 143–144
  title tags, 134–135
  traffic and rankings, 145–146
  URLs
    with single keyword, 130
    structure, 131–134
Bing
  dominance, 158, 337, 351, 371
  Google *v.*, 158, 350, 371
  image search, 363–364
  JavaScript links, 49
  Microsoft and, 348–351
  opinion on SEO, 154
  Seattle Space Needle and, 412
  Toolbox, 41–42
  universal search, 356
Bird, Sarah, 340
Bit.ly, 26
BitTorrent, brand searching on, 103
black hat Internet marketers, 336–337
black holes, 47, 48, 144–145
blended search, 356–357

blocking. *See also* meta robots; robots.txt
  IP, 144
  pages, from search engines, 144–145
blogs
  about SEO conferences, 416
  Google Blog Search, 100–101, 286, 288
  search, comprehensive informational site audit, 276, 330
  SEO, 337–338
body text keywords, 186, 217
BOM (byte-order mark), 62
branded queries, 270
branding
  brand and domain mentions in search engines, 264, 288–289
  brand search engine result page, 97–100
  brand searching, in social media, 100–103
  5-minute brand reputation audit, 97–103
breadcrumbs, 224, 225, 249, 321
Brin, Sergey, 6–7
bring it back to clients, 150
broad searches, 356, 357
browser preparation, 15-minute SEO audit, 86–88
  disable cookies, 86–87
  disable JavaScript, 87–88
  switch user agent to Googlebot, 87
Bruce Clay, Inc., 345
buying
  competition websites, 113
  help of social media influencers, 126
  links, 125–126, 156, 336
  search engine ads, 113
byte-order mark (BOM), 62

C

cache command, 53
canonical URLs, 89
canonicalization. *See also* duplicate content
  cheat sheet, 397–398
  errors, 24–26, 108
  "First Things First" list, 108
  forward slashes and, 25–26
  rel="canonical" tag, 114, 115, 127, 140–142, 396
  "see all" version, 34
canonicalized duplicate content, 194, 242
canonicalized site versions, 194, 241
Cascading Style Sheets. *See* CSS
case
  search engine commands, 55
  URL structure, 38

Internet Information Services. *See* IIS

Internet marketing, 335–340. *See also* SEO conferences;
    SEO industry
  black hat, 336–337
  Google Alerts, 416
  gray hat, 336
  SEO Pyramid, 340–343
  white hat, 336

interviews, SEO consulting and, 176

intitle command, 54, 114

inurl command, 54–55, 102, 162

involvement, with SEO communities, 337–340

IP blocking, 144

IP-based cloaking, 80

ISAPI Rewrite, 133

J

jargon, SEO, 276, 331, 404

Java, 50

JavaScript
  best practice, 143
  disable, 87–88, 90
  Java *v.*, 50
  links, 49
  relocation commands, 25

K

keynotes, SEO conferences, 411

keywords
  meta, 50, 130, 139, 142–143, 185
  research, pricing for, 174
  stuffing, 334
  URL optimization, 130

keyword density, 12, 69, 186, 334

Keyword Density & Prominence Analyzer, Ranks.nl, 70–72

Keyword Density Tool, Dave Naylor's, 69, 71–72

keyword inclusion, 188, 221

keyword targeting
  comprehensive e-commerce site audit, 268–269, 315–316
  comprehensive informational site audit, 185, 210–211
  search engine commands and, 52

Keywords report, GWT, 65

kilobytes downloaded per day, Crawl Stats report, 67

Krum, Cindy, 339

L

Labs reports, GWT, 67–68

Laferney, David, 404

leaders, SEO, 343–345

lectures, SEO conferences, 411

links (hyperlinks). *See also* inbound links
  Brin and, 6–7
  buying, 125–126, 156, 336
  extraneous, 91, 131
  15-minute SEO audit, 95
  footer, 147–148
  "Google Search Engine Ranking Factors" survey, 155, 156
  HTML-based, 49, 51
  importance, 95, 155, 156, 195
  JavaScript, 49
  manipulation, 10
  natural, 126
  navigational, 51, 83, 109, 110, 112, 131, 147
  Page and, 6–7
  paid, 119, 156, 194, 335
  poison links, 121–122
  ranking metrics and, 155, 156
  relevancy, 13–14, 134
  root domains linking, 74, 75, 76, 95
  SEO problems and, 107, 122
  sources, 13, 124
  subcategory pages and, 33

link acquisition practices, 194, 244

link brokers, 126

link building
  comprehensive e-commerce site audit, 274–275, 326–328
    content currently attracting links, 275, 327–328
    inbound link types, 275, 326
  low-risk techniques, 122–125
  pricing for, 173
  risky techniques, 125–126

link farms, 104, 119, 194, 244, 264, 336

link juice (ranking power)
  canonical tagging, 142
  category pages, 31, 33, 91
  homepages, 268
  JavaScript links, 49
  meta robots, 145, 228
  MusicArtistDatabase.com, 246
  `robots.txt`, 145
  SellTheWidget.com, 297, 321, 322
  site architecture, 28–29
  subcategory pages, 33, 91
  301 redirects, 25, 78, 142, 144, 207, 241, 242, 284, 390
  302 redirects, 25, 78, 390
  website pyramid structure, 29

link magnets, 35, 125

link popularity, 6–11

   comprehensive e-commerce site audit, 264, 286

   domain popularity, 8–11, 75

   link profiles and, 8

   page popularity, 8–11

   relevancy and, 14

   solutions to problems, 109–113

   top ten lists, 9–10

link profiles. *See also* inbound links

   identification, 108

   popularity and, 8

link pyramid, 28–29, 92, 112, 131, 132

linkable content, 41

Links To Your Site report, GWT, 65

Linkscape Links, 198, 253

Linkscape metrics, 264, 287

link-worthiness, 91

   comprehensive informational site audit, 195–197, 247–251

      content value, 196–197, 250

      design quality, 196, 248

      share-ability/accessibility, 197, 251

      user experience, 196, 249

   pages, 126

Live HTTP Headers tool, 76–78

local events, SEO, 338

local search

   determining locality, 357–359

   ranking factors, 360–362

long domain names, 22

long URLs, 188, 222

Lopez, Jen, 340

Lord, Joanna, 339

low-risk link building techniques, 122–125

lunch meetings, SEO consulting and, 176

M

Malware report, GWT, 66

manual review penalties, 103, 104–105. *See also* penalties

marketing events, general, 338

Marketing Pilgrim, 338

mass directory submission, 337

master services agreement, 166–167

Matt Cutts blog, 338. *See also* Cutts, Matt

Media Temple, 384

Messages page, GWT, 61

meta descriptions

   best practice, 135–136, 137

   defined, 45

   effective, 45–46

   15-minute SEO audit, 94

   HTML Suggestions report, 67

   on-page/content optimization, 186, 214–215

   for people, 46

   relevance and, 137

   textual additions for, 46

meta directives. *See* meta robots

meta keywords, 50, 130, 139, 142–143, 185

meta redirects, 82

meta refreshes, 25, 82, 144

meta robots (meta directives), 48

   best practice, 144–145

   cheat sheet, 398–400

   defined, 46–47

   "First Things First" list, 108

   "index, follow," 48

   "index, nofollow," 48

   "noindex, follow," 48

   "noindex, nofollow," 48, 108, 116, 144–145, 194, 208, 228, 229, 243, 295, 312

   robots.txt *v.*, 47, 144–145

metrics. *See also* ranking metrics

   comprehensive e-commerce site audit

      Linkscape metrics, 264, 287

      metrics to track daily, 270, 317–318

      third-party traffic metrics (monthly), 264–265, 290

   comprehensive informational site audit, 197–198, 252–256

      Linkscape Links, 198, 253

      mozRank, 198, 255

      mozTrust, 198, 256

      PageRank, 198, 254

microsite, 113

Microsoft, 348–351. *See also* Bing; Google

   company culture, 349

   IAYF, 350

   people at, 349–350

   technology, 350–351

Microsoft Internet Information Services. *See* IIS

Mihm, David, 360

minus sign (-), 54. *See also* search engine queries

mod_rewrite, 133, 398

most pressing and valuable changes

   comprehensive e-commerce site audit, 262, 284

   comprehensive informational site audit, 184, 207–208

SEOMOZ PRO
INDUSTRY LEADING SEO SOFTWARE

HELLO my name is ROGER @SEOmoz

cut here

Step One
Cut out Roger.

Step Two
Build a paper airplane.

Step Three
Insert Roger into plane.

Step Four
Toss the paper airplane.

Readers of SEO Secrets can try it free for 30 days!

✔Campaign software for easy SEO management

✔Dozens of tools & valuable SEO resources

✔The largest SEO communit on the web